Second SIGHAN Workshop on Chinese Language Processing 2003

Sapporo, Japan
11-12 July 2003

ISBN: 978-1-62748-369-8

Printed from e-media with permission by:

Curran Associates, Inc.
57 Morehouse Lane
Red Hook, NY 12571

Some format issues inherent in the e-media version may also appear in this print version.

Printed by Curran Associates, Inc. (2013)

For permission requests, please contact the Association for Computational Linguistics at the address below.

Association for Computational Linguistics
209 N. Eighth Street
Stroudsburg, Pennsylvania 18360

Phone: 1-570-476-8006
Fax: 1-570-476-0860

acl@aclweb.org

Additional copies of this publication are available from:

Curran Associates, Inc.
57 Morehouse Lane
Red Hook, NY 12571 USA
Phone: 845-758-0400
Fax: 845-758-2634
Email: curran@proceedings.com
Web: www.proceedings.com

TABLE OF CONTENTS

PREFACE

This year's workshop is special. First, Sighan organized the First Chinese Word Segmentation Bakeoff, and this workshop will include presentations from the participating sites and discussion about the bakeoff and further contests. Second, many of us have been affected one way or another by SARS in the past half year. It is important to keep carrying out our research while helping our countries and people to get through the tough time.

Our first thanks go to Sighan and ACL for sponsoring the workshop. We would also like to thank all those who submitted their work to the workshop and who participated in the Word Segmentation Bakeoff. In total, we received twenty-nine workshop papers, and thirteen sites from Mainland China, Hong Kong, Taiwan, Singapore, Japan, and United States participated in the bakeoff.

Richard Sproat has put tremendous effort in organizing the bakeoff. We would also like to thank the four sites (Academia Sinica, the City University of Hong Kong, Peking University, and the University of Pennsylvania) for providing the training and testing data, and Tom Emerson for maintaining the workshop and bakeoff websites.

Our programming committee has done a terrific job, considering the problems caused by SARS in Asia, and the short time span between the submission deadline and the time of acceptance notices.

In closing we would like to thank you for attending the workshop, and we wish you have a great time at the workshop.

Qing Ma and Fei Xia
May 25, 2003

PROGRAM COMMITTEE:

Qing Ma	Ryukoku University, Japan, Co-chair
Fei Xia	IBM, USA, Co-chair

Joyce Chai	Michigan State University, USA
Keh-Jiann Chen	Academia Sinica, Taiwan
Zhendong Dong	Hownet designer, China
Tom Emerson	Basis Technology Corp, USA
Changning Huang	Microsoft, China
Chu-ren Huang	Academia Sinica, Taiwan
K.L.Kwok	Queens College, USA
Tom Lai	City University of Hong Kong
Sujian Li	Peking University, China
Tan Chew Lim	National University of Singapore
Dekang Lin	University of Alberta, Canada
Kim-Teng Lua	National University of Singapore
Masaki Murata	Communications Research Laboratory, Japan
Martha Palmer	University of Pennsylvania, USA
Shimei Pan	IBM, USA
Fuji Ren	Tokushima University, Japan
Bangalore Srinivas	AT&T, USA
Keh-Yih Su	Behavior Design Corporation, Taiwan
Maosong Sun	Tsinghua University, China
Bing Swen	Peking University, China
Banjamin Tsou	City University of Hong Kong
Amy Weinberg	University of Maryland, USA
Andi Wu	Microsoft, USA
Dekai Wu	Hong Kong Science and Technology University
Nianwen Xue	University of Pennsylvania, USA
Jin Yang	Systran, USA
Shiwen Yu	Peking University, China
Qiang Zhou	Tsinghua University, China

WORKSHOP WEBSITE:

http://www.sighan.org/swclp2/

Unsupervised Training for Overlapping Ambiguity Resolution in Chinese Word Segmentation

Mu Li, Jianfeng Gao, Changning Huang
Microsoft Research, Asia
Beijing 100080, China
{t-muli,jfgao,cnhuang}@microsoft.com

Jianfeng Li
University of Science and Technology of China
Hefei, 230027, China
jackwind@mail.ustc.edu.cn

Abstract

This paper proposes an unsupervised training approach to resolving overlapping ambiguities in Chinese word segmentation. We present an ensemble of adapted Naïve Bayesian classifiers that can be trained using an unlabelled Chinese text corpus. These classifiers differ in that they use context words within windows of different sizes as features. The performance of our approach is evaluated on a manually annotated test set. Experimental results show that the proposed approach achieves an accuracy of 94.3%, rivaling the rule-based and supervised training methods.

1 Introduction

Resolving segmentation ambiguities is one of the fundamental tasks for Chinese word segmentation, and has received considerable attention in the research community. Word segmentation ambiguities can be roughly classified into two classes: overlapping ambiguity (OA), and combination ambiguity (CA). In this paper, we focus on the methods of resolving overlapping ambiguities.

Consider a Chinese character string ABC, if it can be segmented into two words either as AB/C or A/BC depending on different context, ABC is called an overlapping ambiguity string (OAS). For example, given a Chinese character string "各国有" (*ge4-guo2-you3*), it can be segmented as either "各 | 国有" (each state-owned) in Sentence (1) of Figure 1, or "各国 | 有" (every country has) in Sentence (2).

(1) 在 (in) | 各 (each) | 国有 (state-owned) | 企业 (enterprise) | 中 (middle)
(in each state-owned enterprise)

(2) 在 (in) | 人权 (human rights) | 问题 (problem) | 上 (on) | 各国 (every country) | 有 (have) | 共同点 (common ground)
(Regarding human rights, every country has some common ground)

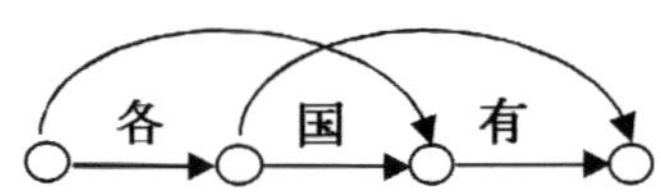

Figure 1. Overlapping ambiguities of Chinese character string "各国有"

Our method of resolving overlapping ambiguities contains two procedures. One is to construct an ensemble of Naïve Bayesian classifiers to resolve ambiguities. The other is an unsupervised method for training the Naïve Bayesian classifiers which compose the ensemble. The main issue of the unsupervised training is how to eliminate the negative impact of the OA errors in the training data. Our solution is to identify all OASs in the training data and replace them with a single special token. By doing so, we actually remove the portion of training data that are likely to contain OA errors. The classifiers are then trained on the processed training data.

Our approach is evaluated on a manually annotated test set with 5,759 overlapping segmentation ambiguities. Experimental results show that an accuracy of 94.3% is achieved.

This remainder of this paper is structured as follows: Section 2 reviews previous work. Section 3 defines overlapping ambiguous strings in Chinese. Section 4 describes the evaluation results. Section 5 presents our conclusion.

2 Previous Work

Previous methods of resolving overlapping ambiguities can be grouped into rule-based approaches and statistical approaches.

Maximum Matching (MM) based segmentation (Huang, 1997) can be regarded as the simplest rule-based approach, in which one starts from one end of the input sentence, greedily matches the longest word towards the other end, and repeats the process with the rest unmatched character sequences until the entire sentence is processed. If the process starts with the beginning of the sentence, it is called Forward Maximum Matching (FMM). If the process starts with the end of the sentence, it is called Backward Maximum Matching (BMM). Although it is widely used due to its simplicity, MM based segmentation performs poorly in real text.

Zheng and Liu (1997) use a set of manually generated rules, and reported an accuracy of 81% on an open test set. Swen and Yu (1999) presents a lexicon-based method. The basic idea is that for each entry in a lexicon, all possible ambiguity types are tagged; and for each ambiguity types, a solution strategy is used. They achieve an accuracy of 95%. Sun (1998) demonstrates that most of the overlapping ambiguities can be resolved without taking into account the context information. He then proposes a lexicalized rule-based approach. His experiments show that using the 4,600 most frequent rules, 51% coverage can be achieved in an open test set.

Statistical methods view the overlapping ambiguity resolution as a search or classification task. For example, Liu (1997) uses a word unigram language model, given all possible segmentations of a Chinese character sequence, to search the best segmentation with the highest probability. Similar approach can be traced back to Zhang (1991). But the method does not target to overlapping ambiguities. So the disambiguation results are not reported. Sun (1999) presents a hybrid method which incorporates empirical rules and statistical probabilities, and reports an overall accuracy of 92%. Li (2001) defines the word segmentation disambiguation as a binary classification problem. Li then uses Support Vector Machine (SVM) with mutual information between each Chinese character pair as a feature. The method achieves an accuracy of 92%. All the above methods utilize a supervised training procedure. However, a large manually labeled training set is not always available. To deal with the problem, unsupervised approaches have been proposed. For example, Sun (1997) detected word boundaries given an OAS using character-based statistical measures, such as mutual information and difference of t-test. He reported an accuracy of approximately 90%. In his approach, only the statistical information within 4 adjacent characters is exploited, and lack of word-level statistics may prevent the disambiguation performance from being further improved.

3 Ensemble of Naïve Bayesian Classifier for Overlapping Ambiguity Resolution

3.1 Problem Definition

We first give the formal definition of overlapping ambiguous string (OAS) and longest OAS.

An OAS is a Chinese character string O that satisfies the following two conditions:

a) There exist two segmentations Seg_1 and Seg_2 such that $\forall w_1 \in Seg_1, w_2 \in Seg_2$, where Chinese words w_1 and w_2 are different from either literal strings or positions;

b) $\exists w_1 \in Seg_1, w_2 \in Seg_2$, where w_1 and w_2 overlap.

The first condition ensures that there are ambiguous word boundaries (if more than one word segmentors are applied) in an OAS. In the example presented in section 1, the string "各国有" is an OAS but "各国有企业" is not because the word "企业" remains the same in both FMM and BMM segmentations of "各 | 国有 | 企业" and "各国 | 有 | 企业". The second condition indicates that the ambiguous word boundaries result from crossing brackets. As illustrated in Figure 1, words "各国" and "国有" form a crossing bracket.

The longest OAS is an OAS that is not a substring of any other OAS in a given sentence. For example, in the case "生活水平" (*sheng1-huo2-shui3-ping2*, living standard), both "生活水" and "生活水平" are OASs, but only "生活水平" is the longest OAS because "生活水" is a substring of "生活水平". In this paper, we only consider the longest OAS because both left and right boundaries of the longest OAS are determined.

Furthermore, we constrain our search space within the FMM segmentation O_f and BMM segmentation O_b of a given longest OAS. According to Huang (1997), two important properties of OAS has been identified: (1) if the FMM segmentation is the same as its BMM segmentation ($O_f = O_b$), for example "搜索引擎" (*sou1-suo3-yin3-qing2*, Search Engine), the probability that the MM segmentation is correct is 99%; Otherwise, (2) if the FMM segmentation differs from its BMM segmentation ($O_f \neq O_b$), for example "各国有", the probability that at least one of the MM segmentation is correct is also 99%. So such a strategy will not lower the coverage of our approach.

Therefore, the overlapping ambiguity resolution can be formulized as a binary classification problem as follows:

Given a longest OAS O and its context feature set C, let $G(Seg, C)$ be a score function of Seg for $seg \in \{O_f, O_b\}$, the overlapping ambiguity resolution task is to make the binary decision:

$$seg = \begin{cases} O_f & G(O_f, C) > G(O_b, C) \\ O_b & G(O_f, C) < G(O_b, C) \end{cases} \quad (1)$$

Note that $O_f = O_b$ means that both FMM and BMM arrive at the same result. The classification process can then be stated as:

a) If $O_f = O_b$, then choose either segmentation result since they are same;

b) Otherwise, choose the one with the higher score G according to Equation (1).

For example, in the example of "搜索引擎", if $O_f = O_b$ = "搜索 | 引擎", then "搜索 | 引擎" is selected as the answer. In another example of "各国有" in sentence (1) of Figure 1, O_f = "各国 | 有", O_b = "各 | 国有". Assume that C = {在, 企业}, i.e., we used a context window of size 3; then the segmentation "各国 | 有" is selected if $G(\text{"各国|有"}, \{在, 企业\}) > G(\text{"各|国有"}, \{在, 企业\})$, otherwise "各 | 国有" is selected.

3.2 Naïve Bayesian Classifier for Overlapping Ambiguity Resolution

Last section formulates the overlapping ambiguity resolution of an OAS O as the binary classification between O_f and O_b. This section describes the use of the adapted Naïve Bayesian Classifier (NBC) (Duda and Hart, 1973) to address problem. Here, we use the words around O within a window as features, with $w_{-m}...w_{-1}$ denoting m words on the left of the O and $w_1...w_n$ denoting n words on the right of the O. Naïve Bayesian Classifier assumes that all the feature variables are conditionally independent. So the joint probability of observing a set of context features $C = \{w_{-m}...w_{-1}, w_1...w_n\}$ of a segmentation Seg (O_f or O_b) of O is as follows:

$$p(w_{-m}, w_{-1,} w_1, ...w_n, Seg) = p(Seg) \prod_{i=-m,...-1,1,...n} p(w_i \mid Seg) \quad (2)$$

Assume that Equation (2) is the score function in Equation (1) G, we then have two parameters to be estimated: $p(Seg)$ and $p(w_i|Seg)$. Since we do not have enough labeled training data, we then resort to the redundancy property of natural language. Due to the fact that the OAS occupies only in a very small portion of the entire Chinese text, it is feasible to estimate the word co-occurrence probabilities from the portion of corpus that contains no overlapping ambiguities. Consider an OAS 信心地 (*xin4-xin1-de*, confidently). The correct segmentation would be "信心 | 地", if 充满 (*cong1-man3*, full of) were its context word. We note that 充满 appears as the left context word of 信心 in both strings 充满信心地 and 充满信心和勇气 (勇气, *yong3-qi4*, courage). While the former string contains an OAS, the latter does not. We then remove all OAS from the training data, and estimate the parameters using the training data that do not contain OAS. In experiments, we replace all longest OAS that has $O_f \neq O_b$ with a special token `[GAP]`. Below, we refer to the processed corpus as tokenized corpus.

Note that Seg is either the FMM or the BMM segmentation of O, and all OASs (including Seg) have been removed from the tokenized corpus, thus there are no statistical information available to estimate $p(Seg)$ and $p(w_{-m}...w_{-1}, w_1...w_n|Seg)$ based on the Maximum Likelihood Estimation (MLE) principle. To estimate them, we introduce the following two assumptions.

1) Since the unigram probability of each word w can be estimated from the training data, for a given segmentation $Seg = w_{s1}...w_{sk}$, we assume that each word w of Seg is generated independently. The probability $p(Seg)$ is approxi-

mated by the production of the word unigram probabilities:

$$p(Seg) = \prod_{w_i \in Seg} p(w_i) \quad (3)$$

2) We also assume that left and right context word sequences are only conditioned on the leftmost and rightmost words of *Seg*, respectively.

$$\begin{aligned} & p(w_{-m}...w_{-1}, w_1...w_n \mid Seg) \\ & = p(w_{-m}...w_{-1} \mid w_{s1}) p(w_1...w_n \mid w_{sk}) \\ & = \frac{p(w_{-m}...w_{-1}, w_{s1}) p(w_{sk}, w_1...w_n)}{p(w_{s1}) p(w_{sk})} \end{aligned} \quad (4)$$

where the word sequence probabilities $P(w_{-m}, ..., w_{-1}, w_{s1})$ and $P(w_{sk}, w_1, ..., w_n)$ are decomposed as productions of trigram probabilities. We used a statistical language model toolkit described in (Gao et al, 2002) to build trigram models based on the tokenized corpus.

Although the final language model is trained based on a tokenized corpus, the approach can be regarded as an unsupervised one from the view of the entire training process: the tokenized corpus is automatically generated by an MM based segmentation tool from the raw corpus input with neither human interaction nor manually labeled data required.

3.3 Ensemble of Classifiers and Majority Vote

Given different window sizes, we can obtain different classifiers. We then combine them to achieve better results using the so-called ensemble learning (Peterson 2000). Let NBC(l, r) denote the classifier with left window size l and right window size r. Given the maximal window size of 2, we then have 9 classifiers, as shown in Table 1.

	$L = 0$	$l = 1$	$l = 2$
$r = 0$	NBC(0, 0)	NBC(1, 0)	NBC(2,0)
$r = 1$	NBC(0,1)	NBC(1,1)	NBC(2,1)
$r = 2$	NBC(0,2)	NBC(1,2)	NBC(2,2)

Table 1. Bayesian classifiers in the ensemble

The ensemble learning suggests that the ensemble classification results are based on the majority vote of these classifiers: The segmentation that is selected by most classifiers is chosen.

4 Experiments and Discussions

4.1 Settings

We evaluate our approach using a manually annotated test set, which was selected randomly from People's Daily news articles of year 1997, containing approximate 460,000 Chinese characters, or 247,000 words. In the test set, 5759 longest OAS are identified. Our lexicon contains 93,700 entries.

4.2 OAS Distribution

We first investigate the distribution of different types of OAS in the test set. In our approach, the performance upper bound (i.e. oracle accuracy) cannot achieve 100% because not all the OASs' correct segmentations can be generated by FMM and BMM segmentation. So it is very useful to know to what extent our approach can deal with the problem.

The results are shown in Table 2. We denote the entire OAS data set as *C*, and divide it into two subsets *A* and *B* according to the type of OAS. It can be seen from the table that in data set *A* (O_f=O_b), the accuracy of MM segmentation achieves 98.8% accuracy. Meanwhile, in data set *B* ($O_f \neq O_b$) the oracle recall of candidates proposed by FMM and BMM is 95.7% (97.2% in the entire data set *C*). The statistics are very close to those reported in Huang (1997).

A $OAS_{Of=Ob}$ 2763 47.98%	$O_f = O_b =$ COR 2731 47.42%
	$O_f = O_b \neq$ COR 32 0.56%
B $OAS_{Of \neq Ob}$ 2996 52.02%	$O_f =$ COR $\vee$ $O_b =$ COR 2866 49.77%
	$O_f \neq$ COR $\wedge$ $O_b \neq$ COR 130 2.26%

Table 2. Distribution of OAS in the test set

Here are some examples for the overlapping ambiguities that cannot be covered by our approach. For errors resulting from $O_f = O_b \neq$ COR, a typical example in the literature is 结合成分子时 (jie2-he2-cheng2-fen1-zi3-shi2, 结合 | 成 | 分子 |

时). For errors caused by $O_f \neq O_b$ and $O_f \neq$ COR $\wedge$ $O_b \neq$ COR, 出现在世纪(之初) (chu1-xian4-zai4-shi4-ji4, 出现 | 在 | 世纪) serves as a good example. These two types of errors are usually composed of several words and need a much more complicated search process to determine the final correct output. Since the number of such errors is very small, they are not target of our approach in this paper.

4.3 Experimental Results of Ensemble of Naïve Bayesian Classifiers

The classifiers are trained from the People's Daily news articles of year 2000, which contain over 24 million characters. The training data is tokenized. That is, all OAS with $O_f \neq O_b$ are replaced with the token `[GAP]`. After tokenization, there are 16,078,000 tokens in the training data in which 203,329 are `[GAP]`, which is 1.26% of the entire training data set. Then a word trigram language model is constructed on the tokenized corpus, and each Bayesian classifier is built given the language model.

	$l = 0$	$l = 1$	$l = 2$
$r = 0$	88.73%	88.85%	88.95%
$r = 1$	89.09%	89.39%	89.39%
$r = 2$	88.95%	89.39%	89.35%

Table 3. Accuracy of each individual classifier

Table 3 shows the accuracy of each classifier on data set *B*. The performance of the ensemble based on majority vote is 89.79% on data set *B*, and the overall accuracy on *C* is 94.13%. The ensemble consistently outperforms any of its members. Classifiers with both left and right context features perform better than the others because they are capable to segment some of the context sensitive OAS. For example, contextual information is necessary to segment the OAS "看台上"(*kan4-tai2-shang4*, on the stand) correctly in both following sentences:

你 | 看 | 台上 | 那个 | 演员
(Look at the performer in the stage)
站 | 在 | 最高 | 一 | 层 | 看台 | 上
(Stand in the highest stand)

Both Peterson (2000) and Brill (1998) found that the ultimate success of an ensemble depends on the assumption that classifiers to be combined make complementary errors. We investigate this assumption in our experiments, and estimate the oracle accuracy of our approach. Result shows that only 6.0% (180 out of 2996) of the OAS in data set *B* that is classified incorrectly by all the 9 classifiers. In addition, we can see from Table 2, that 130 instances of these 180 errors are impossible to be correct because neither O_f nor O_b is the correct segmentation. Therefore, the oracle accuracy of the ensemble is 94.0%, which is very close to 95.7%, the theoretical upper bound of our approach in data set *B* described in Section 4.2. However, our majority vote based ensemble only achieves accuracy close to 90%. This analysis thus suggests that further improves can be made by using more powerful ensemble strategies.

4.4 Lexicalized Rule Based OAS Disambiguation

We also conduct a series of experiments to evaluate the performance of a widely used lexicalized rule-based OAS disambiguation approach. As reported by Sun (1998) and Li (2001), over 90% of the OAS can be disambiguated in a context-free way. Therefore, simply collecting large amount of correctly segmented OAS whose segmentation is independent of its context would yield pretty good performance.

We first collected 730,000 OAS with $O_f \neq O_b$ from 20 years' People's Daily corpus which contains about 650 million characters. Then approximately 47,000 most frequently occurred OASs were extracted. For each of the extracted OAS, 20 sentences that contain it were randomly selected from the corpus, and the correct segmentation is manually labeled. 41,000 lexicalized disambiguation rules were finally extracted from the labeled data, whose either MM segmentation (O_f or O_b) gains absolute majority, over 95% in our experiment. The rule set covers approximately 80% occurrences of all the OASs in the training set, which is very close to that reported in Sun (1998). Here is a sample rule extracted: 信心地 => 信心 | 地. It means that among the 20 sentences that contain the character sequence "信心地", at least 19 of them are segmented as "信心 | 地".

The performance of the lexicalized rule-based approach is shown in Table 4, where for comparison we also include the performance of using only FMM or BMM segmentation algorithm.

	Accuracy	
	Data set B	Data set C
FMM	49.44%	73.12%
BMM	46.31%	71.51%
Rule + FMM	83.10%	90.65%
Rule + BMM	84.43%	91.33%
NBC(0, 0)	88.73%	93.70%
Ensemble	89.79%	94.13%

Table 4. Performance comparison

In Table 4, Rule + FMM means if there is no rule applicable to an OAS, FMM segmentation will be used. Similarly, Rule + BMM means that BMM segmentation will be used as backup. We can see in Table 4 that rule-based systems outperform their FMM and BMM counterparts significantly, but do not perform as well as our method, even when no context feature is used. This is because that the rules can only cover about 76% of the OASs in the test set with precision 95%, and FMM or BMM performs poorly on the rest of the OASs. Although the precision of these lexicalized rules is high, the room for further improvements is limited. For example, to achieve a higher coverage, say 90%, much more manually labeled training data (i.e. 81,000 OAS) are needed.

5 Conclusion and Future work

Our contributions are two-fold. First, we propose an approach based on an ensemble of adapted naïve Bayesian classifiers to resolving overlapping ambiguities in Chinese word segmentation. Second, we present an unsupervised training method of constructing these Bayesian classifiers on an unlabeled training corpus. It thus opens up the possibility for adjusting this approach to a large variety of applications. We perform evaluations using a manually annotated test set. Results show that our approach outperforms a lexicalized rule-based system. Future work includes investigation on how to construct more powerful classifier for further improvements. One promising way is combining our approach with Sun's (1997), with a core set of context free OASs manually labeled to improve accuracy.

Acknowledgements

We would like to thank Wenfeng Yang and Xiaodan Zhu for helpful discussions on this project and Wenfeng's excellent work on the lexicalized disambiguation rule set construction.

References

Eric Brill and Wu Jun. 1998. Classifier combination for improved lexical disambiguation. In *Proceedings of the 36th Annual Meeting of the Association for Computational Linguistics*, Montreal. CA.

Richard Duda and Peter Hart. 1973. *Pattern Classification and Scene Analysis.* Wiley, New York, NY.

Jianfeng Gao and Joshua Goodman, Li Mingjing, Lee Kai-Fu. 2002. Toward a unified approach to statistical language modeling for Chinese. *ACM Transactions on Asian Language Information Processing,* 1 (1):3-33.

Changning Huang. 1997. Segmentation problem in Chinese Processing. (In Chinese) *Applied Linguistics.* 1:72-78.

Rong Li, Shaohui Liu, Shiwei Ye and Zhongzhi Shi. 2001. A Method of Crossing Ambiguities in Chinese word Segmentation Based on SVM and k-NN. (In Chinese) *Journal of Chinese Information Processing*, 15(6): 13-18.

Ting Liu, Kaizhu Wang and Xinghai Jiang. 1997. The Maximum Probability Segmentation Algorithm of Ambiguous Character Strings. (In Chinese) *Language Engineering*. Tsinghua University Press. pp.182-187.

Ted Pedersen. 2000. A Simple Approach to Building Ensembles of Naive Bayesian Classifiers for Word Sense Disambiguation. In *Proceedings of the First Annual Meeting of the North American Chapter of the Association for Computational Linguistics*. Seattle, WA. pp. 63-69

Maosong Sun, Changning Huang and Benjamin K. Tsou. 1997. *Using Character Bigram for Ambiguity Resolution In Chinese Words Segmentation.* (In Chinese) Computer Research and Development, 34(5): 332-339

Maosong Sun and Zhengping Zuo. 1998. Overlapping ambiguity in Chinese Text. (In Chinese) *Quantitative and Computational Studies on the Chinese Language*, HK, pp. 323-338

Maosong Sun, Zhengping Zuo and Changning Huang. 1999. Algorithm for solving 3-character crossing ambiguities in Chinese word segmentation. (In Chinese) *Journal of Tsinghua University Science and Technology*, 39(5).

Bing Swen and Shiwen Yu. 1999. A Graded Approach for the Efficient Resolution of Chinese Word Segmentation Ambiguities. In *Proceedings of 5th Natural Language Processing Pacific Rim Symposium*. pp. 19-24

Junsheng Zhang, Zhida Chen and Shunde Chen. 1991. Constraint Satisfaction and Probabilistic Chinese Segmentation. (In Chinese) In *Proceedings of ROCLING IV (R.O.C. Computational Linguistics Conference)*. pp. 147-165

Jiaheng Zheng and Kaiying Liu. 1997. The Research of Ambiguity Word – Segmentation Technique for the Chinese Text. (In Chinese) *Language Engineering*, Tsinghua University Press, pp. 201-206

Class Based Sense Definition Model for Word Sense Tagging and Disambiguation

Tracy Lin
Department of Communication Engineering
National Chiao Tung University,
1001, Ta Hsueh Road, Hsinchu, 300, Taiwan, ROC
tracylin@cm.nctu.edu.tw

Jason S. Chang
Department of Computer Science
National Tsing Hua University
101, Kuangfu Road, Hsinchu, 300, Taiwan, ROC
jschang@cs.nthu.edu.tw

Abstract

We present an unsupervised learning strategy for word sense disambiguation (WSD) that exploits multiple linguistic resources including a parallel corpus, a bilingual machine readable dictionary, and a thesaurus. The approach is based on Class Based Sense Definition Model (CBSDM) that generates the glosses and translations for a class of word senses. The model can be applied to resolve sense ambiguity for words in a parallel corpus. That sense tagging procedure, in effect, produces a semantic bilingual concordance, which can be used to train WSD systems for the two languages involved. Experimental results show that CBSDM trained on Longman Dictionary of Contemporary English, English-Chinese Edition (LDOCE E-C) and Longman Lexicon of Contemporary English (LLOCE) is very effectively in turning a Chinese-English parallel corpus into sense tagged data for development of WSD systems.

1. Introduction

Word sense disambiguation has been an important research area for over 50 years. WSD is crucial for many applications, including machine translation, information retrieval, part of speech tagging, etc. Ide and Veronis (1998) pointed out the two major problems of WSD: sense tagging and data sparseness. On one hand, tagged data are very difficult to come by, since sense tagging is considerably more difficult than other forms of linguistic annotation. On the other hand, although the data sparseness is a common problem, it is especially severe for WSD. The problems were attacked in various ways. Yarowsky (1992) showed a class-based approach under which a very large untagged corpus and thesaurus can be used effectively for unsupervised training for noun homograph disambiguation. However, the method does not offer a method that explicitly produces sense tagged data for any given sense inventory. Li and Huang (1999) described a similar unsupervised approach for Chinese text based on a Chinese thesaurus. As noted in Merialdo (1994), even minimal hand tagging improved on the results of unsupervised methods. Yarowsky (1995) showed that the learning strategy of bootstrapping from small tagged data led to results rivaling supervised training methods. Li and Li (2002) extended the approach by using corpora in two languages to bootstrap the learning process. They showed *bilingual bootstrapping* is even more effective. The bootstrapping approach is limited by lack of a systematic procedure of preparing seed data for any word in a given sense inventory. The approach also suffers from errors propagating from one iteration into the next. Li and Huang

Another alternative involves using a parallel corpus as a surrogate for tagged data. Gale, Church and Yarowsky (1992) exploited the so-called *one sense per translation constraint* for WSD. They reported high precision rates of a WSD system for two-way disambiguation of six English nouns based on their translations in an English-French Parallel corpus. However, when working with a particular sense inventory, there is no obvious way to know whether the one sense per translation constraint holds or how to determine the relevant translations automatically.

Diab and Resnik (2002) extended the translation-based learning strategy with a weakened constraint that many instances of a word in a parallel corpus often correspond to lexically varied but semantically consistent translations. They proposed to group those translations into a *target set*, which can be automatically tagged with correct senses based on the hypernym hierarchy of WordNet. Diab and Resnik's work represents a departure from previous unsupervised approaches in that no seed data is needed and explicit tagged data are produced for a given sense inventory (WordNet in their case). The system trained on the tagged data was shown to be on a par with the best "supervised training" systems in SENSEVAL-2 competition. However, Diab and Resnik's method is only applicable to nominal WordNet senses. Moreover, the method is seriously hampered by noise and semantic inconsistency in a target set. Worse still, it is not always possible to rely on the hypernym hierarchy for tagging a target set. For instance, the relevant senses of the target set of {**serve**, **tee off**} for the Chinese counterpart "發球" [**faqiu**] do not have a common hypernym:

Sense 15
serve – (put the **ball** into play; as in **games** like tennis)
⇨ move – (have a turn; make one's move in a game)
Sense 1
Tee off – (strike a golf **ball** from a tee at the start of a **game**)
⇨ play – (participating in game or sports)
⇨ compete – (compete for something)

This paper describes a new WSD approach to simultaneously attack the problems of tagging and data sparseness. The approach assumes the availability of a parallel corpus of text written in *E* (the first language, L1[+]) and *C* (the second language, L2), an L1 to L2 bilingual machine readable dictionary *M*, and a L1 thesaurus *T*. A so-called *Mutually Assured Resolution of Sense* Algorithm (*MARS*) and Class Based Sense Definition Model (CBSDM) are proposed to identify the word senses in *I* for each word in a semantic class of words *L* in *T*. Unlike Diab and Resnik, we do not apply the MARS algorithm directly to *target sets* to avoid the noisy words therein. The derived classes senses and their relevant glosses in L1 and L2 make it possible to build Class Based Sense Definition and Translation Models (CBSDM and CBSTM), which subsequently can be applied to assign sense tags to words in a parallel corpus.

The main idea is to exploit the defining L1 and L2 words in the glosses to resolve the sense ambiguity. For instance, for the class containing "*serve*" and "*tee off*," the approach exploits common defining words, including "*ball*" and "*game*" in two relevant **serve**-15 and **tee off**-1 to assign the correct senses to "*serve*" and "*tee off*." The character bigram "發球" [**faqiu**] in an English-Chinese MRD:

serve v **10** [I∅; T1] to begin play by striking (the ball) to the opponent 發球 (LDOCE E-C p. 1300),

would make it possible to align and sense tag "*serve*" or "*tee off*" in a parallel corpus such as the bilingual citations in Example 1:

(1C) 發球前先喝一小瓶蓋酒。
(1E) drink a capful before **teeing off** at each hole. (Source: *Sinorama, 1999, Nov. Issue, p.15, Who Played the First Stroke?*).

That effectively attaches semantic information to bilingual citations and turns a parallel corpus into a Bilingual Semantic Concordance (BSC). The BSC enables us to simultaneously attack two critical WSD problems of sense tagging difficulties and data sparseness, thus provides an effective approach to WSD. BSC also embodies a projection of the sense inventory from L1 onto L2, thus creates a new sense inventory and semantic concordance for L2. If *I* is based on WordNet for English, it is then possible to obtain an L2 WordNet. There are many additional applications of BSC, including bilingual lexicography, cross language information retrieval, and computer assisted language learning.

The remainder of the paper is organized as follows: Sections 2 and 3 lay out the approach and describe the MARS and SWAT algorithms. Section 4 describes experiments and evaluation. Section 5 contains discussion and we conclude in Section 6.

2. Class Based Sense Definition Model

We will first illustrate our approach with an example. A formal treatment of the approach will follow in Section 2.2.

2.1 An example

[+] This has nothing to do with the direction of translation and is not to be confused with the native and second language distinction made in the literature of Teaching English As a Second Language (TESL) and Computer Assisted Language Learning.

To make full use of existing machine readable dictionaries and thesauri, some kind of linkage and integration is necessary (Knight and Luk, 1994). Therefore, we are interested in linking thesaurus classes and MRD senses: Given a thesaurus class *S*, it is important that the relevant senses for each word *w* in *S* is determined in a MRD-based sense inventory *I*. We will show such linkage is useful for WSD and is feasible, based solely on the words of the glosses in *I*. For instance, given the following set of word (N060) in Longman Lexicon of Contemporary English (McArthur 1992):

L = {**difficult**, **hard**, **stiff**, **tough**, **arduous**, **awkward**}.

Although those words are highly ambiguous, the juxtaposition immediately brings to mind the relevant senses. Specifically for the sense inventory of LDOCE E-C, the relevant senses for *L* are as follows:

- **dfficult** *adj* **1**. not easy; hard to do, make, understand, etc. 不容易 [bu rongyi] ; 難 [nan]
- **hard** *adj* **2**. difficult (to do or understand) 難的 [nan de]; 困難的 [kunnan de]
- **stiff** *adj* **6**. difficult to do 難做的 [nanzuo de] ; 棘手的 [jishou de]
- **tough** *adj* **4**. difficult to do; not easy; demanding effort 難做的 [nanzuo de] ; 費力的 [feili de]
- **arduous** *adj* **1**. needing much effort; difficult 費力的 [feilide] ; 艱難的 [jian-nan de]
- **awkward** *adj* **2**. not well made for use; difficult to use; causing difficulty 難於使用的 [nan yu shi-yong de] ; 不便的 [buban de]

Therefore, we have the intended senses, *S*

S = {**difficult-1**, **hard-2**, **stiff-6**, **tough-4**, **arduous-1**, **awkward-2**}.

It is reasonable to assume each sense in *I* is accompanied by a sense definition written in the same language (L1). We use D(*S*) to denote the glosses of *S*. Therefore we have

D(*S*) = "not easy; hard to do, make, understand, etc.; difficult to do or understand; difficult to do; difficult to do; not easy; demanding effort; needing much effort; difficult; not well made for use; difficult to use; causing difficulty;"

The intuition of bringing out the intended senses of semantically related words can be formalized by Class Based Sense Definition Model (CBSDM), which is a *micro* language model generating D(*S*), the glosses of *S* in *I*. For simplicity, we assume an unigram language model P(*d*) that generates the content words *d* in the glosses of *S*. Therefore, we have

D(*S*) = "easy hard do make understand difficult do understand difficult do difficult do easy demanding effort needing much effort difficult well made use difficult use causing difficulty"

If we have the relevant senses, it is a simple matter of counting to estimate P(*d*). Conversely, with P(*d*) available to us, we can pick the relevant sense of *S* in *I* which is most likely generated by P(*d*). The problem of learning the model P(*d*) lend itself nicely to an iterative relaxation method such as the Expectation and Maximization Algorithm (Dempster, Laird, Rubin, 1977).

Initially, we assume all senses of *S* word in *I* is equally likely and use all the defining words therein to estimate P(*d*) regardless of whether they are relevant. For LDOCE senses, initial estimate of the relevant glosses is as follows:

D(*S*) = "easy hard do make understand people unfriendly quarrelling pleased ... firm stiff broken pressed bent difficult do understand forceful needing using force body mind ...bent painful moving moved ... strong weakened suffer uncomfortable conditions cut worn broken ...needing effort difficult lacking skill moving body parts body CLUMSY made use difficult use causing difficulty"

Table 1. The initial CBSDM for n-word list {difficult, hard, stiff, tough, arduous, awkward} based on the relevant and irrelevant LDOCE senses, *n* = 6.

Defining word *d*	Count, *k*	P(*d*) = *k*/*n*
Difficult	5	0.83
Effort	3	0.50
Understand	2	0.33
Bad	2	0.33
Bent	2	0.33
Body	2	0.33
Broken	2	0.33
Difficulty	2	0.33
Easy	2	0.33
Firm	2	0.33
Hard	2	0.33
Moving	2	0.33
Needing	2	0.33
Water	2	0.33

As evident from Table 1, the initial estimates of P(*d*) are quite close to the true probability distribution (based on the relevant senses only). The three top ranking defining words "*difficult*," "*effort*," and "*understand*" appear in glosses of relevant senses, and not in irrelevant senses. Admittedly, there are still some noisy, irrelevant words such as "*bent*" and "*broken.*" But they do not figure prominently in the model from the start and will fade out gradually with successive iterations of re-estimation. We estimate the probability of a particular sense *s* being in *S* by P(D(*s*)), the probability of its gloss under P(*d*). For intance, we have

P(**hard**-1) = P(D(**hard**-1)) = P("firm and stiff; which ..."),

P(**hard**-2) = P(D(**hard**-2)) = P("difficult to do or understand").

On the other hand, we re-estimate the probability P(*d*) of a defining word *d* under CBSDM by how often *d* appears in a sense *s* and P(*s*). P(*d*) is positively prepositional to the frequency of *d* in D(*s*) and to the value of P(*s*). Under that re-estimation scheme, the defining words in relevant senses will figure more prominently in CBSDM, leading to more accurate estimation for probability of *s* being in *S*. For instance, in the first round, "*difficult*" in the gloss of **hard**-2 will weigh twice more than "*firm*" in the gloss of irrelevant **hard**-1, leading to relatively higher unigram probability for "*difficult.*" That in turn makes **hard**-2 even more probable than **hard**-1. See Table 2.

Table 2. First round estimates for P(*s*), the probability of sense *s* in *S*.

Sense*	Definition	P(*s*)
hard-1	**firm** and stiff; which cannot easily be broken	0.2857
hard-2	**difficult** to do or understand	0.7143
stiff-1	not easily bent	0.2857
stiff-6	**difficult** to do	0.7143

* in LDOCE.

** Assuming $P(s) \approx \max_{d \in D(s)} P(d)$

Often the senses in *I* are accompanied with glosses written in a second language (L2); exclusively (as in a simple bilingual word list) or additionally (as in LDOCE E-C). Either way, the words in L2 glosses can be incorporated into D(*s*) and P(*d*). For instance, the character unigrams and/or overlapping bigrams in the Mandarin glosses of *S* in LDOCE E-C and their appearance counts and probability are shown in Table 3.

Table 3. Classes Based Sense Translation Model for {difficult-1, hard-2, stiff-6, tough-4, arduous-1, awkward-2} in LDOCE*.

Translation	Count	Prob	Translation	Count	Prob
難	6	1.00	棘	1	0.17
力	2	0.33	艱	1	0.17
不	2	0.33	難做	3	0.50
做	2	0.33	費力	2	0.33
費	2	0.33	不容	2	0.33
手	1	0.17	不便	1	0.17
用	1	0.17	困難	1	0.17
困	1	0.17	使用	1	0.17
使	1	0.17	於使	1	0.17
於	1	0.17	容易	1	0.17
易	1	0.17	棘手	1	0.17
便	1	0.17	艱難	1	0.17
容	1	0.17			

* After removing the stop word 的 [**de**]

We call the part of CBSDM that are involved with words written in L2, *Class Based Sense Translation Model.* CBSTM trained on a thesaurus and a bilingual MRD can be exploited to align words and translation counter part as well as to assign word sense in a parallel corpus. For instance, given a pair of aligned sentences in a parallel corpus:

(2C) 一位接近李約瑟的學者分析他所以能成就如此巨構，實有旁人**難**及的條件。

(2E) A scholar close to Needham analyses the reasons that he was able to achieve this huge work as being due to a combination of factors that would be **hard** to find in any other person. (*Source: 1990, Dec Issue Page 24, Giving Justice Back to China --Dr. Joseph Needham and the History of Science and Civilisation in China*)

It is possible to apply CBSTM to obtain the following pair of translation equivalent, (難 [**nan**], "hard") and, at the same time, determine the intended sense. For instance, we can label the citation with **hard**-2_{LDOCE}, leading to the following quadruple:

(3) (**hard**, 難 [nan], **hard**-2 $_{LDOCE}$, (2C, 2E))

After we have done this for all pairs of word and translation counterpart, we would in effect establish a Bilingual Semantic Concordance (BSC).

2.2 The Model

We assume that there is a Class Based Sense Definition Model, which can be viewed as a language model that generates the glosses for a class of senses *S*. Assume that we are given *L*, the words of *S* but not explicitly the intended senses *S*. In addition, we are given a sense inventory *I* in the form of an MRD with the regular glosses, which are written in L1 and/or L2. We are concerned with two problems: (1) Unsupervised training of *M*, CBSDM for *S;* (2) Determining *S* by identifying a relevant sense in *I*, if existing, for each word in *L*. Those two problems can be solved based on Maximum Likelihood Principle: Finding *M* and *S* such that *M generates* the glosses of *S* with maximum probability. For that, we utilize the Expectation and Maximization Algorithm to derive *M* and *S* through *Mutually Assured Resolution of Sense Algorithm* (MARS) given below:

Mutual Assured Resolution of Sense Algorithm

Determine the intended sense for each of a set of semantic related words.

Input: (1) Class of words $L = \{w_1\ w_2 \dots w_n\}$;
(2) Sense inventory *I*.

Output: (1) Senses *S* from *I* for words in *L;*
(2) CBSTM *M* from L1 to L2.

1. Initially, we assume that each of the senses $w_{i,j}$, j = 1, m_i in *I* is equally probable to be in *S* with probability $P(w_{i,j} \mid i, L) = \frac{1}{m_i}$, j = 1, m_i; where m_i is the number of senses in *I* for the word w_i.
2. Estimate CBSDM P(d | L) for L,
$$P(d \mid L) = \frac{\sum_i \max_{j,k} P(w_{i,j} \mid i, L) EQ(d, d_{i,j,k})}{n},$$
where d is a unigram or overlapping bigram in L1 or L2, $d_{i,j,k}$ = the kth word in D($w_{i,j}$), and $EQ(x, y)$ = 1, if $x = y$ and 0 otherwise;
3. Re-estimate P($w_{i,j}$ | i,L) according to $d_{i,j,k}$, $k = 1, n_{i,j}$:
$$P_1(w_{i,j} \mid i, L) = 0.5 \max_k P(d_{i,j,k} \mid L) + 0.5 \sum_k \frac{1}{n_{i,j}} P(d_{i,j,k} \mid L),$$
$$P(w_{i,j} \mid i, L) = \frac{P_1(w_{i,j} \mid i, L)}{\sum_{j=1,\ m_i} P_1(w_{i,j} \mid i, L)};$$
4. Repeat Steps 2 and 3 until the values of P(d | L) and P($w_{i,j}$ | i, L) converge;
5. For each i, find the most probable sense w_{i,j^*}, j^*=argmax$_j$ P($w_{i,j}$ | i, L) ;
6. Output $S = \{ w_{i,j^*} \mid j^* = \text{argmax}_j\ P(w_{i,j} \mid i, L)\}$;
7. Estimate and output CBSTM for L,
$$P(c \mid L) = \frac{\sum_{i=1,n} I(c \in t_{i,j^*})}{n},$$
where c is a unigram or overlapping bigram in L2 and $t_{i,j}$ is the L2 gloss of $w_{i,j}$.

Note that the purpose of Step 2 is to estimate how likely a word will appear in the definition of S based on the definining word for the senses, $w_{i,j}$ and relevant probability P($w_{i,j}$ | i,L). This likelihood of the word d being used to define senses in questions is subsequently used to re-estimate P($w_{i,j}$ | i,L), the likelihood of the jth sense, $w_{i,j}$ of w_i being in the intended senses of L.

3. Application to Word Sense Tagging

Armed with the Class Based Sense Translation Model, we can attack the word alignment and sense tagging problems simultaneously. Each word in a pair of aligned sentences in a parallel corpus will be considered and assigned a counterpart translation and intended sense in the given context through the proposed algorithm below:

Simutaneous Word Alignment and Tagging Algorithm (SWAT)

Align and sense tag words in a give sentence and translation.

Input: (1) Pair of sentences (*E*, *C*);
(2) Word *w*, POS *p* in question;
(3) Sense Inventory *I;*
(4) CBSTM, P(c|L).

Output: (1) Translation *c* of *w* in *C;*
(2) Intended sense *s* for *w.*

1. Perform part of speech tagging on *E;*
2. Proceed if *w* with part of speech *p* is found in the results of tagging *E;*
3. For all classes *L* to which (*w*, *p*) belongs and all words *c* in *C*:
$$L^* = \arg\max_L \left(\max_{LINK(w,c)} P(c \mid L) \right),$$
$$c^* = \arg\max_c \left(P(c \mid L^*) \right),$$
where LINK(x, y) means x and y are two word aligned based on Competitive Linking Alignment
4. Output c^* as the translation;
5. Output the sense of w in L^* as the intended sense.

To make sense tagging more precise, it is advisable to place constraint on the translation counterpart *c* of *w*. SWAT considers only those translations *c* that has been linked with *w* based the Competitive

Linking Algorithm (Melamed 1997) and logarithmic likelihood ratio (Dunning 1993).

Table 4. The experimental results of assigning LDOCE senses to classes of LLOCE.

Word	Class	pos	Sense**	Ex.
Star	K082	N	**8** a famous or very skilful performer. 明星；主角；名角	Y
Star	L002	N	**1** a brightly-burning heavenly body of great size, … 星	Y
Interest	F028	N	**2** a readiness to give attention. … 趣味；引起注意之性質	Y
Interest	F228	N	**1** a readiness to give attention 興趣	Y
Interest	J112	N	**6** money paid for the use of money 利息	Y
Interest	K006	N	**3** an activity, subject, etc., which one gives time and attention to 所愛好之事物；嗜好	Y
Issue	A020	N	**7** children 孩子；子嗣	Y
Issue	G180	N	**4** something printed, brought out again … 發行之印刷物	Y
Issue	G243	N	**2b** something which comes or is given out 流來或給出之事物	N
Issue	N153	N	**6** the result 結果	Y
Serve	C263	V	**9** to spend (a period of time) in prison 服刑	Y
Serve	D108	V	**5** to be good enough or satisfying for… 適合	N
Serve	E015	V	**7** to offer (food, a meal, etc.) for eating 送（食物、餐食等）	Y
Serve	I028	V	**1** to work (faithfully) for; do a useful job for 服務；為效力	N
Hard	N060	A	**2** difficult (to do or understand) 難的；困難的	Y
Hard	N264	A	**1** firm and stiff; … 堅硬	Y

4. Experiments and evaluation

In order to assess the feasibility of the proposed approach, we carried out experiments and evaluation on an implementation of MARS and SWAT based on LDOCE E-C, LLOCE, and Sinorama.

First experiment was involved with the trainability of CBSDM and CBSTM via MARS. The second experiment was involved with the effectiveness of using SWAT and CBSTM to annotate a parallel corpus with sense information. Evaluation was done on a set of 14 nouns, verbs, adjectives, and adverbs studies in previous work. The set includes the nouns *"bass," "bow," "cone," "duty," "gallery," "mole," "sentence," "slug," "taste," "star," "interest," "issue,"* the adjective *"hard,"* and the verb *"serve."*

Table 5. Evaluation of the MARS Algorithm based on 12 nouns, 1 verb, 1 adjective in LDOCE.

Word	Pos	#Senses	#Done	#Correct	Prec (LB*)	Prec.
Bass	N	4	1	1	0.25	1.00
Bow	N	5	2	2	0.25	1.00
Cone	N	3	3	2	0.33	0.67
Duty	N	2	2	2	0.13	1.00
Galley	N	3	3	2	0.33	0.67
Mole	N	3	2	2	0.33	1.00
Sentence	N	2	2	2	1.00	1.00
Slug	N	2	2	2	0.20	1.00
Taste	N	6	1	1	0.17	1.00
Star	N	8	2	2	0.13	1.00
Interest	N	6	4	4	0.17	1.00
Issue	N	7	4	3	0.14	0.75
Serve	V	13	4	2	0.08	0.50
Hard	A	12	2	2	0.08	1.00
Avg.		4.14	1.36	1.29	0.26	0.90

* The lower bound of precision of picking one sense in random.

Table 6. Experimental results of sense tagging the Sinorama parallel Corpus.

Word	Instance	#done	#correct	Precision
Star	173	86	82	0.95
Hard	325	37	33	0.89

4.1 Experiment 1: Training CBSDM

We applied MARS to assign LDOCE senses to word classes in LLOCE. Some results related to the test set are shown in Tables 4. The evaluation in Tables indicates that MARS assigns LDOCE senses to an LLOCE class with a high average precision rate of 90%.

4.2 Experiment 2: Sense Tagging

We applied SWAT to sense tag English words in some 50,000 reliably aligned sentence pairs in Sinorama parallel Corpus based on LDOCE sense inventory. The results are shown in Tables 6. Evaluation indicates an average precision rate of around 90%.

5. Discussion

The proposed approach offers a new method for automatic learning for the task of word sense disambiguation. The class based approach attacks the problem of tagging and data sparseness in a way similar to the Yarowsky approach (1992) based on thesaurus categories. We differ from the Yarowsky's approach, in the following ways:

i. The WSD problem is solved for two languages instead of one within a single sense inventory. Furthermore, an explicit sense tagged corpus is produced in the process.
ii. It is possible to work with any number of sense inventories.
iii. The method is applicable not only to nouns but also to adjectives and verbs, since it does not rely on topical context, which is effective only for nouns as pointed out by Towell and Voorhees (1998).

The approach is very general and modular and can work in conjunction with a number of learning strategies for word sense disambiguation (Yarowsky, 1995; Li and Li, 2002).

The approach is limited by the comprehensiveness of L2 glosses in MRD to cover in-context translations. For instance, the translation equivalent ("hard", "吃力") in (3) is not covered by CBSTM for N060 words trained on LDOCE E-C.

(3C) 不少雄中學生念起現在的課本都覺得很吃力
(3E) At Kaohsiung High, ... quite a few of the students find the textbooks hard to follow. (*Source: Sinorama, 2000, May Issue Page 4, Star Wars--The Controversy over Elite High Schools)*

That limitation can be partially alleviated by a smoothing technique of backing off from the probability of rare translation to that of its more frequent synonym in an L2 thesaurus. For instance, P("吃力" | N060) = 0 under maximum likelihood estimation, but using the back-off scheme, we have

P("吃力" |N060) = *c* P("困難" |N060),
for some constant *c*.

By backing off to the probability of "困難," the most frequent synonym of "吃力" (Mei, et al. 1984), we are able to correctly align and tag "*hard*" In Example 3.

6. Conclusion

In this paper, we present the Mutual Assured Resolution of Sense (MARS) Algorithm for assigning relevant senses to word classes in a given sense inventory (i.e. LDOCE or WordNet). We also describe the SWAT Algorithm for automatic sense tagging of a parallel corpus.

We carried out experiments on an implementation of the MARS and SWAT Algorithms for all the senses in LDOCE and LLOCE. Evaluation on a set of 14 highly ambiguous words showed that very high precision CBSDM and CBSTM can be constructed. High applicability and precision rates were achieved, when applying CBSTM to sense tagging of a Chinese-English parallel corpus.

A number of interesting future directions present themselves. First, it would be interesting to see how effectively we can broaden the coverage of CBSTM via backing off smoothing. Second, a CBSTM trained directly on a parallel corpus would be more effective in word alignment and sense tagging. The approach of training CBSTM on the L2 glosses in a bilingual MRD may lead to occasional mismatch between MRD translations and in-context translations. Third, there is a lack of research for a more abstractive and modular representation of sense differences and commonality. There is potential of developing Sense Definition Model to identify and represent semantic and stylistic differentiation reflected in the MRD glosses pointed out in DiMarco, Hirst and Stede (1993). Last but not the least, it would be interesting to apply MARS to both LDOCE E-C and WordNet and project WordNet's sense inventory to a sencond language via CBSDM and a parallel corpus, thus creating a Chinese WordNet and semantic concordance.

Acknowledgement

We acknowledge the support for this study through grants from National Science Council and Ministry of Education, Taiwan (NSC 90-2411-H-007-033-MC and MOE EX-91-E-FA06-4-4).

References

Dagan, Ido; A. Itai, and U. Schwall (1991). Two languages are more informative than one. *Proceedings of the 29th Annual Meeting of the Association for Computational Linguistics,* 18-21 June 1991, Berkeley, California, 130-137.

Dempster, A., N. Laird, and D. Rubin (1977). Maximum likelihood from incomplete data via the EM algorithm. *Journal of the Royal Statistical Society, Series B*, 39(1):1–38.

Diab, M. and P. Resnik, (2002). An Unsupervised Method for Word Sense Tagging using Parallel Corpora, *Proceedings of ACL*, 255-262.

DiMarco, C., G. Hirst, M. Stede, (1993). "The semantic and stylistic differentiation of synonyms and near-synonyms." In: *Working notes of the AAAI Spring Symposium on Building Lexicons for Machine Translation.* Stanford University.

Dunning, T (1993) Accurate methods for the statistics of surprise and coincidence, Computational Linguistics 19:1, 61-75.

Gale, W., K. Church, and D. Yarowsky, (1992). Using Bilingual Materials to Develop Word Sense Disambiguation Methods. In *Proceedings, Fourth International Conference on Theoretical and Methodological Issues in Machine Translation.* Montreal, 101-112, 1992.

Ide, N. and J. Véronis (1998). Word sense disambiguation: The state of the art. *Computational Linguistics,* 24:1, 1-40.

Knight, K, and A. Luk, (1994). Building a Large-Scale Knowledge Base for Machine Translation, *Proc. of the National Conference on Artificial Intelligence (AAAI).*

Knight, K., I. Chander, M. Haines, V. Hatzivassiloglou, E. Hovy, M. Iida, S. Luk, A. Okumura, R. Whitney, K. Yamada, (1994). "Integrating Knowledge Bases and Statistics in MT, *Proc. of the Conference of the Association for Machine Translation in the Americas (AMTA).*

Leacock, C., G. Towell, and E. Voorhees (1993). Corpus-based statistical sense resolution. *Proceedings of the ARPA Human Language Technology Worskshop*, San Francisco, Morgan Kaufman.

Li, C, and H. Li (2002). Word Translation Disambiguation Using Bilingual Bootstrapping, *Proceedings of the 40th Annual Meeting of the Association for Computational Linguistics (ACL)*, Philadelphia, July 2002, 343-351.

Li, Juanzi and C. Huang (1999). A Model for Word Sense Disambiguation. In Computational Linguistics and Chinese Language Processing,4(2), August 1999, pp.1-20

McArthur, T. (1992) *Longman Lexicon of Contemporary English*, Longman Group (Far East) Ltd., Hong Kong.

Mei, J. J., et al. (1984) Tongyici Cilin, Shanghai, Commercial Press. (in Chinese)

Melamed, I.D. (1997). "A Word-to-Word Model of Translational Equivalence". In Procs. of the ACL97. pp 490-497. Madrid Spain.

Merialdo, B, (1994). Tagging English Text with a Probabilistic Model, *Computational Linguistics*, 20(2):155-171.

Miller, G., A, R.. Beckwith, C. Fellbaum, D. Gross and K.J. Miller. (1990). WordNet: An on-line lexical database. *International Journal of Lexicography,* 3(4), 235- 244.

Proctor, P. (1988) Longman English-Chinese Dictionary of Contemporary English, Longman Group (Far East) Ltd., Hong Kong.

Towell, G. and E. Voorhees. (1998) Disambiguating Highly Ambiguous Words. *Computational Linguistics*, vol. 24, no. 1, 125-146.

Yarowsky, D. (1992). Word sense disambiguation using statistical models of Roget's categories trained on large corpora. *Proceedings of the 14th International Conference on Computational Linguistics,* COLING'92, 23-28 August, Nantes, France, 454-460.

Yarowsky, D. (1995). Unsupervised word sense disambiguation rivaling supervised methods. *Proceedings of the 33rd Annual Meeting of the Association for Computational Linguistics*, 189-196

Utterance Segmentation Using Combined Approach Based on Bi-directional N-gram and Maximum Entropy

Ding Liu
National Laboratory of Pattern Recognition
Institute of Automation
Chinese Academy of Sciences
Beijing 100080, China.
dliu@nlpr.ia.ac.cn

Chengqing Zong
National Laboratory of Pattern Recognition
Institute of Automation
Chinese Academy of Sciences
Beijing 100080, China.
cqzong@nlpr.ia.ac.cn

Abstract

This paper proposes a new approach to segmentation of utterances into sentences using a new linguistic model based upon Maximum-entropy-weighted Bi-directional N-grams. The usual N-gram algorithm searches for sentence boundaries in a text from left to right only. Thus a candidate sentence boundary in the text is evaluated mainly with respect to its left context, without fully considering its right context. Using this approach, utterances are often divided into incomplete sentences or fragments. In order to make use of both the right and left contexts of candidate sentence boundaries, we propose a new linguistic modeling approach based on Maximum-entropy-weighted Bi-directional N-grams. Experimental results indicate that the new approach significantly outperforms the usual N-gram algorithm for segmenting both Chinese and English utterances.

1 Introduction

Due to the improvement of speech recognition technology, spoken language user interfaces, spoken dialogue systems, and speech translation systems are no longer only laboratory dreams. Roughly speaking, such systems have the structure shown in Figure 1.

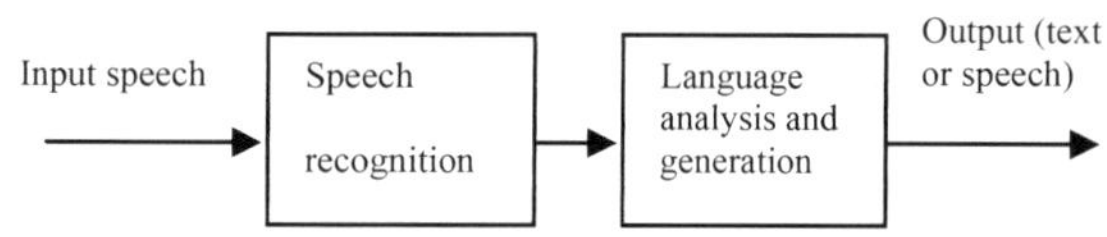

Figure 1. System with speech input.

In these systems, the language analysis module takes the output of speech recognition as its input, representing the current utterance exactly as pronounced, without any punctuation symbols marking the boundaries of sentences. Here is an example: *这边请您坐电梯到 9 楼服务生将在那里等您并将您带到913 号房间* . (*this way please please take this elevator to the ninth floor the floor attendant will meet you at your elevator entrance there and show you to room 913.*) As the example shows, it will be difficult for a text analysis module to parse the input if the utterance is not segmented. Further, the output utterance from the speech recognizer usually contains wrongly recognized words or noise words. Thus it is crucial to segment the utterance before further language processing. We believe that accurate segmentation can greatly improve the performance of language analysis modules.

Stevenson et al. have demonstrated the difficulties of text segmentation through an experiment in which six people, educated to at least the Bachelor's degree level, were required to segment into sentences broadcast transcripts from which all punctuation symbols had been removed. The experimental results show that humans do not always agree on the insertion of punctuation symbols, and that their segmentation performance is not very good (Stevenson and Gaizauskas, 2000). Thus it is a great challenge for computers to perform the task automatically. To solve this problem, many methods have been proposed, which can be roughly classified into two categories. One approach is based on simple acoustic criteria, such as non-speech intervals (e.g. pauses), pitch and energy. We can call this approach *acoustic segmentation*. The other approach, which can be called *linguistic segmentation*, is based on linguistic clues, including lexical knowledge, syntactic structure, semantic information etc. Acoustic segmentation can not always work well, because utterance boundaries do not always correspond to acoustic criteria. For example: *您好<pause>请问<pause>明天的单人间还有吗<pause>或者<pause>标准间也行.* Since the simple acoustic criteria are inadequate, linguistic clues play an indispensable role in utterance segmentation, and many methods relying on them have been proposed.

This paper proposes a new approach to linguistic segmentation using a Maximum-entropy-weighted Bi-directional N-gram-based algorithm (MEBN). To evaluate the performance of MEBN, we conducted experiments in both Chinese and English. All the results show that MEBN outperforms the normal N-gram algorithm. The remainder of this paper will focus on description of our new approach for linguistic segmentation. In Section 2, some related work on utterance segmentation is briefly reviewed, and our motivations are described. Section 3 describes MEBN in detail. The experimental results are presented in Section 4. Finally, Section 5 gives our conclusion.

2 Related Work and Our Motivations

2.1 Related Work

Stolcke et al. (1998, 1996) proposed an approach to detection of sentence boundaries and disfluency locations in speech transcribed by an automatic recognizer, based on a combination of prosodic cues modeled by decision trees and N-gram language models. Their N-gram language model is mainly based on part of speech, and retains some words which are particularly relevant to segmentation. Of course, most part-of-speech taggers require sentence boundaries to be pre-determined; so to require the use of part-of-speech information in utterance segmentation would risk circularity. Cettolo et al.'s (1998) approach to sentence boundary detection is somewhat similar to Stolcke et al.'s. They applied word-based N-gram language models to utterance segmentation, and then combined them with prosodic models. Compared with N-gram language models, their combined models achieved an improvement of 0.5% and 2.3% in precision and recall respectively.

Beeferman et al. (1998) used the CYBERPUNC system to add intra-sentence punctuation (especially commas) to the output of an automatic speech recognition (ASR) system. They claim that, since commas are the most frequently used punctuation symbols, their correct insertion is by far the most helpful addition for making texts legible. CYBERPUNC augmented a standard trigram speech recognition model with lexical information concerning commas, and achieved a precision of 75.6% and a recall of 65.6% when testing on 2,317 sentences from the Wall Street Journal.

Gotoh et al. (1998) applied a simple non-speech interval model to detect sentence boundaries in English broadcast speech transcripts. They compared their results with those of N-gram language models and found theirs far superior. However, broadcast speech transcripts are not really spoken language, but something more like spoken written language. Further, radio broadcasters speak formally, so that their reading pauses match sentence boundaries quite well. It is thus understandable that the simple non-speech interval model outperforms the N-gram language model under these conditions; but segmentation of natural utterances is quite different.

Zong et al. (2003) proposed an approach to utterance segmentation aiming at improving the performance of spoken language translation (SLT) systems. Their method is based on rules which are oriented toward key word detection, template matching, and syntactic analysis. Since this approach is intended to facilitate translation of Chinese-to-English SLT systems, it rewrites long sentences as several simple units. Once again, these results cannot be regarded as general-purpose utterance segmentation. Furuse et al. (1998) similarly propose an input-splitting method for translating spoken language which includes many long or ill-formed expressions. The method splits an input into well-balanced translation units, using a semantic dictionary.

Ramaswamy et al. (1998) applied a maximum entropy approach to the detection of command boundaries in a conversational natural language user interface. They considered as their features words and their distances to potential boundaries. They posited 400 feature functions, and trained their weights using 3000 commands. The system then achieved a precision of 98.2% in a test set of 1900 commands. However, command sentences for conversational natural language user interfaces contain much smaller vocabularies and simpler structures than the sentences of natural spoken language. In any case, this method has been very helpful to us in designing our own approach to utterance segmentation.

There are several additional approaches which are not designed for utterance segmentation but which can nevertheless provide useful ideas. For example, Reynar et al. (1997) proposed an approach to the disambiguation of punctuation marks. They considered only the first word to the left and right of any potential sentence boundary, and claimed that examining wider context was not beneficial. The features they considered included the candidate's prefix and suffix; the presence of particular characters in the prefix or suffix; whether the candidate was honorific (e.g. Mr., Dr.); and whether the candidate was a corporate designator (e.g. Corp.). The system was tested on the Brown Corpus, and achieved a precision of 98.8%. Elsewhere, Nakano et al. (1999) proposed a method for incrementally understanding user utterances whose semantic boundaries were unknown. The method operated by incrementally finding plausible sequences of utterances that play crucial roles in the task execution of dialogues, and by utilizing beam search to deal with the ambiguity of boundaries and with syntactic and semantic ambiguities. Though the method does not require utterance segmentation before discourse processing, it employs special rule tables for discontinuation of significant utterance boundaries. Such rule tables are not easy to maintain, and experimental results have demonstrated only that the method outperformed the method assuming pauses to be semantic boundaries.

2.2 Our motivations

Though numerous methods for utterance segmentation have been proposed, many problems remain unsolved.

One remaining problem relates to the language model. The N-gram model evaluates candidate sentence boundaries mainly according to their left context, and has achieved reasonably good results, but it can't take into account the distant right context to the candidate. This is the reason that N-gram methods often wrongly divide some long sentences into halves or multiple segments. For example: *小王病了一个星期.* The N-gram method is likely to insert a boundary mark between "了" and "一", which corresponds to our everyday impression that, if reading from the left and not considering several more words to the right of the current word, we will probably consider "小王病了" as a whole sentence. However, we find that, if we search the sentence boundaries from right to left, such errors can be effectively avoided. In the present example, we won't consider "一个星期" as a whole sentence, and the search will be continued until the word "小" is encountered. Accordingly, in order to avoid segmentation errors made by the normal N-gram method, we propose a reverse N-gram segmentation method (RN) which does seek sentence boundaries from right to left. Further, we simply integrate the two N-gram methods and propose a bi-directional N-gram method (BN), which takes into account both the left and the right context of a candidate segmentation site. Since the relative usefulness or significance of the two N-gram methods varies depending on the context, we propose a method of weighting them appropriately, using parameters generated by a maximum entropy method which takes as its features information about words in the context. This is our Maximum-Entropy-Weighted Bi-directional N-gram-based segmentation method. We hope MEBN can retain the correct segments discovered by the usual N-gram algorithm, yet effectively skip the wrong segments.

3 Maximum-Entropy-Weighted Bi-directional N-gram-based Segmentation Method

3.1 Normal N-gram Algorithm (NN) for Utterance Segmentation

Assuming that $W_1W_2...W_m$ (where m is a natural number) is a word sequence, we consider it as an n order Markov chain, in which the word $W_i (1 \le i \le m)$ is predicted by the n-1 words to its left. Here is the corresponding formula:

$$P(W_i \mid W_1W_2...W_{i-1}) = P(W_i \mid W_{i-n+1}...W_{i-1})$$

From this conditional probability formula for a word, we can derive the probability of a word sequence $W_1W_2...W_i$:

$$P(W_1W_2..W_i) = P(W_1W_2..W_{i-1}) \times P(W_i \mid W_1W_2..W_{i-1})$$

Integrating the two formulas above, we get:

$$P(W_1W_2..W_i) = P(W_1W_2..W_{i-1}) \times P(W_i \mid W_{i-n+1}..W_{i-1})$$

Let us use SB to indicate a sentence boundary and add it to the word sequence. The value of $P(W_1W_2...W_iSBW_{i+1})$ and $P(W_1W_2...W_iW_{i+1})$ will determine whether a specific word $W_i (1 \le i \le m)$ is the final word of a sentence. We say W_i is the final word of a sentence if and only if $P(W_1W_2...W_iSBW_{i+1}) > P(W_1W_2...W_iW_{i+1})$.

Taking the trigram as our example and considering the two cases where W_{i-1} is and is not the final word of a sentence, $P(W_1W_2...W_iSBW_{i+1})$ and $P(W_1W_2...W_iW_{i+1})$ is computed respectively by the following two formulas:

$$P(W_1W_2..W_iSBW_{i+1}) = P(W_1W_2..SBW_i) \times P(SB \mid SBW_i) \times P(W_{i+1} \mid W_iSB)$$
$$+ P(W_1W_2..W_{i-1}W_i) \times P(SB \mid W_{i-1}W_i) \times P(W_{i+1} \mid W_iSB)$$

$$P(W_1W_2..W_iW_{i+1}) = P(W_1W_2..SBW_i) \times P(W_{i+1} \mid SBW_i)$$
$$+ P(W_1W_2..W_{i-1}W_i) \times P(W_{i+1} \mid W_{i-1}W_i)$$

In the normal N-gram method, the above iterative formulas are computed to search the sentence boundaries from W_1 to W_m.

3.2 Reverse N-gram Algorithm (RN) for Utterance Segmentation

In the *reverse* N-gram segmentation method, we take the word sequence $W_1W_2...W_m$ as a reverse Markov chain in which $W_i (1 \le i \le m)$ is predicted by the *n-1* words to its right. That is:

$$P(W_i \mid W_mW_{m-1}...W_{i+1}) = P(W_i \mid W_{i+n-1}...W_{i+1})$$

As in the N-gram algorithm, we compute the occurring probability of word sequence $W_1W_2...W_m$ using the formula:

$$P(W_mW_{m-1}..W_i) = P(W_mW_{m-1}..W_{i+1}) \times P(W_i \mid W_mW_{m-1}..W_{i+1})$$

Then the iterative computation formula is:

$$P(W_mW_{m-1}..W_i) = P(W_mW_{m-1}..W_{i+1}) \times P(W_i \mid W_{i+n-1}..W_{i+1})$$

By adding SB to the word sequence, we say W_i is the final word of a sentence if and only if $P(W_mW_{m-1}...W_{i+1}SBW_i) > P(W_mW_{m-1}...W_{i+1}W_i)$. Similar to NN, $P(W_mW_{m-1}...W_{i+1}SBW_i)$ and $P(W_mW_{m-1}...W_{i+1}W_i)$ are computed as follows in the trigram:

$$P(W_mW_{m-1}..W_{i+1}SBW_i) = P(W_mW_{m-1}..SBW_{i+1}) \times P(SB \mid SBW_{i+1}) \times P(W_i \mid W_{i+1}SB)$$
$$+ P(W_mW_{m-1}..W_{i+2}W_{i+1}) \times P(SB \mid W_{i+2}W_{i+1}) \times P(W_i \mid W_{i+1}SB)$$

$$P(W_mW_{m-1}..W_{i+1}W_i) = P(W_mW_{m-1}..SBW_{i+1}) \times P(W_i \mid SBW_{i+1})$$
$$+ P(W_mW_{m-1}..W_{i+2}W_{i+1}) \times P(W_i \mid W_{i+2}W_{i+1})$$

In contrast to the normal N-gram segmentation method, we compute the above iterative formulas to seek sentence boundaries from W_m to W_1.

3.3 Bi-directional N-gram Algorithm for Utterance Segmentation

From the iterative formulas of the normal N-gram algorithm and the reverse N-gram algorithm, we can see that the normal N-gram method recognizes a candidate sentence boundary location mainly according to its left context, while the reverse N-gram method mainly depends on its right context. Theoretically at least, it is reasonable to suppose that, if we synthetically consider both the left and the right context by integrating the NN and the RN, the overall segmentation accuracy will be improved.

Considering the word sequence $W_1W_2...W_m$, the candidate sites for sentence boundaries may be found between W_1 and W_2, between W_2 and W_3, ..., or between W_{m-1} and W_m. The number of candidate sites is thus *m-1*. We number those *m-1* candidate sites 1, 2 ... *m-1* in succession, and we use $P_{is}(i)$ $(1 \le i \le m-1)$ and $P_{no}(i)$ $(1 \le i \le m-1)$ respectively to indicate the probability that the current site *i* really is, or is not, a sentence boundary. Thus, to compute the word sequence segmentation, we must compute $P_{is}(i)$ and $P_{no}(i)$ for each of the *m-1* candidate sites. In the bi-directional BN, we compute $P_{is}(i)$ and $P_{no}(i)$ by combining the NN results and RN results. The combination is described by the following formulas:

$$P_{is\_BN}(i) = P_{is\_NN}(i) \times P_{is\_RN}(i)$$

$$P_{no\_BN}(i) = P_{no\_NN}(i) \times P_{no\_RN}(i)$$

where $P_{is\_NN}(i)$, $P_{no\_NN}(i)$ denote the probabilities calculated by NN which correspond to $P(W_1W_2...W_iSBW_{i+1})$ and $P(W_1W_2...W_iW_{i+1})$ in section 3.1 respectively and $P_{is\_RN}(i)$, $P_{no\_RN}(i)$ denote the probabilities calculated by RN which correspond to $P(W_mW_{m-1}...W_{i+1}SBW_i)$ and $P(W_mW_{m-1}...W_{i+1}W_i)$ in section 3.2 respectively.

We say there exits a sentence boundary at site i $(1 \le i \le m-1)$ if and only if $P_{is\_BN}(i) > P_{no\_BN}(i)$.

3.4 Maximum Entropy Approach for Utterance Segmentation

In this section, we explain our maximum-entropy-based model for utterance segmentation. That is, we estimate the joint probability distribution of the candidate sites and their surrounding words. Since we consider information concerning the lexical context to be useful, we define the feature functions for our maximum method as follows:

$$f_{j10}(b,c) = \begin{cases} 1 & if\ (include\ (Prefix(c), S_j)\ \&\&\ b == 0) \\ 0 & else \end{cases}$$

$$f_{j11}(b,c) = \begin{cases} 1 & if\ (include\ (Prefix(c), S_j)\ \&\&\ b == 1) \\ 0 & else \end{cases}$$

$$f_{j20}(b,c) = \begin{cases} 1 & if\ (include\ (Suffix(c), S_j)\ \&\&\ b == 0) \\ 0 & else \end{cases}$$

$$f_{j21}(b,c) = \begin{cases} 1 & if\ (include\ (Suffix(c), S_j)\ \&\&\ b == 1) \\ 0 & else \end{cases}$$

S_j denotes a sequence of one or more words which we can call the Matching String. (Note that S_j may contain the sentence boundary mark 'SB'.) The candidate c's state is denoted by b, where $b=1$ indicates that c is a sentence boundary and $b=0$ indicates that it is not a boundary. *Prefix(c)* denotes all the word sequences ending with c (that is, c's left context plus c) and *Suffix(c)* denotes all the word sequences beginning with c (in other words, c plus its right context). For example: in the utterance: *去<c1>机<c2>场<c3>怎<c4>么<c5>走,* '场', '机场', and '去机场' are *c3*'s Prefix, while '怎', '怎么'and '怎么走' are *c3*'s Suffix. The value of function $include(Prefix(c), S_j)$ is *true* when word sequence S_j is one of c's Prefixes, and the value of function $include(Suffix(c), S_j)$ is *true* when S_j is one of c's Suffixes.

Corresponding to the four feature functions $f_{j10}(b,c)$, $f_{j11}(b,c)$, $f_{j20}(b,c)$, $f_{j21}(b,c)$ are the four parameters α_{j10}, α_{j11}, α_{j20}, α_{j21}. Thus the joint probability distribution of the candidate sites and their surrounding contexts is given by:

$$P(c,b) = \pi \prod_{j=1}^{k} (\alpha_{j10}^{f_{j10}(b,c)} \times \alpha_{j11}^{f_{j11}(b,c)} \times \alpha_{j20}^{f_{j20}(b,c)} \times \alpha_{j21}^{f_{j21}(b,c)})$$

where k is the total number of the Matching Strings and π is a parameter set to make *P(c,1)* and *P(c,0)* sum to 1. The unknown parameters $\alpha_{j10}, \alpha_{j11}, \alpha_{j20}, \alpha_{j21}$ are chosen to maximize the likelihood of the training data using the *Generalized Iterative Scaling* (Darroch and Ratcliff, 1972) algorithm. In the maximum entropy approach, we say that a candidate site is a sentence boundary if and only if P(c, 1) > P(c, 0). (At this point, we can anticipate a technical problem with the maximum approach to utterance segmentation. When a Matching String contains SB, we cannot know whether it belongs to the Prefixes or Suffixes of the candidate site until the left and right contexts of the candidate site have been segmented. Thus if the segmentation proceeds from left to right, the lexical information in the right context of the current candidate site will always remain uncertain. Likewise, if it proceeds from right to left, the information in the left context of the current candidate site remains uncertain. The next subsection will describe a pragmatic solution to this problem.)

3.5 Maximum-Entropy-Weighted Bi-directional N-gram Algorithm for Utterance Segmentation

In the bi-directional N-gram based algorithm, we have considered the left-to-right N-gram algorithm and the right-to-left algorithm as having the same significance. Actually, however, they should be assigned differing weights, depending on the lexical contexts. The combination formulas are as follows:

$$P_{is}(i) = W_{n\_is}(C_i) \times P_{is\_NN}(i) \times W_{r\_is}(C_i) \times P_{is\_RN}(i)$$

$$P_{no}(i) = W_{n\_no}(C_i) \times P_{no\_NN}(i) \times W_{r\_no}(C_i) \times P_{no\_RN}(i)$$

$W_{n\_is}(C_i)$, $W_{n\_no}(C_i)$, $W_{r\_is}(C_i)$, $W_{r\_no}(C_i)$ are the functions of the context surrounding candidate site i which denotes the weights of $P_{is\_NN}(i)$, $P_{no\_NN}(i)$, $P_{is\_RN}(i)$ and $P_{no\_RN}(i)$ respectively. Assuming that the weights of $P_{is\_NN}(i)$ and $P_{no\_NN}(i)$ depend upon the context to the left of the candidate site, and that the weights of

$P_{is\_RN}(i)$ and $P_{no\_RN}(i)$ depend on the context to the right of the candidate site, the weight functions can be rewritten as: $W_{n\_is}(LeftC_i)$, $W_{n\_no}(LeftC_i)$, $W_{r\_is}(RightC_i)$, $W_{r\_no}(RightC_i)$. It is reasonable to assume that as the joint probability $P(LeftC_i, i = SB)$ rises, $P_{is\_NN}(i)$ will increase in significance. (The joint probability in question is the probability of the current candidate's left context, taken together with the probability that the candidate is a sentence boundary.) Therefore the value of $W_{n\_is}(LeftC_i)$ is given by $W_{n\_is}(LeftC_i) = P(LeftC_i, i = SB)$. Similarly we can give the formulas for computing $W_{n\_no}(LeftC_i)$, $W_{r\_is}(RightC_i)$, and $W_{r\_no}(RightC_i)$ as follows:

$$W_{n\_no}(LeftC_i) = P(LeftC_i, i != SB)$$

$$W_{r\_is}(RightC_i) = P(RightC_i, i = SB)$$

$$W_{r\_no}(RightC_i) = P(RightC_i, i != SB)$$

We can easily get the values of $P(LeftC_i, i = SB)$, $P(LeftC_i, i != SB)$, $P(RightC_i, i = SB)$, and $P(RightC_i, i != SB)$ using the method described in the maximum entropy approach section. For example:

$$P(LeftC_i, i = SB) = \pi \prod_{j=1}^{k} \alpha_{j11}^{f_{j11}(1,i)}$$

$$P(LeftC_i, i != SB) = \pi \prod_{j=1}^{k} \alpha_{j10}^{f_{j10}(0,i)}$$

As mentioned in last subsection, we need segmented contexts for maximum entropy approach. Since the maximum entropy parameters for MEBN algorithm are used as modifying NN and RN, we just estimate the joint probability of the candidate and its surrounding contexts based upon the segments by NN and RN. Using $NLeftC_i$ indicate the left context to the candidate *i* which has been segmented by NN algorithm and $RRightC_i$ indicate the right context to *i* which has been segmented by RN, the combination probability computing formulas for MEBN are as follows:

$$P_{is\_MEBN}(i) = P(NLeftC_i, i = SB) \times P_{is\_NN}(i) \times P(RRightC_i, i = SB) \times P_{is\_RN}(i)$$

$$P_{no\_MEBN}(i) = P(NLeftC_i, i != SB) \times P_{no\_NN}(i) \times P(RRightC_i, i != SB) \times P_{no\_RN}(i)$$

We evaluate site *i* as a sentence boundary if and only if $P_{is\_MEBN}(i) > P_{no\_MEBN}(i)$.

4 Experiment

4.1 Model Training

Our models are trained on both Chinese and English corpora, which cover the domains of hotel reservation, flight booking, traffic information, sightseeing, daily life and so on. We replaced the full stops with "SB" and removed all other punctuation marks in the training corpora. Since in most actual systems part of speech information cannot be accessed before determining the sentence boundaries, we use Chinese characters and English words without POS tags as the units of our N-gram models. Trigram and reverse trigram probabilities are estimated based on the processed training corpus by using *Modified Kneser-Ney Smoothing* (Chen and Goodman, 1998). As to the maximum entropy model, the Matching Strings are chosen as all the word sequences occurring in the training corpus whose length is no more than 3 words. The unknown parameters corresponding to the feature functions are generated based on the training corpus using the *Generalized Iterative Scaling algorithm*. Table 1 gives an overview of the training corpus.

Corpus	SIZE	SB Number	Average Length of Sentence
Chinese	4.02MB	148967	8 Chinese characters
English	4.49MB	149311	6 words

Table 1. Overview of the Training Corpus.

4.2 Testing Results

We test our methods using open corpora which are also limited to the domains mentioned above. All punctuation marks are removed from the test corpora. An overview of the test corpus appears in table 2.

Corpus	SIZE	SB Number	Average Length of Sentence
Chinese	412KB	12032	10 Chinese characters
English	391KB	10518	7 words

Table 2. Overview of the Testing Corpus.

We have implemented four segmentation algorithms using NN, RN, BN and MEBN respectively.

If we use "RightNum" to denote the number of right segmentations, "WrongNum" denote the number of wrong segmentations, and "TotalNum" to denote the number of segmentations in the original testing corpus, the precision (P) can be computed using the formula $P=RightNum/(RightNum+WrongNum)$, the recall (R) is computed as $R=RightNum/TotalNum$, and the F-Score is computed as $F\text{-}Score = \frac{2 \times P \times R}{P+R}$.

The testing results are described in Table 3 and Table 4.

Methods	Total Num	Right Num	Wrong Num	Preci-sion	Recall	F-Score
NN	12032	10167	2638	79.4%	84.5%	81.9%
RN	12032	10396	2615	79.9%	86.4%	83.0%
BN	12032	10528	2249	82.4%	87.5%	84.9%
MEBN	12032	10348	1587	86.7%	86.0%	86.3%

Table 3. Experimental Results for Chinese Utterance Segmentation.

Methods	Total Num	Right Num	Wrong Num	Preci-sion	Recall	F-Score
NN	10518	8730	3164	73.4%	83.0%	77.9%
RN	10518	9014	3351	72.9%	85.7%	78.8%
BN	10518	9056	3019	75.0%	86.1%	80.2%
MEBN	10518	8929	2403	78.8%	84.9%	81.7%

Table 4. Experimental Results for English Utterance Segmentation.

From the result tables it is clear that RN, BN, and MEBN all outperforms the normal N-gram algorithm in the F-score for both Chinese and English utterance segmentation. MEBN achieved the best performance which improves the precision by 7.3% and the recall by 1.5% in the Chinese experiment, and improves the precision by 5.4% and the recall by 1.9% in the English experiment.

4.3 Result analysis

MEBN was proposed in order to maintain the correct segments of the normal N-gram algorithm while skipping the wrong segments. In order to see whether our original intention has been realized, we compared the segments as determined by RN with those determined by NN, compare the segments found by BN with those of NN and then compare the segments found by MEBN with those of NN. For RN, BN and MEBN, suppose TN denotes the number of total segmentations, CON denotes the number of correct segmentations overlapping with those found by NN; SWN denotes the number of wrong NN segmentations which were skipped; WNON denotes the number of wrong segmentations not overlapping with those of NN; and CNON denotes the number of segmentations which were correct but did not overlap with those of NN. The statistical results are listed in Table 5 and Table 6.

Methods	TN	CON	SWN	WNON	CNON
RN	13011	9525	1098	1077	870
BN	12777	9906	753	355	622
MEBN	11935	9646	1274	223	678

Table 5. Chinese Utterance Segmentation Results Comparison.

Methods	TN	CON	SWN	WNON	CNON
RN	12365	8223	1077	1271	792
BN	12075	8565	640	488	491
MEBN	11332	8370	1247	486	559

Table 6. English Utterance Segmentation Results Comparison.

Focusing upon the Chinese results, we can see that RN skips 1098 incorrect segments found by NN, and has 9525 correct segments in common with those of NN. It verifies our supposition that RN can effectively avoid some errors made by NN. But because at the same time RN brings in 1077 new errors, RN doesn't improve much in precision. BN skips 753 incorrect segments and brings in 355 new segmentation errors; has 9906 correct segments in common with those of NN and brings in 622 new correct segments. So by equally integrating NN and RN, BN on one hand finds more correct segments, on the other hand brings in less wrong segments than NN. But in skipping incorrect segments by NN, BN still performs worse than RN, showing that it only exerts the error skipping ability of RN to some extent. As for MEBN, it skips 1274 incorrect segments and at the same time brings in only 223 new incorrect segments. Additionally it maintains 9646 correct segments in common with those of NN and brings in 678 new correct segments. In recall MEBN performs a little worse than BN, but in precision it achieves a much better performance than BN, showing that modified by the maximum entropy weights, MEBN makes use of the error skipping ability of RN more effectively. Further, in skipping wrong segments by NN, MEBN even outperforms RN, which indicates the weights we set on NN and RN not only act as modifying parameters, but also have direct beneficial affection on utterance segmentation.

5 Conclusion

This paper proposes a reverse N-gram algorithm, a bi-directional N-gram algorithm and a Maximum-entropy-weighted Bi-directional N-gram algorithm for utterance segmentation. The experimental results for both Chinese and English utterance segmentation show that MEBN significantly outperforms the usual N-gram algorithm. This is because MEBN takes into account both the left and right contexts of candidate sites: it integrates the left-to-right N-gram algorithm and the right-to-left N-gram algorithm with appropriate weights, using clues on the sites' lexical context, as modeled by maximum entropy.

Acknowledgements

This work is sponsored by the Natural Sciences Foundation of China under grant No.60175012, as well as supported by the National Key Fundamental Research Program (the 973 Program) of China under the grant G1998030504.

The authors are very grateful to Dr. Mark Seligman for his very useful suggestions and his very careful proofreading.

References

Beeferman D., A. Berger, and J. Lafferty. 1998. CYBERPUNC: A lightweight punctuation annotation system for speech. In *Proceedings of the IEEE International Conference on Acoustics, Speech and Signal Processing*, Seattle, WA. pp. 689-692.

Beeferman D., A. Berger, and J. Lafferty. 1999. Statistical models for text segmentation. *Machine Learning* 34, pp 177-210.

Berger A., S. Della Pietra, and V. Della Pietra. 1996. A Maximum Entropy Approach to Natural Language Processing. *Computational Linguistics*, 22(1), pp. 39-71.

Cettolo M. and D. Falavigna. 1998. Automatic Detection of Semantic Boundaries Based on Acoustic and Lexical Knowledge. *ICSLP* 1998, pp. 1551-1554.

Chen S. F. and J. Goodman. 1998. An empirical study of smoothing techniques for language modeling. *Technical Report* TR-10-98, Center for Research in Computing Technology, Harvard University. pp.243-255.

Darroch J. N. and D. Ratcliff. 1972. Generalized Iterative Scaling for Log-Linear Models. The *Annals of Mathematical Statistics*, 43(5), pp. 1470-1480.

Furuse O., S. Yamada, and K. Yamamoto. 1998. Splitting Long or Ill-formed Input for Robust Spoken-language Translation. *COLING-ACL* 1998, pp. 421-427.

Gotoh Y. and S. Renals. 2000. Sentence Boundary Detection in Broadcast Speech Transcripts. In *Proc. International Workshop on Automatic Speech Recognition*, pp. 228-235.

Nakano M., N. Miyazaki, J. Hirasawa, K. Dohsaka, and T. Kawabata. 1999. Understanding Unsegmented User Utterances in Real-Time Spoken Dialogue Systems. *Proceedings of the 37th Annual Meeting of the Association for Computational Linguistics (ACL-99)*, College Park, MD, USA, pp. 200-207.

Ramaswamy N. G. and J. Kleindienst. 1998. Automatic Identification of Command Boundaries in a Conversational Natural Language User Interface. *ICSLP* 1998. pp. 401-404.

Reynar J. and A. Ratnaparkhi. 1997. A maximum entropy approach to identifying sentence boundaries. In *Proceedings of the 5th Conference on Applications of Natural Language Processing (ANLP)*, Washington DC, pp. 16-19.

Seligman M. 2000. Nine Issues in Speech Translation. *In Machine Translation,* 15, pp. 149-185.

Stevenson M. and R. Gaizauskas. 2000. Experiments on sentence boundary detection. In *Proceedings of the Sixth Conference on Applied Natural Language Processing and the First Conference of the North American Chapter of the Association for Computational Linguistics*, pp. 24-30.

Stolcke A. and E. Shriberg. 1996. Automatic linguistic segmentation of conversational speech. *Proc. Intl. Conf. on Spoken Language Processing,* Philadelphia, PA, vol. 2, pp. 1005-1008.

Stolcke A., E. Shriberg, R. Bates, M. Ostendorf, D. Hakkani, M. Plauche, G. Tur, and Y. Lu. 1998. Automatic Detection of Sentence Boundaries and Disfluencies based on Recognized Words. *Proc. Intl. Conf. on Spoken Language Processing*, Sydney, Australia, vol. 5, pp. 2247-2250.

Zong, C. and F. Ren. 2003. Chinese Utterance Segmentation in Spoken Language translation. In *Proceedings of the* 4th *international conference on intelligent text processing and Computational Linguistics (CICLing)*, Mexico, Feb 16-22. pp. 516-525.

Zhou Y. 2001. Utterance Segmentation Based on Decision Tree. Proceedings of the 6th *National joint Conference on Computational Linguistics*, Taiyuan, China, pp. 246-252.

Two-Character Chinese Word Extraction Based on Hybrid of Internal and Contextual Measures

Shengfen Luo, Maosong Sun
National Lab. of Intelligent Tech. & Systems
Tsinghua University, Beijing 100084, China
lkc-dcs@mail.tsinghua.edu.cn

Abstract

Word extraction is one of the important tasks in text information processing. There are mainly two kinds of statistic-based measures for word extraction: the internal measure and the contextual measure. This paper discusses these two kinds of measures for Chinese word extraction. First, nine widely adopted internal measures are tested and compared on individual basis. Then various schemes of combining these measures are tried so as to improve the performance. Finally, the left/right entropy is integrated to see the effect of contextual measures. Genetic algorithm is explored to automatically adjust the weights of combination and thresholds. Experiments focusing on two-character Chinese word extraction show a promising result: the F-measure of mutual information, the most powerful internal measure, is 57.82%, whereas the best combination scheme of internal measures achieves the F-measure of 59.87%. With the integration of the contextual measure, the word extraction achieves the F-measure of 68.48% at last.

1 Introduction

New words are generated quite often with the rapid development of Chinese society, resulting that the lexicon of Chinese cannot well meet the requirement of natural language processing. How to extract word automatically from immense text collection has thus become an important problem.

The task of extracting Chinese words with multi-characters from texts is quite similar to that of extracting phrases (e.g., compound nouns) in English, if we regard Chinese characters as English words. Research in word/phrase extraction has been carried out extensively. Currently the mainstream approach is statistic-based. In general, there are two kinds of statistic-based measures for estimating the soundness of an extracted item being a word/phrase: One is the internal measure, which estimates the soundness by the internal associative strength between constituents of the item. Nine widely adopted internal measures are listed in (Schone et al. 2001), including Frequency, Mutual Information, Selectional Association, Symmetric Conditional Probability, Dice Formula, Log-likelihood, Chi-squared, Z-score, Student's t-score. The other kind is the contextual measure, which estimates the soundness by the dependency of the item on its context, such as the left/right entropy (Sornlertlamvanich et al. 2000), and the left/right context dependency (Chien 1999).

This paper firstly analyzes nine internal measures mentioned above, tests and compares their word extraction performance on individual basis, then tries to improve the performance by properly combining these measures. Furthermore, the contextual measure is integrated with internal measures to acquire more improvement. Throughout the experiments, genetic algorithm is explored to adjust weights of combination and thresholds automatically. We only concern two-character word extraction in this paper, because two-character words reflect the most popular word-formation of Chinese and possess the largest proportion in Chinese lexicon.

2 Internal Measures

Nine internal measures are discussed and compared in this section. These measures tend to estimate the internal associative strength from different perspectives, so it is possible to improve the word extraction performance by properly combining them. This paper will try two combination schemes, i.e., direct combination and interval-based combination.

As stated earlier, the evaluation is based on two-character Chinese word extraction. PDR9596, a raw corpus of People Daily of 1995 and 1996 with about 50.0M characters, is used to train the matrix of Chinese character bigrams throughout the experiments. PDA98J, a manually word-segmented corpus composed of People Daily of January 1998 with about 1.3M characters (developed by Institute of Computational Linguistics of Peking University), is further used to exhaustively generate a list of Chinese character bigrams. The list contains 218,863 distinct bigrams. We randomly divide the list into two parts, 9/10 of it as TS1, the rest 1/10 as TS2.

2.1 Nine Widely Adopted Internal Measures

Table 1 lists nine widely adopted internal measures, as mentioned in (Schone 2000). In the table: xy represents any two-character item, $\bar{x}$ stands for all characters except x, N is the size of training corpus, f_x and p_x are frequency and probability of x respectively, f_{xy} and p_{xy} are frequency and probability of xy respectively, and ξ_{xy} is the frequency expectation of xy suppose x and y are independent.

Obviously:

$$\xi_{xy} = p_{xy}N = p_x p_y N = f_x f_y / N$$

Table 1. Nine Widely Adopted Internal Measures

Measure	Marked As	Formula
Frequency	Freq	f_{xy}
Mutual Information	MI	$\log_2 \frac{p_{xy}}{p_x p_y}$
Selectional Association	SA	$\frac{p(x \mid y)MI(xy)}{\sum_z p(z \mid y)MI(zy)}$
Symmetric Conditional Probability	SCP	$\frac{p_{xy}^2}{p_x p_y}$
Dice Formula	Dice	$\frac{2f_{xy}}{f_x + f_y}$
Log-likelihood	LogL	$-2\log\frac{(p_x p_y p_{\bar{x}} p_{\bar{y}})^{f_y}}{(p_{xy} p_{\overline{xy}})^{f_{xy}} (p_{x\bar{y}} p_{\bar{x}y})^{f_{\bar{x}y}}}$
Chi-squared	Chi	$\frac{N(f_{xy} f_{\overline{xy}} - f_{x\bar{y}} f_{\bar{x}y})^2}{(f_{xy} + f_{x\bar{y}})(f_{xy} + f_{\bar{x}y})(f_{\overline{xy}} + f_{x\bar{y}})(f_{\overline{xy}} + f_{\bar{x}y})}$
Z-Score	ZS	$\frac{f_{xy} - \xi_{xy}}{\sqrt{\xi_{xy}(1 - \xi_{xy}/N)}}$
Student's t-Score	TS	$\frac{f_{xy} - \xi_{xy}}{\sqrt{f_{xy}(1 - f_{xy}/N)}}$

Table 2. Comparison of Word Extraction Performance of Internal Measures (Open Test on TS1)

Top 17,333	Freq	MI	SA	SCP	Dice	LogL	Chi	ZS	TS
F-measure (%)	26.28	**54.77**	42.98	51.77	49.37	43.13	52.97	53.20	39.12
Comparison of F-measure: MI > ZS > Chi > SCP >Dice > LogL > SA > TS > Freq									

Table 3. Weights for Direct Combination Scheme (Fitness Function is Based on TS1)

Freq	MI	SA	SCP	Dice	LogL	Chi	ZS	TS
0.000598	0.351393	0.000263	0.146348	0.214541	0.002804	0.035930	0.072293	0.17583
Comparison of weights: MI > Dice > TS > SCP > ZS > Chi > LogL > Freq > SA								

When using these nine measures for word extraction, the hypothesis is same: the larger value of measure means the stronger associative strength between *x* and *y*, and thus the more possibility of *xy* being a word. The criterion of judgment is very simple: *xy* would be accepted as a word if its internal associative strength is larger than a given threshold.

2.2 Word Extraction Performance of Each Internal Measure

The performance of each internal measure is tested on TS1. TS1 contains 196,977 distinct bigrams, among which 17,333 are two-character words according to PDA98J. The procedure of word extraction is to sort the 196,977 candidate bigrams in descending order in terms of the value of the measure to be tested, and then to select the top 17,333 bigrams as words. In this case, the precision rate, recall rate and F-measure are exactly the same. Table 2 shows the comparison of performances of these nine internal measures. Mutual information achieves the best performance with the F-measure of 54.77%.

2.3 Direct Combination of Internal Measures

The first combination scheme is to directly combine the nine measures with appropriate weights. The internal associative strength of an item *xy* is estimated by:

$$score(xy) = \sum_{i=1}^{9} (wt_i \times score_i(xy))$$

where $score_i(xy)$ is the value of *xy* given by the i-th measure, and wt_i is the weight for the i-th measure accordingly (satisfying $\sum_{i=1}^{9} wt_i = 1$).

The determination of weights is not straightforward due to the presence of combinatorial explosion (notice that wt_i is real number). Genetic algorithm (Pan 1998) is explored to adjust the weights automatically, trying to find the optimal one. Let (wt_1, wt_2,…,wt_9) be a possible solution, we set the F-measure of word extraction on TS1 to be the fitness function, and set the size of population to be 25. We simply use the GenocopIII software (Michalewicz) to do the job.

In a PIII650 PC, GenocopIII runs 12 hours, iterates 1,161 generation, and converges to a group of weights (as shown in Table 3). With this group of weights, the F-measure of word extraction on TS1 is 55.44%, improving only 0.67% over the most powerful single measure MI (54.77%). Note this is not a pure open test, because the fitness function of genetic algorithm is based on TS1.

2.4 Interval-based Combination of Internal Measures

The experimental result in section 2.3 shows that it is not so effective to combine the nine measures directly. We try another combination scheme now, i.e., interval-based combination.

2.4.1 The Idea

The idea is as follows: for every measure mentioned above, we first discretize its value range into a number of intervals. Every interval of every measure is then assigned a corresponding probability that indicates the tendency of any item being regarded as a word if its value with respect to this measure falls into this interval. We name this kind of probability 'the interval probability'. The soundness of an item being a word would be the weighted sum of all of its interval probabilities over nine measures.

We describe the idea in a more formal way. Suppose $score_i(xy)$ is the internal associative strength of any item xy with respect to the i th measure, $v_i(xy)$ is its corresponding interval determined by the value of $score_i(xy)$, $pv_i(xy)$ is the interval probability of $v_i(xy)$, then the soundness of xy being word, $pv(xy)$, will be given by:

$$pv(xy) = \sum_{i=1}^{9}(wt_i \times pv_i(xy))$$

where wt_i is the weight for the i-th measure.

If $pv(xy)$ is larger than a threshold, xy would be extracted out as a word.

2.4.2 The Related Issues

Three related issues need to be clarified.

(1) How to discretize the range of a measure with continuous values?

We use D-2, an entropy-based top-down algorithm (Catlett 1991) to discretize the value range by supervised learning. It adopts the information gain as the criterion to decide whether a given training set should be further partitioned or not. Given a set of examples *S*, the information gain caused by a cut point t will be:

$$IG(t,S) = Ent(S) - \frac{|S_1|}{|S|}Ent(S_1) - \frac{|S_2|}{|S|}Ent(S_2)$$

where *Ent(S)* is the entropy of *S*, and S_1 and S_2 are two subsets of *S* partitioned by the cut point t.

It has been proved that the information gain obtains optimal discretization only on boundary points (Fayyad et al. 1992, Elomaa et al. 2000). So only boundary points need to be examined as potential cut points. Suppose T is the set of boundary points, the D-2 algorithm for discretizing set S is:

ALGORITHM DISCRETE (*S,T*)

BEGIN

Step1. For each t in *T*, calculate $IG(t,S)$

Step2. Select $t_0 = \arg\max_t(IG(t,S))$, S is partitioned into two subsets: S_1, S_2

Step3. If stopping criteria are satisfied,

Step4. then DO NOT partition S, Return Φ.
// Φ is an empty set

Step5. else $P1$ = DISCRETE(S_1, T_1)
$P2$ = DISCRETE(S_2, T_2)
$P = P1 + \{t_0\} + P2$, Return P.
//P is the set of cut points for discretizing S

END

This algorithm only considers two stopping criteria. One is the minimal number of samples in an interval, the other is the minimum information gain. With this algorithm, we finally get a set of cut points each measure, which discretize the value range to variable-length intervals.

(2) How to assign the interval probability to each interval?

After discretization, training examples (i.e., a list of Chinese character bigrams) will be distributed to a certain interval according to its value of a given measure. Let v_{ij} represent the j-th interval of the i-th measure, then $pv(v_{ij})$, the interval probability of v_{ij}, is defined as:

$$pv(v_{ij}) = \frac{\#\ of\ \ bigrams\ being\ words\ in\ \ v_{ij}}{\#\ of\ \ bigrams\ in\ \ v_{ij}}$$

(3) How to set the weights for combining all $pv_i(xy)$ in the process of word extraction?

Genetic algorithm is again invoked to adjust the weight wt_i. The configuration of GenecopIII is the same as that in session 2.3.

2.4.3 Effect of the Stopping Criteria and Discretization Strategy on Combination

The stopping criteria and discretization strategy take effect on the word extraction performance of interval-based combination.

First, have a look at the effect of stopping criteria. In DISCRETE, two stopping criteria are needed to set. We fix the minimal number of samples in one interval on 50 arbitrarily. And, we change the setting of the minimum information gain. In Table 4, performances under five different minimum information gains are compared, marked as D1, D2 ,..., D5 respectively. It can be seen that, the smaller the minimal information gain, the finer the granularity of discretization, and the better the performance of word extraction. But if the discretization is too grainy, it may cause over-fitting problem. Compared with D4 and D5, D3 achieves nearly the same performance but has a much rough discretization. So, we set the minimum information gain to be 0.0001 (D3) in the following experiments.

Second, observe the effect of the discretization strategy. The equal-length discretization is compared to the variable-length discretization. We divide the value range of each measure into equal-length intervals, and let the number of intervals be identical to that in D3 accordingly. As shown in Table 4, the equal-length discretization only achieves the F-measure of 55.56%, which is much less than D3 (57.45%). This means the entropy-based discretization is more reasonable than equal-length discretization, and the discretization strategy has significant impact on the performance of interval-based combination.

2.4.4 Reduction of Measures for Combination

To improve the performance of word extraction through combination, the premise is that there must be enough mutual supplements among those measures. However, if the combination involves too many measures, interference may become obvious. We try to reduce the number of measures for combination.

The reduction procedure is recursive: It first compares the performance after removing any of the n measures, then reduces the one that can bring the most improvement of performance if it is removed. Repeat this reduction procedure in the left n-1 measures, until the performance cannot improve anymore.

Table 5 shows the reduction procedure of the nine internal measures. It indicates that, excluding SA and SCP, the interval-based combination of other seven measures could achieve the best F-measure of 57.77%, with the weights in Table 6. That result is 3.00% higher than that of the most powerful internal measure MI (54.77%).

Note again that all tests in section 2.4 are not pure open, because all the related parameters such as granularity of discretization, reduction of measures and adjustment of combination weights, are based on TS1.

Table 4. Effect of the Stopping Criteria and Discretization Strategy (Based on TS1)

Entropy-based Discretization		F-measure (%)	Number of Partitions								
	Min Gain		Freq	MI	SA	SCP	Dice	LogL	Chi	ZS	TS
D1	0.001	55.92	80	117	88	63	122	126	237	189	66
D2	0.0005	56.75	104	341	230	96	255	314	380	343	625
D3	0.0001	57.45	340	1449	641	109	471	1390	949	1411	1234
D4	0.00005	57.67	385	1660	693	113	543	1777	1316	1555	1808
D5	0.00001	57.69	423	2204	754	120	581	2522	2375	2233	2304
Equal-length Discretization		55.56	340	1449	641	109	471	1390	949	1411	1234

Table 5. The Reduction Procedure of the Nine Measures (Based on TS1)

N	F-measure (%) after Removing									Action
	Freq	MI	SA	SCP	Dice	LogL	Chi	Zs	Ts	
9	57.62	55.09	57.63	**57.69**	57.48	57.65	57.64	57.50	57.37	Reduce SCP
8	57.71	55.19	**57.77**		57.63	57.60	57.40	57.36	57.49	Reduce SA
7	57.67	55.25			57.66	57.71	57.74	57.64	57.48	No Reduction

Table 6. Weights for Interval-based Combination (Based on TS1)

Freq	MI	SA	SCP	Dice	LogL	Chi	ZS	TS
0.00034	0.47238	0	0	0.00238	0.00125	0.09339	0.25636	0.17390
Comparison of weights: MI > ZS > TS > Chi > Dice > Freq								

Table 7. Open Test for Effect of Internal Measures, the Contextual Measures and the Hybrid (on TS2)

	Precision(%)	Recall(%)	F-measure(%)	Setting t_1 and t_2 for Left/Right Entropy
MI	56.72	58.97	57.82	N.A.
Comb	60.41	59.35	59.87	N.A.
MI+Le/Re	83.53	54.88	66.24	MI-tuned threshold
Comb+Le/Re*	85.69	55.76	67.56	MI-tuned threshold
Comb+Le/Re	85.71	57.02	68.48	Comb-tuned threshold

3 The Contextual Measure

This section turns to discuss how to make use of contextual measures. The most commonly used contextual measure is the left/right entropy:

$$Le(xy) = -\sum_{\forall a \in A} p(axy \mid xy) \cdot \log_2 p(axy \mid xy)$$

$$\mathrm{Re}(xy) = -\sum_{\forall b \in A} p(xyb \mid xy) \cdot \log_2 p(xyb \mid xy)$$

where: xy is the candidate item, a, b are Chinese characters belonging to A, the set of Chinese characters.

In the sight of entropy, the larger the value of $Le(xy)$ and $Re(xy)$, the more various the characters coming after/before xy, and thus the more possible xy to be a word.

4 The Hybrid of Internal and Contextual Measures

Combining the contextual measure with internal measures, the word extraction process would become like this: First, any candidate item xy not satisfying the contextual condition is rejected. The contextual condition is, $Le(xy)>t_1$ and $Re(xy)>t_2$. Second, those residual candidates will be extracted out as words if their internal measure or combination of internal measures is high than a given threshold t_3. In this paper, we try two alternatives of hybrid for comparison: one is the contextual measure with mutual information, the best single internal measure; another one is the contextual measure with Comb, the best result of interval-based combination of seven internal measures (Freq, MI, Dice, LogL, Chi, ZS, TS).

We need to determine three thresholds in above process, Threshold t_3 are set as the value to select the top 17,333 candidates from TS1: according to experiments in section 2, MI will choose t_3=4.0, while Comb will choose t_3=0.26. To set appropriate thresholds t_1 and t_2, we still employ genetic algorithm. We let a group of threshold (t_1, t_2) be a possible solution, and let the F-measure of word extraction on TS1 be fitness. Two groups of thresholds can be thus obtained:

(1) MI-tuned thresholds: t_1=2.2, t_2=1.4.

(2) Comb-tuned thresholds: t_1=1.8, t_2=1.2.

To further investigate the effect of internal measures, the contextual measure and the hybrid, we conduct a series of open tests on TS2, as demonstrated in Table 7. Since the left/right entropy would become less reliable in cases that the occurrences of contexts are not sufficient, we drop out those candidates whose frequencies are no more than 5 in TS2. After dropping, TS2 contains 14,867 candidates, out of which 1,589 are words according to PDA98J.

In the first two rows of Table 7, the best single internal measure, MI, and our best combination of internal measures Comb are open tested. The successive three rows show the effect of contextual measures. The row of 'MI+Le/Re' selects MI as the internal measure, and use the MI-tuned thresholds as t_1 and t_2. The rows of 'Comb+Le/Re*' and 'Comb+Le/Re' both select Comb as the internal measure, but use different t_1 and t_2: The former uses MI-tuned thresholds, while the latter uses Comb-tuned thresholds.

From Table 7, we can draw several conclusions: (1) With open test, the F-measure of MI, the best single internal measure, is 57.82%, whereas the F-measure of our interval-based combination is 59.87%; (2) The integration of the commonly used contextual measure, the left/right entropy with internal measures, can bring a large improvement of about 8%~9%; (3) There is only a modest difference between the performances of

'Comb+Le/Re*' and 'Comb+Le/Re', and two group of thresholds adjusted by different internal measures have small difference as well.

5 Conclusion

This paper focuses on the research of pure statistic-based measures for automatic extraction of two-character Chinese words. Two kinds of statistic-based measures are discussed: internal measures and contextual measures. Nine internal measures are tested and compared. Two schemes are tried to improve the performance by properly combining these nine measures. Experimental results in open tests show that, the best combination scheme, interval-based combination, achieves the F-measure of 59.87%, improving 2.05% over the best single internal measure mutual information. On the other hand, the left/right entropy, a kind of contextual measure, is integrated to acquire further improvement in word extraction. With the left/right entropy and interval-based combination of internal measures, the F-measure ultimately achieves 68.48%. Another point of this paper is that, weights for combination and thresholds for left/right entropy are adjusted automatically by genetic algorithm, rather than manually.

Future work will extend the proposed method to automatic extraction of multi-character Chinese words. Other useful information, such as lexicon and semantic resource, are expected to be included for consideration so as to further improve the performance.

Acknowledgements

This research is supported by the National '973' Plan of China under grant no G1998030507 and NSFC under grant no 60083005.

References

Catlett. (1991) On changing continuous attributes into odered discrete attributes. In Proceedings of the European Working Session on Learning, Berlin, Germany. pp. 164-178

Chien, L.F. (1999) Pat-tree-based adaptive keyphrase extraction for intelligent Chinese information retrieval. Information Processing and Management vol.35 pp.501-521

Elomaa T., Rousu J., (2000) Generalizing boundary points. In Proceedings of the 17th National Conference on Artificial Intelligence, Menlo Park, CA.

Fayyad, U., Irani, K., (1992) On the handling of continuous-valued attributes in decision tree generation. Machine Learning. Vol.(8) pp.87-102

Pan, Z.J., (1998) Evolution Computing. Tsinghua University Press, Beijing.

Sornlertlamvanich V., Potipiti T., Charoenporn T. (2000) Automatic corpus-based Thai word extraction with the C4.5 learning algorithm. In Proceedings of COLING 2000.

Schone, P., Jurafsky D. (2001) Is knowledge-free induction of multiword unit dictionary headwords a solved problem? In proceedings of EMNLP 2001.

Michalewicz, Z., Genocop III, available at:

http://www.coe.uncc.edu/~gnazhiya/gchome.html

A Bottom-up Merging Algorithm for Chinese Unknown Word Extraction

Wei-Yun Ma
Institute of Information science,
Academia Sinica
ma@iis.sinica.edu.tw

Keh-Jiann Chen
Institute of Information science,
Academia Sinica
kchen@iis.sinica.edu.tw

Abstract

Statistical methods for extracting Chinese unknown words usually suffer a problem that superfluous character strings with strong statistical associations are extracted as well. To solve this problem, this paper proposes to use a set of general morphological rules to broaden the coverage and on the other hand, the rules are appended with different linguistic and statistical constraints to increase the precision of the representation. To disambiguate rule applications and reduce the complexity of the rule matching, a bottom-up merging algorithm for extraction is proposed, which merges possible morphemes recursively by consulting above the general rules and dynamically decides which rule should be applied first according to the priorities of the rules. Effects of different priority strategies are compared in our experiment, and experimental results show that the performance of proposed method is very promising.

1 Introduction and Related Work

Chinese sentences are strings of characters with no delimiters to mark word boundaries. Therefore the initial step for Chinese processing is word segmentation. However, occurrences of unknown words, which do not listed in the dictionary, degraded significantly the performances of most word segmentation methods, so unknown word extraction became a key technology for Chinese segmentation.

For unknown words with more regular morphological structures, such as personal names, morphological rules are commonly used for improving the performance by restricting the structures of extracted words (Chen et. al 1994, Sun et. al 1994, Lin et. al 1994). However, it's not possible to list morphological rules for all kinds of unknown words, especially those words with very irregular structures, which have the characteristics of variable lengths and flexible morphological structures, such as proper names, abbreviations etc. Therefore, statistical approaches usually play major roles on irregular unknown word extraction in most previous work (Sproat & Shih 1990, Chiang et. al 1992, Tung and Lee 1995, Palmer 1997, Chang et. al 1997, Sun et. al 1998, Ge et. al 1999).

For statistical methods, an important issue is how to resolve competing ambiguous extractions which might include erroneous extractions of phrases or partial phrases. They might have statistical significance in a corpus as well. Very frequently superfluous character strings with strong statistic associations are extracted. These wrong results are usually hard to be filtered out unless deep content and context analyses were performed. To solve this problem, the idea of unknown word detection procedure prior to extraction is proposed. Lin et al. (1993) adopt the following strategy: First, they decide whether there is any unknown word within a detected region with fix size in a sentence, and then they extract the unknown word from the region by a statistical method if the previous answer is "yes". A limitation of this method is that it restricts at most one unknown word occurs in the detected region, so that it could not deal with occurrences of consecutive unknown words within a sentence. Chen & Ma (2002) adopt another strategy: After an initial segmentation process, each monosyllable is decided whether it is a common word or a morpheme of unknown word by a set of syntactic discriminators. The syntactic discriminators are a set of syntactic patterns containing monosyllabic, words which are learned from a large word segmented corpus, to discriminate between monosyllabic words and morphemes of unknown words. Then more deep analysis can be carried out at the detected unknown word morphemes to extract unknown words.

In this paper, in order to avoid extractions of superfluous character strings with high frequencies, we proposed to use a set of general rules, which is formulated as a context free grammar rules of composing detected morphemes and their adjacent tokens, to match all kinds of unknown words, for instance which includes the rule of (UW → UW UW). To avoid too much superfluous extractions caused by the over general rules, rules are appended with linguistic or statistical constraints. To disambiguate between rule applications and reduce the complexity of the rule matching, a bottom-up merging algorithm for extraction is proposed, which merges possible morphemes recursively by consulting above general rules and dynamically decides which rule should be applied first according to the priorities of the rules.

The paper is organized into 7 sections. In the next section, we provide an overview of our system. Section 3 briefly introduce unknown word detection process and makes some analysis for helping the derivation of general rules for unknown words. In section 4, we derive a set of general rules to represent all kinds of unknown words, and then modify it by appending rules constraints and priorities. In section 5, a bottom-up merging algorithm is presented for unknown word extraction. In section 6, the evaluation of extraction is presented; we also compare the performances to different priority strategies. Finally, in section 7, we make the conclusion and propose some future works.

2 System Overview

The purpose to our unknown word extraction system is to online extract all types of unknown words from a Chinese text. Figure 1 illustrates the block diagram of the system proposed in this paper. Initially, the input sentence is segmented by a conventional word segmentation program. As a result, each unknown word in the sentence will be segmented into several adjacent tokens (known words or monosyllabic morphemes). At unknown word detection stage, every monosyllable is decided whether it is a word or an unknown word morpheme by a set of syntactic discriminators, which are learned from a corpus. Afterward, a bottom-up merging process applies the general rules to extract unknown word candidates. Finally, the input text is re-segmented by consulting the system dictionary and the extracted unknown word candidates to get the final segmented result.

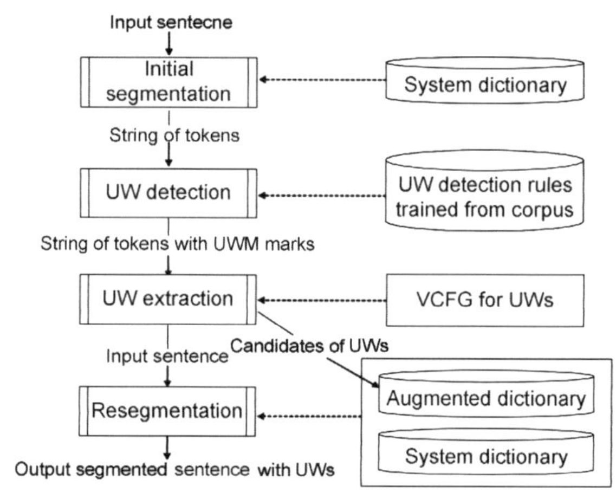

Figure 1. Flowchart of the system

(1) 若 能 提升 毛利率
if can increase gross profit rate
"if gross profit rate can be increased…"

(2) after first step word segmentation:
若 能 提升 毛 利 率
after unknown word detection:
若 能 提升 毛(?) 利(?) 率(?)
after unknown word extraction:
若 能 提升 毛利率

For example, the correct segmentation of (1) is shown, but the unknown word "毛利率" is segmented into three monosyllabic words after the first step of word segmentation process as shown in (2). The unknown word detection process will mark the sentence as "若() 能() 提升() 毛(?) 利(?) 率(?)", where (?) denotes the detected monosyllabic unknown word morpheme and () denotes common words. During extracting process, the rule matching process focuses on the morphemes marked with (?) only and tries to combine them with left/right neighbors according to the rules for unknown words. After that, the unknown word "毛利率" is extracted. During the process, we do not need to take care of other superfluous combinations such as "若能" even though they might have strong statistical association or co-occurrence too.

3 Analysis of Unknown Word Detection

The unknown word detection method proposed by (Chen & Bai 1998) is applied in our system. It adopts a corpus-based learning algorithm to derive a set of syntactic discriminators, which are used to distinguish whether a monosyllable is a word or an unknown word morpheme after an initial segmentation process. If all occurrences of monosyllabic words are considered as morphemes of unknown words, the recall of the detection will be about 99%, but the precision is as low as 13.4%.

The basic idea in (Chen & Bai 1998) is that the complementary problem of unknown word detection is the problem of monosyllabic known-word detection, i.e. to remove the monosyllabic known-words as the candidates of unknown word morphemes. Chen and Bai (1998) adopt ten types of context rule patterns, as shown in table 1, to generate rule instances from a training corpus. The generated rule instances were checked for applicability and accuracy. Each rule contains a key token within curly brackets and its contextual tokens without brackets. For some rules there may be no contextual dependencies. The function of each rule means that in a sentence, if a character and its context match the key token and the contextual tokens of the rule respectively, this character is a common word (i.e. not a morpheme of unknown word).

For instance, the rule "{Dfa} Vh" says that a character with syntactic category Dfa is a common word, if it follows a word of syntactic category Vh.

Rule type	Example
char	{的}
word char	不 {願}
char word	{全} 世界
category	{T}
{category} category	{Dfa} Vh
category {category}	Na {Vcl}
char category	{就} VH
category char	Na {上}
category category char	Na Dfa {高}
char category category	{極} Vh T

Table1. Rule types and Examples

The final rule set contains 45839 rules and were used to detect unknown words in the experiment. It achieves a detection rate of 96%, and a precision of 60%. Where detection rate 96% means that for 96% of unknown words in the testing data, at least one of its morphemes are detected as part of unknown word and the precision of 60% means that for 60% of detected monosyllables in the testing data, are actually morphemes. Although the precision is not high, most of over-detecting errors are "isolated", which means there are few situations that two adjacent detected monosyllabic unknown morphemes are both wrong at the mean time. These operative characteristics are very important for helping the design of general rules for unknown words later.

4 Rules for Unknown Words

Although morphological rules work well in regular unknown word extraction, it's difficult to induce morphological rules for irregular unknown words. In this section, we try to represent a common structure for unknown words from another point of view; an unknown word is regarded as the combination of morphemes which are consecutive morphemes/words in context after segmentation, most of which are monosyllables. We adopt context free grammar (Chomsky 1956), which is the most commonly used generative grammar for modelling constituent structures, to express our unknown word structure.

4.1 Rule Derivation

According to the discussion in section 3, for 96% of unknown words, at least one of its morphemes are detected as part of unknown word, which motivates us to represent the unknown word structure with at least one detected morpheme. Taking this phenomenon into our consideration, the rules for modeling unknown words and an unknown word example are presented as follows.

UW →	UW UW	(1)
	| ms(?) ms(?)	(2)
	| ms(?) ps()	(3)
	| ms(?) ms()	(4)
	| ps() ms(?)	(5)
	| ms() ms(?)	(6)
	| ms(?) UW	(7)
	| ms() UW	(8)
	| ps() UW	(9)
	| UW ms(?)	(10)
	| UW ms()	(11)
	| UW ps()	(12)

Notes: There is one non-terminal symbol. "UW" denotes "unknown word" and is also the start symbol. There are three terminal symbols, which includes ms(?), which denotes the detected monosyllabic unknown word morpheme, ms() , which denotes the monosyllable that is not detected as the morpheme, and ps(), which denotes polysyllabic (more than one syllable) known word.

Table 2. General rules for unknown words

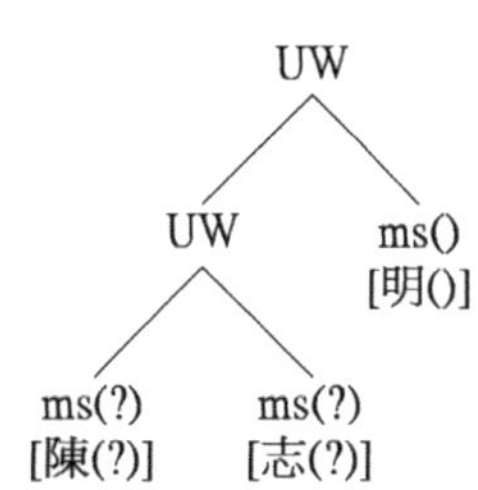

Figure 2. A possible structure for the unknown word "陳志明"(Chen Zhi Ming), which is segmented initially and detected as "陳(?) 志(?) 明()", and "明" was marked incorrectly at detection stage.

There are three kinds of commonly used measures applied to evaluate grammars: 1. generality (recall), the range of sentences the grammar analyzes correctly; 2. selectivity (precision), the range of non-sentences it identifies as problematic and 3. understandability, the simplicity of the grammar itself (Allen 1995). For generality, 96% unknown words have this kind of structure, so the grammar has high generality to generate unknown words. But for selectivity, our rules are over-generation. Many patterns accepted by the rules are not words. The main reason is that rules have to include non-detected morphemes for high generality. Therefore selectivity is sacrificed momentary. In next section, rules would be constrained by linguistic and text-based statistical constraints to compensate the selectivity of the grammar. For understandability, you can find each rule in (1)-(12) consists of just two right-hand side symbols. The reason for using this kind of presentation is that it regards the unknown word structure as a series of combinations of consecutive two morphemes, such that we could simplify the analysis of unknown word structure by only analyzing its combinations of consecutive two morphemes.

4.2 Appending Constraints

Since the general rules in table 2 have high generality and low selectivity to model unknown words, we append some constraints to restrict their applications. However, there are tradeoffs between generality and selectivity: higher selectivity usually results in lower generality. In order to keep high generality while assigning constraints, we assign different constraints on different rules according to their characteristics, such that it is only degraded generality slightly but selectivity being upgraded significantly.

The rules in table 2 are classified into two kinds: one kind is the rules which both its right-hand side symbols consist of detected morphemes, i.e, (1), (2), (7), and (10), the others are the rules that just one of its right-hand side symbols consists of detected morphemes, i.e, (3), (4), (5), (6), (8), (9), (11), and (12). The former is regarded as "strong" structure since they are considered to have more possibility to compose an unknown word or an unknown word morpheme and the latter is regarded as "weak" structure, which means they are considered to have less possibility to compose an unknown word or an unknown word morpheme. The basic idea is to assign more constraint on those rules with weak structure and less constraint on those rules with strong structure.

The constraints we applied include word length, linguistic and statistical constraints. For statistical constraints, since the target of our system is to extract unknown words from a text, we use text-based statistical measure as the statistical constraint. It is well known that keywords often reoccur in a document (Church 2000) and very possible the keywords are also unknown words. Therefore the reoccurrence frequency within a document is adopted as the constraint. Another useful statistical phenomenon in a document is that a polysyllabic morpheme is very unlikely to be the morphemes of two different unknown words within the same text. Hence we restrict the rule with polysyllabic symbols by evaluating the conditional probability of polysyllabic symbols. In addition, syntactic constraints are also utilized here. For most of unknown word morphemes, their syntactic categories belong to "bound", "verb", "noun", and "adjective" instead of "conjunction", "preposition"...etc. So we restrict the rule with non-detected symbols by checking whether syntactic categories of its non-detected symbols belong to "bound", "verb", "noun", or "adjective". To avoid unlimited recursive rule application, the length of matched unknown word is restricted unless very strong statistical association do occur between two matched tokens. The constraints adopted so far are presented in table 3. Rules might be restricted by multi-constraints.

$Freq_{docu}(LR)>=Threshold$	(3) (4) (5) (6) (8) (9) (11) (12)
$P_{docu}(L\|R)=1$	(1) (3) (7) (8) (9) (12)
$P_{docu}(R\|L)=1$	(1) (5) (9) (10) (11) (12)
Category(L) is bound, verb, noun or adjective	(5) (6) (8) (9)
Category(R) is bound, verb, noun or adjective	(3) (4) (11) (12)

Notes: L denotes left terminal of right-hand side
R denotes right terminal of right-hand side
Threshold is a function of Length(LR) and text size. The basic idea is larger amount of length(LR) or text size matches larger amount of Threshold.

Table 3. Constraints for general rules

4.3 Priority

To scheduling and ranking ambiguous rule matching, each step of rule matching is associated with a measure of priority which is calculated by the association strength of right-hand side symbols. In our extracting algorithm, the priority measure is used to help extracting process dynamically decide which rule should be derived first. More detail discussion about ambiguity problem and complete disambiguation process are presented in section 5.

We regard the possibility of a rule application as co-occurrence and association strength of its right-hand side symbols within a text. In other words, a rule has higher priority of application while its right-hand side symbols are strongly associated with each other, or co-occur frequently in the same text. There have been many statistical measures which estimate co-occurrence and the degree of association in previous researches, such as mutual information (Church 1990, Sporat 1990), t-score (Church 1991), dice matrix (Smadja 1993, 1996). Here, we adopt four well-developed kinds of statistical measures as our priority individually: mutual information (MI), a variant of mutual information (VMI), t-score, and co-occurrence. The formulas are listed in table 4. MI mainly focuses on association strength, and VMI and t-score consider both co-occurrence and association strength. The performances of these four measures are evaluated in our experiments discussed in section 6.

$$co-occurence(L,R) = f(L,R)$$

$$MI(L,R) = \log\frac{P(L,R)}{P(L)P(R)}$$

$$VMI(L,R) = f(L,R)MI(L,R)$$

$$t-score(L,R) = \frac{f(L,R) - \frac{f(L)f(R)}{N}}{\sqrt{f(L,R)}}$$

Notes: f(L,R) denotes the number of occurrences of L,R in the text; N denotes the number of occurrences of all the tokens in the text; length(*) denotes the length of *.

Table 4. Formulas of 4 kinds of priority

5 Unknown Word Extraction

5.1 Ambiguity

Even though the general rules are appended with

well-designed constraints, ambiguous matchings, such as, overlapping and covering, are still existing. We take the following instance to illustrate that: "拉法葉" (La Fa Yeh), a warship name, occurs frequently in the text and is segmented and detected as "拉(?) 法(?) 葉(?)". Although "拉法葉" could be derived as an unknown word "((拉法)葉)" by rule 2 and rule 10, "拉法" and "法葉" might be also derived as unknown words "(拉法)" and "(法葉)" individually by the rule 2. Hence there are total three possible ambiguous unknown words and only one is actually correct.

Several approaches on unsupervised segmentation of Chinese words were proposed to solve overlapping ambiguity to determine whether to group "xyz" as "xy z" or "x yz", where x, y, and z are Chinese characters. Sproat and Shih (1990) adopt a greedy algorithm: group the pair of adjacent characters with largest mutual information greater than some threshold within a sentence, and the algorithm is applied recursively to the rest of the sentence until no character pair satisfies the threshold. Sun et al. (1998) use various association measures such as t-score besides mutual information to improve (Sproat & Shih 1990). They developed an efficient algorithm to solve overlapping character pair ambiguity.

5.2 Bottom-up Merging Algorithm

Following the greedy strategy of (Sproat & Shih 1990), here we present an efficient bottom-up merging algorithm consulting the general rules to extract unknown words. The basic idea is that for a segmented sentence, if there are many rule-matched token pairs which also satisfy the rule constraints, the token pair with the highest rule priority within the sentence is merged first and forms a new token string. Same procedure is then applied to the updated token string recursively until no token pair satisfied the general rules. It is illustrated by the following example:

=====================================

System environment:

Co-occurrence priority is adopted.

Text environment:

"陳志強" (Chen Zhi Qiang), an unknown word, occurs three times.

"造勢" (take an electing activity), an unknown word, occurs two times.

"陳志強造勢" (Chen Zhi Qiang took an electing activity), a sentence, occurs one time.

Input: 陳志強造勢

After initial segmentation and detection:

陳(?) 志(?) 強(?) 造(?) 勢(?)

[3] 3 1 2 priority

After first iteration:

陳志(uw) 強(?) 造(?) 勢(?)

[3] 1 2 priority

After second iteration:

陳志強(uw) 造(?) 勢(?)

[2] priority

After third iteration:

陳志強(uw) 造勢(uw)

=====================================

Figure 3. Extraction process of input "陳志強造勢".

By the general rules and greedy strategy, besides overlapping character pair ambiguity, the algorithm is able to deal with more complex overlapping and coverage ambiguity, even which result from consecutive unknown words. In finger 3, input sentence "陳志強造勢" is derived as the correct two unknown words "((陳志)強)" and "(造勢)" by rule (2), rule (10), and rule (2) in turn. "陳志強" and "造勢" are not further merged. That is because P(造勢|陳志強)<1 violates the constraint of rule (1). Same reason explains why "陳志強" and "造" do not satisfy rule (10) in the third iteration.

By this simple algorithm, unknown words with unlimited length all have possibilities to be extracted. Observing the extraction process of "陳志強", you can find, in the extraction process, boundaries of unknown words might extend during iteration until no rule could be applied.

6 Experiment

In our experiments, a word is considered as an unknown word, if either it is not in the CKIP lexicon or it is not identified by the word segmentation program as foreign word (for instance English) or a number. The CKIP lexicon contains about 80,000 entries.

6.1 Evaluation Formulas

The extraction process is evaluated in terms of precision and recall. The target of our approach is to extract unknown words from a text, so we define "correct extractions" as unknown word types correctly extracted in the text. The precision and recall formulas are listed as follows:

NC_i = number of correct extractions in document i
NE_i = number of extracted unknown words in document i
NT_i = number of total unknown words in document i

$$\text{Precision rate} = \frac{\sum_{i=1}^{i=150} NC_i}{\sum_{i=1}^{i=150} NE_i} \qquad \text{Recall rate} = \frac{\sum_{i=1}^{i=150} NC_i}{\sum_{i=1}^{i=150} NT_i}$$

6.2 Data Sets

We use the Sinica balanced corpus version 3.0 as our training set for unknown word detection, which contains 5 million segmented words tagged with pos. We randomly select 150 documents of Chinese news on the internet as our testing set. These testing data are segmented by hand according to *the segmentation standard for information processing* designed by the Academia Sinica (Huang et.al 1997). In average, each testing text contains about 300 words and 16.6 unknown word types.

6.3 Results

Based on the four priority measures listed in table 4, the bottom-up merging algorithm is applied. The performances are shown in table 5.

Priority \ Evaluation	Match#	Extract#	Precision	Recall
Co-occurrence	1122	1485	76%	45%
MI	1112	1506	74%	45%
VMI	1125	1499	75%	45%
t-score	1125	1494	75%	45%

Note: There are total 2498 reference unknown word types

Table 5. Experimental results of the four different priority measures

In table 5, comparing co-occurrence and MI, we found that the performance of co-occurrence measure is better than MI on both precision and recall. The possible reason is that the characteristic of reoccurrence of unknown words is more important than morphological association of unknown words while extracting unknown words from a size-limited text. That is because sometimes different unknown words consist of the same morpheme in a document, and if we use MI as the priority, these unknown words will have low MI values of their morphemes. Even though they have higher frequency, they are still easily sacrificed when they are competed with their adjacent unknown word candidates. This explanation is also proved by the performances of VMI and t-score, which emphasize more importance on co-occurrence in their formulas, are better than the performance of MI. According to above discussions, we adopt co-occurrence as the priority decision making in our unknown word extraction system.

In our final system, we adopt morphological rules to extract regular type unknown words and the general rules to extract the remaining irregular unknown words and the total performance is a recall of 57% and a precision of 76%. An old system of using the morphological rules for names of people, compounds with prefix or suffix were tested, without using the general rules, having a recall of 25% and a precision of 80%. The general rules improve 32% of the recall and without sacrificing too much of precision.

7 Conclusion and Future Work

In this research, Chinese word segmentation and unknown word extraction has been integrated into a frame work. To increase the coverage of the morphological rules, we first derive a set of general rules to represent all kinds of unknown words. To avoid extracting superfluous character strings, we then append these rules with linguistic and statistical constraints. We propose an efficient bottom-up merging algorithm by consulting the general rules to extract unknown words and using priority measures to resolve the rule matching ambiguities. In the experiment, we compare effects of different priority strategies, and experimental results show that the co-occurrence measure performances best.

It is found that the performance of unknown word detection would affect the entire performance significantly. Although the performance of unknown word detection is not bad, there is still room for improvement. The possible strategies for improvement in our future work include using contextual semantic relations in detection, and some updated statistical methods, such as support vector machine, maximal entropy and so on, to achieve better performance of unknown word detection.

References

[1] Chen, H.H., & J.C. Lee, 1994,"The Identification of Organization Names in Chinese Texts", *Communication of COLIPS*, Vol.4 No. 2, 131-142.

[2] Sun, M. S., C.N. Huang, H.Y. Gao, & Jie Fang, 1994, "Identifying Chinese Names in Unrestricted Texts", *Communication of COLIPS*, Vol.4 No. 2, 113-122

[3] Lin, M. Y., T. H. Chiang, & K. Y. Su, 1993," A Preliminary Study on Unknown Word Problem in Chinese Word Segmentation," Proceedings of ROCLING VI, pp. 119-137

[4] Richard Sproat and Chilin Shih, "A Statistical Method for Finding Word Boundaries in Chinese Text," *Computer Processing of Chinese and Oriental Languages,* 4, 336-351, 1990

[5] Sun, Maosong, Dayang Shen, and Benjamin K. Tsou. 1998. Chinese Word Segmentation without Using Lexicon and Hand-crafted Training Data. In Proceedings of COLING-ACL '98,pages 1265-1271

[6] Ge, Xianping, Wanda Pratt, and Padhraic Smyth. 1999. Discovering Chinese Words from Unsegmented Text. In SIGIR '99, pages 271-272

[7] Palmer, David. 1997. A Trainable Rule-based Algorithm for Word Segmentation. In Proceedings of the Association for Computational Linguistics

[8] Chiang, T. H., M. Y. Lin, & K. Y. Su, 1992," Statistical Models for Word Segmentation and Unknown Word Resolution," Proceedings of ROCLING V, pp. 121-146

[9] Chang, Jing-Shin and Keh-Yih Su, 1997a. "An Unsupervised Iterative Method for Chinese New Lexicon Extraction", to appear in International Journal of Computational Linguistics & Chinese Language Processing, 1997

[10] C.H. Tung and H. J. Lee , "Identification of unknown words from corpus," *International Journal of Computer Processing of Chinese and Oriental Languages,* Vol. 8, Supplement, pp. 131-146, 1995

[11] Chen, K.J. & Wei-Yun Ma, 2002. Unknown Word Extraction for Chinese Documents. In Proceedings of COLING 2002, pages 169-175

[12] Chen, K.J. & Ming-Hong Bai, 1998, "Unknown Word Detection for Chinese by a Corpus-based Learning Method," international Journal of Computational linguistics and Chinese Language Processing, Vol.3, #1, pp.27-44

[13] Church, Kenneth W., 2000, "Empirical Estimates of Adaptation: The Chance of Two Noriegas is Closer to p/2 than p*p", Proceedings of Coling 2000, pp.180-186.]

[14] Allen James 1995 Natural Language understandding. Second Edition, page 44

[15] Chen, K.J. & S.H. Liu, 1992,"Word Identification for Mandarin Chinese Sentences," *Proceedings of 14th Coling*, pp. 101-107

[16] Huang, C. R. Et al.,1995,"The Introduction of Sinica Corpus," *Proceedings of ROCLING VIII*, pp. 81-89.

[17] Huang, C.R., K.J. Chen, & Li-Li Chang, 1997, "Segmentation Standard for Chinese Natural Language Processing," International Journal of Computational Linguistics and Chinese Language Processing, Accepted.

[18] Chomsky, N. 1956 Three models for the description of language. IRE Transactions on Information Theory, 2, 113-124

[19] Church, K. and Hanks, P., "Word Association Norms, Mutual Information and Lexicography," Computational Linguistics, Vol.16, March. 1990, pp.22-29

[20] Smadja, Frank, "Retrieving Collocations from Text: Xtract," Computational Linguistics, Vol. 19 , No. 1, 1993, pp.143-177

[21] Smadja, Frank, McKeown, K.R. and Hatzivasiloglou, V. "Translating Collocations for Bilingual Lexicons," Computational Linguistics, Vol. 22, No.1, 1996

[22] Church, K, W. Gale, P. Hanks, and D. Hindle. 1991 "Using Statistics in Lexical Analysis," in Zernik (ed.) Lexical Acquisition: Exploiting On-Line Resources to Build a Lexicon, pp. 115-164, Lawrence Erlbaum Associates Publishers

The Effect of Rhythm on Structural Disambiguation in Chinese

Honglin Sun **Dan Jurafsky**
Center for Spoken Language Research
University of Colorado at Boulder
{honglin.sun, jurafsky}@colorado.edu

Abstract

The length of a constituent (number of syllables in a word or number of words in a phrase), or *rhythm,* plays an important role in Chinese syntax. This paper systematically surveys the distribution of rhythm in constructions in Chinese from the statistical data acquired from a shallow tree bank. Based on our survey, we then used the rhythm feature in a practical shallow parsing task by using rhythm as a statistical feature to augment a PCFG model. Our results show that using the probabilistic rhythm feature significantly improves the performance of our shallow parser.

1 Introduction

Syntactic research indicates that prosodic features, including stress, rhythm, intonation, and others, have an impact on syntactic structure. For example, normally in a coordination construction like "A and B", A and B are interchangeable, that is to say, you can say "B and A" and the change of word order does not change the meaning. However, sometimes A and B are not interchangeable. Quirk et al.(1985) gives the following examples:

man and woman * woman and man
ladies and gentleman *gentleman and ladies

Obviously, the examples above cannot be explained by gender preference. A reasonable explanation is that the length of the words (perhaps in syllables) is playing a role; the first constituent tends to be shorter than the second constituent.

This feature of the length in syllables of a constituent plays an even more important role in Chinese syntax than in English (Feng, 2000). For example, in the verb-object construction in Chinese, there is a preference for the object to be equal to or longer than the verb. Thus while both "种"(plant) and "种植"(plant) are verbs and have the same meaning, "种/plant 树/tree" is grammatical while "种植/plant 树/tree" is ungrammatical. However, both verbs allow bi-syllabic nouns as objects (e.g., "果树"(fruit tree), "棉花"(cotton) etc.). The noun phrases formed by "noun + verb" give us another example in which rhythm feature places constraints on syntax, as indicated in the following examples (ungrammatical with *):

棉花/cotton 种植/planting
*棉花/cotton 种/planting
*花/flower 种植/planting
*花/flower 种/planting

"棉花/cotton 种植/planting" is grammatical but "棉花/cotton 种/planting", "花/flower 种植/planting" and "花/flower 种/planting" are all ungrammatical, although "棉花/cotton" and "花/flour", "种植/planting" and "种/planting" have the same POS and the same or similar meaning. The only difference lies in that they have different number of syllables or different length.

This paper systematically surveys the effect of rhythm on Chinese syntax from the statistical data from a shallow tree bank. Based on the observation that rhythm places constraints on syntax in Chinese, we try to deploy a feature based on rhythm to improve disambiguation in a probabilistic parser by mixing the rhythm feature into a statistical parsing model.

The rest of the paper is organized as follows: we present specific statistical analyses of rhythm feature in Chinese syntax in Section 2. Section 3 introduces the content chunk parsing which is the task in our experiment. Section 4 presents the statistical model used in our experiment in which a probabilistic rhythm feature is integrated. Section 5 gives the experimental results and finally Section 6 draws some conclusions.

2 Analysis of Rhythmic Constraints

We divide our analysis of the use of rhythm in Chinese phrases into two categories, based on two types of phrases in Chinese: (1) simple phrases, containing only words, i.e. all the child nodes are POS tag in the derivation tree; and (2) complex phrases in which at least one constituent is a phrase itself, i.e. it has at least one child node with phrase type symbol (like NP, VP) in its derivation tree.

Below we will give the statistical analysis of the distribution of rhythm feature in different constructions from both simple and complex phrases. The corpus from which the statistical data is drawn contains 200K words of newspaper text from the People's Daily. The texts are word-segmented, POS tagged and labeled with content chunks. The content chunk is a phrase containing only content words, akin to a generalization of a BaseNP. These content chunks are parsed into binary shallow trees. More details about content chunks can be found in Section 3.

2.1 Rhythm feature in simple phrases

Simple phrases contain two lexical words (since, as discussed above, our parse trees are binary). The rhythm feature of each word is defined to be the number of syllables in it. Thus the rhythm feature for a word can take on one of the following three values: (1) monosyllabic; (2) bi-syllabic; and (3) multi-syllabic, meaning with three syllables or more.

Since each binary phrase contains two words, the set of rhythm features for a simple phrase is:

F = { (0，0), (0,1), (0,2), (1,0), (1,1), (1,2), (2,0), (2,1), (2,2) }

where 0, 1, 2 represent monosyllabic, bi-syllabic and multi-syllabic respectively.

In the following sections, we will present three case studies on the distributions of rhythm feature in different constructions: (1) verbs as modifier or head in NP; (2) the contrast between NPs and VPs formed by " verb + noun" sequences; (3) "noun + verb" sequences.

2.1.1 Case 1: Verb as modifier/head in NP

In Chinese, verbs can function as modifier or head in a noun phrase without any change of forms. For example, in "果树/fruit tree 栽培/growing", "栽培" is the head while in "栽培/growing 技术/technique", "栽培" is a modifier. However, in such constructions, there are strong constraints on the length of both verbs and nouns. Table 1 gives the distributions of the rhythm feature in the rule "NP -> N V"('N' and 'V' represent noun and verb respectively) in which the verb is the head and "NP -> V N" in which the verb is a modifier.

Table 1 Distribution of rhythm feature in NP with verb as modifier or head

	[0,0]	[0,1]	[0,2]	[1,0]	[1,1]	[1,2]	[2,0]	[2,1]	[2,2]	Total
NP -> V N	0	4	0	0	1275	4	0	88	0	1371
NP -> N V	13	10	0	401	2328	91	0	44	2	2889

Table 2 Distribution of rhythm feature in NP and VP formed by "V N"

	[0,0]	[0,1]	[0,2]	[1,0]	[1,1]	[1,2]	[2,0]	[2,1]	[2,2]	Total
VP -> V N	826	640	49	80	1221	121	0	11	1	2777
NP -> V N	13	10	0	401	2328	91	0	44	2	2889

Table 3 Distribution of rhythm feature in phrases formed by "N V" sequence

	[0,0]	[0,1]	[0,2]	[1,0]	[1,1]	[1,2]	[2,0]	[2,1]	[2,2]	Total
NP -> N V	0	4	0	0	1275	4	0	88	0	1371
NC -> N V	384	578	42	1131	3718	143	90	435	15	6536
S -> N V	28	1	2	17	347	22	2	43	8	470

Table 1 indicates that in both rules, the rhythm pattern [1,1], ie. "bi-syllabic + bi-syllabic", prevails. In the rule "NP -> V N", this pattern accounts for 93% among the nine possible patterns while in the rule "NP -> N V", this pattern accounts for 81%. We can also find that in both cases, [0,2] and [2,0] are prohibited, that is to say, both verbs and nouns cannot be longer than two syllables.

2.1.2 Case 2: Contrast between NP and VP formed by "V N" sequence

The sequence "V N"("verb + noun") can constitute an NP or a VP. The rhythm patterns in the two types of phrases are significantly different, however, as shown in Table 2. We see that in the NP case, verbs are mainly bi-syllabic. The total number of examples with bi-syllabic verbs in NP is 2820, accounting for 98% of all the cases. On the other hand, mono-syllabic verbs are less likely to appear in this position. The total number of examples with mono-syllabic verbs in NP is 23, accounting for only 0.8% of all the cases. That is to say, the likelihood of bi-syllabic verbs appearing in this syntactic position is 122 times the likelihood of mono-syllabic verbs. On the other hand, there is no big difference between bi-syllabic verbs and mono-syllabic verbs in the VP formed by "V + N". The ratios of bi-syllabic and mono-syllabic verbs in VP are 48 % and 55% respectively. The statistical facts tell us that for a "verb + noun" sequence, if the verb is not bi-syllabic then it is very unlikely to be an NP. Figure 1 depicts more clearly the difference between NP and VP formed by "V N" sequence in the distribution of rhythm feature.

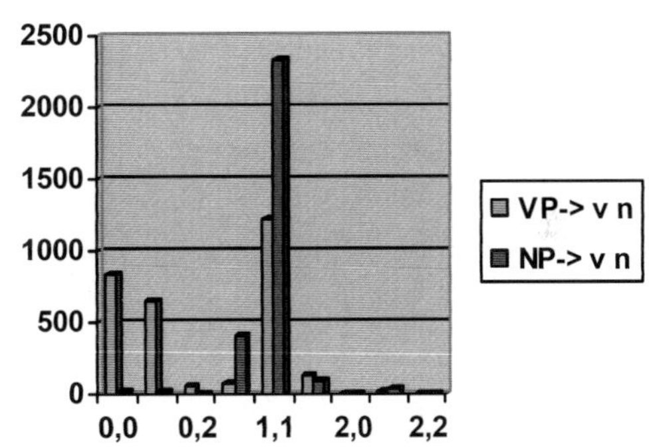

Figure 1 Distributions of rhythm feature in NP and VP formed by "verb + noun"

2.1 3 Case 3: "N V" sequence

An "N V"("noun + verb") sequence can be mainly divided into three types by the dominating phrasal category:

(1) NP(noun phrase), e.g. "果树/fruit tree 栽培/growth";

(2) S(subject-verb construction), e.g. "彩旗/colored flag 飘扬/flutter";

(3)NC(non-constituent), eg. "经济/economy 发展/develop" in "中国/China 的/DE 经济/economy 发展/develop 得/DE 很/very 快/fast". ('China's economy develops very fast')

Table 3 gives the distribution of rhythm feature in the three types of cases.

We see in Table 3, in rule "NP -> N V", that the verb cannot be mono-syllabic since the first row is 0 in all the patterns in which verb is mono-syllabic([0,0], [1,0],[2,0]). The "bi-syllabic + bi-syllabic" ([1,1]) pattern accounts for 93% (1275/1371) of the total number. Let's look at the cases with mono-syllabic verbs in all the three types. The total number of such examples is 1652 in the corpus (adding all the numbers in columns [0,0], [1,0] and [2,0] on the three rows). Among these 1652 cases, there is not one example in which the "N V" is an NP. The sequence has a probability of 3%(47/1652) to be an S and 97 %(1605/1652) of being an NC(non-constituent).

2.2 Rhythm feature in complex phrases

Just as we saw with two word simple phrases, the rhythm feature also has an effect on complex phrases where at least one component is a phrase, i.e. spanning over two words or more. For example, for the following fragment of a sentence:

跨/stride 进/into 三峡/the Three Gorges 工程/project 大门/gate

'enter into the gate of the Three Gorges Project'

according to PCFG, the parse as indicated in Figure 2 (a) is incorrectly assigned the greatest

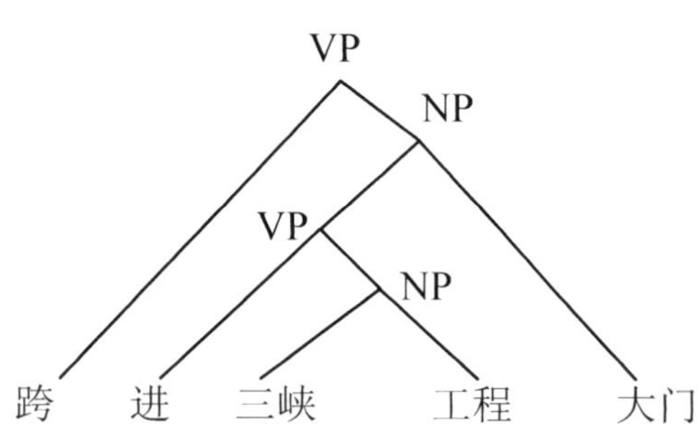

(a)

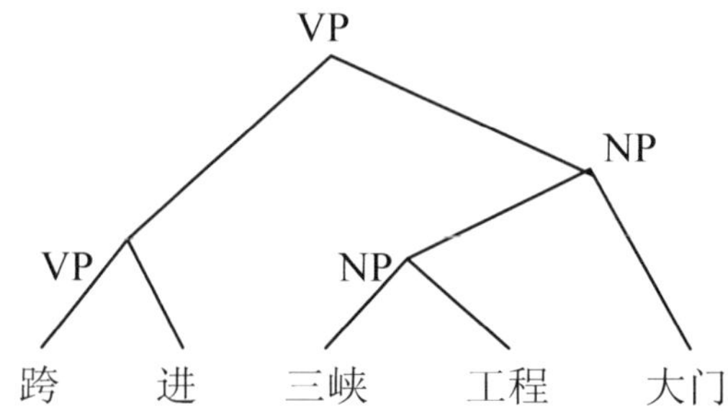

(b)

Figure 2 (a) incorrect parse and (b) correct parse

probability but the correct parse is that given in Figure 2 (b). One major error in (a) is that it applies the rule "NP-> VP N" (i.e. "进 三峡 工程" modifying "大门"). This rule has 216 occurrences in the corpus, of which 168 times it contains a VP of 2 words, 30 times a VP of 3 words and 18 times a VP of more than 3 words. These statistics indicate that this rule prefers to choose a short VP acting as the modifier of a noun, as in "NP(VP(种/grow 粮/grain) 大户/large family)" and "NP(VP(学/learn 雷锋/Lei Feng) 标兵/model)". But in the example in Figure 2(a), the VP contains 3 words, so it is less likely to be a modifier in an NP.

When a phrase works as a constituent in a larger phrase, its rhythm feature is defined as the number of words in it. Thus a phrase may take on one of the three values for the rhythm feature: (1) two words; (3) three words; and (3) more than three words. Similar to that in the simple phrases, we may use 0, 1, 2 to represent the three values respectively. Therefore, for every construction containing two constituents, its rhythm feature can be described by a 3×3 matrix uniformly. For example, in the examples for rule "NP -> VP N" above, the feature value for "NP(VP(种/grow 粮/grain) 大户/large family)" is [0, 1] in which 0 indicates the VP contains 2 words and 1 represents that the noun is bi-syllabic. The rule helps to interpret the meaning of the feature value, i.e. the value is for a word or a phrase. For example, for rule "VP -> V N", feature value [0, 1] means that the verb is mono-syllabic and the noun is bi-syllabic, while for rule "NP-> VP N", feature [0,1] means that the VP contains two words and the noun is bi-syllabic.

3 Content Chunk Parsing

We have chosen the task of content chunk parsing to test the usefulness of our rhythm feature to Chinese text. In this section we address two questions: (1) What is a content chunk? (2) Why are we interested in content chunk parsing?

A content chunk is a phrase formed by a sequence of content words, including nouns, verbs, adjectives and content adverbs. There are three kinds of cases for the mapping between content word sequences and content chunks:

(1) A content word sequence is a content chunk. A special case of this is that a whole sentence is a content chunk when all the words in it are content words, eg. [[前景/Prospect 公司/company]NP [推出/release [高级/advanced [电脑/computer [排版/typesetting 系统/system]NP]NP]NP]VP ('Prospect Company released an advanced computer typesetting system.').

(2) A content word sequence is not a content chunk. For example, in "中国/China 的/AUX 经济/economy 发展/develop 得/AUX 很/very 快/fast"('China's economy develops very fast.'), "经济/economy 发展/develop" is a content word sequence, but it's not a phrase in the sentence.

(3) A part of a content word sequence is a content chunk. For example, in "私营/private 经济/economy 发展/develop 的/AUX 势头/trend 很/very 好/good"('The developmental trend of private economy is very good.'), "私营/private 经济/economy 发展/develop" is a content word sequence, but it's not a phrase; only "私营/private 经济/economy" in it is a phrase.

The purpose of content chunk parsing is to recognize phrases in a sequence of content words. Specifically speaking, the content chunking contains two subtasks: (1) to recognize the maximum phrase in a sequence of content words; (2) to analyze the hierarchical structure within the phrase down to words. Like baseNP chunking(Church, 1988; Ramshaw & Marcus 1995), content chunk parsing is also a kind of shallow parsing. Content chunk parsing is deeper than baseNP chunking in two aspects: (1) a content chunk may contain verb phrases and other phrases even a full sentence as long as the all the components are content words; (2) it may contain recursive NPs. Thus the content chunk can supply more structural information than a baseNP.

The motives for content chunk parsing are two-fold: (1) Like other shallow parsing tasks, it can simplify the parsing task. This can be explained in two aspects. First, it can avoid the ambiguities brought up by functional words. In Chinese, the most salient syntactic ambiguities are prepositional phrases and the "DE" construction. For prepositional phrases, the difficulty lies in how to determine the right boundary, because almost any constituent can be the object of a preposition. For "DE" constructions, the problem is how to determine its left boundary, since almost any constituent can be followed by "DE" to form a "DE" construction. Second, content chunk parsing can simplify the structure of a sentence. When a content chunk is acquired, it can be replaced by its head word, thus reducing the length of the original sentence. If we get a parse from the reduced sentence with a full parser, then we can get a parse for the original sentence by replacing the head-word nodes with the content chunks from which the head-words are extracted. (2) The content chunk parsing may be useful for applications like information extraction and question answering. When using template matching, a content chunk may be just the correct level of shallow structure for matching with an element in a template.

4 PCFG + PF Model

In the experiment we propose a statistical model integrating probabilistic context-free grammar (PCFG) model with a simple probabilistic features (PF) model. In this section we first give the definition for the statistical model and then we will give the method for parameter estimation.

4.1 Definition

According to PCFG, each rule r used to expand a node n in a parse is assigned a probability, i.e.:

$$P(r(n)) = P(\beta \mid A) \tag{1}$$

where A -> β is a CFG rule. The probability of a parse T is the product of each rule used to expand each node n in T:

$$P(T \mid S) = \prod_{n \in T} P(r(n)) \tag{2}$$

We expand PCFG by the way that when a left hand side category A is expanded into a string β, a feature set FS related to β is also generated. Thus, a probability is assigned for expansion of each node n when a rule r is applied:

$$P(r(n)) = P(FS, \beta \mid A) \tag{3}$$

where A -> β is a CFG rule and FS is a feature set related to β. From Equation (3) we get:

$$P(r(n)) = P(FS \mid \beta, A) * P(\beta \mid A) \tag{4}$$

where P(FS| β, A) is probabilistic feature(PF) model and P(β | A) is PCFG model. PF model describes the probability of each feature in feature set FS taking on specific values when a CFG rule A -> β is given. To make the model more practical in parameter estimation, we assume the features in feature set FS are independent from each other, thus:

$$P(FS \mid \beta, A) = \prod_{Fi \in FS} P(Fi \mid \beta, A) \tag{5}$$

Under this PCFG+PF model, the goal of a parser is to choose a parse that maximizes the following score:

$$Score(T \mid S) = \arg\max_{T} \prod_{i=1}^{n} P(FS_i, \beta_i \mid A_i) \tag{6}$$

Our model is thus a simplification of more sophisticated models which integrate PCFGs with features, such as those in Magerman(1995), Collins(1997) and Goodman(1997). Compared with these models, our model is more practical when only small training data is available, since we assume the independence between features. For example, in Goodman's probabilistic feature grammar (PFG), each symbol in a PCFG is replaced by a set of features, so it can describe specific constraints on the rule. In the PFG model the generation of each feature is dependent on all the previously generated features, thus likely leading to severe sparse data problem in parameter estimation. Our simplified model assumes independence between the features, thus data sparseness problem can be significantly alleviated.

4.2 Parameter Estimation

Let F be a feature associated with a string β, where the possible values for F are $f_1, f_2, \ldots, f_n$, E is the set of observations of rule A → β in the training corpus, and thus E can be divided into n disjoint subsets: $E_1, E_2, \ldots, E_n$, corresponding to $f_1, f_2, \ldots, f_n$ respectively. The probability of F taking on a value of f_i given A → β can be estimated as follows, according to MLE:

$$P(F = f_i \mid \beta, A) = \frac{|E_i|}{|E|} \tag{7}$$

This indicates that feature F adds constraints on CFG rule A → β by dividing Ω, the state space of A → β, into n disjoint subspaces $\omega_1, \omega_2, \ldots, \omega_n$, and each case of F taking a value of f_i given A → β is viewed as a random event.

5 Experimental Results

5.1 Training and Test Data

A Chinese corpus of 200K words extracted from the People's Daily are segmented, POS-tagged and hand-labeled with content chunks in which all the trees are binary. The corpus is divided into two parts: (1) 180K for training set and (2) 20K for test set.

5.2 Metrics and results

We take two kinds of criteria to measure the system's performance: labeled and unlabeled. According to the labeled criterion, a recognized phrase is correct only if a phrase with the same starting position, ending position and the same label is found in the gold standard. According to the unlabeled criterion, a recognized phrase is correct as long as a phrase with the same starting position and ending position is found in the gold standard.

Table 4 Experimental Results

	Labeled			Unlabeled		
	P	R	F	P	R	F
PCFG	49.91	64.96	56.45	53.33	80.73	65.66
PCFG+RF in simple phrases	53.25	68.46	59.90	57.46	81.21	67.30
PCFG +RF in all the phrases	56.47	72.08	63.33	60.07	83.57	69.90

Table 5 Effect of rhythm feature on structural disambiguation

Word sequence	Rule	P(β|A)	RF	P(RF=[0, 1] |A, β)	P(RF=(0, 1), β)|A)
国 捐躯 country sacrifice	NC→ N V	0.120273	[0,1]	0.08843	0. 010636
国 捐躯	S → N V	0.161679	[0,1]	0.00292	0. 000344
国 捐躯	NP→ N V	0.063159	[0,1]	0.00213	0. 000184
国 捐躯	V → N V	0.011573	[0,1]	0.0	0. 0

Within each criterion, precision, recall and F-measure are given as metrics for the system's performance. Precision represents how many phrases are correct among the phrases recognized, recall represents how many phrases in the gold standard are correctly recognized, and F-measure is defined as follows:

$$F-measure=\frac{Precision\times Recall\times 2}{Precision+Recall}$$

Table 4 gives the experimental results in three different conditions: the first row gives the result of PCFG model; the second row gives the result of PCFG model integrated with rhythm feature model (RF) where only the features of simple phrases are considered; the last row gives the result of PCFG model plus RF where the rhythm features in all the phrases are considered. The results indicate that the rhythm features in both simple and complex phrases contribute to the improvement of performance over PCFG model. We see that the rhythm feature improves the labeled F-measure 6.88 percent and the unlabeled F-measure 4.24 percent over the unaugmented PCFG model.

5.3 Effect of rhythm feature on parsing

The experiment shows that the rhythm feature can help the performance of a parser in Chinese. Specifically, the effects of rhythm feature on parsing are shown in two ways:

(1) Help for the disambiguation of phrasal type.

Table 5 shows the difference of the results between PCFG model and PCFG + RF model for the sequence "国/country 捐躯/sacrifice" in the sentence "该/the 校/school 有/have 900 学子

/students 为/for 国/country 捐躯/sacrifice“ (‘900 students from this school gave their lives for their country’).

In the sentence above, “国/country” is the object of preposition “为/for”, “国/country 捐躯/sacrifice” is not a constituent. But the unaugmented PCFG model incorrectly parses it as a S(subject-predicate construction). Contrarily, according to PCFG+RF model, the type with greatest probability is the (correct) NC(non-constituent) parse.

(2) Help for pruning.

Let’s give an example to explain it. For the sentence “解决/solve 居民/resident 吃/eat 菜/vegetable 问题/problem 十分/very 困难/difficult”(‘It’s very difficult to solve the vegetable problem for the residents.’), the number of edges generated by the PCFG is 1236, but the number decreases to 348 after the rhythm feature is applied, thus pruning 73% of the edges. As indicated in Table 1, in the rule “NP -> N V”, P(RF = [1,0]) = 0, so “[居民/N 吃/V]NP” is pruned after adding RF. Similarly, in rule “NP -> V N”, P(RF = [0, 1]) = 0.003, so “[吃/V 菜/N]NP” is pruned since it has very low probability. With these two edges pruned, more potential edges containing them will not be generated.

6 Conclusion

In this paper, we systematically survey the distribution of rhythm (number of syllables per word or numbers of words per phrase for a constituent) in different constructions in Chinese. Our analysis suggests that rhythm places strong constraints on Chinese syntax. Based on this observation, we used the rhythm feature in a practical shallow parsing task in which a PCFG model is augmented with a probabilistic representation of the rhythm feature. The experimental results show that the probabilistic rhythm feature aids in disambiguation in Chinese and thus helps to improve the performance of a Chinese parser. We can expect that the performance of the parser may further improve when more features are considered under the probabilistic feature (PF) model.

Acknowledgments

This research was partially supported by the NSF, via a KDD extension to NSF IIS-9978025.

References

Church,,K.,1988.A stochastic parts program and noun phrase parser for unrestricted text. In *Proceedings of the Second Conference on Applied Natural Language Processing*, pp.136-143.

Collins, M. 1997. Three generative lexicalized models for statistical parsing, in *Proceedings of the 35th Annual Meeting of the ACL*, pp. 16-23.

Feng, Shengli. 2000. *The Rhythmic syntax of Chinese*(in Chinese), Shanghai Education Press.

Goodman, J. 1997. Probabilistic Feature Grammars, In *Proceedings of the International Workshop on Parsing Technologies*, September 1997

Magerman, D. 1995. Statistical decision-tree models for parsing, in *Proceedings of the 33rd Annual Meeting of the Association for Computational Linguistics*, pp.276-283.

Quirk et al. 1985. *A Comprehensive Grammar of English Languge*, Longman.

Ramshaw L., and Marcus M. 1995. Text chunking using transformation-based learning. In *Proceedings of the Third Workshop on Very Large Corpora*.pp.86-95.

Annotating the Propositions in the Penn Chinese Treebank

Nianwen Xue
Dept. of Computer and Info. Science
University of Pennsylvania
Philadelphia, PA 19104, USA
xueniwen@linc.cis.upenn.edu

Martha Palmer
Dept. of Computer and Info. Science
University of Pennsylvania
Philadelphia, PA 19104, USA
mpalmer@linc.cis.upenn.edu

Abstract

In this paper, we describe an approach to annotate the propositions in the Penn Chinese Treebank. We describe how diathesis alternation patterns can be used to make coarse sense distinctions for Chinese verbs as a necessary step in annotating the predicate-structure of Chinese verbs. We then discuss the representation scheme we use to label the semantic arguments and adjuncts of the predicates. We discuss several complications for this type of annotation and describe our solutions. We then discuss how a lexical database with predicate-argument structure information can be used to ensure consistent annotation. Finally, we discuss possible applications for this resource.

1 Introduction

Linguistically interpreted corpora are instrumental in supervised machine learning paradigms of natural language processing. The information encoded in the corpora to a large extent determines what can be learned by supervised machine learning systems. Therefore, it is crucial to encode the desired level of information for its automatic acquisition. The creation of the Penn English Treebank (Marcus et al., 1993), a syntactically interpreted corpus, played a crucial role in the advances in natural language parsing technology (Collins, 1997; Collins, 2000; Charniak, 2000) for English. The creation of the Penn Chinese Treebank (Xia et al., 2000) is also beginning to help advance technologies in Chinese syntactic analysis (Chiang, 2000; Bikel and Chiang, 2000). Since the treebanks are generally syntactically oriented (cf. Sinica Treebank (Chen et al., to appear)), the information encoded there is "shallow". Important information useful for natural language applications is missing. Most notably, significant regularities in the predicate-argument structure of lexical items are not captured. Recent effort in semantic annotation, the creation of the Penn Proposition Bank (Kingsbury and Palmer, 2002) on top of the Penn English Treebank is beginning to address this issue for English. In this new layer of annotation, the regularities of the predicates, mostly verbs, are captured in the predicate-argument structure. For example, in the sentences "The Congress passed the bill" and "The bill passed", it is intuitively clear that "the bill" plays the same role in the two occurrences of the verb "pass". Similar regularities also exist in Chinese. For example, in "这/this 条/CL 法案/bill 通过/pass 了/AS" and "议会/Congress 通过/pass 了 /AS 这/this 条/CL 法案/bill", "法案/bill" also plays the same role for the verb "通过/pass" even though it occurs in different syntactic positions (subject and object respectively).

Capturing such lexical regularities requires a "deeper" level of annotation than generally provided in a typical syntactically oriented treebank. It also requires making sense distinctions at the appropriate granularity. For example, the regularities demonstrated for "pass" does not exist in other senses of this verb. For example, in "He passed the exam" and "He passed", the object "the exam" of the transitive use of "pass" does not play the same role as the subject "he" of the intransitive use. In fact, the subject plays the same role in both sentences.

However, how deep the annotation can go is constrained by two important factors: how consistently human annotators can implement this type of annotation (the **consistency** issue) and whether the annotated information is learnable by machine (the **learnability** issue). Making fine-grained sense distinctions, in particular, has been known to be difficult for human annotators as well as machine-learning systems (Palmer et al., submitted). It seems generally true that structural information is more learnable than non-structural information, as evidenced by the higher parsing accuracy and relatively poor fine-grained WSD accuracy. With this in mind, we will propose a level of semantic annotation that still can be captured in structural terms and add this level of annotation to the Penn Chinese Treebank. The rest of the paper is organized as follows. In Section 2, we will discuss the annotation model in detail and describe our representation scheme. We will discuss some complications in Section 3 and some implementation issues in Section 4. Possible applications of this resource are discussed in Section 5. We will conclude in Section 6.

2 Annotation Model

In this section we describe a model that annotates the predicate-argument structure of Chinese predicates. This model captures the lexical regularities by assuming that different instances of a predicate, usually a verb, have the same predicate argument structure if they have the same sense. Defining sense has been one of the most thorny issues in natural language research (Ide and Vronis, 1998), and the term "sense" has been used to mean different things, ranging from part-of-speech and homophones, which are easier to define, to slippery fine-grained semantic distinctions that are hard to make consistently. Determining the "right" level of sense distinction for natural language applications is ultimately an empirical issue, with the best level of sense distinction being the level with the least granularity and yet sufficient for a natural language application in question. Without gearing towards one particular application, our strategy is to use the structural regularities demonstrated in Section 1 to define sense. Finer sense distinctions without clear structural indications are avoided. All instances of a predicate that realize the same set of semantic roles are assumed to have one sense, with the understanding that not all of the semantic roles for this verb sense have to be realized in a given verb instance, and that the same semantic role may be realized in different syntactic positions. All the possible syntactic realizations of the same set of semantic roles for a verb sense are then **alternations** of one another. This state of affairs has been characterized as **diathesis alternation** and used to establish cross-predicate generalizations and classifications (Levin, 1993). It has been hypothesized and demonstrated that verbs sharing the same disthesis alternation patterns also have similar meaning postulates. It is equally plausible to assume then that verb instances having different diathesis alternation patterns also have different semantic properties and thus different senses.

Using diathesis alternation patterns as a diagnostic test, we can identify the different senses for a verb. Alternating **syntactic frames** for a particular verb sense realizing the same set of semantic roles (we call this **roleset**) form a **frameset** and share similar semantic properties. It is easy to see that each frameset, a set of syntactic frames for a verb, corresponds with one roleset and vice versa. From now on, we use the term **frameset** instead of **sense** for clarity. Each frameset consists of one or more syntactic frames and each syntactic frame realizes one or more semantic roles. One frame differs from another in the number and type of arguments its predicate actually takes, and one frameset differs from another in the total number and type of arguments its predicate CAN take. This is illustrated graphically in Figure 1.

Annotating the predicate-argument structure involves mapping the frameset identification information for a predicate to an actual predicate instance in the corpus and assign the semantic roles to its arguments based on the syntactic frame of that predicate instance. It is hoped that since framesets are defined through diathesis alternation of syntactic frames, the distinctions made are still structural in nature and thus are machine-learnable and can be consistently annotated by human annotators.

So far our discussion has focused on semantic ar-

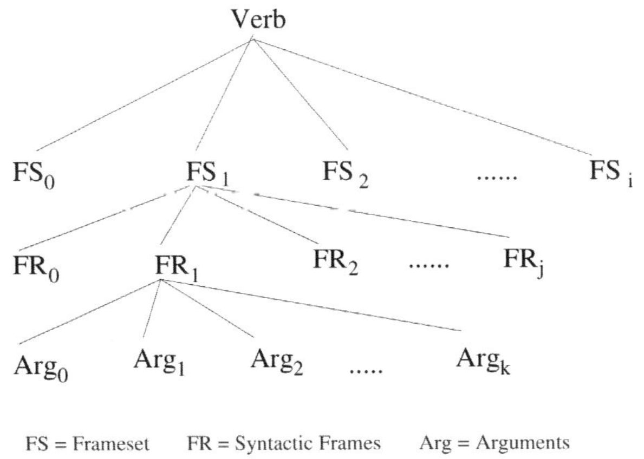

Figure 1: Annotation model

guments, which play a central role in determining the syntactic frames and framesets. There are other elements in a proposition: semantic adjuncts. Compared with semantic arguments, semantic adjuncts do not play a role in defining the syntactic frames or framesets because they occur in a wide variety of predicates and as a result are not as discriminative as semantic arguments. On the other hand, since they can co-occur with a wide variety of predicates, they are more generalizable and classifiable than semantic arguments. In the next section, we will describe a representation scheme that captures this dichotomy.

2.1 Representing arguments and adjuncts

Since the number and type of semantic arguments for a predicate are unique and thus define the semantic roles for a predicate, we label the arguments for a predicate with a contiguous sequence of integers, in the form of *argN*, where N is the integer between 0 and 5. Generally, a predicate has fewer than 6 arguments. Since semantic adjuncts are not subcategorized for by the predicate, we use one label *argM* for all semantic adjuncts. *ArgN* identifies the arguments while *argM* identifies all adjuncts. An *argN* uniquely identifies an argument of a predicate even if it occupies different syntactic positions in different predicate instances. Missing arguments of a predicate instance can be inferred by noting the missing argument labels.

Additionally, we also use secondary tags to generalize and classify the semantic arguments and adjuncts when possible. For example, an adjunct receiving a TMP tag if it is a temporal adjunct. The secondary tags are reserved for semantic adjuncts, predicates that serve as arguments, as well as certain arguments for phrasal verbs. The 18 secondary tags and their descriptions are presented in Table 1.

11 functional tags for semantic adjuncts	
ADV	adverbial, default tag
BNF	beneficiary
CND	condition
DIR	direction
DGR	degree
FRQ	frequency
LOC	locative
MNR	manner
PRP	purpose or reason
TMP	temporal
TPC	topic
1 functional tag for predicate as argument	
PRD	predicate
6 functional tags for arguments to phrasal verbs	
AS	为, 是, 作, 做
AT	在, 于
INTO	成, 入, 进
ONTO	上
TO	到, 至
TOWARDS	向, 往

Table 1: List of functional tags

3 Complications

In this section we discuss several complications in annotating the predicate-argument structure as described in Section 2. Specifically, we discuss the phenomenon of "split arguments" and the annotation of nominalized verbs (or deverbal nouns).

3.1 Split Arguments

What can be characterized as "split arguments" are cases where a constituent that occurs as one argument in one sentence can also be realized as multiple arguments (generally two) for the same predicate in another sentence, without causing changes in the meaning of the sentences. This phenomenon surfaces in several different constructions. One such construction involves "possessor raising", where the possessor (in a broad sense) raises to a higher position. Examples 1a and 1b illustrate this. In 1a, the possessor originates from the subject position and raises to the topic[1] position, while in 1b, the possessor originates from the object position and raises

[1]In Chinese, it is possible to have a topic in addition to the subject. The topic is higher than the subject and plays an important role in the sentence (Li and Thompson, 1976).

to the subject position. The exact syntactic analysis is not important here, and what is important is that one argument in one sentence becomes two in another. The challenge is then to capture this regularity when annotating the predicate-argument structure of the verb.

1. Possessor Raising

a. Subject to Topic

```
(IP (NP-PN-TPC 中国/China)
    (NP-TMP 去年/last year)
    (NP-SBJ 进出口/import-export
            总值/total volume)
    (VP 逾/exceed
        (QP-OBJ 三千二百五十亿/325 Billion
                (CLP 美元/US. Dollar))))
```

逾/exceed
arg0-**psr**: 中国/China
arg0-**pse**: 进出口/import-export 总值/total volume
arg1: 三千二百五十亿/325 Billion 美元/US. Dollar

```
(IP (NP-TMP 去年/last year)
    (NP-SBJ (DNP (NP-PN 中国/China)
                 的/DE)
            (NP 进出口/import-export
                总值/volume))
    (VP 逾/exceed
        (QP-OBJ 三千二百五十亿/325 Billion
                (CLP 美元/US. Dollar))))
```

逾/exceed
arg0: 中国/China 的/DE 进出口/import-export 总值/volume
arg1: 三千二百五十亿/325 Billion 美元/US. Dollar

b. Object to Subject

```
(IP (NP-SBJ (NP-PN 中国/China)
            (NP 经济/economy
                增长/expansion))
    (VP (ADVP 也/also)
        (ADVP 将/will)
        (VP 放慢/slow down
            (NP-OBJ 速度/speed)))
```

放慢/slow down
arg1-**psr**: 中国/China 经济/economy 增长/expansion
arg1-**pse**: 速度/speed

```
(IP (NP-SBJ (DNP (NP (NP-PN 中国/China)
                     (NP 经济/economy
                         增长/expansion))
                 的)
            (NP 速度/speed))
    (VP (ADVP 也/also)
        (ADVP 将/will)
        (VP 放慢/slow down))
```

放慢/slow down
arg1: 中国/China 经济/economy 增长/expansion 的/DE 速度/speed

Another case of "split arguments" involves the coordinated noun phrases. In 2a, for example, the coordinated structure as a whole is an argument to the verb "签订/sign". In contrast, in 2b, one piece of the argument, "中国 /China" is realized as a noun phrase introduced by a preposition. There is no apparent difference in meaning for the two sentences.

2. Coordination vs. Prepositional phrase

```
a. (IP (NP-PN-SBJ 缅甸/Burma
                  和/and
                  中国/China)
       (VP (ADVP 已/already)
           (VP 签订/sign
               了/ASP
               (NP-OBJ 边境/border
                       贸易/trade
                       协定/agreement))))
```

签订/sign
arg0: 缅甸/Burma 和/and 中国/China
arg1: 边境/border 贸易/trade 协定/agreement

```
b. (IP (NP-PN-SBJ 缅甸/Burma)
       (VP (ADVP 已/already)
           (PP 同/with
               (NP-PN 中国/China))
           (VP 签订/sign
               了/ASP
               (NP-OBJ 边境/border
                       贸易/trade
                       协定/agreement))))
```

签订/sign
arg0-**crd**: 缅甸/Burma
arg0-**crd**: 中国/China
arg1: 边境/border 贸易/trade 协定/agreement

There are two ways to capture this type of regularity. One way is to treat each piece as a separate argument. The problem is that for coordinated noun phrases, there can be arbitrarily many coordinated constituents. So we adopt the alternative approach of representing the entire constituent as one argument. When the pieces are separate constituents, they will receive the same argument label, with different secondary tags indicating they are parts of a larger constituent. For example, in 1, when possessor raising occurs, the possessor and possessee receive the same argument label with different secondary tags *psr* and *pse*. In 2b, both "中国/China" and "缅甸/Burma" receive the label *arg0*, and the secondary label *crd* indicates each one is a part of the coordinated constituent.

3.2 Nominalizations

Another complication involves nominalizations (or deverbal nouns) and their co-occurrence with light and not-so-light verbs. A nominalized verb, while serving as an argument to another predicate (generally a verb), also has its own predicate-argument structure. For example, in 3, the predicate-argument structure for "怀疑/doubt" should be "怀疑 (读者, 这条 新闻)", where all the arguments of "怀疑/doubt" are embedded in the NP headed by "怀疑/doubt". The complication arises when the nominalized noun is a complement to another verb, as in 4, where the subject "读者/reader" is an argument to both the verb "产生/produce" and the nominalized verb "怀疑/doubt". More interestingly, the other argument "这/this 条/CL 新闻/news" is realized as an adjunct to the verb (introduced by a preposition) even though it bears no apparent thematic relationship to it.

It might be tempting to treat the verb "产生/develop" as a "light verb" that does not have its own predicate-argument structure, but this is questionable because "产生/doubt" can also take a noun that is not a nominalized verb: "我/I 对/towards 她/she 产生/develop 了/LE 感情/feeling". In addition, there is no apparent difference in meaning for "产生/develop" between this sentence and 4, so there is little basis to say these are two different senses of this verb. So we annotate the predicate-argument structure of both the verb "产生 (读者, 怀疑)" and the nominalized verb "怀疑 (读者, 这 条 新闻)".

```
3. (IP (NP-SBJ (NP 读者/reader)
               (DNP (PP 对/towards
                        (NP (DP 这/this
                                (CLP 条/CL))
                            (NP 新闻/news)))
                    的)
               (NP 怀疑/doubt))
       (VP 加深/deepen
           了/LE))
加深/deepen
arg1:读者/reader 对/towards 这/this 条/CL
     新闻/news
```

```
4. (IP (NP-SBJ 读者/reader)
       (VP (PP-DIR 对/towards
                   (NP (DP 这/this
                           (CLP 条/CL))
                       (NP 新闻/news)))
           (ADVP 也/too)
           (VP 会/will
               (VP 产生/develop
                   (NP-OBJ 怀疑/doubt)))))
产生/develop
arg0: 读者/reader
arg1: 怀疑/doubt
```

4 Implementation

To implement the annotation model presented in Section 2, we create a lexical database. Each entry is a predicate listed with its framesets. The set of possible semantic roles for each frameset are also listed with a mnemonic explanation. This explanation is not part of the formal annotation. It is there to help human annotators understand the different semantic roles of this frameset. An annotated example is also provided to help the human annotator.

As illustrated in Example 5, the verb "通过/pass" has three framesets, and each frameset corresponds with a different meaning. The different meanings can be diagnosed with diathesis alternations. For example, when "通过/pass" means "pass through", it allows dropped object. That is, the object does not have to be syntactically realized. When it means "pass by vote", it also has an intransitive use. However, in this case, the verb demonstrates "subject of the intransitive / object of the transitive" alternation. That is, the subject in the intransitive use refers to the same entity as the object in the transitive use. When the verb means "pass an exam, test, inspection", there is also the transitive/intransitive alternation. Only in this case, the object of the transitive counterpart is now part of the subject in the intransitive use. This is the argument-split problem discussed in the last section. The three framesets, representing three senses, are illustrated in 5.

5. Verb: 通过/pass
Frameset.01: 穿越,穿过/pass through
Roles: arg0("passer"), arg1("place")
Example:
(IP (NP-SBJ 火车/train)
    (VP (ADVP 正在/now)
        (VP 通过/pass
            (NP-OBJ 遂道/tunnel))))
通过.01/pass
arg0: 火车/train
arg1: 遂道/tunnel
argM-ADV: 正在/now

(IP (NP-SBJ 火车/train)
    (VP (ADVP 正在/now)
        (VP 通过/pass)))
通过.01/pass
arg0: 火车/train
argM-ADV: 正在/now

Frameset.02: 及格,合格(考试,比赛等)/pass
    (an exam, etc.)
(IP (NP-SBJ (DNP (NP 他/he)
            的/DE)
        (NP 药检/drug inspection))
    (VP (ADVP 没/not)
        (VP 通过/pass)))
通过.02/pass
arg1: 他/he 的/DE 药检/drug inspection

(IP (NP-SBJ (NP 他/he)
    (VP (ADVP 没/not)
        (VP 通过/pass)))
            (NP-OBJ 药检/drug inspection))
通过.02/pass
arg1-psr: 他/he
arg1-pse: 药检/drug inspection

Frameset.03: 表决通过/pass (a bill, a law, etc.)
(IP (NP-PN-SBJ 美国/the U.S.
            国会/Congress)
    (VP (NP-TMP 最近/recently)
        (VP 通过/pass
            了/ASP
            (NP-OBJ 州际/interstate
                银行法/banking law))))
通过.03/pass
arg0: 美国/the U.S.
arg1: 州际/interstate 银行法/banking law

(IP (NP-SBJ (ADJP 州际/interstate)
            (NP 银行法/banking law))
    (VP (NP-TMP 最近/recently)
        (VP 通过/pass
            了/ASP)))
通过.03/pass
arg1: 州际/interstate 银行法/banking law

The human annotator can use the information specified in this entry to annotate all instances of "通过/pass" in a corpus. When annotating a predicate instance, the annotator first determines the syntactic frame of the predicate instance, and then determine which frameset this frame instantiates. The frameset identification is then attached to this predicate instance. This can be broadly construed as "sense-tagging", except that this type of sense tagging is coarser, and the "senses" are based on structural distinctions rather than just semantic nuances. A distinction is made only when the semantic distinctions also coincide with some structural distinctions. The expectation is that this type of sense tagging is much amenable to automatic machine-learning approaches. The annotation does not stop here. The annotator will go on identifying the arguments and adjuncts for this predicate instance. For the arguments, the annotator will determine which semantic role each argument realizes, based on the set of possible roles for this frameset, and attach the appropriate semantic role label (*argN*) to it. For adjuncts, the annotator will determine the type of adjunct this is and attach a secondary tag to *argM*.

5 Applications

A resource annotated with predicate-argument structure can be used for a variety of natural language applications. For example, this level of abstraction is useful for Information Extraction. The argument role labels can be easily mapped to an Information Extraction template, where each role is mapped to a piece of information that an IE system is interested in. Such mapping will not be as straightforward if it is between surface syntactic entities such as the subject and IE templates.

This level of abstraction can also provide a platform where lexical transfer can take place. It opens up the possibility of linking a frameset of a predicate in one language with that of another, rather than using bilingual (or multilingual) dictionaries where one word is translated into one or more words in a different language. This type of lexical transfer has several advantages. One is that the transfer is made more precise, in the sense that there will be more cases where one-to-one mapping is possible. Even in cases where one-to-one mapping is still not possible, the identification of the framesets of a predicate will narrow down the possible lexical choices. For example, *sign.02* in the English Proposition Bank (Kingsbury and Palmer, 2002) will be linked to "签订.01/enter into an agreement". This type of linking rules out "签署" as a possible translation for *sign.02*, even though it is a translation for other framesets of the word *sign*.

The transfer will also be more precise in another sense, that is, the predicate-argument structure of a word instance will be preserved during the transfer process. Knowing the arguments of a predicate instance can further constrain the lexical choices and rule out translation candidates whose predicate-argument structures are incompatible. For example, if the realized arguments of "sign.01" of the English Proposition Bank in a given sentence are the signer, the document, and the signature, among the translation candidates "签署, 签" ("签订.01/enter into an agreement" is ruled out as a possibility for this frameset), only "签" is possible, because "签署" can only take two arguments, namely, the signer and the document.

6. 他/he 在/at 这/this 个/CL 文件/document 上/LC 签/sign 了/LE 自己/self 的/DE 名字/name
"He signed his name on this document."

One might argue that the syntactic subcategorization frame obtained from the syntactic parse tree can also constrain the lexical choices. For example, knowing that "sign" has a subject, an object and a prepositional phrase should be enough to rule out "签署" as a possible translation. This argument breaks down when there are lexical divergences. The "document" argument of "签字" can only be realized as a prepositional phrase in Chinese while in English it can only be realized the direct object of "sign". If the syntactic subcategorization frame is used to constrain the lexical choices for "sign", "签字" will be incorrectly ruled out as a possible translation. There will be no such problem if the more abstract predicate-argument structure is used for this purpose. Even when the document is realized as a prepositional phrase, it is still the same argument. Of course, "签署/sign" is also a possible translation. So compared with the surface syntactic frames, the predicate-argument structure constrains the lexical choices without incorrectly ruling out legitimate translation candidates. This is understandable because the predicate-structure abstracts away from the syntactic idiosyncracies of the different languages and thus are more transferable across languages.

7. 他/he 在/at 这/this 个/CL 文件/document 上/LC 签字/sign
他/he 签署/sign 这/this 个/CL 文件/document
"He signed this document."

Annotating the predicate-argument structure as described in previous sections will not reduce the lexical choices to one-to-one mappings in call cases. For example, "统一" can be translated into "standardize" or "unite", even though there is only one frameset for both finer senses of this verb. It is conceivable that one might want to posit two framesets, each for one finer sense of this verb. This is essentially a trade-off: either one can conduct deep analysis of the source language, resolve all sense ambiguities on the source side and have a more straightforward mapping, or one takes the one-to-many mappings and select the correct translation on the target language side. Hopefully, the annotation of the predicate-argument provides just the right level of abstraction and the resource described here, with each predicate annotated with its arguments and adjuncts in context, enables the automatic acquisition of the predicate-argument structure.

6 Summary

In this paper, we described an approach to annotate the propositions in the Penn Chinese Treebank. We described how diathesis alternation patterns can be used to make coarse sense distinctions for Chinese verbs as a necessary step in annotating the predicate-structure of predicates. We also described the representation scheme we use to label the semantic arguments and adjuncts of the predicates. We discussed several complications for this type of annotation and described our solutions. We then discussed how a lexical database with predicate-argument structure information can be used to ensure consistent annotation. Finally, we discussed possible applications for this resource.

7 Acknowledgement

This work is supported by MDA904-02-C-0412.

References

Daniel M. Bikel and David Chiang. 2000. Two statistical parsing models applied to the chinese treebank. In *Proceedings of the 2nd Chinese Language Processing Workshop*, Hong Kong, China.

Eugene Charniak. 2000. A Maximum-Entropy-Inspired Parser. In *Proc. of NAACL-2000*.

Keh-Jiann Chen, Chu-Ren Huang, Feng-Yi Chen, Chi-Ching Luo, Ming-Chung Chang, and Chao-Jan Chen. to appear. Sinica Treebank: Design Criteria, representational issues and immplementation. In Anne Abeille, editor, *Building and Using Syntactically Annotated Corpora*. Kluwer.

David Chiang. 2000. Statisitical parsing with an automatically-extracted tree adjoining grammar. In *Proceedings of the 38th Annual Meeting of the Association for Computational Linguistics*, pages 456-463, Hong Kong.

Mike Collins. 1997. Three Generative, Lexicalised Models for Statistical Parsing. In *Proc. of ACL-1997*.

Mike Collins. 2000. Discriminative Reranking for Natural Language Parsing. In *Proc. of ICML-2000*.

N. Ide and J. Vronis. 1998. Word sense disambiguation: The state of the art. *Computational Linguistics*, 24(1):1–40.

Paul Kingsbury and Martha Palmer. 2002. From treebank to propbank. In *Proceedings of the 3rd International Conference on Language Resources and Evaluation (LREC2002)*, Las Palmas, Spain.

Beth Levin. 1993. *English Verbs and Alternations: A Preliminary Investigation*. Chicago: The Unversity of Chicago Press.

Charles Li and Sandra Thompson. 1976. Subject and Topic: A new typology of language. In Charles Li, editor, *Subject and Topic*. Academic Press.

M. Marcus, B. Santorini, and M. A. Marcinkiewicz. 1993. Building a Large Annotated Corpus of English: the Penn Treebank. *Computational Linguistics*.

Martha Palmer, Hoa Trang Dang, and Christiane Fellbaum. submitted. Making fine-grained and coarse-grained sense distinctions, both manually and automatically. *Journal of Natural Language Engineering*.

Fei Xia, Martha Palmer, Nianwen Xue, Mary Ellen Okurowski, John Kovarik, Fu-Dong Chiou, Shizhe Huang, Tony Kroch, and Mitch Marcus. 2000. Developing Guidelines and Ensuring Consistency for Chinese Text Annotation. In *Proc. of the 2nd International Conference on Language Resources and Evaluation (LREC-2000)*, Athens, Greece.

CHINERS: A Chinese Named Entity Recognition System for the Sports Domain

Tianfang Yao Wei Ding Gregor Erbach
Department of Computational Linguistics
Saarland University
Germany
yao@coli.uni-sb.de wding@mpi-sb.mpg.de
gor@acm.org

Abstract

In the investigation for Chinese named entity (NE) recognition, we are confronted with *two principal challenges*. *One* is how to ensure the quality of word segmentation and Part-of-Speech (POS) tagging, because its consequence has an adverse impact on the performance of NE recognition. *Another* is how to flexibly, reliably and accurately recognize NEs. In order to cope with the challenges, we propose a system architecture which is divided into two phases. In the *first* phase, we should *reduce* word segmentation and POS tagging *errors* leading to the second phase *as much as possible*. For this purpose, we utilize *machine learning techniques* to repair such errors. In the *second* phase, we design *Finite State Cascades (FSC)* which can be *automatically* constructed depending on the recognition rule sets as a shallow parser for the recognition of NEs. The advantages of that are *reliable*, *accurate* and *easy to do maintenance* for FSC. Additionally, to recognize *special NEs*, we work out the corresponding strategies to enhance the correctness of the recognition. The experimental evaluation of the system has shown that the total average recall and precision for six types of NEs are *83%* and *85%* respectively. Therefore, the system architecture is *reasonable* and *effective*.

1 Introduction

The research for Chinese information extraction is one of the topics in the project COLLATE[1] (*Computational Linguistics and Language Technology for Real World Applications*). The main motivation is to investigate the strategies for information extraction for such language, *especially in some special linguistic phenomena*, to build a reasonable information extraction model and to implement an application system. *Chinese Named Entity Recognition System* (*CHINERS*) is a component of Chinese information extraction system which is being developed. CHINERS is mainly based on machine learning and shallow parsing techniques. We adopt *football competition news* as our corpus, because there exist a variety of named entities (NEs) and relations in the news. Among the NEs we select six of them as the recognized objects, that is, *personal name* (*PN*), *date or time* (*DT*), *location name* (*LN*), *team name* (*TN*), *competition title* (*CT*) and *personal identity* (*PI*). e.g. 莫晨月(Mo Chenyue), 卡洛斯 (Carlos); ９月１９日 (Sept. 19), 本周五 (this Friday), 前７０分钟 (former 70 minutes); 上海 (Shanghai), 柏林 (Berlin); 中国队 (China Team), 四川队 (Sichuan Team), 上海申花队

[1] COLLATE is a project dedicated to building up a German competence center for language technology in Saarbrücken, Germany.

(Shanghai Shenhua Team), 拜仁慕尼黑队 (Bayern München); 全国女足超级联赛 (National Woman Football Super League Matches), 泰王杯国际足球邀请赛 (Thailand King's Cup International Football Tournament); 门将 (goalkeeper), 前锋 (forward), 外援 (foreign player), 主教练 (chief coach), 裁判员 (judge), 记者 (correspondent), etc.

Figure 1 shows the system architecture. The system is principally composed of *three components*. The *first* one is *Modern Chinese Word Segmentation and POS Tagging System* from Shan Xi University, China (Liu, 2000), which is our baseline system. The *second* one is an *error repairer* which is used to repair the word segmentation and POS tagging errors from the above system. The *third* one is a shallow parser which consists of *Finite State Cascades* (*FSC*) with three recognition levels. The *dotted line* shows the flow process for the *training texts*; while the *solid line* is the one for the *testing texts*. When training, the texts are segmented and tagged, then the error repairing candidate rules are produced and some of them are selected as the regular rules under the appropriate conditions. Thereafter, the errors caused during word segmentation and POS tagging in testing texts can be automatically repaired through such regular rules. Among the six types of NEs, *PN, DT and LN are tagged by the first component and repaired by the second component*. They are *immediately recognized after error repairing*; while TN, CT and PI are recognized and then tagged by the third component.

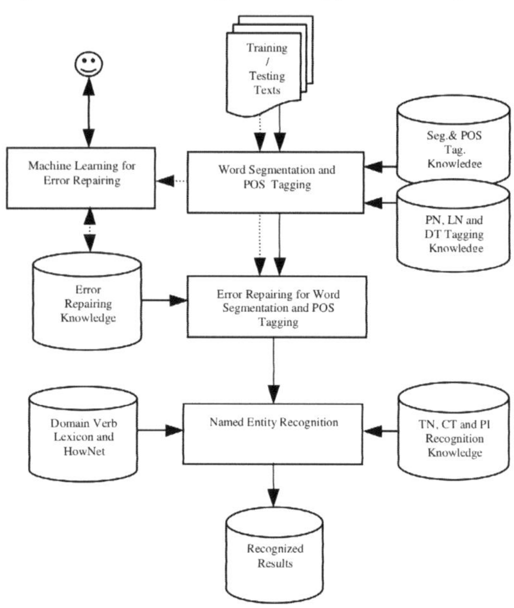

Figure 1: System architecture

In Section 2, an effective repairing approach for Chinese word segmentation and POS tagging errors will be presented. Next, Section 3 will aim to illustrate the principle of an automatically constructed FSC and NE recognition procedure. On the basis of that, Section 4 will show the three experimental conditions and results. Finally, Section 5 will draw some conclusions and introduce future work.

2 Repairing the Errors for Word Segmentation and POS Tagging

For the purpose of *ensuring good quality* in segmenting word and tagging POS, we compared different existing Chinese word segmentation and POS tagging systems and introduced one of them (Liu, 2000) as the first component in our system. Unfortunately, we found there still are considerable errors of word segmentation and POS tagging when we use this system to process our texts on sports domain. For example:

Error$_1$: `大(large)|A|连队(company)|N`
Correct$_1$: `大连(Dalian)|N5|队(team)|N`
Error$_2$: `、|W|上三路(Shang Shan Road)|N5|'|W`
Correct$_2$: `、|W|上三路(upper three paths)|N|'|W`

In the above examples, A, N, N5, and W represent an adjective, a general noun, a Chinese LN, and a punctuation respectively. According to the domain knowledge, the word "大连" is a city name as a constituent of TN, which should not be segmented; while the word "上三路" is an attack strategy of the football match, it should not be tagged as a Chinese LN. Obviously, these errors will have an unfavorable effect on the consequent recognition for NEs.

In order to improve the quality for word segmentation and POS tagging, there may be two ways to achieve such goal:

- *Develop a novel general Chinese word segmentation and POS tagging system*, which will have higher performance than the current systems of the same kind or
- *Utilize a baseline system* with good quality and further improve its performance on a specific domain, so that it can be suitable to real-world application.

We have chosen the *second* way in our investigation. First, the research of word segmentation and POS tagging is a *secondary* task for us in the project. In order to ensure the overall quality of the system, we have to enhance basic quality. Second, it is more effective to improve the quality for word segmentation and POS tagging on a *specific* domain.

The *transformation based error-driven machine learning* approach (Brill, 1995) is adopted to repair word segmentation and POS tagging errors, because it is suitable for fixing Chinese word segmentation and POS tagging errors as well as producing effective repairing rules automatically. Following (Hockenmaier and Brew, 1998; Palmer, 1997) we divide the error repairing operations of word segmentation into three types, that is, *concat*, *split* and *slide*. In addition, we add *context-sensitive* or *context-free* constraints in the rules to repair the errors of word segmentation and POS tagging. It is important that the *context constraints* can help us *distinguish different sentence environments*. The error repairing rules for word segmentation and POS tagging are defined as follows:

rectify_segmentation_error (operator, old_word(s)_and_tag(s), repairing_mode, new_tag(s), preceding_context_constraint, following_context_constraint)

rectify_tag_error (old_word_and_tag, new_tag, preceding_context_constraint, following_context_constraint)

Using these rules, we can move the word segmentation position newly and replace an error tag with a correct tag. e.g. 国|N|足|N|抵|V|沪|N (The national football team arrived in Shanghai). The word "国足" (the national football team) is an abbreviated TN that should not be segmented; while the word "沪" (Hu) is an abbreviated Chinese LN for Shanghai. We can use the following two rules to repair such errors:

rectify_segmentation_error (*concat*, 国|N|足|N, 1, J, _|_, 抵|V)

rectify_tag_error (沪|N, J, 抵|V, _|_)

Here, the digit 1 means the *operation number* of *concat*. J is a POS tag for the *abbreviated word*. After the errors are repaired, the correct result is 国足|J|抵|V|沪|J .

In the *training* algorithm (Yao et al., 2002), the error positions are determined by comparing between manually error-repaired text and automatically processed text from the baseline system. Simultaneously, the error environments are recorded. Based on such information, the candidate transformation rules are generated and the final error repairing rules are selected depending on their *error repairing number* in the *training* set. In order to use these rules with *priority*, the rules in the final rule library are sorted.

Considering the requirements of context constraints for different rules, we manually divide the rule context constraints into three types: *whole POS context constraint*, *preceding POS context constraint* and *without context constraint*. Hence, each error repairing rule can be used in accordance with either common or individual cases of errors. In the *testing* algorithm (Yao et al., 2002), the usage of error repairing rules with context constraints is *prior* to those without context constraints, the employment of error repairing rules for word segmentation has *priority* over those for POS tagging. Thus, it ensures that the rules can repair *more* errors. At the same time, it prevents *new errors* occur during repairing existing errors.

3 Named Entity Recognition

3.1 An Automatically Constructed FSC

After error repairing, the text with repaired word segmentations and POS tags is used as the input text for NE recognition.

We make use of *Finite-State Cascades* (*FSC*) (Abney, 1996) as a shallow parser for NE recognition in our system. An FSC is *automatically* constructed by the NE recognition rule sets and consists of three recognition levels. Each level has a *NE recognizer*, that is, TN, CT and PI recognizer (Other three NEs, namely, PN, DT and LN are immediately recognized after error repairing).

In order to build a *flexible* and *reliable* FSC, we propose the following construction algorithm to *automatically* construct FSC by the recognition rule sets.

The NE recognition rule is defined as follows:

> Recognition Category → POS Rule | Semantic Constraint$_1$ | Semantic Constraint$_2$ | … | Semantic Constraint$_n$

The NE recognition rule is composed of POS rule and its corresponding semantic constraints. The rule sets include 19 POS tags and 29 semantic constraint tags.

Four adjacent matrices, *POS matrix*, *POS index matrix*, *semantic index matrix* and *semantic constraint matrix*, are used in this algorithm as data structure. The POS matrix is used for the corresponding POS tags between two states. The POS index matrix provides the position of indexes related with POS tags between two states in the semantic index matrix. The semantic index matrix indicates the position of semantic constraints for each POS tag in semantic constraint matrix. The semantic constraint matrix saves the semantic constraint information for each POS tag in the POS matrix. We store the information for both the multi-POS tags between two states and the POS tags that have multi-semantic constraints in these matrices. As an example, Figure 2 shows that the following CT recognition rule set is used to build a *deterministic* finite automaton, that is, *CT recognizer*, using the above adjacent matrices. In the figure of the automaton, the semantic constraints in the rule set is *omitted*.

Rule$_1$: B + KEY_WORD | Rank + CompetitionTitleKeyword
Rule$_2$: J + KEY_WORD | AbbreviationName + CompetitionTitleKeyword
Rule$_3$: N + KEY_WORD | AbbreviationName + CompetitionTitleKeyword | CTOtherName + CompetitionTitleKeyword | Range + CompetitionTitleKeyword
Rule$_4$: N1 + KEY_WORD | CountryName + CompetitionTitleKeyword
Rule$_5$: N7 + KEY_WORD | CityName + CompetitionTitleKeyword | ContinentName + CompetitionTitleKeyword | CountryName + CompetitionTitleKeyword

In the POS tags, B, N1, and N7 represent a discrimination word, a proper noun and a transliterated noun separately. In the semantic constraint tags, Rank and Range mean the competition rank and range, such as super, woman etc.

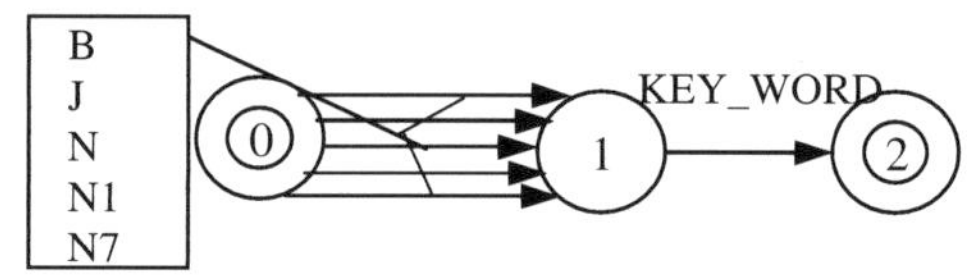

POS adjacent matrix

	0	1	2
0		B/J/N/N1/N7	
1			KEY_WORD
2			

POS index adjacent matrix

	0	1	2
0		0	
1			1
2			

Semantic index adjacent matrix

	B	J	N	N1	N7	KEY_WORD
0	0	1	2	3	4	
1						5

Semantic constraint adjacent matrix

	Abbreviation-Name	City-Name	Competition-TitleKeyword	Continent-Name	CTOther-Name	Country-Name	Range	Rank
0	0	0	0	0	0	0	0	1
1	1	0	0	0	0	0	0	0
2	1	0	0	0	1	0	1	0
3	0	0	0	0	0	1	0	0
4	0	1	0	1	0	1	0	0
5	0	0	1	0	0	0	0	0

Figure 2: An example to build a deterministic finite automaton using four adjacent matrices

The construction algorithm is summarized as follows:

- Input a NE recognition rule set and initialize four adjacent matrices.
- Get the first POS tag of a POS rule, start from the *initial state* of the NE recognizer, add its corresponding edge into the POS adjacent matrix under correct construction

condition (see *below explanation*). At the same time, add its corresponding semantic constraints into the semantic constraint adjacent matrix by the POS and semantic index adjacent matrices.

- If a tag's edge is successfully added, but it doesn't arrive in the final state, *temporarily*, push its POS tag, semantic constraints and related states (edge information) into a stack. If the next tag's edge isn't successfully added, pop the last tag's edge information from the stack. If the added edge arrives in the final state, pop all tag's edge information of the POS rule and add them into the POS and the semantic constraints adjacent matrix.
- If *all* existing states in the NE recognizer are tried, but the current edge can not be added, add a *new* state to the NE recognizer. In the following adding edge procedure, *share* the existing edge with tag's edge to be added *as much as possible*.
- If *all* the POS rules are processed, the construction for certain NE recognition level of FSC is completed.

It is important that the *correct construction condition* in the procedure of adding POS tag's edge must be met. For example, whether its corresponding semantic constraints *conflict* with the existing edge's semantic constraints between two states or the *in-degree of starting state* and the *out-degree of arriving state* must be less than or equal to 1, etc in the NE recognizer. Otherwise *give up* adding this tag's edge. Figure 3 is a part of the constructed recognition level of FSC for CT.

The construction algorithm is a rule-driven algorithm. It only depends on the format of rules. Therefore, it is *easy* to *change* the *size* of POS and semantic constraint tags or *easy* to *add*, *modify* or *delete* the rules. Additionally, the algorithm can be applied to build all the recognition levels, it is also *easy* to *expand* the NE recognizers in FSC for *new NEs*.

3.2 Recognition Procedure

When FSC has been constructed, we use it to recognize *TN*, *CT* and *PI*. First of all, input the text to be processed and different resources, such as *country name*, *club name*, *product name library* and *HowNet knowledge lexicon* (Dong and Dong, 2000). Then attach *keyword*, *potential personal identity*, *digital* or *alphabetic string*, and *other semantic constraint tags* to the corresponding constituents in a sentence. Thirdly, match the words one by one with a NE recognizer. Start from the *initial state*, match the POS tag's edge in the POS adjacent matrix, then match its corresponding semantic constraint tags in the semantic constraint adjacent matrix through two index adjacent matrices. If it is successful, push the related information into the stack. Otherwise find *another edge* that can be matched. Until arriving in the *final state*, pop the recognized named entity from the stack. Fourthly, if the current word is not successfully matched and the stack is not empty, pop the information of the *last* word and *go on* matching this word with other edges. If some words are successfully matched, the following words will be matched until *all* of the words in the sentence are tried to match. Finally, if there is still a sentence which is not processed in the text, *continue*. Otherwise finish the NE recognition procedure.

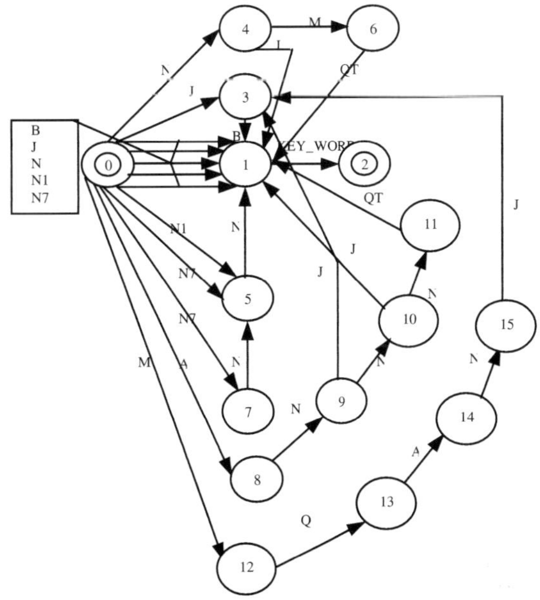

Figure 3: A part of the constructed recognition level of FSC for CT

The matching algorithm guarantees that any NE match is a match with *maximum length*. Because the finite automaton in FSC is *deterministic* and has *semantic constraints*, it can process ambiguous linguistic cases. Therefore, it has *reliability* and *accuracy* during the NE recognition procedure.

The following is an example to give the NE recognition procedure with FSC. L_1 to L_3 represent three *NE recognition levels* of FSC, namely, *TN*, *CT* and *PI* recognition levels. Every level has its NE recognition rule set.

上海|N5|申花|N|队|N|在|P|百事可乐|N|甲|N|A|QT|联赛|N|中|F|击败|V|对手|N|吉林|N5|敖东|N|队|N|。|W1|

Shanghai Shenhua Team defeated the opponent - Jilin Aodong Team in the Pepsi First A League Matches.

```
L3  ----TN P ------CT F V PI----TN W1
L2  ----TN P ------CT F V N ----TN W1
L1  ----TN P N N QT N F V N ----TN W1
L0  N5 N N P N N QT N F V N N5 N N W1
```

3.3 Some Special Named Entities

Sometimes there are TNs or CTs *without keyword* in sentences. For instance, TNs without keyword:

Ex.1: 上视队一球小胜大连。(Shanghai Television Team feebly won one ball against Dalian.)

Ex.2: 中国取胜瑞典并不容易。(It is not easy that China wants to win Sweden.)

Ex.3: 沪连之战。(the fight between Shanghai and Dalian.)

For such special cases, we propose the following strategy for recognizing TN without keyword:

Step 1: Collect *domain verbs* and their *valence constraints* (Lin et al., 1994)

We organize domain verb lexicon and collect domain verbs, such as 胜 (win), 负于(lose), 对 (vs.), 进攻(attack), 防守 (guard), 迎战(take on), 瓦解(disintegrate), and their corresponding valence constraints. For instance, the valence constituents for the verb "胜" in our domain are defined as follows:

Basic Format: *Essiv* win *Object* ($Team_1$ win_1 $Team_2$; $Person_1$ win_2 $Person_2$; Personal $Identity_1$ win_3 Personal $Identity_2$; ...)

Extended Format: *Link* + Basic Format; *Accompaniment* + Basic Format; ...

In the basic format, *Essiv* is a subject that represents a *non-spontaneous* action and state in an event. *Object* is a direct object that deals with an non-spontaneous action. In the extended format, *Link* indicates a type, identity or role of the subject. In general, it begins with the word "作为..." (As ...). *Accompaniment* expresses an indirect object that is accompanied or excluded. It often begins with the word "除了..." (Except ...).

Step 2: Keep the *equity* of domain verbs and analyze the constituents of TN candidates

According to the valence constraints, we examine whether the constituents in both sides of domain verbs are identical with the valence basic format or extended format, e.g. in Ex. 1 the team $name_1$ should be balanced with the team $name_2$ in the light of the valence basic format of domain verb 胜 (win_1). Besides, the candidate of team $name_2$ is checked, its constituent is a city name (Dalian) that can be as a constituent of team name.

Step 3: Utilize *context clue* of TN candidates

We find whether there is a TN that is equal to current TN candidate with the keyword through the context of the TN candidate in the text, in order to enhance the correctness of TN recognition. As an example, in Ex. 2, depending on Step 2, a team name can occur on both sides of the domain verb 取胜 (win victory). A country name can be a constituent of team name. At the same time, the context of two TN candidates will be examined. Finally, if there is such context clue, the candidates are determined. Otherwise, continue to recognize the candidates by the next step.

Step 4: Distinguish *team* name from *location* name

Because a LN can be a constituent of a TN, we should distinguish TNs without keywords from LNs. With the help of other constituents (e.g. *nouns*, *propositions* etc.) in a sentence, the differences of both NEs can be distinguished to a certain extent. In Ex. 3 the noun 战 (fight) is an analogy for the match in sports domain. Therefore, here "沪" (Shanghai) and "连" (Dalian) represent two TNs separately. But it is still difficult to further improve the precision of TN recognition. (see the third experimental result.)

4 System Implementation and Experimental Results

CHINERS has been implemented with Java 2 (ver.1.4.0) under Windows 2000. The user interface displays the result of word segmentation and POS tagging from the baseline system, the error repairing result, the recognized result for six types of NEs and the statistic report for error repairing and NE recognition. The recognized text can be entered from a disk or directly downloaded from WWW (http://www.jfdaily.com/). HowNet knowledge lexicon is used to provide English and concept explanation for Chinese words in the recognized results. Except the error repairing rule library (for the most part) and HowNet knowledge lexicon, other resources have been manually built.

To evaluate this system, we have completed *three different* experiments. The *first* one is *only* for the performance of error repairing component. The *second* one is about comparison for NE recognition performance *with* or *without* error repairing. The *third* one is to test the recognition performance for TNs and CTs *without keyword*. The training set consists of 94 texts including 3473 sentences (roughly 37077 characters) from *Jiefang Daily* in 2001. The texts come from the *football sports news*. After machine learning, we obtain 4304 transformation rules. Among them 2491 rules are for word segmentation error repairing, 1813 rules are for POS tagging error repairing. There are 1730 rules as *concat* rules, 554 rules as *split* rules and 207 rules as *slide* rules in the word segmentation error repairing rules. Subsequently, we distinguish above rules into *context-sensitive* or *context-free* category *manually*. In the error repairing rules for word segmentation, 790, 315 and 77 rules are as *concat*, *split* and *slide* context-sensitive rules respectively; while 940, 239 and 130 rules are as *concat*, *split* and *slide* context-free rules separately. In the error repairing rules for POS tagging, 1052 rules are context-sensitive rules and 761 are context-free rules. The testing set is a separate set, which contains 20 texts including 658 sentences (roughly 8340 characters). The texts in the testing set have been randomly chosen from *Jiefang Daily* in May 2002. The texts also come from *football sports news*.

Table 1 and 2 show the first experimental results for the performance in different cases. These results indicate that the average F-measure of *word segmentation* has increased by *5.11%*; while one of *POS tagging* has even increased by *12.54%*.

In addition, using *same* testing set, we give the second and third experimental results in Figure 4, 5 and Table 3. In Figure 4 and 5, the performance of

	Average Recall	Average Precision	Average F-measure
Without Error Repairing	80.41	74.73	77.47
With Error Repairing	92.39	87.75	90.01

Table 1: Performance for word segmentation

	Average Recall	Average Precision	Average F-measure
Without Error Repairing	91.07	84.67	87.75
With Error Repairing	95.08	90.74	92.86

Table 2: Performance for POS tagging

six types of NEs has *manifestly* been improved. The *total average recall* is increased from 58% to *83%*, and the *total average precision* has also increased from 65% to *85%*. In Table 3, the average recall for TN without keyword has exceeded the average recall of TN in Figure 4; the average recall and precision of CT without keyword have also exceeded the average recall and precision of CT in Figure 4 and 5. But the average precision of TN *only* reaches 66%. We analyze the error reasons for the recognition of TN without keyword. Among 19 errors there are 17 errors from the wrong recognition for LN and 2 errors from imperfect recognition for TN. That is to say, the Step 4 of the recognition strategy in section 3.3 should be *further* improved.

In short, the experimental results have shown that the performance of whole system has been *significantly* improved after error repairing for

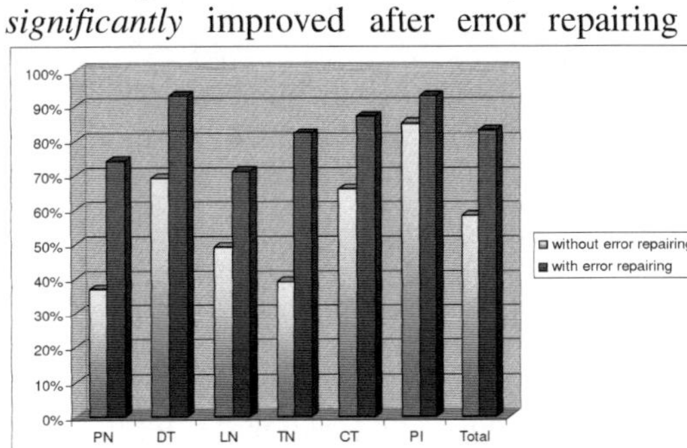

Figure 4: Recall comparison

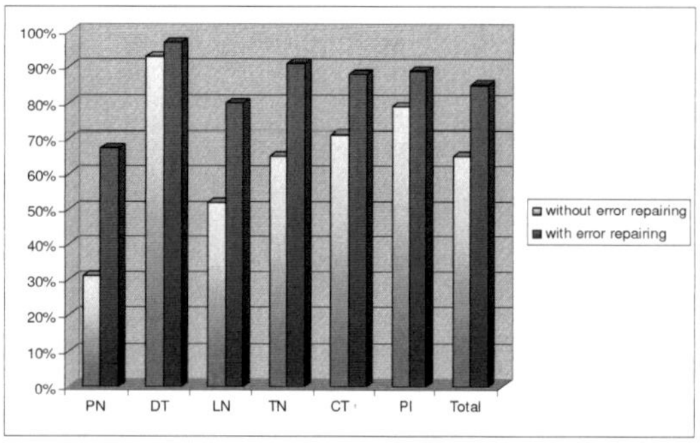

Figure 5: Precision comparison

	Total Number	Total Recognized Number / (Total Error Number)	Average Recall	Average Precision
TN without keyword	65	56 / (19)	86.15	66.07
CT without keyword	45	44 / (1)	97.78	97.73

Table 3: Recognition performance for TN and CT without keyword

word segmentation and POS tagging as well as the recognition for special NEs. It also proves that the system architecture is *reasonable* and *effective*.

5 Conclusions and Future Work

During the research for Chinese NE recognition, we noted that the errors from word segmentation and POS tagging have *adversely* affected the performance of NE recognition to a certain extent. We utilize transformation based error-driven machine learning to perform error repairing for word segmentation and POS tagging *simultaneously*. In the error repairing procedure, we add *context-sensitive* or *context-free* constraints in the rules. Thus, the introduction of *further errors* during error repairing can be *avoided*. In order to recognize NEs *flexibly*, *reliably* and *accurately*, we design and implement a FSC as a shallow parser for the NE recognition, which can be *automatically* constructed on basis of the recognition rule sets. In accordance with special NEs, additionally, we hit on the corresponding solutions for the recognition correctness.

The experimental results have shown that the performance of word segmentation and POS tagging has been improved, *leading* to an improved performance for NE recognition in our system. Such a *hybrid* approach used in our system synthesizes the advantages of *knowledge engineering* and *machine learning*.

For future work we will focus on *relation extraction*. On one hand, we will build an ontology including sports objects, movements and properties as a knowledge base to support corpus annotation. On the other hand, we utilize machine learning to automatically build relation pattern library for relation recognition.

Acknowledgement

This work is a part of the *COLLATE project* under contract no. 01INA01B, which is supported by the *German Ministry for Education and Research*.

References

S. Abney. 1996. *Partial Parsing via Finite-State Cascades*. In Proceedings of the ESSLLI '96 Robust Parsing Workshop. Prague, Czech Republic.

E. Brill. 1995. *Transformation-Based Error-Driven Learning and Natural Language Processing: A Case Study in Part of Speech Tagging*. Computational Linguistics. Vol. 21, No. 4:543-565.

Z. Dong and Q. Dong. 2000. *HowNet*. http://www.keenage.com/zhiwang/e_zhiwang.html.

J. Hockenmaier and C. Brew. 1998. *Error-Driven Learning of Chinese Word Segmentation*. Communications of COLIPS 8 (1):69-84. Singapore.

X. Lin et al. 1994. *Dictionary of Verbs in Contemporary Chinese*. Beijing Language and Culture University Press. Beijing China. (In Chinese)

K. Liu. 2000. *Automatic Segmentation and Tagging for Chinese Text*. The Commercial Press, Beijing, China. (In Chinese)

D. Palmer. 1997. *A Trainable Rule-Based Algorithm for Word Segmentation*. In Proceedings of the 35th Annual Meeting of the Association for Computational Linguistics (ACL '97): 321-328. Madrid, Spain.

T. Yao, W. Ding, and G. Erbach. 2002. *Repairing Errors for Chinese Word Segmentation and Part-of-Speech Tagging*. In Proc. of the First International Conference on Machine Learning and Cybernetics 2002 (ICMLC 2002) , Beijing, China.

Chinese Lexical Analysis Using Hierarchical Hidden Markov Model

Hua-Ping ZHANG[1] **Qun LIU**[1,2] **Xue-Qi CHENG**[1] **Hao Zhang**[1] **Hong-Kui Yu**[1]
[1]Inst. of Computing Tech., The Chinese Academy of Science, Beijing, 100080 CHINA
[2]Inst. of Computational Linguistics, Peking University, Beijing, 100871 CHINA
Email: zhanghp@software.ict.ac.cn

Abstract

This paper presents a unified approach for Chinese lexical analysis using hierarchical hidden Markov model (HHMM), which aims to incorporate Chinese word segmentation, Part-Of-Speech tagging, disambiguation and unknown words recognition into a whole theoretical frame. A class-based HMM is applied in word segmentation, and in this level unknown words are treated in the same way as common words listed in the lexicon. Unknown words are recognized with reliability in role-based HMM. As for disambiguation, the authors bring forth an n-shortest-path strategy that, in the early stage, reserves top N segmentation results as candidates and covers more ambiguity. Various experiments show that each level in HHMM contributes to lexical analysis. An HHMM-based system ICTCLAS was accomplished. The recent official evaluation indicates that ICTCLAS is one of the best Chinese lexical analyzers. In a word, HHMM is effective to Chinese lexical analysis.

1 Introduction

Word is the independent and meaningful atom in natural language. Unlike English and Spanish, there is no delimiter to mark word boundaries and no explicit definition of words in some Asian languages. As for Chinese language processing, the fundamental task is word segmentation, which transforms Chinese character string into words sequence. It is prerequisite to POS tagger, parser and other deep processing, and the lexical result is the basis of further applications such as machine translation, information retrieval and information extraction.

Since the first system CDWS appeared in 1983, word segmentation has been researched intensively. Many solutions were proposed and could be broadly categorized into rules-based approaches that make use of linguistic knowledge and statistical approaches that train on corpus after machine learning. The classic rule-based approaches include maximum matching and shortest path (SP), which achieve the minimum number of segmented words. Zhang and Liu (2002) present an extended SP algorithm named "n-shortest paths". Some researchers introduce more complicated rules, such as error-driven learning (Hockenmaier and Brew, 1998) and parsing (Wu and Jiang, 1998). Rule is the only feasible way to segment words unless necessary resources such as large amount of corpus are available. With the development of hand-corrected resource, statistical approaches became more popular. The language models commonly applied are n-gram (Zhang and Liu, 2002; Gao et al., 2001), EM (Peng and Schuurmans, 2001), and channel noise model. As far as we know, however, there is yet neither purely rule-based system nor purely statistical one. It tends to tackle Chinese lexical problem with mixture of rules and statistical information. On one hand, trainable rules (Palmer, D. 1997) seem more adaptive and efficient in that rule-based approaches benefit from frequency of rule occurrence, on the other hand, statistical solutions employ rules to detect ambiguity, numeric expression, time and other named entities. Apart from the above approaches, we also notice some other promising ideas such as compression-based (Teahan et al., 2001), classifier-based (Xue and Susan, 2002) and self-supervised segmentation without lexicon. According to recent reports, word segmentation has achieved good result in precision, especially on texts that do not contain ambiguity or out-of-vocabulary words.

However, segmentation ambiguity and unknown words[1] cause bottlenecks and greatly degrade performance in word segmentation. Ambiguous or unknown string is hard to be correctly segmented; at the same time, it also influences on segmenting its neighboring words. What's worse, ambiguity often occurs with unknown words. Take "克林顿对内塔尼亚胡说"(*Clinton said to Netanyahu*) as exemplification, "内塔尼亚胡"(*Netanyahu*) is unknown transliterated personal name, and both "对内" (*for home*) and "胡说" (*talk nonsense*) has two ambiguous segmentations: split into halves or not. Here, it's difficult to identify unknown word "内塔尼亚胡" because of the ambiguities, while disambiguation is also difficult to accomplish before unknown words detection. Therefore, the final lexical result is very likely to be "克林顿/对内/塔尼亚/胡说" instead of "克林顿/对/内塔尼亚胡/说".

Historically, much effort has been made in the two sub-problems of word segmentation. Almost all previous solutions (Chunyu et al. 2002; Zhang, 1998; Zheng, 1999) of disambiguation attempt to cover each possible case with trivial rules, while recently statistical approaches are applied in some special categories of ambiguity. For instance, vector space model was applied in combinational ambiguity (Luo et al. 2002). Concerning unknown word, we only need focus on unknown named entities, including personal name (PER), location name (LOC), and organization name (ORG). The motivation in named entity recognition is to utilize its components and contexts. Like word segmentation and disambiguation, the usual approach is to apply rules (Sun, 1993;Tan, 1999;Luo and Ji, 2001; Luo and Song, 2001). Recognition rules are summarized on name libraries or different linguistic phenomena. Compared with rules-based approach, machine learning from large corpus seems easy but better in performance. The statistical approaches proposed recently include hidden Markov model (Zhang and Liu, 2002; Zhang et al. 2002), agent-based (Ye, 2003), class-based trigram model (Sun et al., 2002).

After nearly 20 years of hard work, rapid progresses are made on word segmentation, disambiguation and unknown word recognition research individually. To the best of our knowledge, however, all the achievement has not ever, all the achievement has not integrated into a unified model with a general theoretical basis. In previous lexical analyzers, so-called word segmentation algorithm actually only employs on common words listed in the lexicon, while disambiguation and unknown word recognition have their own independent mechanism and become distinct processes from segmentation. Without scientific quantification, unknown words and disambiguation result could not compete with other segmentation candidates. In a word, previous work lacks a whole frame incorporating the different sub-tasks in lexical analysis, while there is also no consistent mechanism to evaluate various lexical results Therefore, previous lexical system is difficult achieve better performance on real texts that contain irregular character strings mentioned above.

This paper presents an HHMM-based approach for Chinese lexical analysis. It aims to utilize a general model to proceed all steps in lexical analysis, including word segmentation, disambiguation, unknown words recognition and part-of speech (POS) tagging. In the preprocessing, top n segmentation candidates covering the possible ambiguity are provided using n-shortest-path algorithm (Zhang and Liu, 2002). Then, simple unknown named entities like personal names and location names are identified on the candidate set using class-based HMM. Following that, a higher level of HMM could be employed on recognizing organization and other recursive named entity, which includes another simple unknown word. Unknown words recognized with credible probability are added to class-based HMM for word segmentation. In this level of HHMM, unknown words and ambiguity are treated in the same way as common words. POS tagging is the top level in HHMM. After HHMM-based approach applied, Chinese lexical analysis system ICTCLAS achieves well in segmentation and POS tagging. The official evaluation, which was held by the National Foundation of 973 Plan of China, shows that ICTCLAS rank top and it is one of the best Chinese lexical analyzers.

The structure of this paper is as follows. The next section reviews HHMM and presents the framework of HHMM-based Chinese lexical analysis. Then we explain the class-based HMM for word segmentation. Next we detail role-based unknown words recognition and n-shortest-path disambiguation. The following section describes

1 We define unknown words to be those neitheri ncluded in the core lexicon nor recognized through FSA.

various experiments designed to evaluate lexical analysis performance and contribution from different level in HHMM.

2 HHMM and Chinese lexical analysis

2.1 An overview of HHMM

Hidden Markov model (HMM, L.R. Rabiner, 1989) has become the method of choice for modeling stochastic processes and sequence in natural language processing, because HMM is very rich in mathematical structure and hence can form theoretical basis for use. However, compared with the sophisticated phenomena in natural language, traditional HMM seems hard to use due to the multiplicity of length scales and recursive nature of the sequences. Therefore Shai Fine et al (1998) proposed hierarchical hidden Markov model, which is a recursive and generalized HMM.

Based on Shai's work, we give a formal description of HHMM. An HHMM is specified by a six-tuple (S , O , Π, A, B, D), where D is the depth of levels, S and O are the finite set of states and the final output alphabet or intermediate output, and Π,A and B are the probabilities of the initial state, state transitions and emissions of symbol or intermediate output, respectively. The contrast between traditional HMM and HHMM lies in:

1) The state set S can be classified into different sub-sets according to its level. A state in S is annotated with q_i^d ($0<d\le D$, $0<i\le|S^d|$), where d is the level index, i is the state index and S^d is the set of state in level d. When d=D, q_i^d is called terminal state because its observation is symbols, or else, it is called internal state whose observation is from its child HMM in (d+1)th level.

2) Every internal state q^d ($0<d<D$) has its child states, which form an independent HMM. In the child HMM, the state transitive probabilities are $A(q^d)=(a_{ij}(q^d)), and, a_{ij}(q^d)=P(q_j^{d+1}|q_i^{d+1})$.

And the initial distribution vector is like $\Pi(q^d)=(\pi^d(q_i^{d+1}))=(P(q_i^{d+1}\mid q^d))$, where $P(q_i^{d+1}\mid q^d)$ is defined to be the probability that state q^d initially activates its child state q_i^{d+1}.

3) Only the bottom HMM can observe the symbols. The corrcsponding symbol emission probabilities are $B(q^D)=(b_k(q^D)))$, where $b_k(q^D)=P(o_k|q^D)$ and O_k. is in symbol set. For the d (d<D) level HMM, state sequence in its child HMM could be viewed as its observation. The emission probabilities could be estimated as above.

All in all, HHMM includes D levels of HMM while each level is independent HMM. Moreover, each HMM only links with its parent and child. The whole parameters set of HHMM is denoted by

$$\lambda=\{(\lambda(q^d)\}_{d\in\{1,\ldots,D\}}$$
$$=\{\{A(q^d)\}_{d\in\{1,\ldots,D-1\}},\{\Pi(q^d)\}_{d\in\{1,\ldots,D-1\}},\{B(q^D)\}\}.$$

Actually, HMM is the specific form of HHMM with D=1.

2.2 Framework of HHMM-based lexical analysis

As illustrated in Figure 1, HHMM-based Chinese lexical analysis comprises five levels: atom segmentation, simple and recursive unknown words recognition, class-based segmentation and POS tagging. In the whole frame, class-based segmentation graph, which is a directed graph designed for word segmentation, is an essential intermediate data structure that links disambiguation, unknown words recognition with word segmentation and POS tagging.

Atom segmentation, the bottom level of HHMM, is an initial step. Here, atom is defined to be the minimal segmentation unit that cannot be split in any stage. The atom consists of Chinese character, punctuation, symbol string, numeric expression and other non-Chinese char string. Any word is made up of an atom or more. Atom segmentation is to segment original text into atom sequence and it provides pure and simple source for its parent HMM. For instance, a sentence like "2002.9，ICTCLAS 的自由源码开始发布" (The free source codes of ICTCLAS was distributed in September, 2002) would be segmented as atom sequence "2002.9/，/ICTCLAS/的/自/由/源/码/开/始/发/布/". In this HMM, the original symbol is observation while the atom is state. We skip the

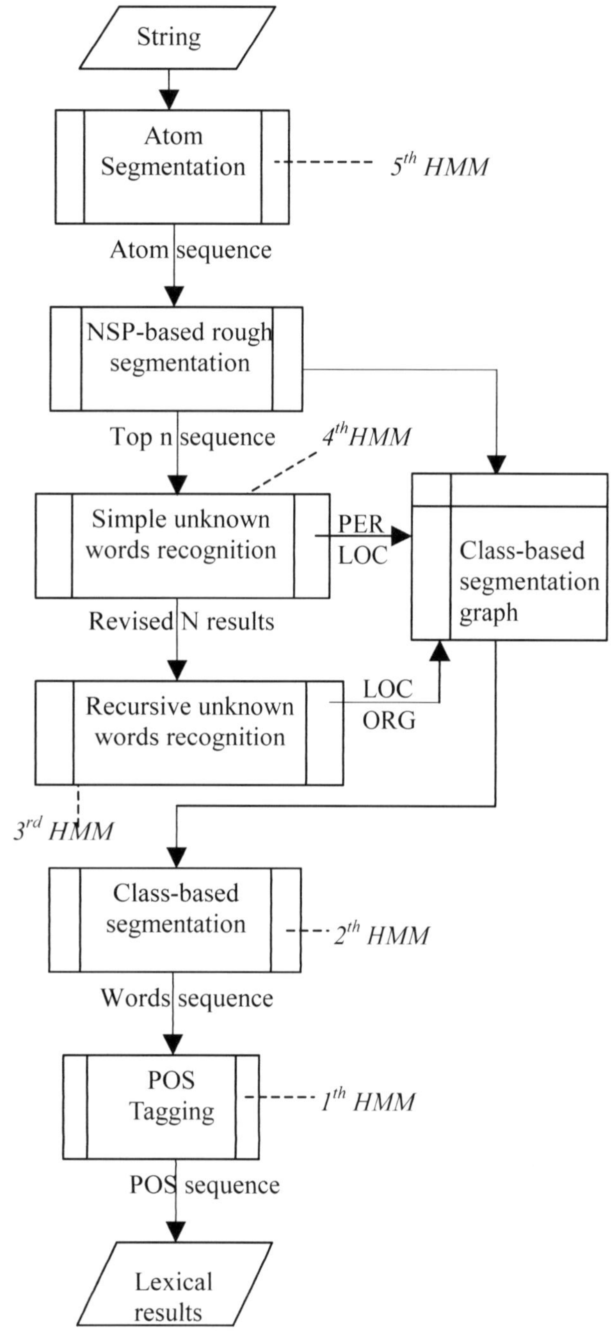

Figure 1. HHMM-based Chinese lexical analysis

detail of operation in that it's a simple application on the basis of HMM. POS tagging using HMM is also skipped because role tagging, which presented in section 5, is similar to it in nature. The other levels of HHMM will be provided in the next parts.

3 Class-based HMM for word segmentation

We apply to word segmentation class-based HMM, which is a generalized approach covering both common words and unknown words.

Given a word w_i, class c_i is defined in Figure 2. Suppose |LEX| to be the lexicon size, then the total number of word classes is |LEX|+9.

$$c_i=\begin{cases} w_i & \text{iff } w_i \text{ is listed in the segmentation lexicon;} \\ \text{PER} & \text{iff } w_i \text{ is unlisted}^* \text{ personal name;} \\ \text{LOC} & \text{iff } w_i \text{ is unlisted location name;} \\ \text{ORG} & \text{iff } w_i \text{ is unlisted organization name;} \\ \text{TIME} & \text{iff } w_i \text{ is unlisted time expression;} \\ \text{NUM} & \text{iff } w_i \text{ is unlisted numeric expression;} \\ \text{STR} & \text{iff } w_i \text{ is unlisted symbol string;} \\ \text{BEG} & \text{iff beginning of a sentence} \\ \text{END} & \text{iff ending of a sentence} \\ \text{OTHER} & \text{otherwise.} \end{cases}$$

* "unlisted" is referred as being outside the lexicon

Figure 2: Class Definition of word w_i

Given the atom sequence A=$(a_1,\ldots a_n)$, let W=$(w_1,\ldots w_m)$ be the words sequence, C=$(c_1,\ldots c_m)$ be a corresponding class sequence of W, and W$^{\#}$ be the choice of word segmentation with the maximized probability, respectively. Then, we could get:

$$W^{\#}=\arg\max_{W} P(W|A)=\arg\max_{W} P(W,A)/P(A)$$

For a specific atom sequence A, P(A) is a constant and P(W,A)= P(W). So,

$$W^{\#}=\arg\max_{W} P(W)$$

On the basis of Baye's Theorem, it can be induced that:

$$W^{\#}=\arg\max_{W} P(W|C)P(C)$$

W$^{\#}$ can be found with another level of HMM if class c_i is viewed as state while word w_i is output. Therefore:

$$W^{\#}\approx \arg\max_{w_1 w_2 \ldots w_m} \prod_{i=1}^{m} p(w_i \mid c_i)\,p(c_i \mid c_{i-1}),$$

where c_0 is begin of sentence.

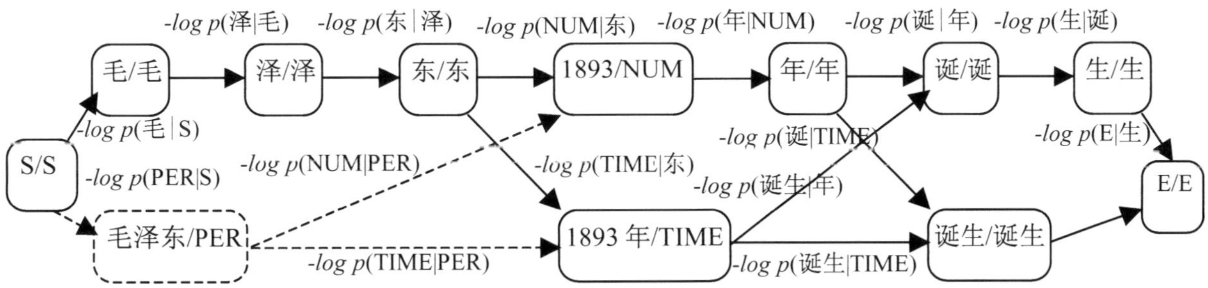

Figure3. Class-based word segmentation

Note:

1. The original sentence is "毛泽东 1893 年诞生" (Mao Ze-Dong was born in the year of 1893). Its atom sequence is "毛/泽/东/1893/年/诞/生/" after atom segmentation;
2. The node format is "word/class" (w_i / c_i) and the weight on the node is $-log\ p\ (w_i \mid c_i)$;
3. Weight on the directed edge is $-\log p\ (c_i \mid c_{i-1})$;
4. "毛泽东" (Mao Ze-Dong) is personal name outside the lexicon.The node " 毛泽东/PER" and the related edges with dash line is inserted after unknown words recognition.

For convenience, we often use the negative log probability instead of the proper form. That is:

$$W^{\#} = \underset{W}{\arg\min} \sum_{i=1}^{m} [-\ln p(w_i \mid c_i) - \ln p(c_i \mid c_{i-1})]$$

According to the word class definition, if w_i is listed in lexicon, then c_i is w_i, and $p(w_i|c_i)$ is equal to 1.0. Otherwise, $p(w_i|c_i)$ is probability that class c_i initially activates w_i, and it could be estimated in its child HMM for unknown words recognition.

As demonstrated in Figure 3, we provide the process of class-based word segmentation on "毛泽东 1893 年诞生" (Mao Ze-Dong was born in the year of 1893). The significance of our method is: it covers the possible ambiguity. Moreover, unknown words, which are recognized in the following steps, can be added into the segmentation graph and proceeded as any other common words.

After transformation through class-based HMM, word segmentation becomes single-source shortest paths problem. Hence the best choice $W^{\#}$ of word segmentation is easy to find using Djikstra's algorithm.

4 NSP-based disambiguation strategy

Segmentation ambiguous error is made mainly because of improper decision in the earlier stage. For example, overlapping ambiguity in "结合/成/分子/时" (When combining into molecule) and combining ambiguity in "这/个/人/手/上/有/痣"(The person has naevi on his hand) are difficult to solve only in the initial stage of word segmentation. However, it's simple to find the correct result among the possible candidates in POS tagging or further processes. Therefore, the initial process should not make the final decision, but provide candidates covering the correct segmentation.

We take n-shortest-path (NSP, Zhang and Liu, 2002) algorithm as the disambiguation strategy. NSP, which selects n shortest paths, is an extension of Djikstra's algorithm. The motivation in disambiguation using NSP is covering more ambiguity with top n results in rough segmentation, which is the initial step in lexical analysis and produces candidate results.

Considering efficiency and performance, rough segmentation coverage, which is percentage of correct results, should be much higher while the average size of candidate set should be as small as possible. Compared with NSP, full segmentation, which produces all the possible segmentation paths, suffers from large amount of candidates, while other approaches lose so many correct results. As shown in Table 1, NSP-based rough segmentation enjoys two good properties: higher coverage and fewer candidates. In other word, NSP is effective strategy for disambiguation.

Approach	Max Size	AV Size	Coverage
MM	1	1	85.46%
SP	1	1	91.80%
ML	1	1	93.50%
FS	>3,424,507	>391.79	100.00%
NSP	8	5.82	99.92%

Table 1. Comparison between NSP and other approaches of rough segmentation

Note:

1) MM: maximum matching; SP: shortest path; ML: Maximum likelihood; FS: Full segmentation
2) Max size and AV size is the maximum and average size of segmentation candidate set, respectively;
3) Coverage=# of correctly segmented/# of sentence*100%
4) The size of testing set is 2 million Chinese characters.

5 Unknown words recognition using role-based HMM

The task includes: locating the boundary of a unknown word w_i, identifying the word class c_i, and computing the probability $p(w_i|c_i)$, which is required in class-based segmentation. Here, we introduce two levels of HMM to recognize simple and recursive unknown words on the rough segmentation set.

5.1 Role set for unknown words recognition

In the same way of class-based HMM for word segmentation, here we classify word class into various role according to its linguistic features shown in unknown words recognition. In table 2, we present a simplified role set for unknown personal name recognition. Role is similar as word class. Their difference is: a word has only a word class, but a word class has one role or more.

Role	Significance	Sample
A	Previous context	***来到***/于/洪/洋/的/家
B	Next context	黄/文/***摄***
C	Surname	***欧阳***/修
D	First token of 2-Hanzi given name	朱/***镕***/基/总理
E	Second token of 2-Hanzi* given name	朱/镕/***基***/总理
H	Suffix	王/***总***; 刘/***老***
L	Token in transliterated name	***蒙***/帕/蒂/・/梅/拉/费
Z	Remote context	***深切***/缅怀/邓/小/平
…		

Table 2. Simplified role set of personal names

* Hanzi: Chinese character

5.2 Role tagging and Recognizing Unknown words recognition

Given a word sequence $W=(w_1,\ldots w_n)$, we could get its class result $C=(c_1,\ldots c_n)$. Now we could tag W with role $R=(r_1,\ldots r_n)$, where all roles are from the same set. Among all the roles sequence, we select the sequence $R^{\#}$ with the maximum probability as the final choice. Through the same induction detailed in section 3, we could get

$$R^{\#} = \arg\min_{R} \sum_{i=1}^{n}[-\ln p(c_i \mid r_i) - \ln p(r_i \mid r_{i-1})]$$

It is a tagging process and we make use of Viterbi algorithm (L.R.Rabiner, 1988) that selects the global optimum among all the state sequences. Here, tagging word class sequence"毛 / 泽 / 东 /TIME/诞生" (Mao Ze-Dong was born in sometime.) with personal roles, we could get $R^{\#}$="毛/C 泽/D 东/E TIME/B 诞生/Z" through Vitebi selection.

Unknown words are recognized through maximum pattern matching on role sequence. For instance, "C", "D","E" is surname, first and second token of 2-Hanzi given name, respectively. So token sequence tagged with role "CDE" is likely to form a traditional Chinese personal name. Therefore, "毛泽东" will be recognized as a Chinese personal name according to its roles.

Let w_i be recognized unknown word and c_i be the word class, we estimate the probability $p(w_i|c_i)$ with the following formula:

$$p(w_i \mid c_i) = \prod_{j=0}^{k-1} p(c_{p+j} \mid r_{p+j}) \times \prod_{j=1}^{k-1} p(r_{p+j} \mid r_{p+j-1});$$

where w_i is made up of tokens from pth to (p+k-1)th.

Hence p(毛泽东|PER)=p(毛|C) p(泽|D) p(东|E) p(D|C)p(E|D). Finally unknown word "毛泽东" and p(毛泽东|PER) can be added into the class-based HMM, shown as dashed area in Figure 3.

5.3 Recursive unknown word recognition

Organization name like "周恩来和邓颖超纪念馆"(Memorial Hall of Zhou En-Lai and Deng Yun-Chao) and some sophisticated location name like "张自忠路"(Zhang Zi-Zhong Road) often include one or more unknown words. We call them "recursive unknown word".

Our solution is: Firstly, recognizing non-recursive unknown words in the lower level of role-based HMM, then revising the word class sequence with the recognized results; next applying another role HMM to recognize the recursive ones. Take the original word class sequence "周/恩/来/和/邓/颖/超/纪念馆" as exemplification. In the first step, "周恩来" and "邓颖超" would be recognized as personal name. Then, the original class sequence could be replaced with "PER/和/PER/纪

念馆". Based on the revised class result, the higher role-based HMM could recognize the recursive unknown word "周恩来和邓颖超纪念馆" as an organization name. Our method utilizes previous results and greatly reduces data sparseness.

The role training set is transformed from corpus tagged with POS. Zhang and Liu (2002) provided the algorithm for role data conversion, model training, named entity recognition and the other procedures in role-based HMM.

6 Experiments

An HHMM-based Chinese lexical system ICTCLAS was accomplished. The following experiments are performed on ICTCLAS.

As commonly used, we conduct our evaluations on terms of segmentation accuracy (SEG), accuracy of POS tagging (TAG1) with 24 tags, accuracy of POS tagging (TAG2) with 48 tags, precision of named entity recognition (P), recall of named entity recognition (R) and F-measure (F) that is weighted combination of P and R. They are calculated as following:

SEG= # of correctly segmented words/ # of words;
TAG1= # of correctly tagged 24-tag POS/ # of words;
TAG2= # of correctly tagged 48-tag POS/ # of words;
P= # of correct recognized NE/# of recognized NE;
R= # of correct recognized NE/# of NE×100%;

$F=\frac{R\times P\times(1+\beta^2)}{R+P\times\beta^2}$, here β is assigned with 1, and F is called F-1.

6.1 Chinese Lexical analysis and HHMM

On 1,108,049-word news corpus from the Peple 's Daily, we conduct four experiments:

1) BASE: ICTCLAS with only class-based segmentation and POS tagging;
2) +PER: Adding role-based HMM for personal name recognition to BASE;
3) +LOC: Adding role-based HMM for location name recognition to +PER;
4) +ORG: Adding role-based HMM for location name recognition to +LOC.

Figure 4 gives the contrast among the four experiments in performance. It indicates that: firstly, every level in HHMM contributes to lexical analysis. For instance, SEG increases from 96.55% to 97.96% after personal HMM is added. If all levels of HMM are integrated, ICTCLAS achieves 98.25% SEG, 95.63% TAG1 and 93.38% TAG2. Secondly, low levels in HHMM benefits from the higher one. After organization recognition is applied, F-1 value of organization adds by 25.91%, furthermore, the performance of segmentation, POS tagging and recognition of personal and location name improves, too. It is because high level not only solves its own problem, but also helps the lower HMMfilter improper candidate. For exa m-ple, in the sentence "刘庄的水很甜"(The water in Liu village is sweet), "刘庄"(Liu village) is very likely to be incorrectly recognized as a personal name in +PER experiment. However, it will be revised as a location name in +LOC experiment.

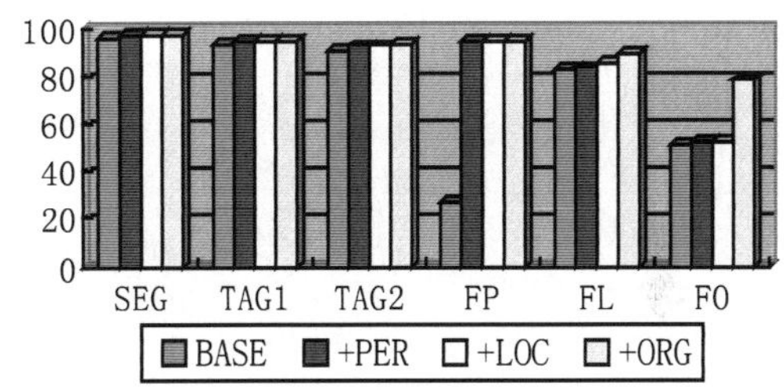

Figure 4. Contrast among 4 cases in performance
Note:
FP: F-1 value of personal name recognition;
FL: F-1 value of location name recognition;
FO: F-1 value of organization name recognition

6.2 Official evaluation on ICTCLAS

On July 6, 2002, ICTCLAS participated the official evaluation, which was held by the National Foundation of 973 Project of China. The open evaluation is conducted on real texts from six domains. The performance of ICTCLAS lists as Table 3.

Domain	Words	SEG	TAG1	RTAG
Sport	33,348	97.01%	86.77%	89.31%
Int. news	59,683	97.51%	88.55%	90.78%
Literature	20,524	96.40%	87.47%	90.59%
Law	14,668	98.44%	85.26%	86.59%
Theoretics	55,225	98.12%	87.29%	88.91%
Economics	24,765	97.80%	86.25%	88.16%
Total:	208,213	97.58%	87.32%	89.42%

Table 3. Official evaluation result of ICTCLAS
Note:
1) RTAG=TAG1/SEG*100%
2) The result about POS is not comparable because our tag set is greatly different from theirs.

Compared with other systems, ICTCLAS ranked top in the evaluation, and it is one of the best Chinese lexical analyzer.

7 Conclusion

Our contributions are:

1) Applying HHMM to different lexical tasks, including word segmentation, POS tagging, unknown words recognition, and disambiguation.
2) Using class-based HMM for word segmentation, which integrates common words and unknown ones into a unified frame.
3) Proposing NSP strategy for segmentation disambiguation.
4) Bringing forth role-based HMM to recognize simple and recursive unknown words.

Various experiments show that each level in HHMM contributes to the final performance. Evaluation on ICTCLAS confirms that HHMM-based Chinese lexical analysis is effective.

8 Acknowledgements

The authors wish to thank Prof. Shiwen Yu of Peking University for the training corpus. And we acknowledge our debt to Gang Zou, Dr. Bin Wang, Dr. Jian Sun, Ji-Feng Li and other colleagues. Huaping Zhang would especially express gratitude to his graceful girl friend Feifei and her family for their encouragement during the hard work. We also thank three anonymous reviewers for their elaborate and helpful comments.

References

Andi Wu ,Zixin Jiang. *Word Segmentation in Sentence Analysis*. 1998 International Conference on Chinese Information Processing, Beijing, 1998. 169-180.

Chunyu Kit,Haihua Pan and Hongbiao Chen. *Learning Case-based Knowledge for Disambiguating Chinese Word Segmentation: A preliminary study*. First SIGHAN Workshop attached with the 19th COLING, 2002.8, pp.63-70

Dai, Y., Khoo, C.S.G. and Loh, T.E. 1999. *A new statistical formula for Chinese text segmentation incorporating contextual information.* Proc ACM SIGIR99, pp. 82-89.

Gao Shan, Zhang Yan. *The Research on Integrated Chinese Word Segmentation and Labeling based on trigram statistical model*, proceeding of natural language understanding and machine translation, Beijing, Tsinghua University Press. 2001.116-122; (in Chinese)

Hockenmaier, J. and Brew, C. .1998. *Error-driven learning of Chinese word segmentation*. In J. Guo, K. T. Lua, and J. Xu, editors, 12th Pacific Conference on Language and Information, pp. 218-229, Singapore. Chinese and Oriental Languages Processing Society.

Lawrence. R.Rabiner.1989. *A Tutorial on Hidden Markov Models and Selected Applications in Speech Recognition*. Proceedings of IEEE 77(2): pp.257-286.

Luo Xiao, Sun, Maosong Benjamin K Tsou. *Covering Ambuguity Resolution in Chinese Word Segmentation Based on Contextual Information*. the 19th COLING, 2002.8, pp.598-604

Luo Z. and Song R. 2001. *Integrated and Fast Recognition of Proper Noun in Modern Chinese Word Segmentation*. Proceedings of International Conference on Chinese Computing 2001, Singapore, pp. 323-328.

Nianwen Xue and Susan P. Converse. *Combining Classifiers for Chinese Word Segmentation*, First SIGHAN Workshop attached with the 19th COLING, 2002.8, pp.63-70.

Palmer, D. 1997. *.A trainable rule-based algorithm for word segmentation*. Proceedings of the 35th Annual Meeting of the Association for Computational Linguistics (ACL '97), Madrid, 1997.

Peng, F. and Schuurmans, D. (2001). *A hierarchical EM approach to word segmentation*. In 6th Natural Language Processing Pacific Rim Symposium (NLPRS-2001)

Shai Fine, Yoram Singer, and Naftali Tishby.1998. *The hierarchical Hidden Markov Model: Analysis and applications*. Machine Learning, 32:41

Sun J., Gao J. F., Zhang L., Zhou M Huang, C.N.2002. *Chinese Named Entity Identification Using Class-based Language Model*, Proc. of the 19th International Conference on Computational Linguistics, Taipei, pp 967-973

Sun M.S. (1993) English Transliteration Automatic Recognition. In "Computational Language Research and Development", L. W. Chen & Q. Yuan, ed., Beijing Institute of Linguistic Press.

Tan H. Y. (1999) *Chinese Place Automatic Recognition Research.* In "Proceedings of Computational Language ", C. N. Huang & Z.D. Dong, ed., Tsinghua Univ. Press, Beijing, China

Teahan, W. J. and Wen, Y. and McNab, R. and Witten I. H. 2001, *A Compression-based Algorithm for Chinese Word Segmentation*. In Comput. Ling., 26(3):375-393.

Xiao Luo, Maosong Sun, Benjamin K Tsou. *Covering Ambuguity Resolution in Chinese Word Segmentation Based on Contextual Information*. the 19th COLING, 2002.8, pp.598-604

Ye S.R, Chua T.S., Liu J. M. 2002. *An Agent-based Approach to Chinese Named Entity Recognition*, Proc. of the 19th International Conference on Computational Linguistics, Taipei, pp 1149-1155

Zhang Hua-Ping, Liu Qun. *Model of Chinese Words Rough Segmentation Based on N-Shortest-Paths Method*. Journal of Chinese information processing, 2002,16(5):1-7 (in Chinese)

ZHANG Hua-Ping, LIU Qun, Zhang Hao and Cheng Xue-Qi. 2002. *Automatic Recognition of Chinese Unknown Words Recognition*. Proc. of COLING 2002

Modeling of Long Distance Context Dependency in Chinese

GuoDong ZHOU
Institute for Infocomm Research
21 Heng Mui Keng Terrace
Singapore, 119613
zhougd@i2r.a-star.edu.sg

Abstract

Ngram modeling is simple in language modeling and has been widely used in many applications. However, it can only capture the short distance context dependency within an N-word window where the largest practical N for natural language is three. In the meantime, much of context dependency in natural language occurs beyond a three-word window. In order to incorporate this kind of long distance context dependency, this paper proposes a new MI-Ngram modeling approach. The MI-Ngram model consists of two components: an ngram model and an MI model. The ngram model captures the short distance context dependency within an N-word window while the MI model captures the long distance context dependency between the word pairs beyond the N-word window by using the concept of mutual information. It is found that MI-Ngram modeling has much better performance than ngram modeling. Evaluation on the XINHUA new corpus of 29 million words shows that inclusion of the best 1,600,000 word pairs decreases the perplexity of the MI-Trigram model by 20 percent compared with the trigram model. In the meanwhile, evaluation on Chinese word segmentation shows that about 35 percent of errors can be corrected by using the MI-Trigram model compared with the trigram model.

1 Introduction

Language modeling is the attempt to characterize, capture and exploit the regularities and constraints in natural language. Among various language modeling approaches, ngram modeling has been widely used in many applications, such as speech recognition, machine translation (Katz 1987; Jelinek 1989; Gale and Church 1990; Brown et al. 1992; Yang et al. 1996; Bai et al 1998; Zhou et al 1999; Rosenfeld 2000; Gao et al 2002). Although ngram modeling is simple in nature and easy to use, it has obvious deficiencies. For instance, ngram modeling can only capture the short distance context dependency within an N-word window where currently the largest practical N for natural language is three.

In the meantime, it is found that there always exist many preferred relationships between words. Two highly associated word pairs are 不仅/而且 ("not only/but also") and 医生/护士 ("doctor/nurse"). Psychological experiments in Meyer et al. (1975) indicated that the human's reaction to a highly associated word pair was stronger and faster than that to a poorly associated word pair. Such preference information is very useful for natural language processing (Church et al. 1990; Hiddle et al. 1993; Rosenfeld 1994; Zhou et al.1998; Zhou et al 1999). Obviously, the preference relationships between words can expand from a short to long distance. While we can use traditional ngram modeling to capture the short distance context dependency, the long distance context dependency should also be exploited properly.

The purpose of this paper is to propose a new MI-Ngram modeling approach to capture the context dependency over both a short distance and a long distance. Experimentation shows that this new MI-Ngram modeling approach can significantly decrease the perplexity of the new MI-Ngram model compared with traditional ngram model. In the meantime, evaluation on Chinese word segmentation shows that this new approach can significantly reduce the error rate.

This paper is organized as follows. In section 2, we describe the traditional ngram modeling approach and discuss its main property. In section 3, we propose the new MI-Ngram modeling approach to capture context dependency over both a short distance and a long distance. In section 4, we measure the MI-Ngram modeling approach and evaluate its application in Chinese word segmentation. Finally we give a summary of this paper in section 5.

2 Ngram Modeling

Let $S = w_1^m = w_1 w_2 ... w_m$, where w_i's are the words that make up the hypothesis, the probability of the word string $P(S)$ can be computed by using the chain rule:

$$P(S) = P(w_1)\prod_{i=2}^{m} P(w_i \mid w_1^{i-1}) \tag{2.1}$$

By taking log function to both sides of equation (2.1), we have the log probability of the word string $\log P(S)$:

$$\log P(S) = \log P(w_1) + \sum_{i=2}^{m} \log P(w_i \mid w_1^{i-1}) \tag{2.2}$$

So, the classical task of statistical language modeling becomes how to effectively and efficiently predict the next word, given the previous words, that is to say, to estimate expressions of the form $P(w_i \mid w_1^{i-1})$. For convenience, $P(w_i \mid w_1^{i-1})$ is often written as $P(w_i \mid h)$, where $h = w_1^{i-1}$, is called history.

Ngram modeling has been widely used in estimating $P(w_i \mid h)$. Within an ngram model, the probability of a word occurring next is estimated based on the $n-1$ previous words. That is to say,

$$P(w_i \mid w_1^{i-1}) \approx P(w_i \mid w_{i-n+1}^{i-1}) \tag{2.3}$$

For example, in bigram model (n=2), the probability of a word is assumed to depend only on the previous word:

$$P(w_i \mid w_1^{i-1}) \approx P(w_i \mid w_{i-1}) \tag{2.4}$$

And the probability $P(w_i \mid w_{i-1})$ can be estimated by using maximum likelihood estimation (MLE) principle:

$$P(w_i \mid w_{i-1}) = \frac{C(w_{i-1} w_i)}{C(w_{i-1})} \tag{2.5}$$

Where $C(\bullet)$ represents the number of times the sequence occurs in the training data. In practice, due to the data sparseness problem, some smoothing techniques, such as linear interpolation (Jelinek 1989; Chen and Goodman 1999) and back-off modeling (Katz 1987), are applied.

Obviously, an ngram model assumes that the probability of the next word w_i is independent of word string w_1^{i-n} in the history. The difference between bigram, trigram and other ngram models is the value of N. The parameters of an ngram are thus the probabilities:

$$P(w_n \mid w_1 ... w_{n-1}) \quad \text{For all } w_1, w_w, ..., w_n \in V.$$

Given $S = w_1 w_2 ... w_m$, an ngram model estimates the log probability of the word string $P(S)$ by re-writing equation (2.2):

$$\log P_{ngram}(S) = \log P(w_1) + \sum_{i=2}^{n-1} \log P(w_i \mid w_1^{i-1}) + \sum_{i=n}^{m} \log P(w_i \mid w_{i-n+1}^{i-1}) \tag{2.6}$$

Where m is the string length, w_i is the i-th word in string S.

From equation (2.3) $P(w_i \mid w_1^{i-1}) \approx P(w_i \mid w_{i-n+1}^{i-1})$, we have:

$$\frac{P(w_1^{i-1} w_i)}{P(w_1^{i-1})} \approx \frac{P(w_{i-n+1}^{i-1} w_i)}{P(w_{i-n+1}^{i-1})}$$

$$\frac{P(w_1^{i-1} w_i)}{P(w_1^{i-1})P(w_i)} \approx \frac{P(w_{i-n+1}^{i-1} w_i)}{P(w_{i-n+1}^{i-1})P(w_i)}$$

$$\log \frac{P(w_1^{i-1} w_i)}{P(w_1^{i-1})P(w_i)} \approx \log \frac{P(w_{i-n+1}^{i-1} w_i)}{P(w_{i-n+1}^{i-1})P(w_i)} \tag{2.7}$$

Obviously, we can get

$$MI(w_1^{i-1}, w_i, d=1) \approx MI(w_{i-n+1}^{i-1}, w_i, d=1) \quad (2.8)$$

where $MI(w_1^{i-1}, w_i, d=1) = \log \frac{P(w_1^{i-1} w_i)}{P(w_1^{i-1})P(w_i)}$ is the mutual information between the word string pair (w_1^{i-1}, w_i) and $MI(w_{i-n+1}^{i-1}, w_i, d=1) = \log \frac{P(w_{i-n+1}^{i-1} w_i)}{P(w_{i-n+1}^{i-1})P(w_i)}$ is the mutual information between the word string pair (w_{i-n+1}^{i-1}, w_i). d is the distance of two word strings in the word string pair and is equal to 1 when the two word strings are adjacent.

For a word string pair (A, B) over a distance d where A and B are word strings, mutual information $MI(A,B,d)$ reflects the degree of preference relationship between the two strings over a distance d. Several properties of mutual information are apparent:

- For the same distance d, $MI(A,B,d) \neq MI(B,A,d)$.
- For different distances d_1 and d_2, $MI(A,B,d_1) \neq MI(A,B,d_2)$.
- If A and B are independent over a distance d, then $MI(A,B,d) = 0$.

$MI(A,B,d)$ reflects the change of the information content when the word strings A and B are correlated. That is to say, the higher the value of $MI(A,B,d)$, the stronger affinity A and B have. Therefore, we can use mutual information to measure the preference relationship degree between a word string pair.

From the view of mutual information, an ngram model assumes the mutual information independency between (w_1^{i-n}, w_i). Using an alternative view of equivalence, an ngram model is one that partitions the data into equivalence classes based on the last n-1 words in the history.

As trigram model is most widely used in current research, we will mainly consider the trigram-based model. By re-writing equation (2.6), the trigram model estimates the log probability of the string $P(S)$ as:

$$\begin{aligned} \log P_{Trigram}(S) &= \log P(w_1) \\ &+ \log(w_2 \mid w_1) \\ &+ \sum_{i=3}^{m} \log P(w_i \mid w_{i-2}^{i-1}) \end{aligned} \quad (2.9)$$

3 MI-Ngram Modeling

Given history $H = w_1^{i-1} = w_1 w_2 ... w_{i-1}$, we can assume $X = w_2^{i-1} = w_2 w_3 ... w_{i-1}$. Then we have

$$H = w_1 X \quad (3.1)$$

and

$$P(w_i \mid H) = P(w_i \mid w_1 X). \quad (3.2)$$

Since

$$\begin{aligned} \log P(w_i \mid H) &= \log \frac{P(Hw_i)}{P(H)} \\ &= \log P(w_i) + \log \frac{P(Hw_i)}{P(H)P(w_i)} \\ &= \log P(w_i) + MI(w_i, H, 1) \end{aligned} \quad (3.3)$$

Here we assume

$$\begin{aligned} MI(H, w_i, d=1) &= MI(X, w_i, d=1) \\ &+ MI(w_1, w_i, d=i) \end{aligned} \quad (3.4)$$

where $H = w_1^{i-1}$, $X = w_2^{i-1}$ and $i > N$. That is to say, the mutual information of the next word with the history is assumed equal to the summation of that of the next word with the first word in the history and that of the next word with the rest word string in the history.

We can re-writing equation (3.3) by using equation (3.4):

$$\begin{aligned} &\log P(w_i \mid H) \\ &= \log P(w_i) + MI(H, w_i, 1) \\ &= \log P(w_i) + MI(X, w_i, 1) + MI(w_1, w_i, i) \end{aligned}$$

$$= \log P(w_i) + \log \frac{P(w_i X)}{P(w_i)P(X)} + MI(w_1, w_i, i)$$

$$= \log \frac{P(w_i X)}{P(X)} + MI(w_1, w_i, i)$$

$$= \log P(w_i \mid X) + MI(w_1, w_i, i) \quad (3.5)$$

Then we have

$$\log P(w_i \mid w_1^{i-1}) = \log P(w_i \mid w_2^{i-1}) + MI(w_1, w_i, i) \quad (3.6)$$

By applying equation (3.6) repeatedly, we have:

$$\log P(w_i \mid w_1^{i-1})$$

$$= \log P(w_i \mid w_2^{i-1}) + MI(w_1, w_i, i)$$

$$= \log P(w_i \mid w_3^{i-1}) + MI(w_2, w_i, i-1) + MI(w_1, w_i, i)$$

.. .. ..

$$= \log P(w_i \mid w_{i-n+1}^{i-1}) + \sum_{k=1}^{k=i-n} MI(w_k, w_i, i-k+1) \quad (3.7)$$

Obviously, the first item in equation (3.7) contributes to the log probability of ngram within an N-word window while the second item is the summation of mutual information which contributes to the long distance context dependency of the next word w_i with the individual previous word $w_j (1 \le j \le i-N, i > N)$ over the long distance outside the N-word window.

By using equation (3.7), equation (2.2) can be re-written as:

$$\log P(S) = \log P(w_1) + \sum_{i=2}^{m} \log P(w_i \mid w_1^{i-1})$$

$$= \log P(w_1) + \sum_{i=2}^{i=n} \log(w_i \mid w_1^{i-1}) + \log P(w_{n+1} \mid w_1^{n}) + \sum_{i=n+2}^{m} \log P(w_i \mid w_1^{i-1})$$

$$= \log P(w_1) + \sum_{i=2}^{i=n} \log(w_i \mid w_1^{i-1}) + \log P(w_{n+1} \mid w_2^{n}) + MI(w_{n+1}, w_1, n+1) + \sum_{i=n+2}^{m} \log P(w_i \mid w_1^{i-1})$$

.. .. ..

$$= \log P(w_1) + \sum_{i=2}^{i=n} \log(w_i \mid w_1^{i-1}) + \sum_{i=n+1}^{m} \log P(w_i \mid w_{i-2}^{i-1}) + \sum_{i=n+1}^{m} \sum_{k=1}^{k=i-n} MI(w_k, w_i, i-k+1) \quad (3.8)$$

In equation (3.8), the first three items are the values computed by the trigram model as shown in equation (2.9) and the forth item $\sum_{i=n+1}^{m} \sum_{k=1}^{k=i-n} MI(w_k, w_i, i-k+1)$ contributes to summation of the mutual information of the next word with the words over the long distance outside the N-word window. That is, the new model as shown in equation (3.8) consists of two components: an ngram model and an MI model. Therefore, we call equation (3.8) as an MI-Ngram model and equation (3.8) can be re-written as:

$$\log P_{MI-Ngram}(S) = \log P_{Ngram}(S) + \sum_{i=n+1}^{m} \sum_{k=1}^{k=i-n} MI(w_k, w_i, i-k+1) \quad (3.9)$$

As a special case N=3, the MI-Trigram model estimate the log probability of the string as follows:

$$\log P_{MI-Trigram}(S) = \log P_{Trigram}(S) + \sum_{i=4}^{m} \sum_{k=1}^{k=i-3} MI(w_k, w_i, i-k+1) \quad (3.10)$$

Compared with traditional ngram modeling, MI-Ngram modeling incorporates the long distance context dependency by computing mutual information of the long distance dependent word pairs. Since the number of possible long distance dependent word pairs may be very huge, it is impossible for MI-Ngram modeling to incorporate all of them. Therefore, for MI-Ngram modeling to be practically useful, how to select a reasonable number of word pairs becomes very important. Here two approaches are used (Zhou et al 1998 and 1999). One is to restrict the window size of possible word pairs by computing and comparing the perplexities[1] (Shannon C.E. 1951) of various long distance bigram models for different distances. It is found that the bigram perplexities for different distances outside the 10-word window become stable. Therefore, we only consider MI-Ngram modeling with a window size of 10 words. Another is to adapt average mutual information to select a reasonable number of long distance dependent word pairs. Given distance d and two words A and B, its average mutual information is computed as:

$$
\begin{aligned}
& AMI(A,B,d) \\
& = P(A,B,d)\log\frac{P(A,B,d)}{P(A)P(B)} \\
& + P(A,\overline{B},d)\log\frac{P(A,\overline{B},d)}{P(A)P(\overline{B})} \\
& + P(\overline{A},B,d)\log\frac{P(\overline{A},B,d)}{P(\overline{A})P(B)} \\
& + P(\overline{A},\overline{B},d)\log\frac{P(\overline{A},\overline{B},d)}{P(\overline{A})P(\overline{B})}
\end{aligned}
\quad (3.11)
$$

Compared with mutual information, average mutual information takes joint probabilities into consideration. In this way, average mutual information prefers frequently occurred word pairs. In our paper, different numbers of long distance dependent word pairs will be considered in MI-Ngram modeling within a window size of 10 words to evaluate the effect of different MI model size.

4 Experimentation

As trigram modeling is most widely used in current research, only MI-Trigram modeling is studied here. Furthermore, in order to demonstrate the effect of different numbers of word pairs in MI-Trigram modeling, various MI-Trigram models with different numbers of word pairs and the same window size of 10 words are trained on the XINHUA news corpus of 29 million words while the lexicon contains about 56,000 words. Finally, various MI-Trigram models are tested on the same task of Chinese word segmentation using the Chinese tag bank PFR1.0[2] of 3.69M Chinese characters (1.12M Chinese Words).

Table 1 shows the perplexities of various MI-Trigram models and their performances on Chinese word segmentation. Here, the precision (P) measures the number of correct words in the answer file over the total number of words in the answer file and the recall (R) measures the number of correct words in the answer file over the total number of

---

[1] Perplexity is a measure of the average number of possible choices there are for a random variable. The perplexity PP of a random variable X with entropy $H(X)$ is defined as:

$$PP(X) = 2^{H(X)}$$

Entropy is a measure of uncertainty about a random variable. If a random variable X occurs with a probability distribution $P(x)$, then the entropy $H(X)$ of that event is defined as:

$$H(X) = -\sum_{x\in X} P(x)\log_2 P(x)$$

Since $x\log_2 x \to 0$ as $x \to 0$, it is conventional to use the relation $0\log_2 0 = 0$ when computing entropy.

The units of entropy are bits of information. This is because the entropy of a random variable corresponds to the average number of bits per event needed to encode a typical sequence of event samples from that random variable' s distribution.

[2] PFR1.0 is developed by Institute of Computational Linguistics at Beijing Univ. Here, only the word segmentation annotation is used.

words in the key file. F-measure is the weighted harmonic mean of precision and recall: $F = \frac{(\beta^2+1)RP}{\beta^2 R + P}$ with β^2=1.

Table 1 shows that

- The perplexity and the F-measure rise quickly as the number of word pairs in MI-Trigram modeling increases from 0 to 1,600,000 and then rise slowly. Therefore, the best 1,600,000 word pairs should at least be included.
- Inclusion of the best 1,600,000 word pairs decreases the perplexity of MI-Trigram modeling by about 20 percent compared with the pure trigram model.
- The performance of Chinese word segmentation using the MI-Trigram model with 1,600,000 word pairs is 0.8 percent higher than using the pure trigram model (MI-Trigram with 0 word pairs). That is to say, about 35 percent of errors can be corrected by incorporating only 1,600,000 word pairs to the MI-Trigram model compared with the pure trigram model.
- For Chinese word segmentation task, recalls are about 0.7 percent higher than precisions. The main reason may be the existence of unknown words. In our experimentation, unknown words are segmented into individual Chinese characters. This makes the number of segmented words in the answer file higher than that in the key file.

It is clear that MI-Ngram modeling has much better performance than ngram modeling. One advantage of MI-Ngram modeling is that its number of parameters is just a little more than that of ngram modeling. Another advantage of MI-Ngram modeling is that the number of the word pairs can be reasonable in size without losing too much of its modeling power. Compared to ngram modeling, MI-Ngram modeling also captures the long-distance context dependency of word pairs using the concept of mutual information.

Table 1: The effect of different numbers of word pairs in MI-Trigram modeling with the same window size of 10 words on Chinese word segmentation

Number of word pairs	Perplexity	Precision	Recall	F-measure
0	316	97.5	98.2	97.8
100,000	295	97.9	98.4	98.1
200,000	281	98.1	98.6	98.3
400,000	269	98.2	98.7	98.4
800,000	259	98.2	98.8	98.5
1,600,000	250	98.4	98.8	98.6
3,200,000	245	98.3	98.9	98.6
6,400,000	242	98.4	98.9	98.6

6 Conclusion

This paper proposes a new MI-Ngram modeling approach to capture the context dependency over both a short distance and a long distance. This is done by incorporating long distance dependent word pairs into traditional ngram model by using the concept of mutual information. It is found that MI-Ngram modeling has much better performance than ngram modeling.

Future works include the explorations of the new MI-Trigram modeling approach in other applications, such as Mandarin speech recognition and PINYIN to Chinese character conversion.

References

Bai S.H., Li H.Z., Lin Z.M. and Yuan B.S. 1989. Building class-based language models with contextual statistics. *Proceedings of International Conference on Acoustics, Speech and Signal Processing (ICASSP'1998). pages173-176.*

Brown P.F. et al. 1992. Class-based ngram models of natural language. *Computational Linguistics* 18(4), 467-479.

Chen S.F. and Goodman J. 1999. An empirical study of smoothing technique for language modeling. *Computer, Speech and Language.* 13(5). 359-394.

Church K.W. et al. 1991. Enhanced good Turing and Cat-Cal: two new methods for estimating probabilities of English bigrams. *Computer, Speech and Language* 5(1), 19-54.

Gale W.A. and Church K.W. 1990. Poor estimates of context are worse than none. *Proceedings of DARPA Speech and Natural Language Workshop*, Hidden Valley, Pennsylvania, pages293-295.

Gao J.F., Goodman J.T., Cao G.H. and Li H. 2002. Exploring asymmetric clustering for statistical language modelling. *Proceedings of the Fortieth Annual Meeting of the Association for Computational Linguistics (ACL'2002).* Philadelphia. pages183-190.

Hindle D. et al. 1993. Structural ambiguity and lexical relations. *Computational Linguistics* 19(1), 103-120.

Jelinek F. 1989. Self-organized language modeling for speech recognition. In *Readings in Speech Recognition.* Edited by Waibel A. and Lee K.F. Morgan Kaufman. San Mateo. CA. pages450-506.

Katz S.M. 1987. " Estimation of Probabilities from Sparse Data for the Language Model Component of a Speech Recognizer". *IEEE Transactions on Acoustics. Speech and Signal Processing.* 35. 400-401.

Meyer D. et al. 1975. Loci of contextual effects on visual word recognition. In *Attention and Performance V*, edited by P.Rabbitt and S.Dornie. pages98-116. Acdemic Press.

Rosenfeld R. 1994. Adaptive statistical language modeling: A Maximum Entropy Approach. *Ph.D. Thesis*, Carneige Mellon University.

Rosenfeld R. 2000. Two decades of language modelling: where do we go from here. *Proceedings of IEEE.* 88:1270-1278. August.

Shannon C.E. 1951. Prediction and entropy of printed English. *Bell Systems Technical Journal* 30, 50-64.

Yang Y.J. et al. 1996. Adaptive linguistic decoding system for Mandarin speech recognition applications. *Computer Processing of Chinese & Oriental Lan*guages 10(2), 211-224.

Zhou GuoDong and Lua Kim Teng, 1998. Word Association and MI-Trigger-based Language Modeling. *Proceedings of the Thirtieth-sixth Annual Meeting of the Association for Computational Linguistics and the Seventeenth International Conference on Computational Linguistics (COLING-ACL'1998).* Montreal, Canada. pages10-14. August.

Zhou GuoDong and Lua KimTeng. 1999. Interpolation of N-gram and MI-based Trigger Pair Language Modeling in Mandarin Speech Recognition, *Computer, Speech and Language*, 13(2), 123-135.

A Chinese Efficient Analyser Integrating Word Segmentation, Part-Of-Speech Tagging, Partial Parsing and Full Parsing

GuoDong ZHOU
Institute for Infocomm Research
21 Heng Mui Keng Terrace
Singapore, 119613
zhougd@i2r.a-star.edu.sg

Jian SU
Institute for Infocomm Research
21 Heng Mui Keng Terrace
Singapore, 119613
sujian@ i2r.a-star.edu.sg

Abstract

This paper introduces an efficient analyser for the Chinese language, which efficiently and effectively integrates word segmentation, part-of-speech tagging, partial parsing and full parsing. The Chinese efficient analyser is based on a Hidden Markov Model (HMM) and an HMM-based tagger. That is, all the components are based on the same HMM-based tagging engine. One advantage of using the same single engine is that it largely decreases the code size and makes the maintenance easy. Another advantage is that it is easy to optimise the code and thus improve the speed while speed plays a critical important role in many applications. Finally, the performances of all the components can benefit from the optimisation of existing algorithms and/or adoption of better algorithms to a single engine. Experiments show that all the components can achieve state-of-art performances with high efficiency for the Chinese language.

1 Introduction

Traditionally, a text parser outputs a complete parse tree for each input sentence, achieving a speed in the order of 10 words per second (wps) (Abney 1997). However, for many applications like text mining, a parse tree is not necessary and a speed of 10 wps is unacceptable when we have to process millions of words in thousands of documents in a reasonable time (Feldman 1997). Therefore, there is a compromise between speed and performance in many applications.

The objective of this paper is to develop an efficient analyser for the Chinese language, exploring different intermediate forms, achieving a target speed in the region of 1,000 wps for full parsing, 2,000 wps for partial parsing and 10,000 wps for word segmentation and part-of-speech tagging, with state-of-art performances.

The layout of this paper is as follows. Section 2 describes the Chinese efficient analyser. Section 3 presents the HMM and the HMM-based tagger. Sections 4 and 5 describe the applications of the HMM-based tagger in integrated word segmentation and part-of-speech tagging, partial parsing, and full parsing respectively. Section 6 gives the experimental results. Finally, some conclusions are drawn with possible extensions of future work in section 7.

2 Chinese Efficient Analyser

The Chinese efficient analyser can be described by the example as shown in Figure 1. Here, "." in Figure 1 means that the current node has not been chunked till now. For convenience, it is regarded as a "special chunk" in this paper and others as "normal chunks". Therefore, every node in Figure 1 can be represented as a 3tuple $c_i(p_i, w_i)$, where c_i is the i-th chunk in the input chunk sequence and

- w_i is the head word of c_i and p_i is the POS tag of w_i when $c_i \neq .$ (c_i is a normal chunk). In this case, we call node $c_i(p_i, w_i)$ a normal chunk node.

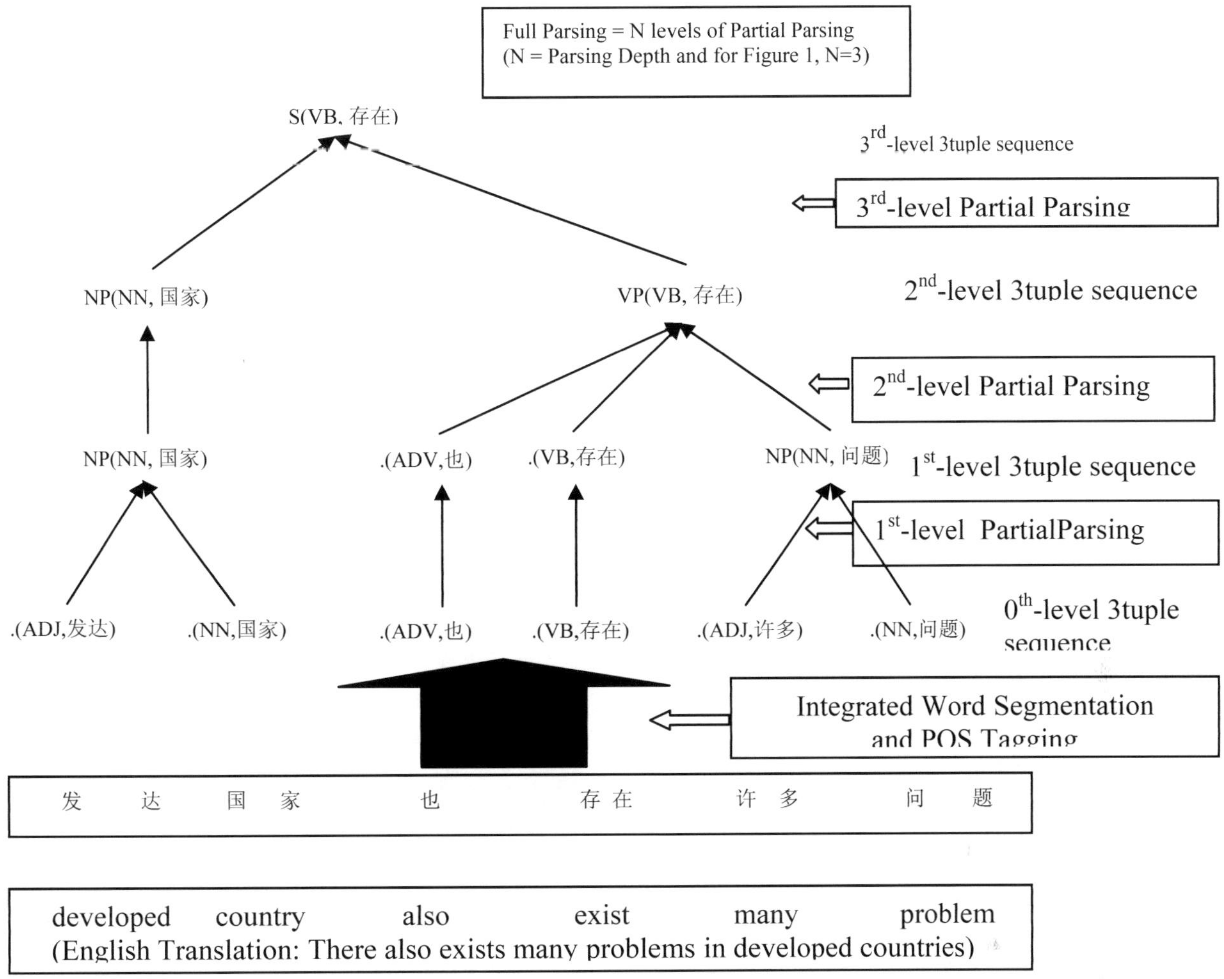

Figure 1: An Example Sentence "发达国家也存在许多问题" of the Chinese Efficient Analyser

- w_i is just the word linked with c_i and p_i is the POS tag of w_i when $c_i = .$ (c_i is a special chunk). In this case, we call node $c_i(p_i, w_i)$ a special chunk or POS node.

Figure 1 shows that, sequentially from bottom to top,

1) Given a Chinese sentence (e.g. "发达国家也存在许多问题"), it is segmented and tagged into a sequence of special chunk, POS and word 3tuples (.(ADJ, 发达) .(NN, 国家) .(ADV, 也) .(VB, 存在) .(ADJ, 许多) .(NN, 问题)) via the integrated word segmentation and POS tagging. In this paper, this resulting 3tuple sequence is called "0th-level 3tuple sequence".

2) The 0th-level 3tuple sequence is then chunked into 1st-level 3tuple sequence (NP(NN, 国家) .(ADV, 也) .(VB, 存在) NP(NN, 问题)) via 1st-level partial parsing, while POS nodes .(ADJ, 发达) and .(NN, 国家) are chunked into a normal chunk node NP(NN, 国家), and POS nodes .(ADJ, 许多) .(NN, 问题) into NP(NN, 问题).

3) The 1st-level 3tuple sequence is further chunked into 2nd-level 3tuple sequence (NP(NN, 国家) VP(VB, 存在)) via 2nd-level partial parsing, while mixed POS and normal chunk nodes .(ADV, 也) .(VB, 存在) NP(NN, 问题) are chunked into a normal chunk node VP(VB, 存在).

4) Finally, 2nd-level 3tuple sequence is chunked into 3rd-level 3tuple sequence (S(VB, 存在)) via 3rd-level partial parsing, while normal chunk nodes NP(NN, 国家) and VP(VB, 存在) are chunked into a normal chunk node S(VB, 存在).
5) In this way, full parsing is completed with a fully parsed tree after several levels (3 in the example of Figure 1) of cascaded partial parsing.

3 HMM-based Tagger

The Chinese efficient analyser is based on the HMM-based tagger described in Zhou et al 2000a. Given a token sequence $G_1^n = g_1 g_2 \cdots g_n$, the goal of tagging is to find a stochastic optimal tag sequence $T_1^n = t_1 t_2 \cdots t_n$ that maximizes

$$\log P(T_1^n \mid G_1^n) = \log P(T_1^n) + \log \frac{P(T_1^n, G_1^n)}{P(T_1^n) \cdot P(G_1^n)}$$

By assuming mutual information independence:

$$MI(T_1^n, G_1^n) = \sum_{i=1}^{n} MI(t_i, G_1^n) \text{ or}$$

$$\log \frac{P(T_1^n, G_1^n)}{P(T_1^n) \cdot P(G_1^n)} = \sum_{i=1}^{n} \log \frac{P(t_i, G_1^n)}{P(t_i) \cdot P(G_1^n)}$$

we have:

$$\log P(T_1^n \mid G_1^n) = \log P(T_1^n) - \sum_{i=1}^{n} \log P(t_i) + \sum_{i=1}^{n} \log P(t_i \mid G_1^n)$$

Both the first and second items correspond to the language model component of the tagger. We will not discuss these two items further in this paper since they are well studied in ngram modeling. This paper will focus on the third item $\sum_{i=1}^{n} \log P(t_i \mid G_1^n)$, which is the main difference between our tagger and other HMM-based taggers. Ideally, it can be estimated by using the forward-backward algorithm (Rabiner 1989) recursively for the first-order (Rabiner 1989) or second-order HMMs (Watson et al 1992). To simplify the complexity, several context dependent approximations on it will be attempted in this paper instead, as detailed in sections 3 and 4.

All of this modelling would be for naught were it not for the existence of an efficient algorithm for finding the optimal state sequence, thereby "decoding" the original sequence of tags. The stochastic optimal tag sequence can be found by maximizing the previous equation over all the possible tag sequences. This is implemented via the well-known Viterbi algorithm (Viterbi 1967) by using dynamic programming and an appropriate merging of multiple theories when they converge on a particular state. Since we are interested in recovering the tag state sequence, we pursue 16 theories at every given step of the algorithm.

4 Word Segmentation and POS Tagging

Traditionally, in Chinese Language Processing, word segmentation and POS tagging are implemented sequentially. That is, the input Chinese sentence is segmented into words first and then the segmented result (in the form of word lattice or N-best word sequences) is passed to POS tagging component. However, this processing strategy has following disadvantages:

- The word lexicons used in word segmentation and POS tagging may be different. This difference is difficult to overcome and largely drops the system accuracy although different optimal algorithms may be applied to word segmentation and POS tagging.
- With speed in consideration, the two-stage processing strategy is not efficient.

Therefore, we apply the strategy of integrating word segmentation and POS tagging in a single stage. This can be implemented as follows:

1) Given an input sentence, a 3tuple (special chunk, POS and word) lattice is generated by skimming the sentence from left-to-right, and looking up the word and POS lexicon to determine all the possible words and get POS tag probability distribution for each possible word.

2) Viterbi algorithm is applied to decode the 3tuple lattice to find the most possible POS tag sequence.

3) In this way, the given sentence is segmented into words with POS tags.

The rationale behind the above algorithm is the ability of HMM in parallel segmentation and classification (Rabiner 1989).

In order to overcome the coarse n-gram models raised by the limited number of orignial POS tags used in current Chinese POS tag bank (corpus), a word clustering algorithm (Bai et al 1998) is applied to classify words into classes first and then the N (e.g. N=500) most frequently occurred word class and POS pairs are added to the original POS tag set to achieve more accurate models. For example, ADJ(<许多>) represents a special POS tag ADJ which pairs with the word class <许多>. Here, <许多> is a word class label. For convenience and clarity, we use the most frequently occurred word in a word class as the label to represent the word class.

5 Partial Parsing and Full Parsing

As discussed in section 2, obviously partial parsing can have different levels and full parsing can be achieved by cascading several levels of partial parsing (e.g. 3 levels of cascaded partial parsing can achieve full parsing for the example as shown in Figure 1).

In this paper, a certain level (e.g. l-th level) of partial parsing is implemented via a chunking model, built on the HMM-based tagger as described in section 2, with $(l-1)$-th level 3tuple sequence as input. That is, for the l-th level partial parsing, the chunking model has the $(l-1)$-th level 3tuple sequence $G_1^n = g_1 g_2 \cdots g_n$ (Here, 3tuple $g_i = c_i(p_i, w_i)$) as input. In the meantime, chunk tag t_i used in the chunking model is structural and consists of following three parts:

- **Boundary Category B**: It is a set of four values 0, 1, 2, 3, where "0" means that the current 3tuple is a whole chunk, "1" means that the current 3tuple is at the beginning of a chunk, "2" means that the current 3tuple is in the middle of a chunk and "3" means that the current stuple is at the end of a chunk.
- **Chunk Category C**: It is used to denote the output chunk category of the chunking model, which includes normal chunks and the special chunk ("."). The reason to include the special chunk is that some of POS 3tuple in the input sequence may not be chunked in the current chunking stage.
- **POS Category POS**: Because of the limited number in boundary category and output chunk category, the POS category is added into the structural tag to represent more accurate models.

Therefore, t_i can be represented by $b_i\_c_i\_pos_i$, where b_i is the boundary type of t_i, c_i is the output chunk type of t_i and pos_i is the POS type of t_i. Obviously, there exist some constraints between t_{i-1} and t_i on the boundary categories and output chunk categories, as briefed in table 1, where "valid"/"invalid" means the chunk tag sequence $t_{i-1}t_i$ is valid/invalid while "validon" means $t_{i-1}t_i$ is valid on the condition $c_{i-1} = c_i$.

	0	1	2	3
0	Valid	Valid	Invalid	Invalid
1	Invalid	Invalid	Valid on	Validon
2	Invalid	Invalid	Valid	Valid
3	Valid	Valid	Invalid	Invalid

Table 1: Constraints between t_{i-1} and t_i (Column: b_{i-1} in t_{i-1}; Row: b_i in t_i)

For the example as shown in Figure 1, we can see that:

- In the 1st-level partial parsing, the input 3tuple sequence is the 0th-level 3tuple sequence .(ADJ, 发达) .(NN, 国家) .(ADV, 也) .(VB, 存在) .(ADJ, 许多) .(NN, 问题) and the output tag sequence 1_NP_ADJ 3_NP_NN 0_._ADV 0_._VB 1_NP_ADJ 3_NP_NN, from where derived is the 1st-level 3tuple sequence NP(NN, 国家) .(ADV, 也) .(VB, 存在) NP(NN, 问题).

- In the 2nd-level partial parsing, the input 3tuple sequence is the 1st-level 3tuple sequence NP(NN, 国家) .(ADV, 也) .(VB, 存在) NP(NN, 问题) and the output tag sequence 0_NP_NN 1_VP_ADV 2_VP_VB 3_VP_NN, from where derived is the 2nd-level 3tuple sequence NP(NN, 国家) VP(VB, 存在).
- In the 3rd-level partial parsing, the input 3tuple sequence is the 2nd-level 3tuple sequence NP(NN, 国家) VP(VB, 存在) and the output tag sequence 1_S_NN 3_S_VB, from where derived is the 3rd-level 3tuple sequence S(VB, 存在). In this way, a fully parsed tree is reached.
- In the cascaded chunking procedure, necessary information is stored for back-tracing. Partially/fully parsed trees can be constructed by tracing from the final 3tuple sequence back to 0th-level 3tuple sequence. Different levels of partial parsing can be achieved according to the need of the application.

6 Experimental Results

The Chinese efficient analyser is implemented in C++, providing a rapid and easy code-compile-train-test development cycle. In fact, many NLP systems suffer from a lack of software and computer-science engineering effort: running efficiency is key to performing numerous experiments, which, in turn, is key to improving performance. A system may have excellent performance on a given task, but if it takes long to compile and/or run on test data, the rate of improvement of that system will be contrained compared to that which can run very efficiently. Moreover, speed plays a critical role in many applications such as text mining.

All the experiments are implemented on a Pentium II/450MHZ PC. All the performances are measured in precisions, recalls and F-measures. Here, the precision (P) measures the number of correct units in the answer file over the total number of units in the answer file and the recall (R) measures the number of correct units in the answer file over the total number of units in the key file while F-measure is the weighted harmonic mean of precision and recall: $F = \frac{(\beta^2+1)RP}{\beta^2 R + P}$ with $\beta^2=1$.

6.1 Word Segmentation and POS Tagging

Table 2 shows the integrated word segmentation and POS tagging results on the Chinese tag bank PFR1.0 of 3.69M Chinese characters (1.12 Chinese Words) developed by Institute of Computational Linguistics at Beijing Univ. Here, 80% of the corpus is used as formal training data, another 10% as development data and remaining 10% as formal test data.

Function	P	R	F	Speed
Word Segment.	97.5	98.2	97.8	11,000 wps
POS Tagging	93.5	94.1	93.8	

Table 2: Performances of Word Segmentation and POS Tagging (wps: words per second)

The word segmentation corresponds to bracketing of the chunking model while POS tagging corresponds to bracketing and labelling. Table 2 shows that recall (P) is higher than precision (P). The main reason may be the existence of unknown words. In the Chinese efficient analyser, unknown words are segmented into individual Chinese characters. This makes the number of segmented words/POS tagged words in the system output higher than that in the correct answer.

6.2 Partial Parsing and Full Parsing

Table 3 shows the results of 1st-level partial parsing and full parsing, using the PARSEVAL evaluation methodology (Black et al 1991) on the UPENN Chinese Tree Bank of 100k words developed by Univ. of Penn. Here, 80% of the corpus is used as formal training data, another 10% as development data and remaining 10% as formal test data.

Function	P	R	F	Speed
Partial Parsing	85.1	82.5	83.8	4500 wps
Full Parsing	77.1	70.3	73.7	2100 wps

Table 3: Performances of 1st-level Partial Parsing and Full Parsing (wps: words per second)

Table 3 shows that the performances of partial parsing and full parsing are quite low, compared to those of state-of-art partial parsing and full parsing for the English language (Zhou et al 2000a; Collins 1997). The main reason behind is the small size of the training corpus used in our experiments. However, the Chinese PENN Tree Bank is the largest corpus we can find for partial parsing and full parsing. Therefore, developing a much larger Chinese tree bank (comparable to UPENN English Tree Bank) becomes an urgent task for the Chinese language processing community. Actually, the best individual system (Zhou et al 2000b) in CoNLL'2000 chunking shared task for the English language (Tjong et al 2000) used the same HMM-based tagging engine.

7 Conclusion

This paper presents an efficient analyser for the Chinese language, based on a HMM and a single engine -- HMM-based tagger. Experiments show that the analyser achieves state-of-art performance at very high speed, which can meet the requirement of speed-critical applications such as text mining.

Our future work includes:

- Syntactic analysis of the partial/full parsing results into a meaningful intermediate form.
- Research and development of Chinese named entity recognition using the same HMM-based tagger and its integration to the Chinese efficient analyser.

Acknowledgements

Thanks go to Institute of Computational Linguistics at Beijing Univ. and LDC at Univ. of Penn. for free research use of their Chinese Tag Bank and Chinese Tree Bank.

References

Abney S. 1997. Part-of-Speech Tagging and Partial Parsing. *Corpus-based Methods in Natural Language Processing*. Edited by Steve Young and Gerrit Bloothooft. Kluwer Academic Publishers, Dordrecht.

Bai ShuanHu, Li HaiZhou, Lin ZhiWei and Yuan BaoSheng. 1998. Building class-based language models with contextual statistics. *Proceedings of International Conference on Acoustics, Speech and Signal Processing (ICASSP'1998)*. pages173-176. Seattle, Washington, USA.

Black E. and Abney S. 1991. A Procedure for Quantitatively Comparing the Syntactic Coverage of English Grammars. *Proceedings of DRAPA workshop on Speech and Natural Language*. pages306-311. Pacific Grove, CA. DRAPA.

Collins M.J. 1997. Three Generative, Lexicalised Models for Statistical Parsing. *Proceedings of the Thirtieth-Five Annual Meeting of the Association for Computational Linguistics (ACL'97)*. pages184-191.

Feldman R. 1997. Text Mining - Theory and Practice. *Proceedings of the Third International Conference on Knowledge Discovery & Data Mining (KDD'1997)*.

Rabiner L. 1989. A Tutorial on Hidden Markov Models and Selected Applications in Speech Recognition. *IEEE 77(*2), pages257-285.

Tjong K.S. Erik and Buchholz S. 2000. Introduction to the CoNLL-2000 Shared Task: Chunking. *Proceedings of the Conference on Computational Language Learning (CoNLL'2000)*. Pages127-132. Lisbon, Portugal. 11-14 Sept.

Viterbi A.J. 1967. Error Bounds for Convolutional Codes and an Asymptotically Optimum Decoding Algorithm. *IEEE Transactions on Information Theory,* IT 13(2), 260-269.

Watson B. and Tsoi A Chunk. 1992. Second order Hidden Markov Models for speech recognition. *Proceeding of the Fourth Australian International Conference on Speech Science and Technology*. pages146-151.

Zhou GuoDong and Su Jian. 2000a. Error-driven HMM-based Chunk Tagger with Context-dependent Lexicon. *Proceedings of the Joint Conference on Empirical Methods on Natural Language Processing and Very Large Corpus (EMNLP/ VLC'2000)*. Hong Kong, 7-8 Oct.

Zhou GuoDong, Su Jian and Tey TongGuan. 2000b. Hybrid Text Chunking. *Proceedings of the Conference on Computational Language Learning (CoNLL'2000)*. Pages163-166. Lisbon, Portugal, 11-14 Sept.

Building A Large Chinese Corpus Annotated With Semantic Dependency

LI Mingqin
Department of Electronic Engineering,
Tsinghua University,
Beijing 100084, China
lmq@thsp.ee.tsinghua.edu.cn

LI Juanzi
Department of Computer Science and Technology,
Tsinghua University,
Beijing 100084, China
ljz@thsp.ee.tsinghua.edu.cn

DONG Zhendong
Research Centre of Computer & Language Engineering,
Chinese Academy of Sciences,
Beijing, 100084,China
dzd@keenage.com

WANG Zuoying
Department of Electronic Engineering,
Tsinghua University,
Beijing 100084, China
wzy-dee@tsinghua.edu.cn

LU Dajin
Department of Electronic Engineering,
Tsinghua University,
Beijing 100084, China
ludj@mail.tsinghua.edu.cn

Abstract

At present most of corpora are annotated mainly with syntactic knowledge. In this paper, we attempt to build a large corpus and annotate semantic knowledge with dependency grammar. We believe that words are the basic units of semantics, and the structure and meaning of a sentence consist mainly of a series of semantic dependencies between individual words. A 1,000,000-word-scale corpus annotated with semantic dependency has been built. Compared with syntactic knowledge, semantic knowledge is more difficult to annotate, for ambiguity problem is more serious. In the paper, the strategy to improve consistency is addressed, and congruence is defined to measure the consistency of tagged corpus.. Finally, we will compare our corpus with other well-known corpora.

1 Introduction

As basic research tools for investigators in natural language processing, large annotated corpora play an important role in investigating diverse language phenomena, building statistical language models, evaluating and comparing kinds of parsing models. At present most of corpora are annotated mainly with syntactic knowledge, though some function tags are added to annotate semantic knowledge. For example, the Penn Treebank (Marcus et al., 1993) was annotated with skeletal syntactic structure, and many syntactic parsers were evaluated and compared on the corpus. For Chinese, some corpora annotated with phrase structure also have been built, for instance the Penn Chinese Treebank (Xia et al., 2000) and Sina Corpus (Huang and Chen, 1992). A syntactic annotation scheme based on dependency was proposed by (Lai and Huang, 2000), and a small corpus was built for testing. However, very limited work has been done with annotation semantic knowledge in all languages. From 1999, Berkeley started FrameNet project (Baker et al., 1998), which produced the frame-semantic descriptions of several thousand English lexical items and backed up these description with semantically annotated attestations from contemporary English corpus. Although few corpora annotated with semantic knowledge are available now, there are some valuable lexical databases describing the lexical semantics in dictionary form, for example English WordNet (Miller et al., 1993) and Chinese HowNet (Dong and Dong, 2001).

For Chinese, many attentions have been naturally paid to researches on semantics, because Chinese is a meaning-combined language, its syntax is very flexible, and semantic rules are more stable than syntactic rules. For instance, in Chinese it is very pervasive that more than one part-of -speeches a word has, and a word does not have tense or voice flectional transition under different tenses or voices. Nevertheless, no large Chinese corpus annotated with semantic knowledge has ever been built at present. In Semantic Dependency Net (SDN), we try to describe deeper semantic dependency relationship between individual words and represent the meaning and structure of a sentence by these dependencies.

Compared with syntactic corpus, it is more difficult to build a semantic corpus, for the granularity of semantic knowledge is smaller, and behaviors of different words differ more greatly. Furthermore, ambiguity in semantics is commoner. Different people may have different opinions on understanding the same word in the same sentence, and even the same people may have different opinions on understanding the same word in different occasions. In this paper, we emphatically discuss the strategy to improve the consistency of Semantic Dependency Net.

The paper is organized as follows. The tagging scheme is discussed in Section 2, which describes the semantic dependency grammar and the tag set of semantic relations. In section 3, we describe the tagging task. First, we briefly introduce the text of this corpus, which has been tagged with semantic classes. Second, we describe the strategy to improve consistency during tagging and checking. At last, congruence is defined to measure the consistency of tagged corpus. In Section 4, we briefly introduce some of the works on the corpus, and indicate the directions that the project is likely to take in the future. Finally, we compare SDN corpus with some other well-known corpora.

Chinese: 杨/Dd15 博士/Ae13 近年来/Ca11 十分/Ka01 重视/Gb21 其/Aa04 发明/Hc05 成果/Da14 的/Kd01 推广/Ie01 使用/Hj28

English: These years, Doctor Yang pays a lot of attention to the popularization and application of his invention.

(a)

Modifier		HeadWord		Semantic Relation
Index	Word	Index	Word	
0	杨/Yang	1	博士/Doctor	限定/Restrictive
1	博士/Doctor	4	重视/pay attention to	经验者/Experiencer
2	近年来/these years	4	重视/pay attention to	时间/Time
3	十分/a lot	4	重视/pay attention to	程度/Degree
4	重视/pay attention to	-1	-1	核心成分/Kernel word
5	其/his	7	成果/production	限定/Restrictive
6	发明/invention	7	成果/production	限定/Restrictive
7	成果/production	9	推广/popularization	内容/Content
8	的/of	7	成果/product	“的”字依存/ 'De' dependency
9	推广/popularization	4	重视/pay attention to	目标/Target
10	使用/application	9	推广/popularization	连接/Connection

(b)

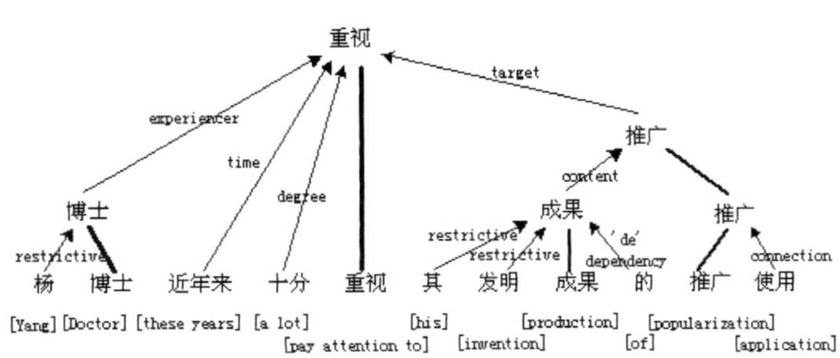

(c)

Figure 1: A sample sentence from the corpus. (a) The sentence tagged with semantic classes; (b) The sentence annotated with semantic dependency; (c) The semantic dependency tree of the sentence, headwords are linked with bold lines, and modifier words are linked with arrow lines.

2 The tagging scheme of semantic dependency

2.1 Semantic dependency grammar

Like Word grammar (Hudson, 1998), We believe that words are the basic units of semantics, and the structure and meaning of a sentence consist mainly of semantic dependencies between individual words. So a sentence could be annotated with a series of semantic dependency relations (Li Juanzi and Wang, 2002). Let S be a sentence composed of words tagged with semantic classes, $S = \{<w_1, s_1>, <w_2, s_2>, \cdots, <w_n, s_n>\}$. A list of semantic dependency relations is defined as: $SRL = \{SR(1), SR(2), \cdots, SR(n)\}$, where $SR(i) = (h_i, r_i)$. SR stands for ' semantic relation'. $SR(i) = (h_i, r_i)$ states that the h_i -th word is the headword to the i-th word with semantic relation r_i. If the word j is the root, $SR(j)$ is defined to be (-1, "kernel word").

For example, a sample sentence from the corpus is shown in Figure 1 (a). The semantic dependency relation list and semantic dependency tree are shown in Figure 1 (b) and (c) respectively. More samples will be seen in Appendix A.

In semantic dependency grammar, the headword of sentence represents the main meaning of the whole sentence, and the headword of constituent represents the main meaning of the constituent. In a compound constituent, the headword inherits the headword of the head sub-constituent, and headwords of other sub-constituents are dependent on that headword. We select the word that can represent the meaning of the constituent to the most extent as headword. For example, the verb is the headword of verb phrase, the object is the headword of preposition phrase, and the location noun is the headword of the location phrase.

At the same time, semantic dependency relations do not damage the phrase structure, that is, all words in the same phrase are in the same subtree whose root is the headword of the phrase. Therefore, when tagging dependency relations, semantic and syntactic restrictions are both taken into account. The structures of dependency tree are mainly determined by syntactic restrictions, and the semantic relations are mainly determined by semantic restrictions. For example, in Figure 1 the phrase "其发明成果的"(of his invention production) modifies the phrase "推广使用" (popularization and application) in syntax, so the word "推广" (popularization) governs the word "成果" (production). However, the production is the content of the action popularization in semantics, so the relation between them is "content".

Our tagging scheme is more concise compared with phrase structure grammar, in which the boundaries of all phrases have to be marked and the corresponding labels have to be tagged. In the semantic dependency grammar, phrases are implicit, but play no part in grammar. More emphasis is paid to the syntactic and semantic functions of the word, especially of the headword.

2.2 The dependency relation tag set

The dependency relation tag set mainly consists of three kinds of relations: semantic relations, syntactic relations and special relations. Semantics is the main content of this corpus, so semantic relations are in the majority, and syntactic relations are used to annotate the special structures that do not have exact sense in terms of semantics. In addition, there are two special relations: "kernel word" is to indicate the headword of a sentence, and "failure" is to indicate the word that cannot be annotated with dependency relations because the sentence is not completed.

The selections of semantic relations were referred to HowNet (Dong and Dong, 2001). HowNet is a lexical database, which describes the relations among words and concepts as a network. In HowNet, senventy-six semantic relations are defined to describe all relations among various concepts, and most of them describe the semantic relations between action and other concepts. With these semantic relations, necessary role frame is further defined. The roles in the necessary role frame must take part in the action in real word, while these roles may not appear in the same sentence. Hong Kong Technology University has successfully tagged a news corpus with the necessary role frame (Yan and Tan, 1999), which shows that these roles can describe all semantic phenomena in real texts.

In order to make tagging task easier and the corpus more suitable for statistical learning, we have pared down some relations in HowNet and got fifty-nine semantic relations. Some HowNet relations seldom occurred in the corpus, and their semantic functions are somewhat similar, so they are merged. Some relations are ambiguous, for example "degree" and "range". In order to improve the consistency, we also merge these two relations.

Semantic relations can describe the relations between notional words, but they cannot annotate function words in some special phrase structures. So nine syntactic relations are added.

The tag set is listed in table 1. Full definition of each dependency relation can be seen in (Li Mingqin et al., 2002).

Semantic Relations (59)	Relevant /关系主体	Possessor /领有者	Existent /存现体	Experiencer /经验者	Agent /施事	Descriptive /描写体
	Possession /占有物	Patient /受事	PartOfTouch /触及部件	Content /内容	Isa /类指	PartOf /部分
	Whole /整体	Result /结果	Target /目标	Cost /代价	ResultEvent /结果事件	EventProcess /事件过程
	Succeeding /接续	Accompaniment /伴随	Modifier /描述	Restrictive /限定	Quantity /数量	Appositive /同位语
	Degree /程度	Manner /方式	Frequency /频率	Times /动量	Scope /范围	Comment /评论
	Time /时间	TimeIni /起始时间	TimeFin /终止时间	DurationAfterEvent /后延时段	Duration /进程时段	Time /时间
	TimeIni /起始时间	TimeFin /终止时间	Duration /进程时段	DurationAfterEvent /后延时段	TimeRange /时距	Location /处所
	LocationIni /原处所	LocationFin /终处所	LocationThru /通过处所	StateIni /原状态	StateFin /终状态	Partner /相伴体
	Contrast /参照体	ContentCompare /比较内容	QuantityCompare /比较量	Means /手段	Instrument /工具	Material /材料
	Source /来源	Cause /原因	Purpose /目的	Accoudingto /根据	Direction /方向	Condition /条件
	Concession /让步	Besides /递进	Conjuncture /并列	Except /除了		
Syntacitc Relations (9)	'De' dependency /"的"字依存	…' Shi' …' de' /…是…的依存	Connection /连接依存	LocationPreposition /方位词依存	Tense&Voice / 时态语态依存	Mood /语气依存
	Correlative /关联词依存	Trend /趋向动词依存	Preposition /介词依存			
Special relaions (2)	Kernel word /核心成分	Failure /依存失败				

Table 1: The dependency relation tag set.

3 The tagging and checking of semantic dependency relations

3.1 Texts of corpus

A part of Tsinghua Corpus (Zhang, 1999) annotated with semantic classes was selected as raw data of our corpus. The texts of Tsinghua corpus come from the news of *People's Daily*. The selected part consists of about 1,000,000 words, approximately 1,500,000 Chinese characters. Its domain covers the politics, economy, science, sports, etc. The proportion of different domains is shown in figure 2.

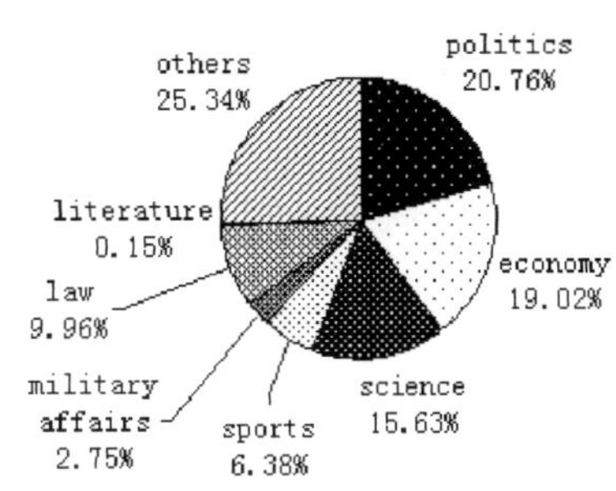

Figure 2: The proportion of texts of different domains

Because Chinese is not written with word delimiters, first the text was segmented into words according to the lexicon of 100,000 words. Then each word was tagged with semantic class, whose definition follows *Tongyici Cilin (Dictionary of Synonymous Words)* (Mei et al., 1983).The semantic classes are organized as a tree, which has three levels. The first level contains 18 classes, the second level contains 101 classes, and the third level contains 1434 classes. These hierarchical semantic classes are helpful to express the superordinate and subordinate information among words.

All the text in Tsinghua Corpus was segmented, tagged and checked manually. Since the corpus was built in 1998, it has been used for several years in the researches on automatic sense tagging and class-based language model. Now, the accuracy of tagging system has reached to 92.7% (Zhang, 1999).

3.2 Tagging tools

A computer-aided tagging tool was developed to assist annotators in tagging semantic dependency relations. To tag a word, annotator only need to select its headword and their relation by clicking mouse. After a sentence has been tagged, the corresponding semantic dependency tree will be displayed to help annotators check the sentence structure.

Two additional functions are also provided in the tool: dependency grammar checking and on-line reference of HowNet. Dependency grammar checking guarantees that the tagged sentence conforms to four axioms of dependency grammar (Robinson, 1970):

(a) One and only one element is independent;
(b) All others depend directly on some element;
(c) No element depends directly on more than one other
(d) If A depends directly on B and some element C intervenes between them (in linear order of string), then C depends directly on A or B or some other intervening element.

During annotating procedure, the tool checks whether the tagged relation conforms to dependency grammar, and prompts the grammar errors in time.

On-line HowNet reference facilitates looking up semantic knowledge and helps to ensure the consistency of tagging. Semantic knowledge is more difficult to grasp than syntactic knowledge. Even for annotators majored in linguistics, it is too difficult to grasp all semantic relations of words only after a short-term training. And different opinions about relations will lead to the inconsistency. However, HowNet defines the necessary role frame for verbs frequently used in real world, and these roles can be mapped to our semantic relations, so HowNet has set up a detail annotating manual for us. For example, in HowNet the role frame of the verb "重视" (pay attention to) is defined as {experiencer, target, cause}. With basic semantic knowledge, annotators can easily identify the relation between "博士" (doctor) and "重视" (pay attention to) as "experiencer", and the relation between "推广" (popularization) and "重视" (pay attention to) as "target". We integrated the on-line reference of HowNet to the tool, which has been proved in practice to be very helpful in improving the consistency and speed of tagging.

3.3 Checking

Our work is the first attempt to annotate semantic dependency relations on a large corpus, and no prior knowledge is available, so the whole corpus is tagged manually. But in checking procedure we have learned some experience and knowledge, which should be used as possible as we can. So we adopt two checking modes. In the first mode—manual checking, checkers correct all errors by hand; in second mode—semiautomatic checking, computer-aided checking tool automatically searches for the errors and then human checkers correct them, and it means checkers need to read only about 1/3 or less questionable sentences.

In semiautomatic checking, all the files are scanned automatically to search for three kinds of errors:

1. To check whether the semantic relations conform to the necessary role frame defined by HowNet.
2. To check whether the relations conform to error rules. Some errors frequently occurred during manual checking. For example, the relation between words "再/又"(again) and a verb must be "frequency", but in incorrect sentences it was tagged otherwise. We summarized these errors, and wrote them as rules.
3. To check whether the score of semantic dependency model (equation 1) is below some threshold. A simple semantic dependency model was built on the corpus. Although the

score of tagged sentence cannot be the criterion of correctness, at least it can show the consistency of a kind of sentences.

$$P(T) = \prod_{k=1}^{n} P(w_k, h(w_k), r_k) \qquad (1)$$

where n is the length of the sentence, w_k is the k-th word in the sentence, $h(w_k)$ is the headword to w_k with semantic relation r_k.

The semiautomatic checking interface could prompt some possible errors, but the necessary role frames defined by HowNet may be not complete, the error rules may be not restrict, and the score of semantic structure model may be not credible. The prompted errors may be false, so the decision whether the error is true and how to correct it must be made by human checkers. This is the reason why it is called semiautomatic checking.

The checking procedure consisted of five rounds of selective manual checking and a round of semiautomatic checking. In tagging procedure, we dispatched the raw files to annotators in a group of 10 files. In a round of selective manual checking, one file in every group was selected to check. All corrections were recorded by the checking interface, and the reasons for corrections were explained by the checker. If too many error sentences occurred in the selected file, all files in this group needed correcting by original annotators after referring to the corrected sentences and their explanations.

After four rounds of selective manual checking, most of errors have been corrected, but there were still some files that have not been checked or corrected. We semi-automatically checked all files. Finally, the fifth round of manual checking was taken.

Fourteen graduate studentstook part in annotating, most of them are majored in linguistics. Seven excellent students were elected for checking among annotators, and they were not allowed to check their own files. According to our statistics, the average speed to annotate by hand is about 1.15 hours per 100 sentences; the average speed to check by hand is about 0.25 hours per 100 sentences; and the speed to check half automatically is about 0.08 hours per 100 sentences. In manual checking procedure, there were 50% of all files that were manually checked, 75.45% that were turned to the original annotator to correct. (When counting the files corrected by original annotators, if the same group of files were corrected in two rounds, we count them as two groups.) And all files were checked in semiautomatic checking procedure.

3.4 Congruence

Under the given annotating manual, consistency is an important criterion to evaluate the corpus. If tagged sentence is independently checked and passed by several experts, the annotation may be credible; otherwise, if some experts do not agree to the annotation, it may be not credible enough. If several experts evaluate tagged sentences independently, the inter-checker agreement is defined as the measure of consistency.

Relation Congruence (RCn) and Sentence Congruence (SCn) are defined. RCn is the number of relations for which n judges agreed, divided by the total number of relations, in which n can be 1, 2, 3. SCn is the number of sentences for which n judges agreed, divided by the total number of sentences, in which n can be 1, 2, 3. For example, if three experts take part in evaluating, RC3 is the percentage of the annotated relation that all three experts are agree to one annotation, and SC1 is the percentage of the annotated sentence for which all three judges' opinions are different from one another.

Before checking, 500 sentences were evaluated by three experts. After checking, 1,400 sentences were evaluated by three experts. In order to balance the coverage and workload of evaluation, another 4,900 sentences were evaluated by two experts. The congruency is shown in table 2.

	RC3	RC2	RC1
Unchecked(500)	90.78%	8.65%	0.57%
Checked(1400)	96.24%	3.64%	0.12%
Checked(4900)	---------	97.56%	2.44%
	SC3	SC2	SC1
Unchecked(500)	69.20%	23.00%	7.80%
Checked(1400)	83.43%	14.07%	2.50%
Checked(4900)	----------	89.10%	10.90%

Table 2: the congruency of data before and after checking

The results show that the quality of corpus is improved greatly after checking, and high relation/sentence congruency of 96.24%/83.43% among three experts was satisfactory.

4 Future works

Although the tagging task is completed, much further work will be needed. A user-friendly, interactive interface for corpus investigation is needed to search the example sentences and to maintain the tagged data. Inconsistencies still exist in the corpus, and it may become more apparent with time. How to reduce inconsistencies is a challenging problem. The role frame of verbs can to be extracted from the corpus, which could be integrated with HowNet to build a larger database. The correlation frame of nouns, which can represent the order of modifier phrases, can be extracted, too.

More statistical researches could be carried out on the corpus. Researches on Chinese information structure have been carried out on the corpus (You et al., 2002). Auto-tagging the semantic dependency structure of this kind is under going. And we hope the SDN corpus could be exploited in more areas: speech recognition, natural language understanding, machine translation, information extraction, and so on.

5 Comparison with other corpora

Our Corpus is compared with other famous corpora for English and Chinese in table 3.

Corpus	Languge	Content	Scale	Institution
SDN	Chinese	Semantic dependency	1,000,000 words	Tsinghua
FrameNet	English	Frame Semantics	250,000 sentences	Berkeley
TreeBank(C)	Chinese	Phrase structure	500,000 words	UPenn

Table 3: Comparison with other corpora

The FrameNet is annotated with semantic knowledge, which emphasizes on describing the frame and scene of several thousands verbs. They first build a frame database, which contains descriptions of each frame of the verbs, and then annotated example sentences of these frames. Unlike FrameNet, we first annotated semantic dependency relations of sentences according to HowNet, and hope to extract frames from the corpus later. FrameNet only described the frame of verbs, while from Semantic Dependency Net the correlation frame of nouns and verbs could be automatically learned by machine.

References

Collin F. Baker, Charles J. Fillmore, John B. Lowe. 1998. The Berkeley FrameNet Project, *Proceedings of the COLING-ACL,* Montreal, Canada.

Zhendong Dong and Qiang Dong. 2001. Construction of a Knowledge System and its Impact on Chinese Research, *Contemporary Linguistics*, 3: 33-44, Beijing.

Chu-Ren Huang and Keh-jiann Chen. 1992. A Chinese Corpus for Linguistics Research. *In the Proceedings of the COLING.* 1214-1217. Nantes, France

Richard Hudson. 1998. Word Grammars, Dependency and Valency, *An International Handbook of Contemporary Research.* Edited by Vilmos Agel, Ludwig M. Eichinger, etc. Berlin, Walter de Gruyter.

Tom B. Y. Lai and Changning Huang. 2000. Dependency-based syntactic analysis of Chinese and Annotation of Parsed Corpus. *The 38th Annual Meeting of the Association for Computational Linguistics,* Hong Kong.

Juanzi Li and Zuoying Wang. 2002. Chinese Statistcal Parser Based on Semantic Dependecies, Tsinghua Science and Technology, 7(6): 591-595.

Mingqin Li, Fang You, Juanzi Li, Zuoying Wang. 2002. Manual of Tagging Semantic Dependency (third Version), Technical Report, Tsinghua University, Department of Electronic Engineering.

Mitchell P. Marcus, Beatrice Santorini, Mary Ann Marcinkiewicz. 1993. Building a large annotated corpus of English: The Penn Treebank. *Computational Linguistics*, 19(2): 313-330.

Jiaju Mei, Yiming Zhu and YunQi Gao, Yin Hongxiang, Edited. 1983. *Tongyici Cilin (Dictionary of Synonymous Words)*, Shanghai Cishu Publisher.

George A. Miller, Richard Beckwith, Christiane Fellbaum, Derek Gross, and Katherine Miller. 1993. Introduction to WordNet: An On-line Lexical Database, *Five papers on WordNet, CSL Report 43*, Cognitive Science Laboratory. Princeton University.

Jane J. Robinson. 1970. Dependency Structures and Transformation Rules. *Lanuage,* 46: 259-285.

Fei Xia, Martha Palmer, Nianwen Xue, Mary Ellen Okurowski, John Kovarik, Fu-Dong Chiou, Shizhe Huang, Tony Kroch, and Mitch Marcus. 2000. *Proceedings of the second International Conference on*

Language Resources and Evaluation (LREC 2000), Athens, Greece.

Guowei Yan and Huimin Tan. 1999. Corpus Annotating Mannual Based on HowNet (Jiyu ZhiWang de Yuliao Biaozhu Shouce), Technical Report, the Department of computer science, Hong Kong University of Sience of Techonolgy. http://www.keenage.com

Fang You, Juanzi Li and Zuoying Wang. 2002. An approach Based HowNet for Extracting Chinese Message Structure, *Computer Engineering and Applications*, 38: 56-58.

Jianping Zhang. 1999. A Study of Language Model and Understanding Algorithm for Large Vocabulary Spontaneous Speech Recognition. Doctor Dissertation, The Department of Electronic Engineering, Tsinghua University, Beijing.

Appendix A. samples from corpus

Sentence 1: 其中 提到 东京 上野 的 樱花 烂漫 的 时节

0 其中	1 提到	范围/Scope
1 提到	-1 -1	核心成分/Kernel word
2 东京	3 上野	限定/Restrictive
3 上野	8 时节	限定/Restrictive
4 的	3 上野	"的"字依存/'De' dependency
5 樱花	6 烂漫	描写体/Descriptive
6 烂漫	8 时节	限定/Restrictive
7 的	6 烂漫	"的"字依存/'De' dependency
8 时节	1 提到	内容/Content

Sentence 2: 在 北京 虽 也 见过 天坛 公园 自 日本 移植 的 樱花

0 在	1 北京	介词依存/Preposition
1 北京	4 见过	处所/Location
2 虽	4 见过	关联词依存/Correlative
3 也	4 见过	评论/Comment
4 见过	-1 -1	核心成分/Kernel word
5 天坛	6 公园	限定/Restrictive
6 公园	11 樱花	限定/Restrictive
7 自	8 日本	介词依存/Preposition
8 日本	9 移植	原处所/LocationIni
9 移植	11 樱花	受事/Patient
10 的	9 移植	"的"字依存/'De' dependency
11 樱花	4 见过	内容/Content

Sentence 3: 诗集 共 收入 年轻 诗人 戈麦 一 百 三 十 多 首 代表 其 各个 时期 的 优秀 作品

0 诗集	2 收入	施事/Agent
1 共	2 收入	评论/Comment
2 收入	-1 -1	核心成分/Kernel word
3 年轻	4 诗人	描述/Modifier
4 诗人	18 作品	限定/Restrictive
5 戈麦	4 诗人	同位语/Appositive
6 一	11 首	数量/Quantity
7 百	6 一	连接依存/Connection
8 三	6 一	连接依存/Connection
9 十	6 一	连接依存/Connection
10 多	6 一	连接依存/Connection
11 首	18 作品	数量/Quantity
12 代表	18 作品	关系主体/Relevant
13 其	15 时期	限定/Restrictive
14 各个	15 时期	限定/Restrictive
15 时期	12 代表	类指/Isa
16 的	12 代表	"的"字依存/'De' dependency
17 优秀	18 作品	描述/Modifier
18 作品	2 收入	受事/Patient

Sentence 4: 相信 会 得到 喜爱 中国 传统 文化 的 人士 青睐

0 相信	-1 -1	核心成分/Kernel word
1 会	2 得到	评论/Comment
2 得到	0 相信	内容/Content
3 喜爱	8 人士	经验者/Experiencer
4 中国	6 文化	限定/Restrictive
5 传统	6 文化	限定/Restrictive
6 文化	3 喜爱	目标/Target
7 的	3 喜爱	"的"字依存/'De' dependency
8 人士	9 青睐	限定/Restrictive
9 青睐	2 得到	占有物/Possession

Sentence 5: 在 如 镜 似 毯 的 滩涂 上

0 在	6 滩涂	介词依存/Preposition
1 如	6 滩涂	关系主体/Relevant
2 镜	1 如	参照体/Contrast
3 似	1 如	连接依存/Coordination
4 毯	3 似	参照体/Contrast
5 的	1 如	"的"字依存/'De' dependency
6 滩涂	-1 -1	核心成分/Kernel word
7 上	6 滩涂	方位词依存/LocationPreposition

News-Oriented Automatic Chinese Keyword Indexing

Li Sujian[1] lisujian@pku.edu.cn

Wang Houfeng[1] wanghf@pku.edu.cn

Yu Shiwen[1] Yusw@pku.edu.cn

Xin Chengsheng[2] csxin@peoplemail.com.cn

[1]Institute of Computational Linguistics, Peking University, 100871
[2]The Information Center of PEOPLE'S DAILY, 100733

Abstract

In our information era, keywords are very useful to information retrieval, text clustering and so on. News is always a domain attracting a large amount of attention. However, the majority of news articles come without keywords, and indexing them manually costs highly. Aiming at news articles' characteristics and the resources available, this paper introduces a simple procedure to index keywords based on the scoring system. In the process of indexing, we make use of some relatively mature linguistic techniques and tools to filter those meaningless candidate items. Furthermore, according to the hierarchical relations of content words, keywords are not restricted to extracting from text. These methods have improved our system a lot. At last experimental results are given and analyzed, showing that the quality of extracted keywords are satisfying.

1 Introduction

With more and more information flowing into our life, it is very important to lead people to gain more important information in time as short as possible. Keywords are a good solution, which give a brief summary of a document's content. With keywords, people can quickly find what they are most interested in and read them carefully. That will save us a lot of time. In addition, keywords are also useful to the research of information retrieval, text clustering, and topic search [Frank 1999]. Manually indexing keywords will cost highly. Thus, automatically indexing keywords from text is of great interests.

News is always the main domain that people pay a large amount of attention to. Unfortunately, only a small fraction of documents in this field have keywords. However, compared to unrestricted text, news articles are relatively easy to extract keywords from, because they have the following characteristics. Firstly, a news document is always short in length, and usually, only important words or phrases repeat. Secondly, as a rule, the purpose of news articles is to illustrate an event or a thing for readers. Then this kind of articles usually place more emphasis on some name entities such as persons, places, organizations and so on. Lastly, important content often occurs the first time in the title, or in the anterior part of the whole text, especially the first paragraph or the first sentence in every paragraph. These characteristics will help us in keywords indexing.

Several methods have been proposed for extracting English keywords from text. For example, Witten[1999] adopted Naïve Bayes techniques, and Turney[1999] combined decision trees and genetic algorithm in his system. These systems achieved satisfying results. However, they need a large amount of training documents with keywords, which are just what we are in need of now. For the Chinese language, some researchers adopt the structure of PAT tree and make use of mutual information to obtain keywords [Chien 1997, Yang 2002]. Unfortunately, the construction of PAT tree will cost a lot of space and time. In this paper, aiming at the characteristics of news-oriented articles, resources and techniques of current situation, we will introduce a simple procedure to index keywords from text. Section 2 will describe the architecture of the whole system. In section 3, we will introduce every module in detail, including how to obtain candidate keywords, how to filter out the meaningless items, and how to score possible keyword candidates according to their feature values. In section 4, experimental results will be given and analyzed. At last, we will end with the conclusion.

2 System Overview

Keyword indexing can also be called keyword extraction. The definition of a keyword is not restricted to one word in our conception. Here, a keyword can be seen as a Chinese character string, which might consist of more than one Chinese word. These character strings can summarize the content of the document they are in.

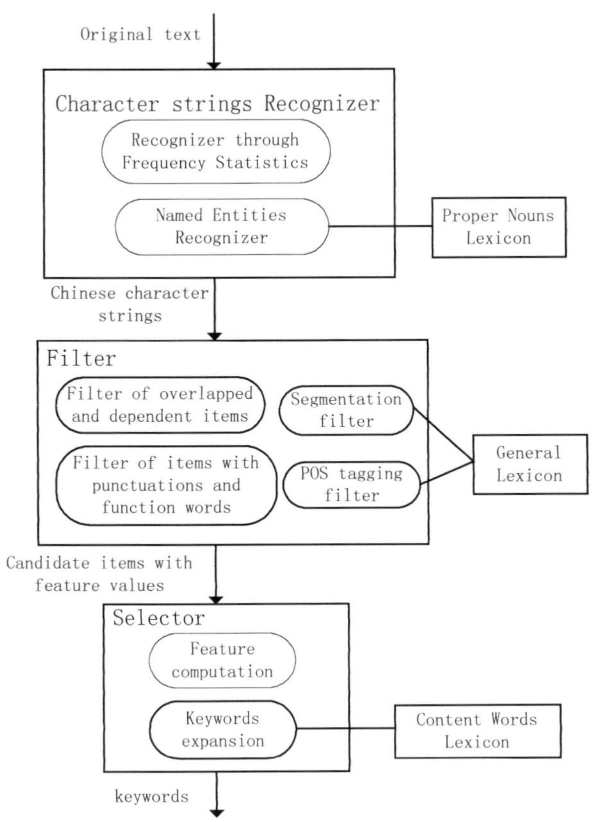

Fig. 1. System Architecture

Aiming at the task of keywords indexing, our system is designed and composed of three modules. As in figure 1, the first module is to recognize some Chinese character strings according to their frequency, and pick out those named entities in the text as the candidate keywords. The second module is a filter to remove all the meaningless character strings from the set of candidates. And the third module is a selector, which evaluates every candidate according to its feature values and choose from the candidate set those keywords with higher score. The higher score a character string has, the more content it will cover of the article it is in.

In our system, there are three kinds of lexicons. The lexicon of proper nouns is used to recognize named entities. The general lexicon includes Chinese words in common use, which is adopted for the segmentation and POS tagging of the text. And the lexicon of content words is used to expand the set of keywords. They will be introduced in detail in the following section.

3 System Design

3.1 Recognizer Module

It can be seen that one document is composed of a set of character strings. Every character string has its frequency in the document. In general, those character strings that occur several times can reflect the topic of the document. So, we take them out as keyword candidates. In addition, named entities, such as person names, place names, organizations, translation terms, titles of person and so on, are usually very important for the document without reference to their frequency. They will also be picked out from the text by named entities recognizer and input into the filter module with other character strings.

Unlike English, there are no explicit word boundaries in Chinese sentences, which makes it especially difficult to tell whether a character string is composed of one word or more than one word. Due to this characteristic, we don't use a dictionary, but get those character strings only according to their frequency statistics. We set a threshold value as 2 for the Chinese character strings considering the length of news documents. Suppose that a character string is $c_1c_2 \ldots c_n$, and $f(c_1c_2 \ldots c_n)$ represents its frequency, then we extract $c_1c_2 \ldots c_n$ from text only if $f(c_1c_2 \ldots c_n)$ equals to or is more than 2. That is, only a character string occurs two or more than two times, it can be selected as a candidate keyword.

There are two kinds of named entities. The first are those which have rules of composition, mainly Chinese names and foreign terms. They can be recognized with statistical and rule-based methods combined. Chinese names are composed of family names and first names, whose lengths are respectively 1 or 2 Chinese characters. Furthermore, there is a relatively stable set of family names, which often provide the anchor to search a name. For foreign terms, there are a relatively set of Chinese characters which are generally used as translation characters. Due to the limitation of the paper's length, we don't introduce the process of recognition in detail here. The other kind of named entities is mainly composed of proper nouns which represent names of places, organizations, person titles, etc. They often occur in news documents, but don't have rules of composition. Thus, we collect such words into our proper nouns lexicon. Then the module can find these named entities through looking up in this lexicon.

3.2 Filter Module

So far, Chinese character strings are generated only through frequency statistics. Thus, some of them stand out just because of simple repetition and are probably not meaningful units of language. We need to filter out those meaningless items. As in figure 1, we adopt four kinds of filters in filter module. They work as follows.

(1) Filter of Overlapped and Dependent Items
For two character strings S1 and S2, with S1 as a substring of S2, and the frequency of S1 is equal to that of S2, then S1 is overlapped by S2. In fact, we can set a threshold t_d for f(S1)-f(S2), where the function f(.) represents the frequency of some character string. If the value of f(S1)-f(S2) is less than t_d, then the string S1 is dependent on S2. Here, the overlapped and dependent substring will be removed from the candidate set.

(2) Filter of Items with Punctuations and Function words
The recognizer module treats equally all symbols in the text, such as Chinese characters and punctuations, etc. Thus when conducting the process of frequency statistics, for a character string, there might exist some punctuations and function words such as '。', '、', '了', '着', etc. These punctuations and function words usually occur in the head or tail of a character string. It's evident that such character strings can't serve as keywords of an article, and they should be deleted from the candidate set.

(3) Segmentation Filter
We find the first occurrence position of every candidate keyword and get the sentence at the position. Then the sentence is segmented. According to the segmented result, we can verify whether the character string is meaningful. First of all, we get the segmentation result of the character string in the segmented sentence. Suppose the character string $c_i \ldots c_j$ in the original text with the sentence $c_1c_2 \ldots c_{i-1}c_i \ldots c_jc_{j+1} \ldots c_n$ as its context, if the segmentation tool segments $c_{i-1}c_i$ or c_jc_{j+1} into one word, then $c_i \ldots c_j$ will not be regarded as an integrated unit. That is, this item will be seen as meaningless and filtered out from the set of candidate keywords. Here we don't adopt the method of conducting frequency statistics of words after segmentation, but use segmentation tool after frequency statistics of character strings. There are some reasons. Above all, although the segmentation technique is relatively mature, its precision is still not high enough. Then, for the same character string, its segmentation results often differ in different sentences. Thus, it's difficult to compute the frequency of a character string precisely. Furthermore, now we only need to segment one sentence for a candidate keyword. That will save us a great deal of time.

(4) POS Filter
Because keywords provide a brief summary for one document, they should be words or phrases that represent some meaning units such as nouns and noun phrases. Therefore, a single word whose part of speech is preposition, adverb, adjective, or conjunctive is filtered out. At the same time, verb phrases, adjective phrases, preposition phrases are also excluded from the candidate set. The same as segmentation filter, we only do the POS tagging for the sentence where every candidate keyword occurs the first time. If a candidate item is made of more than one word, it will have a sequence of POS tags according to which we can assign a phrase category. The POS tags or phrase categories are the basis for POS filtering.

Only conducting frequency statistics of character strings can't refine the candidate set well, and we utilize the relatively mature linguistic segmentation and POS tagging techniques so that we can further improve the quality of the candidate keywords. Here, the general lexicon with about 60,000 Chinese words is applied to the processes of segmentation and POS tagging.

3.3 Selector Module

After several filtering, now we can get a reduced set of candidate keywords. Most character strings in the set are meaningful and reflect the content of the document to some extent. For every candidate now, we adopt several features to describe it. The features include frequency, length, position of the first occurrence, part of speech and whether it is a proper noun or in a pair of specific punctuations, as in table 1. At the same time, through the processing of several linguistic tools in filter module, we can assign a value to every feature in every candidate item.

feature	meaning of feature
freq	Frequency of an item
len	Length of an item
is_noun	Whether an item is a noun phrase
in_title	Whether the first occurrence of an item is in the title of one document
in_seg1	Whether the first occurrence of an item is in the first paragraph of one document
is_proper	Whether an item is a proper noun, for example: person name, organization, translation term, place name, title of a person etc.
in_sign	Whether an item is bracketed by a pair of specific punctuations such as ‘《》’ and ‘“ ”’.

Table 1. Features of candidate keywords

We can find that the candidate set is still too large to select from it the keywords. Then we will conduct feature calculation to refine the candidate set. We have known that every candidate item has a feature-value set. These feature values are our basis to evaluate every candidate item. We compute a score for every candidate keyword through the module of feature computation. The higher the score, the more relevant the candidate is to the document.

We compute the percentage how much manually indexed keywords of different lengths cover in the set of automatically generated candidates. As in figure 2, Length represents the length of keywords and percentage denotes the corresponding percentage that keywords of this length are in the set. The higher the percentage, the more likely the keywords of this length are to be selected. Therefore, we can make a conclusion that the score of a candidate is directly proportional to the percentage of its length. Then we can acquire the relation between score and length of a candidate. At the same time, we can also see that the score is directly proportional to a candidate's frequency. In addition, score is relevant to other features in table 1. Thus, we get formula 1, as following.

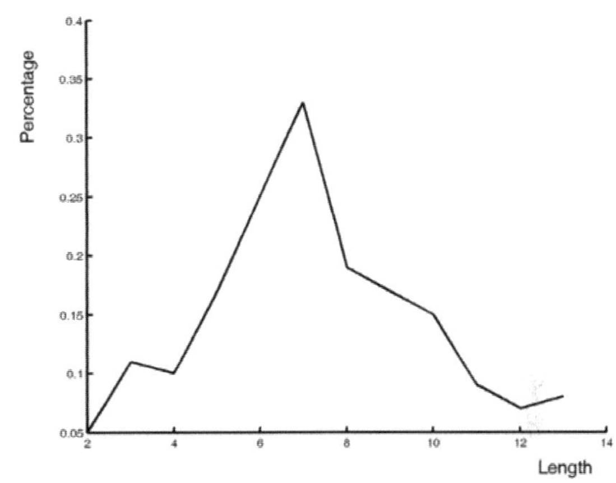

Fig. 2. Relations between Percentage Selected and Length of Keywords

$$score(ck) = Freq(ck) * \ln \frac{100}{(len(ck) - 7.1)^2} * \prod_{fi \in F} w_i^{fi(ck)} \qquad (1)$$

$$f_i(ck) = \begin{cases} 1 & \text{if ck satisfies the } i^{th} \text{ feature} \\ 0 & \text{otherwise} \end{cases}$$

Where ck represents a candidate keyword, the function freq(ck) gets the frequency of ck, len(ck) represents its length, that is, the number of Chinese characters every item includes. F represents all the binary features of a candidate keyword as in table 1. Every feature except the features of freq and len are denoted by f_i. $f_i(ck)$ is a binary function and its value is 0 or 1. If a candidate item ck satisfies the ith feature, then the value is set to 1, otherwise, it's set to 0. w_i is the corresponding weight of feature f_i. For features is_noun, in_title, in_seg1, is_proper and in_sign, we set their weights to 7, 13, 5, 11 and 3 respectively by experience. After each candidate keyword gets a score, we choose those whose scores rank higher as keywords.

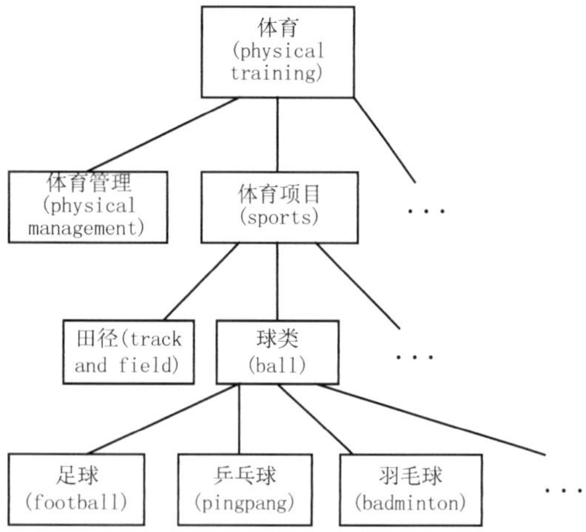

Fig. 3. A Sample Tree Structure of Content Words

Now the keywords we get are all selected from the original text. However, some keywords may express the content of the document, but they don't occur in the text. Therefore, we have constructed one list of content words with hierarchical relations as in figure 3. That is content words lexicon. The lexicon contains about 1,200 words which are often used as keywords. As the content words lexicon available now, we can look up in it and expand obtained keywords to a higher level, i.e., if a selected keyword has a parent in the lexicon, the parent word will be expanded as a keyword.

4 Experimental Results and Analysis

We select 37 news articles from China Daily as our testing material from which experts have manually extracted keywords. There are 23 articles about national politics, 10 articles of international politics, and 4 sports news articles. Here, we automatically extracted keywords from them and evaluated the results with the standard measures of precision and recall, which are defined as follows:

$$P = \frac{\text{number of genuine keywords recognized}}{\text{number of keywords indexing automatically}}$$

$$R = \frac{\text{number of genuine keywords recognized}}{\text{number of keywords indexing manually}}$$

Where P represents precision, and R represents recall. In general, these two measures in one system are opposite to each other. When precision is higher, recall will be lower. Otherwise, when precision is improved, recall will decrease. In table 2, we illustrate our experimental results. The first three rows give measures for articles about different styles and the figures in parentheses represent the number of articles. The fourth row gives the average measure of our system. For comparison, we also illustrate the results of Chien's [1997] PAT-tree-based method from his experiments in the last row. From this table, we can see that more emphasis is placed on precision in Chien's system. However, we incline to enhancing recall when precision and recall are assured relatively balanced. When precision is lower, perhaps more noise is introduced into the set of candidate keywords. Because we have adopted segmentation and POS tagging tools which can verify whether a candidate character string is a meaningful unit and found that the noise introduced now is more or less relevant to the content of the article, we don't have to worry more about precision. Therefore, we hope to generate more keywords automatically under the condition that the number of noise words is accepted.

	Recall	Precision
National politics (23)	0.452	0.401
International Politics (10)	0.644	0.594
Sports news (4)	0.629	0.482
Average	0.523	0.462
Chien's (exact match)	0.30	0.43

Table 2. Experimental Results

It has to be pointed out that there are no satisfactory results in extracting keywords from texts [Chien, 1997]. Although some keywords extracted are the same as manually extracted ones in meaning, they are often different due to one or two characters mismatched. According to our analysis of experimental results, though only 46% of extracted keywords appear in the set of manual keywords, the rest are also relevant to the text and adapt to the need of information retrieval. At the same time, about 52% of the manual keywords are generated by the automatically indexing method, however, we can often find a substitute for most of the rest in the set of automatically generated keywords.

Most of the keywords missed occur only once in the text, but they are mostly proper nouns of places, organizations or titles of person. And this reveals that we need to further improve the techniques to recognize proper nouns.

5 Conclusion and Future Work

We have described a system for automatically indexing keywords from texts. One document is inputted into the recognizer module, the filter module and the selector module consecutively, with keywords output. Here we utilize the mature techniques available now such as string frequency statistics, segmentation and POS tagging tools. Then, according to features, we propose our method to evaluate directly every candidate keyword and select those with higher scores as keywords. At the same time, we break through the tradition of generating keywords only from the original text and acquire some keywords through looking up in the lexicon of content words with hierarchical relations. The experimental results show that our system can perform comparably to the state of the art.

Owing to the limit of the training corpus, the parameters in scoring formula are set by experience values. With our method, we can cumulate more and more documents with keywords. Then we can adopt machine-learning methods to conduct keyword indexing, which can make parameters more objective. That will be our further work.

References

[Chien 1997] Chien, L. F., PAT-Tree-Based Keyword Extraction for Chinese Information Retrieval, Proceedings of the ACM SIGIR International Conference on Information Retrieval, 1997, pp. 50--59.

[Frank 1999] Frank E., Paynter G.W., Witten I.H., Gutwin C., and Nevill-Manning C.G., Domain-specific keyphrase extraction, Proc. Sixteenth International Joint Conference on Artificial Intelligence, Morgan Kaufmann Publishers, San Francisco, CA, 1999, pp. 668-673.

[Lai 2002] Yu-Sheng Lai, Chung-Hsien Wu, Meaningful term extraction and discriminative term selection in text categorization via unknown-word methodology, ACM Transactions on Asian Language Information Processing (TALIP), Vol.1, No.1, March 2002, pp. 34-64.

[Liu 1998] Liu Ting, Wu Yan, Wang Kaizhu, An Chinese Word Automatic Segmentation System Based on String Frequency Statistics Combined with Word Matching, Journal of Chinese Information Processing, Vol.12, No.1, 1998, pp. 17-25.

[Ong 1999] T. Ong and H. Chen, Updateable PAT-Tree Approach to Chinese Key Phrase Extraction Using Mutual Information: A Linguistic Foundation for Knowledge Management, Proceedings of the Second Asian Digital Libaray Conference, Taipei, Taiwan, Novemeber 8-9, 1999.

[Turney 1999] Turney, P.D., Learning to Extract Keyphrases from Text, NRC Technical Report ERB-1057, National Research Council, Canada, 1999.

[Witten 1999] Witten I.H., Paynter G.W., Frank E., Gutwin C., and Nevill-Manning C.G., KEA: Practical automatic keyphrase extraction, Proc. DL '99, 1999, pp. 254-256.

[Yang 2002] Wenfeng Yang, Chinese keyword extraction based on max-duplicated strings of the documents, Proceedings of the 25th annual international ACM SIGIR conference on Research and development in information retrieval, 2002, pp. 439-440.

Semantic Maps for Word Alignment in Bilingual Parallel Corpora

Qing Ma
Ryukoku University
Otsu 520-2194, Japan
qma@math.ryukoku.ac.jp

Yujie Zhang
Communications Research Laboratory
Kyoto 619-0289, Japan
yujie@crl.go.jp

Masaki Murata
Communications Research Laboratory
Kyoto 619-0289, Japan
murata@crl.go.jp

Hitoshi Isahara
Communications Research Laboratory
Kyoto 619-0289, Japan
isahara@crl.go.jp

Abstract

Effective self-organizing techniques for constructing monolingual semantic maps of Japanese and Chinese have already been developed. By extending the monolingual map to a bilingual semantic map, we have proposed a semantics-based approach for word alignment in a Japanese/Chinese bilingual corpus.

1 Introduction

Acquiring translation knowledge from a bilingual parallel corpus requires alignment not only at the sentence level but also at the word level. If a bilingual corpus is aligned at the word level, translation words that are not in a dictionary, such as those depending on domain or time, might be obtained, or, multiple translation candidates might be scored. Furthermore, translation patterns based on the relations of words at the phrase or clause level might be automatically acquired (Brown, 1997). Thus, alignment is a very important, fundamental task in natural language processing (NLP). The research related to this topic includes a series of statistical models (e.g., Brown, et al., 1988; Brown, et al., 1993; Macklovitch and Hanna, 1996), a method using dynamic programming (Dagan, 1993), a statistical approach introducing contextual information (Varea, et al., 2002), and structure alignment methods (Kaji, et al., 1992; Matsumoto, et al., 1993; Wu, 1995; Imamura, 2001). All of these approaches, however, are based on either statistical information or grammatical structure, but not on meaning.

Automatic methods for constructing monoligual semantic maps of Japanese or Chinese have already been proposed (Ma, et al., 2002). In a monoligual semantic map, words with similar meanings are placed at the same or neighboring points, so that the distance between the points represents the semantic similarity of the words. If a bilingual semantic map could be automatically constructed by accepting translation pairs of sentences as inputs, word alignment would be easily obtained from the map. Since the bilingual semantic map, like the monolingual semantic map, would provide results with visibility and continuity, it would be easy to handle one-to-many or many-to-one alignment. Furthermore, bilingual maps can perhaps be expected to be applied in foreign language learning or foreign language writing by using bilingual parallel corpora. The most important factor is that the translations should usually be free. There is an evident limitation of existing alignment methods that rely on statistical or grammatical information, which suggests the necessity to develop an approach based on meaning.

This paper proposes a new method for automatically constructing bilingual semantic maps of Japanese and Chinese. the method accepts translation pairs of Japanese and Chinese sentences as inputs, with the aiming of providing word alignment based on meaning[1] . We used the Kyoto University Japanese corpus and its translated Chinese corpus to conduct an experiment and confirm the effectiveness of the proposed method. The necessary training data for automatically constructing semantic maps was obtained from eight years of a Japanese newspaper, Mainichi Shinbun.

[1] Since present semantic maps are constructed basically on co-occurrent information, the method proposed is not strictly a semantic approach. However, since our final goal is to develop true semantic maps, and alignment based on meaning itself is a very important idea, we use the expression "based on meaning", without fear of misunderstanding.

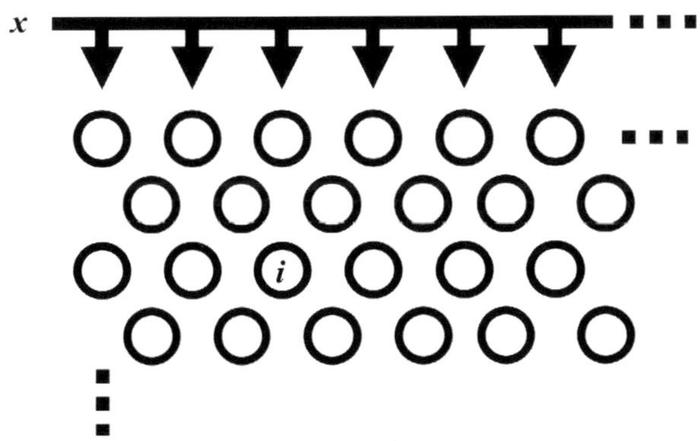

Figure 1: Two-dimensional SOM.

2 Self-organizing Neural Networks

As an automatic method for constructing semantic maps, we have adopted a self-organizing neural network, which was proposed by Kohonen in the early 1980s (see details in Kohonen, 1997) and is called a self-organizing map (SOM). An SOM can be visualized as a two-dimensional array (Figure 1) of nodes on which a high-dimensional input vector can be mapped in an orderly manner through a learning process. It is as if some meaningful nonlinear coordinate system for different input features was created over the network. Such a learning process is competitive and unsupervised and is called a self-organizing process.

Suppose input $x = [\xi_1, \xi_2, \cdots, \xi_n]^T \in \Re^n$, where $\Re^n$ is an n-dimensional space. Each node i is then associated with a parametric reference vector m_i, which equals $[\mu_{i1}, \mu_{i2}, \cdots, \mu_{in}]^T \in \Re^n$, whose element μ_{ij} is a scalar weight between node i and input element ξ_j and is gradually modified in the learning process. When input vector $x \in \Re^n$ is given, it is compared to all reference vectors $m_i \in \Re^n$, which are associated by each node and is gradually modified in the learning process, and the network responses comply with the two different stages, learning and mapping, as follows. In the mapping stage, only the node whose reference vector has the smallest Euclidean distance to the input vector is activated. This node, c, is called the best-matching node or winner. It can thus be defined by

$$c = argmin_i\{||x - m_i||\}. \qquad (1)$$

In the learning stage, on the other hand, not only the best-matching node but also its neighboring nodes are activated and their reference vectors are changed so that they are closer to the same input vector x. This results in a local relaxation or smoothing effect on the reference vectors of the nodes in the neighborhood, which leads to global ordering in continued learning. This gradual adapttaion of the reference vectors can be expressed as

$$m_i(t+1) = m_i(t) + h_{ci}(t)[x(t) - m_i(t)], \qquad (2)$$

where $h_{ci}(t)$ is the neighborhood function. For convergence, it is necessary that $h_{ci}(t) \to 0$ when $t \to \infty$. A widely applied neighborhood function can be written in terms of a Gaussian function:

$$h_{ci}(t) = \alpha(t) \cdot \exp(-\frac{||r_c - r_i||^2}{2\sigma^2(t)}). \qquad (3)$$

Here, $r_c \in \Re^2$ and $r_i \in \Re^2$ are the location vectors of nodes c and i, respectively: Term $\alpha(t)$ is the learning rate and $\sigma(t)$ defines the radius of the neighborhood. Both of the latter terms are monotonically decreasing functions of time, and their exact forms are not critical. They can thus be defined linearly as

$$\alpha(t) = \alpha(0)\frac{T-t}{T}, \qquad (4)$$

and

$$\sigma(t+1) = 1 + (\sigma(t) - 1)\frac{T-t}{T}, \qquad (5)$$

where $\alpha(0)$ is an initial value and T is the total number of learning steps.

The learning process usually consists of an ordering phase and a fine adjustment phase. In the ordering phase, $\alpha(t)$ should start with a value that is close to unity, and the initial radius of the neighborhood can be more than half the diameter of the network. The terms $\alpha(t)$ and $\sigma(t+1)$ then decrease monotonically according to Eqs. (4) and (5). The ordering of m_i occurs during this initial phase, while the remaining steps are only needed for finely adjusting the map. After the ordering phase, the radius may still contain the nearest neighbors of node c, and $\alpha = \alpha(t)$ should attain a low value over a long period.

3 Self-organizing Semantic Map for Word Alignment

3.1 Purpose

When a translation pair of sentences like

(Japanses) 経営 トップ が 低 成長 時代 定着 を 実感 して いる こと を うかがわ せた 。

(Chinese) 由此 可以 看出 ， 最高 経営者 深感 経済 仍 停留 在 低速 増長 時代 。

is given, to self-organize a semantic map for word alignment means to automatically map all the words in the given sentences by employing some kind of unsupervised learning data.

3.2 Learning data

As part of the Japanese-Chinese machine translation project, we are constructing a bilingual parallel corpus based on the Kyoto University Japanese corpus (Kurohashi and Nagao, 1997). The translation pair of sentences were obtained from the corpus. Since the Kyoto University corpus has already been morphologically analyzed, the Japanese sentences were used directly without any analysis, while the translated Chinese sentences were segmented and part-of-speech tagged by using the morphological analysis tool developed by Beijing University (Zhou and Duan, 1994).

To evaluate the two different languages with the same measure, the words appearing in a translated Chinese sentence were given at most five translated Japanese candidate words, which were used instead of the original Chinese words. The candidates were obtained manually[2] from two Chinese-Japanese dictionaries: "Han Ri Ci Dian", published by Jilin Education Publisher, and "Chunichi Daijiten"[3] , published by Taishukan Publishing Co., Ltd. The candidates were selected according to the following order of priority: (1) a word that also appears in the Japanese original sentence; (2) a word that has the same POS as the original Chinese word; (3) a word chosen according to the order listed in the dictionary; and (4) a word that appears in the Kyoto University corpus. Thus, all the words in the translated Chinese sentence in the pair shown above can be rendered in terms of Japanese candidate words as follows:

(Chinese) 由此:これによって 可以:ことができる/てよい 看出:見抜く/看破 ，:， 最高:最高/最も高い 経営者:経営者 深感:実感 経済:経済/生活/経済的 仍:依然として/いまなお 停留:滞在/止まる 在:で/に/している/しつつある 低速:低 増長:増長/ふえる 時代:期/時代 。:。

In this way, we can express a translation pair of sentences in terms of only Japanese words. As this example shows, however, we can recognize translated Japanese candidate words, such as "これによって" or "ことができる/てよい", that do not exist in the original Japanese sentence. This means that it is virtually impossible to perform word alignment by only using surface representations, even if the translation pair of sentences has been unified by a single language.

The actual learning data used in self-organization were obtained in the following way. Each Japanese word appearing in a Japanese sentence was defined in terms of its co-occurrent words (the targeted word itself and the words to its immediate left and right). They were obtained from eight years (1991-1998) of the Japanese newspaper, Mainichi Shinbun, and used as learning data. Each Chinese word appearing in a translated Chinese sentence was defined in terms of the co-occurrent words of its Japanese translation candidates and the Chinese words defined in this way were used as learning data. In the next section, we explicitly describe the construction of the learning data and the coding method used to transform it into inputs for the SOM.

3.3 Data coding

Suppose we are given a Japanese-Chinese translation pair of sentences:

$$J_1, J_2, \cdots, J_m$$

$$C_1 : J_{11}/\cdots/J_{1,n_1}, \cdots, C_n : J_{n1}/\cdots/J_{n,n_n}$$

, where the J_i $(i = 1, \cdots, m)$ are the Japanese words forming the Japanese sentence, the C_i $(i = 1, \cdots, n)$ are the Chinese words forming the translated Chinese sentence, J_{ij} $(i = 1, \cdots, n,\ j = 1, \cdots, n_i)$ is the jth translated Japanese candidate for C_i, $n_i (1 \leq n_i \leq t)$ is the number of candidates for C_i, and t is the maximum number of candidates ($t = 5$ in the paper).

Word w_i $(= J_i)$ of a Japanese sentence is defined by a set of co-occurrent information:

$$w_i = J_i = \{a_1^{(i)}, f_1^{(i)}, \cdots, a_{\alpha_i}^{(i)}, f_{\alpha_i}^{(i)}\}, \qquad (6)$$

where $a_j^{(i)}$ is a co-occurrent word of J_i, $f_j^{(i)}$ is the normalized (i.e., $\sum_{j=1}^{\alpha_i} f_j^{(i)} = 1$) co-occurrence frequency, and α_i is the number of words co-occurring with J_i. Word w_j $(= C_j)$ of a translated Chinese sentence is also defined by a set of co-occurrent information:

$$w_j = C_j = \{J_{j1}, \cdots, J_{j,n_j}\} = \{a_1^{(j)}, f_1^{(j)}, \cdots, a_{\alpha_j}^{(j)}, f_{\alpha_j}^{(j)}\}, \qquad (7)$$

where $a_i^{(j)}$ is a co-occurrent word of either or severals of $J_{j1}, \cdots, J_{j,n_i}$, $f_i^{(j)}$ is the normalized co-occurrence frequnecy (it will be the summation of the frequencies when occuring with severals), and α_i is the number of words co-occuring with J_i.

Since the Chinese words are also defined in terms of co-occurrent Japanese words, there is no need to distinguish between Chinese and Japanese, and it thus becomes possible to apply all existing coding methods for self-organizing monolingual semantic maps. In this paper, the semantic distance d_{ij} between any two words w_i and w_j appearing in a

[2] Since there are no online electronic dictionaries, we have to obtain the data manually at present.

[3] This dictionary was used only when a word had no entry in the former dictionary.

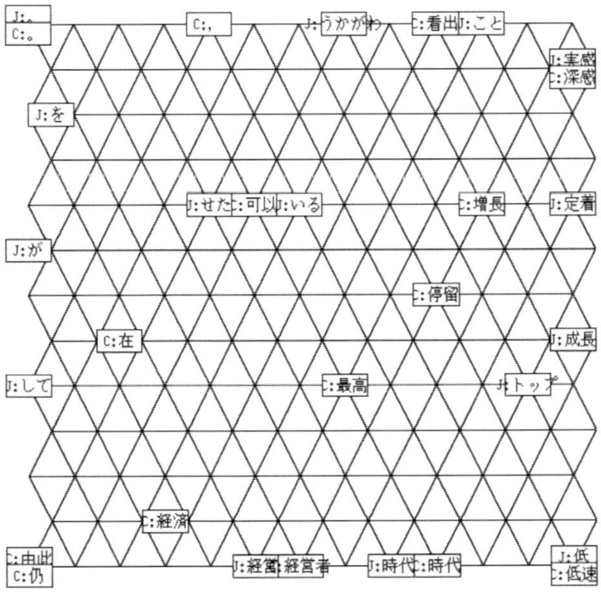

Figure 2: Semantic map obtained by self-organization.

translation pair of sentences is calculated by the following frequency term-weighting method:

$$d_{ij} = \begin{cases} \frac{(F_i - F_{ij}) + (F_j - F_{ij})}{F_i + F_j - F_{ij}} & \text{if } i \neq j \\ 0, & \text{otherwise,} \end{cases} \tag{8}$$

where F_i and F_j are expansions of α_i and α_j, the numbers of co-occurrent words of w_i and w_j, respectively, and F_{ij} is an expansion of c_{ij}, the number of co-occurrent words that both w_i and w_j have in common. The expansion are obtained as follows:

$$F_i = \sum_{x=1}^{x=\alpha_i} f_x^{(i)} \text{ and } F_{ij} = \sum_{x=1}^{x=c_{ij}} f_x^{(ij)}, \tag{9}$$

where $f_x^{(i)}$ is the co-occurrence frequency of word w_i and its co-occurrent word $a_x^{(i)}$, and $f_x^{(ij)}$ is the co-occurrence frequency of words w_i and w_j and their co-occurrent word $a_x^{(i)}$ $(x = 1, \cdots, \alpha_i)$. As a result, we can define a correlative matrix D with the distance d_{ij} as its element. Each word w_i is thus coded with the elements in the i-th row of the correlative matrix D as

$$V(w_i) = [d_{i1}, d_{i2}, \cdots, d_{iN}]^T, \tag{10}$$

where N is the total number of words appearing in the translation pair of sentences (i.e., $N = m + n$), and $V(w_i) \in \Re^N$ is the input to the SOM.

Table 1: Word alignment results obtained from the semantic map

Japanese	Chinese	Correct answer
J:経営:	C:経営者	-
J:トップ	C:停留	C:最高
J:が	C:在	-
J:低	C:低速	C:低速
J:成長	C:停留	C:増長
J:時代	C:時代	C:時代
J:定着	C:増長	C:停留
J:を	C:。	-
J:実感	C:深感	C:深感
J:して	C:在	-
J:いる	C:可以	-
J:こと	C:看出	-
J:を	C:。	-
J:うかがわ	C:看出	C:看出
J:せた	C:可以	C:可以
J:。	C:。	C:。

4 Experimental Results

4.1 Data

Word alignment experiments were performed for ten translation pairs of sentences. The learning data was obtained in the way described in Sec. 3.2. Considering the translation pair of sentences given in Sec. 3.1 as an example, the number of words was $N = m + n = 16 + 15 = 31$, the total number of co-occurrent words was 62,627, and the number of different co-occurrent words was 22,077. Among the 31 words, the period symbol ("。")[4] had the largest number of co-occurrent words (4,180), while the word "うかがわ" in the Japanese sentence and the comma ", " in the translated Chinese sentence had the smallest numbers of co-occurrent words (5 each).

4.2 SOM

We used an SOM consisting of a 13×13 two-dimensional array. The number of input dimensions, N, was 31, the same as the number of words to be mapped. In the ordering phase, the number of learning steps, T, was set to 10,000, the initial value of the learning rate, $\alpha(0)$, was set to 0.1, and the initial radius of the neighborhood, $\sigma(0)$, was set to 13, equal to the diameter of the SOM. In the fine adjustment phase, T was set to 100,000, $\alpha(0)$ was set to 0.01, and $\sigma(0)$ was set to 7. The initial reference vectors $m_i(0)$ consisted of random values between 0 and 1.0.

[4] Although there is actually no need to align period symbols between sentences, this step was not omitted because the sentences were processed mechanically.

Table 2: Baseline word alignment results

Japanese	Chinese	Correct answer
J:経営:	C:経営者	-
J:トップ	C:経営者	C:最高
J:が	C:在	-
J:低	C:低速	C:低速
J:成長	C:時代	C:増長
J:時代	C:時代	C:時代
J:定着	C:深感	C:停留
J:を	C:在	-
J:実感	C:深感	C:深感
J:して	C:在	-
J:いる	C:可以	-
J:こと	C:深感	-
J:を	C:在	-
J:うかがわ	C:深感	C:看出
J:せた	C:可以	C:可以
J:。	C:。	C:。

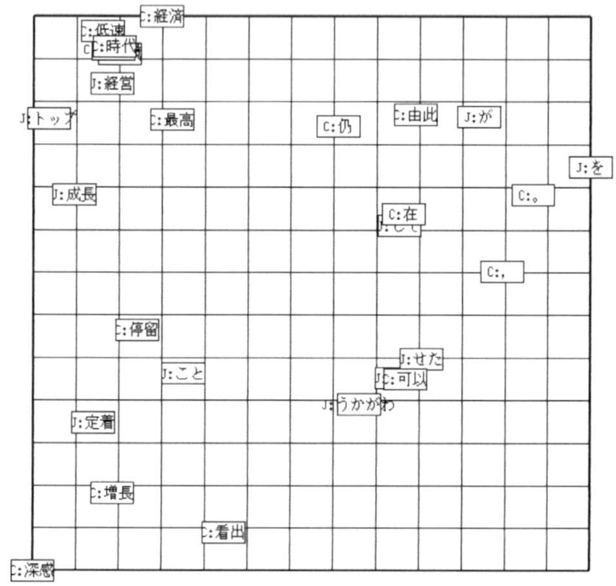

Figure 3: Semantic map by PCA.

4.3 Results

Figure 2 shows the semantic map for word alignment of the translation pair given in Sec. 3.1 as an example. Here, the words tagged with "J" are Japanese words from the Japanese sentence and the words with "C" are Chinese words from the translated Chinese sentence[5] . From the map, we could obtain the word alignment results listed in Table 1 by focusing on each Japanese word and choosing the closest Chinese word to it[6] . The correct answers are also given in the table. From this table, we can see that [J：低, C：低速],[J：時代, C：時代], [J：実感, C：深感],[J：うかがわ, C：看出],[J：せた, C：可以], [J:。, C:。] were aligned correctly. Among these pairs, in the case of [J:うかがわ，C:看出] and [J:せた, C:可以], the Japanese word and the Japanese translation candidates for the Chinese words have different surface representations. The other alignment results are incorrect in the strict sense of the word. Among these apparent mistakes, however, there are some interesting results. For example, for the Japanese word "J:成長", although "C:停留" was aligned as the closest Chinese word, the semantic map shows that the second closest Chinese word is actually "C:増長". That is, if we had included the second closest candidate, we would have obtained the correct answer. Similarly, for "J：トップ", its second candidates is "C：最高", a correct answer. Also, the incorrect alignment results, [J:こと，C:看出] and [J:を，C:。] were due to the fact that there are no Chinese words (or at least none appearing in the sentence) that correspond to these Japanese words. Another problem was incorrect alignment caused by the inconsistency of word segmentation between the Japanese and Chinese sentence, as in the case of [J:経営:, C:経営者]. None of these problems can be resolved by only applying the word alignment technique.

Table 2 lists the baseline word alignment results, which were obtained by focusing on each Japanese word and choosing the Chinese word with the smallest semantic distance d_{ij} which was calculated by Eq. (8). From this table we can see that [J：うかがわ, C：深感] was incorrect, while "J：うかがわ" was correctly aligned by using the semantic map. Also, although incorrect results were obtained both for the semantic map, such as [J:成長, C:停留] or [J:停留, C:増長] and for the baseline such as, [J:成長, C:時代] or [J:停留, C:深感], the results for the semantic map were somewhat correct in meaning, whereas those for the baseline were totally wrong. If we see the second candidates, we can know that the second candidates of "J:成長" and "J: トップ" are "C:深感" and "C:時代" which are incorrect. We can thus say that the method using the semantic map performed better than the baseline method.

Figure 3 shows the word-alignment semantic map obtained by principle component analysis (PCA). By

[5] Because both Japanese and Chinese use Chinese characters, it is necessary to use such symbols to distinguish between languages.

[6] These results were obtained by only selecting the Chinese word closest the Japanese word. If the second closest or third closest words are also used, the word alignment results can include multiple candidates.

comparing it with Figure 2, we can see that the results obtained by PCA would be worse than those obtained by self-organization. For example, the pair [J:うかがわ, C:看出], which has different surface representations, could not be obtained by PCA. "J:成長" also could not be correctly aligned even if the second closest candidate were included. In addition, words tend to cluster together in certain areas and the total disposition of the words is thus imbalanced, which detracts from the semantic map's features of visibility and continuity. We also tried to use hierarchical clustering for word alignment. The results obtained were slightly worse than those obtained with the self-organizing semantic map. For example, [J:うかがわ, C:看出] also could not be correctly obtained with the clustering method. Moreover, because we could not know the semantic distance between words within a group, we could not easily obtain second closest candidates as we could with the semantic map.

5 Conclusion

This paper has proposed a novel word alignment method designed to provide a meaning-based approach. The effectiveness of the proposed method was confirmed through small-scale experiments. In our future work, we are going to conduct numerical evalution through large scale experimental comparison with existing methods. We also plan to develop a word alignment technique for practical use by integrating the proposed method into existing systems.

References

Brown, P. F., Cocke, J., Della Pietra, S. A., Della Pietra, V. J., Jelinek, F., Mercer, R. L., Roossin, P.: A statistical approach to language translation, *COLING'88*, pp. 71-76, 1988.

Brown, P. F., Della Pietra, S. A., Della Pietra, V. J., Mercer, R. L.: The mathematics of statistical machine translation: parameter estimation, *Computational Linguistics*, Vol. 19, No. 2, pp.263-311, 1993.

Brown, R. D.: Automated dictionary example-based translation, *Proceedings of the Seventh International Conference on Theoretical and Methodological Issues in Machine Translation*, pp. 111-118, 1997.

Dagan, I., Church, K. W., Gale, W. A.: Robust bilingual word alignment for machine aided translation, *Proceedings of the Workshop on Very Large Corpora*, pp. 1-8, 1993.

Kurohashi, S., Nagao, M: Kyoto University text corpus project, *Proc. 3rd Annual Meeting of the Association for Natural Language Processing*, pp. 115-118, 1997 (in Japanese).

Kaji, H., Kida, Y., Morimoto Y.: Learning translation templates from bilingual text, *COLING'92*, pp. 672-678, 1992.

Ma, Q., Zhang, M., Murata, M., Zhou, M., Isahara, H.: Self-Organizing Chinese and Japanese Semantic Maps, The 19th International Conference on Computational Linguistics (COLING'2002), Taiwan, pp. 605-611, August, 2002.

Matsumoto, Y., Ishimoto, H, Utsuro, T.: Structural matching of parallel texts, *ACL'93*, pp. 23-30, 1993.

Macklovitch, E., Hannan, M. L.: Line 'em up: advances in alignment technology and their impact on translation support tools, *in Expanding MT Horizons, Second Conference of the Association for Machine Translation in the Americas*, Montreal, pp. 145-156, 1996.

Varea, I. G., Och, F. J., Casacuberta, F.: Improving alignment quality in statistical machine translation using context-dependent maximum entropy models, *COLING2002*, pp. 1051- 1057, 2002.

Wu, D.: An algorithm for simultaneously bracketing parallel texts by aligning words, *ACL-95*, pp. 244-251, 1995.

Imamura, K.: Hierarchical phrase alignment harmonized with parsing, *NLPRS2001*, pp. 377-384, 2001.

Kohonen, T.: Self-organizing maps, Springer, 2nd Edition, 1997.

Zhou, Q. Duan, H.: Segmentation and tagging in modern Chinese corpus, *Chinese Journal of Computers*, Vol. 85, 1994.

Abductive Explanation-based Learning Improves Parsing Accuracy and Efficiency

Oliver Streiter
Language and Law, European Academy, Bolzano, Italy
ostreiter@eurac.edu

Abstract

Natural language parsing has to be accurate and quick. Explanation-based Learning (EBL) is a technique to speed-up parsing. The accuracy however often declines with EBL. The paper shows that this accuracy loss is not due to the EBL framework as such, but to deductive parsing. Abductive EBL allows extending the deductive closure of the parser. We present a Chinese parser based on abduction. Experiments show improvements in accuracy and efficiency.[1]

1 Introduction

The difficulties of natural language parsing, in general, and of parsing Chinese, in particular, are due to local ambiguities of words and phrases. Extensive linguistic and non-linguistic knowledge is required for their resolution (Chang, 1994; Chen, 1996). Different parsing approaches provide different types of knowledge. Example-based parsing approaches offer rich syntagmatic contexts for disambiguation, richer than rule-based approaches do (Yuang et al., 1992). Statistical approaches to parsing acquire mainly paradigmatic knowledge and require larger corpora, c.f. (Carl and Langlais, 2003). Statistical approaches handle unseen events via smoothing. Rule-based approaches use abstract category labels.

[1]This research has been carried out within *Logos Gaias* project, which integrates NLP technologies into a Internet-based natural language learning platform (Streiter et al., 2003).

Example-based parsing generalizes examples during compilation time, e.g. (Bod and Kaplan, 1998), or performs a similarity-based fuzzy match during runtime (Zavrel and Daelemans, 1997). Both techniques may be computationally demanding, their effect on parsing however is quite different, c.f. (Streiter, 2002a).

Explanation-based learning (EBL) is a method to speed-up rule-based parsing via the caching of examples. EBL however trades speed for accuracy. For many systems, a small loss in accuracy is acceptable if an order of magnitude less computing time is required. Apart from speed, one generally recognizes that EBL acquires some kind of knowledge from texts. However, what is this knowledge like if it does not help with parsing? Couldn't a system improve by learning its own output? Can a system learn to parse Chinese by parsing Chinese? The paper sets out to tackle these questions in theory and practice.

1.1 Explanation-based Learning (EBL)

Explanation-based learning techniques transform a general problem solver (PS) into a specific and operational PS (Mitchel et al., 1986). The caching of the general PS's output accounts for this transformation. The PS generates, besides the output, a documentation of the reasoning steps involved (the explanation). This determines which output the system will cache.

The *utility problem* questions the claim of speeding-up applications (Minton, 1990): Retrieving cached solutions in addition to regular processing requires extra time. If retrieval is slow and cached solutions are rarely re-used, the cost-benefit ratio is negative.

The accuracy of the derived PS is generally below that of the general PS. This may be due to the EBL framework as such or the deductive base of the PS. Research in abductive EBL (A-EBL) seems to suggest the latter: A-EBL has the potential to acquire new knowledge (Dimopoulos and Kakas, 1996). The relation between knowledge and accuracy however is not a direct and logical one. The *U-shaped* language learning curves in children exemplifies the indirect relation (Marcus et al., 1992). Wrong regular word forms supplant correct irregular forms when rules are learned. We therefore cannot simply equate automatic knowledge acquisition and accuracy improvement, in particular for complex language tasks.

1.2 EBL and Natural Language Parsing

Previous research has applied EBL for the speed-up of large and slow grammars. Sentences are parsed. Then the parse trees are filtered and cached. Subsequent parsing uses the cached trees. A complex HPSG-grammar transforms into tree-structures with instantiated values (Neumann, 1994). One hash table lookup of POS-sequences replaces typed-feature unification. Experiments conducted in EBL-augmented parsing consistently report a speed-up of the parser and a drop in accuracy (Rayner and Samuelsson, 1994; Srinivas and Joshi, 1995).

A loss of information may explain the drop of accuracy. Contextual information, taken into account by the original parser, may be unavailable in the new operational format (Sima'an, 1997), especially if partial, context-dependent solutions are retrieved. In addition, the set of cached parse trees, judged to be "sure to cache", is necessarily biased (Streiter, 2002b). Most cached tree structures are short noun phrases. Parsing from biased examples will bias the parsing.

A further reason for the loss in accuracy are incorrect parses which leak into the cache. A stricter filter does not solve the problem. It increases the bias in the cache, reduces the size of the cache, and evokes the utility problem.

EBL actually can improve parsing accuracy (Streiter, 2002b) if the grammar does not derive the parses to be cached via deduction but via abduction. The deductive closure[2] which cannot increase with EBL from deductive parsing may increase with abductive parsing.

2 A Formal View on Parsing and Learning

We use the following notation throughout the paper: $\mu \rightarrow (y) = x$ (function μ applied to y yields x), $\mu \mapsto (y) = x$ (relation μ applied to y yields x). $< ... >$ and $\{...\}$ represent tuples and sets respectively. The $\#$ prefix denotes the cardinality of a collection, e.g. $\#\{o_1, o_2\} = 2$.

Uppercase variables stand for collections and lowercase variables for elements. Collections may contain the anonymous variable ϵ (the variable _ in PROLOG). Over-braces or under-braces should facilitate reading: $\underbrace{1+1}_{2} = \underbrace{2*1}_{2}$.

A theory $\mathcal{T}$ is $< \mathcal{A}, \mathcal{I}, \mathcal{R} >$ where $\mathcal{R}$ is a set of rules r. $\mathcal{A}$ and $\mathcal{I}$ are two disjoint sets of attributes a and i (e.g. $\mathcal{A} = \{"noun", "verb", ...\}; \mathcal{I} = \{"Bob", "hill", ...\}$). A rule is written as $r =< o, a >$ or $r \mapsto (o) = a$. A rule specifies the relation between an observable fact o and an attribute a assigned to it. $\mathcal{O}$ is the set of observable data with each $o \in \mathcal{O}$ being a tuple $o =< a, i >$.[3]

$\mathcal{C}$ is the set of data classified according to $\mathcal{T}$, with $c =< o, a >$. o, i and a may have an internal structure in the form of ordered or unordered collections of more elementary o, i and a respectively.

Transferring this notation to the description of parsing, $\mathcal{T}$ is a syntactic formalism and $\mathcal{R}$ a grammar. $\mathcal{A}$ is the union of syntax trees and morpho-syntactic tags. $\mathcal{O}$ is a corpus tagged with $\mathcal{A}$. $\mathcal{I}$ corresponds to a list of words, phrases or sentences (the surface strings). $\mathcal{C}$ is a treebank, a cache of parse trees, or a history of explanations.

$$c_{parse} =<< a_{pos}, i_{lexeme} >, a_{tree} > \quad (1)$$

2.1 Parsing: $\pi \mapsto (o) = \{c_{new}\}$

A **parser** defines a relation between $\mathcal{O}$ and $\mathcal{C}$ (c.f. 2). **Parsing** is a relation between o and a subset of $\mathcal{C}$ (c.f. 3).

$$\pi \mapsto (\mathcal{O}) = \mathcal{C} \quad (2)$$

[2]The deductive closure of the set of axioms $\mathcal{X}$ is the set $\mathcal{S}$ which can be proved from it.

[3]The formalization follows (Dimopoulos and Kakas, 1996).

$$\pi \mapsto (o) = \{c_{new}\} \quad (3)$$

Simplifying, we can assume that π is defined as the set of rules, i.e. $\pi =< \mathcal{O}, \mathcal{C} >= \mathcal{R}$. A specific parser π is derived by the application of θ to the training material (e.g. $\mathcal{C}$): $\theta \mapsto (\mathcal{C}) = \pi$. The set of possible relations θ is Θ. Elements of Θ are caching (no generalization), induction (hypothesis after data inspection) and abduction (hypothesis during classification). Equation (5) describes the cycle of grammar learning and grammar application.

$$\theta \mapsto (\mathcal{C}) = \pi \quad (4)$$

$$\underbrace{(\theta \mapsto (\mathcal{C}_{old}))}_{\pi} \mapsto (\mathcal{O}) = \mathcal{C}_{new} \quad (5)$$

2.1.1 Memory-based Parsing

π is based on *memory* if $(\theta \mapsto (c)) =< c, c >=< r, r >$. γ in (6) is the trivial formalization of caching. Parsing proceeds via recalling ρ defined in (7). The cycle of grammar learning and parsing $\rho \mapsto (\gamma)$ is defined in (8): The training material c_w yields the parsing output c_w.[4]

$$\gamma \mapsto (< o_v, a_w >) = \underbrace{< o_v, a_w >}_{\rho} \quad (6)$$

$$\rho \mapsto (o_v) =< o_v, a_w > \quad (7)$$

$$\overbrace{\overbrace{(\gamma \mapsto (\overbrace{< o_v, a_w >}^{c_w}))}^{\text{learning } \rho \text{ from } c} \mapsto (o_v) = \underbrace{< o_v, a_w >}_{c_w}}^{\text{parsing } o_v} \quad (8)$$

2.1.2 Deduction-based Parsing

Let *delete* be a function which replaces one or more elements of a collection by a named variable or ϵ. π is a deductive inference if r is obtained from an *induction* (a reduction of o with the help of *delete*). The following expressions define induction ι (9), deduction δ (10) and the inductive-deductive cycle $\delta \mapsto (\iota)$ (11):

[4]We use subscripts to indicate the identity of variables. The same subscript of two variables implies the identity of both variables. Different subscripts imply nothing. The variables may be identical or not identical. In memory-based parsing, learning material and parsing output are identical.

$$\iota \mapsto (\underbrace{<< a_w, i_w >, a_v >}_{c_v}) = \underbrace{< \underbrace{delete \rightarrow (< a_w, i_w >)}_{< a_w, \epsilon >}, a_v >}_{r_{v_\epsilon} = \delta} \quad (9)$$

$$\delta \mapsto (\underbrace{< a_w, i_x >}_{o_w}) =<< a_w, i_x >, a_v > \quad (10)$$

$$\overbrace{(\iota \mapsto \overbrace{(<< a_w, i_w >, a_v >)}^{c_v}) \mapsto (< a_w, i_x >)) =}^{\text{parsing } o_z} << a_w, i_x >, a_v > \quad (11)$$

2.1.3 Abduction-based Parsing

Abduction, defined as $\overbrace{(\psi \mapsto (c))}^{\alpha} \mapsto (o)$ is a run-time generalization which is triggered by a concrete o to be classified. We separate ψ and α for presentation purpose only.[5] The relation σ may express a similarity, a temporal or causal relation. (12) and the cycle of $\alpha \mapsto (\psi)$ (13) define abduction.

$$\psi \mapsto (c) = \sigma \mapsto (c) = r \quad (12)$$

$$\overbrace{\overbrace{(\psi \mapsto (<< a_x, i_x >, a_c >))}^{\text{learning } \alpha \text{ from } c} \mapsto \overbrace{(< a_y, i_y >)}^{o_y} =}^{\text{parsing } o_y} < \underbrace{< a_y, i_y >}_{o_y}, a_r > \quad (13)$$

Abduction subsumes reasoning by analogy. Abduction is an analogy, if σ describes a similarity. Reasoning from rain to snow is a typical analogy. Reasoning from wet street to rain is an abductive reasoning. For a parsing approach based on analogy c.f. (Lepage, 1999).

[5]Abduction is a process of hypothesis generation. Deduction and abduction may work conjointly whenever deductive inferences encounter gaps. A deductive inference stops in front of a gap between the premises and a possible conclusion. Abduction creates a new hypothesis, which allows to bridge the gap and to continue the inference.

2.2 Learning: $\mathcal{C} \cup ((\theta \mapsto (\mathcal{C})) \mapsto (o))$

In this section, we formalize EBL. We mechanically substitute θ in the definition of EBL by γ, δ, α to show their learning potentials.

A learning system changes internal states, which influence the performance. The internal states of π are determined by $\mathcal{C}$ and Θ. We assume that, for a given π, Θ remains identical before and after learning. Therefore, the comparison of $\mathcal{C}$ (before learning) with $\mathcal{C} \cup c_{new}$ (after learning) reveals the acquired knowledge.

We define EBL in (14). $(\theta \mapsto (\mathcal{C}))$ is the parser before learning. This parser applies to o and yields c_{new}, formalized as $(\theta \mapsto (\mathcal{C})) \mapsto (o)$. The new parser is the application of Θ to the union of $\mathcal{C}$ and c_{new}.

$$\pi_{new} = \theta \mapsto (\mathcal{C} \cup \underbrace{(\underbrace{(\theta \mapsto (\mathcal{C}))}_{\pi_{old}} \mapsto (o))}_{\{c_{new}\}}) \tag{14}$$

From two otherwise identical parsers, the parser with $c =<< a_o, \epsilon >, a_c >$ not present in the other has a greater deductive closure. The cardinality of $<< a_o, \epsilon >, a_c > \in \mathcal{C}$ reflects an empirical knowledge. The empirical knowledge does not allow to conclude something new, but to resolve ambiguities in accordance with observed data, e.g. for a sub-language as shown in (Rayner and Samuelsson, 1994). Both learning techniques have the potential of improving the accuracy.

2.2.1 Learning through Parsing

A substitution of Θ with γ, δ, α reveals the transformation of c_{old} to c_{new}. We start with caching and recalling (Equation 15).

$$\pi_{new} = \gamma \mapsto (\{c_i\} \cup \underbrace{(\underbrace{(\gamma \mapsto (c_i))}_{\rho} \mapsto (o_i))}_{c_i}) \tag{15}$$

Parsing o_i with the cache of c_i yields c_i. The deductive closure is not enlarged. Quantitative relations with respect to o change in $\mathcal{C}$. If c_i is not cached twice, memory-based EBL is idempotent.[6]

[6] Idempotence is the property of an operation that results in the same state no matter how many times it is executed.

EBL with induction and deduction is shown in (16). Here the subscripts merit special attention: $o =< a_x, i_y >$ is parsed from $c =<< a_x, i_x >, a_v >$. This yields $c_{new} =<< a_x, i_y >, a_v >$. Integrating c_{new} into C changes the empirical knowledge with respect to a and i. If the empirical knowledge does not influence ι, D-EBL is idempotent. The deductive closure does not increase as $<< a_x, \epsilon >, a_v > \in \mathcal{C}$.

$$\pi_{new} = \iota \mapsto (\{< a_x, i_x >, a_v >\} \cup \underbrace{((\iota \mapsto (\underbrace{<< a_x, i_x >, a_v >}_{c})) \mapsto (< a_x, i_y >))}_{<< a_x, i_y >, a_v >}) \tag{16}$$

Abductive EBL (A-EBL) is shown in (17). A-EBL acquires empirical knowledge similarly to D-EBL. In addition, a new $<< a_y, \epsilon >, a_r >$ is acquired. This c_{new} may differ from c_{old} with respect to a_y and/or a_r. In the experiments in A-EBL we reported below, $a_y \neq a_x$ and $a_r = a_c$ holds.

$$\pi_{new} = \psi \mapsto (\{< a_x, i_x >, a_c >\} \cup \underbrace{(\underbrace{(\psi \mapsto (\underbrace{<< a_x, i_x >, a_c >}_{c}))}_{\text{learning } \alpha} \mapsto (\underbrace{< a_y, i_y >}_{o_y}))}_{<< a_y, i_y >, a_r >}) \tag{17}$$

2.2.2 Recursive Rule Application

Parsing is a classification task in which $a \in \mathcal{A}$ is assigned to $o \in \mathcal{O}$. Differently from typical classification tasks in machine learning, natural language parsing requires an open set $\mathcal{A}$. This is obtained via the recursive application of $\mathcal{R}$, which unlike non-recursive styles of analysis (Srinivas and Joshi, 1999) yields $\mathcal{A}$ (syntax trees) of any complexity. Then $delete$ is applied to $\mathcal{A}$ so that $delete \mapsto (A)$ can be matched by further rules (c.f. 18). Without this reduction, recursive parsing could not go beyond memory-based parsing.

$$\begin{aligned} r_m =<< &< a_m, i_m >, \\ &< delete \mapsto (r_p \mapsto (o_p)), i_p >>, \\ &< a_n, < a_m, r_p \mapsto (o_p) >>> \end{aligned} \tag{18}$$

Figure 1: An explanation produced by OCTOPUS. At the top, the final parse obtained via deductive substitutions. Abductive term identification bridges gaps in the deduction (X $\sim$ Y). The marker '?' is a graphical shortcut for the set of lexemes $\{i\}$ in c.

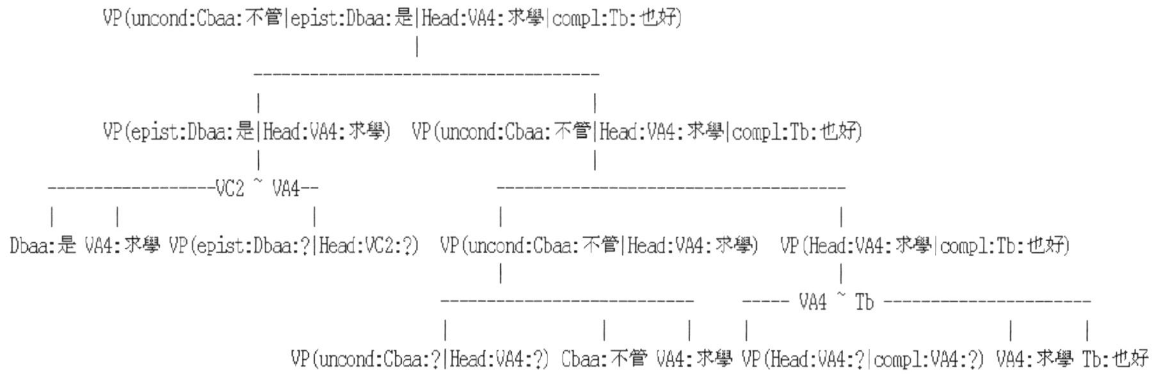

The function $delete$ defines an induction and recursive parsing is thus a deduction. Combinations of memory-based and deduction-based parsing are deductions, combinations of abduction-based parsing with any another parsing are abductions.

Macro Learning is the common term for the combination of EBL with recursive deduction (Tadepalli, 1991). A macro r_{macro} is a rule which yields the same result as a set of rules $\mathcal{R}'$ with $\#\mathcal{R}' \geq 2$ and $r_{macro} \notin \mathcal{R}'$ does. In terms of a grammar, such macros correspond to redundant phrases, i.e. phrases that are obtained by composing smaller phrases of $\mathcal{R}$. Macros represent shortcuts for the parser and, possibly, improved likelihood estimate of the composed structure compared to the estimates under independency assumption (Abney, 1996). When the usage of macros excludes certain types of analysis, e.g. by trying to find longest/best matches we can speak of pruning. This is the contribution of D-EBL for parsing.

3 Experiments in EBL

3.1 Experimental purpose and setup

The aim of the experiments is to verify whether new knowledge is acquired in A-EBL and D-EBL. Secondly, we want to test the influence of new knowledge on parsing accuracy and speed.

The general setup of the experiment is the following. We use a section of a treebank as seed-corpus ($\mathcal{C}_{seed}$). We train the seed-corpus to a corpus-based parser. Using a test-corpus we establish the parsing

Figure 2: The main parsing algorithm of OCTOPUS. The parser interleaves memory-based, deductive, and abductive parsing strategies in five steps: Recalling, non-recursive deduction, deduction via chunk substitution, first with lexemes, then without lexemes and finally abduction.

$\pi \rightarrow (< a, i >)$ {

 # 1 recalling from POS (a) and lexeme (i)
RETURN c IF $(c = \rho \rightarrow (< a, i >))$

 # 2 deduction on the basis of POS (a)
RETURN c IF $(c = \delta(< a, \epsilon >))$

 # 3 deductive, recursive parsing with POS and lexeme
 # Substitutions are defined as in TAGs (Joshi, 2003) IF $((< a_{chunk}, i_{chunk} >, < a_{redu}, i_{redu} >) = best\_chunk \rightarrow (< a, i >))$ {

RETURN $substitution \rightarrow$ (**# deduction**
$\pi \rightarrow (< a_{chunk}, i_{chunk}, >)$,
$\pi \rightarrow (< a_{redu}, i_{redu}) >)$}

 # 4a deductive recursive parsing with lexeme,
 # 4b compared to abductive parsing
IF $((< a_{chunk}, i_{chunk} >, < a_{redu}, i_{redu} >) = best\_chunk \rightarrow (< a, \epsilon >))$ {

RETURN $arg_{max} \rightarrow$(
$\alpha \rightarrow (< a, i >)$, **#abduction**
$substitution \rightarrow$ (**#deduction**
$\pi \rightarrow (a_{chunk}, i_{chunk})$,
$\pi \rightarrow (a_{redu}, i_{redu})))$}

 # 5 abduction as robust parsing solution
RETURN $\alpha \rightarrow (< a, i >)$ }

Figure 3: Abductive parsing with k-nn retrieval and adaptation of retrieved examples.

$\alpha \rightarrow (< a, i >) \{$

RETURN $adaptation \rightarrow (viterbi.align \rightarrow (k.nn.retrieval \rightarrow (< a, i >)))\}$

---

accuracy and speed of the parser ($evaluate(\pi \mapsto (O_{test}))$ =(recall,precision,f-score,time)). Then, we parse a large corpus ($\pi \mapsto (O) = \{c_{new}\}$). A filter criterion that works on the explanation applies. We train those trees which pass the filter to the parser ($\theta \mapsto (C_{seed} \cup \{c_{new}\}) = \pi_{new}$)). Then the parsing accuracy and speed is tested against the same training corpus ($evaluate(\pi_{new} \mapsto (O_{test}))$ =(recall,precision,f-score,time)).

Sections of the Chinese Sinica Treebank (Huang et al., 2000) are used as seed-treebank and gold standard for parsing evaluation. Seed-corpora range between 1.000 and 20.000 trees. We train them to the parser OCTOPUS (Streiter, 2002a). This parser integrates memory- deduction- and abduction-based parsing in a hierarchy of preferences, starting from **1** memory-based parsing, **2** non-recursive deductive parsing, **3** recursive deductive parsing and **5** finally abductive parsing (Fig. 2).

Learning the seed corpora ($\theta \mapsto (c_{1000} \cdots {}_{20.000})$) results in $\pi_{1000} \cdots \pi_{20.000}$. For each $\pi \in \{\pi_{1000} \cdots \pi_{20.000}\}$, a POS tagged corpus $\mathcal{O}$ with $\#\mathcal{O} = 200.000$ is parsed, producing the corpora $\mathcal{C}_{o_{1000}} \cdots \mathcal{C}_{o_{20.000}}$. The corpus used is a subset of the 5 Million word Sinica Corpus (Huang and Chen, 1992).

For every $o \in \mathcal{O}$ the parser produces one parse-tree $c =< o, a >$ and an *explanation*. The explanation has the form of a derivation tree in TAGs, c.f (Joshi, 2003). The deduction and abduction steps are visible in the explanation. Filters apply on the explanation and create sub-corpora that belong to one inference type.

The first filter requires the explanation to contain only one non-recursive deduction, i.e. only parsing step **2**. As deductive parsing is attempted after memory-based parsing (**1**), $i_x \neq i_v$ holds.

A second filter extracts those structures, which are obtained by parsing step **4a** or **5** where only one POS-labels may be different in the last characters (e.g. $\sigma \mapsto$ ("Nab") = "Nac"). The resulting corpora are $\mathcal{C}_{o1000_{deduct}} \cdots \mathcal{C}_{o20.000_{deduct}}$ and $\mathcal{C}_{o1000_{abduct}} \cdots \mathcal{C}_{o20.000_{abduct}}$.

3.2 The Acquired Knowledge

We want to know whether or not new knowledge has been acquired and what the nature of this acquired knowledge is. As parsing was not recursive, we can approach the closure by the types of POS-sequences from all trees and their subtrees in a corpus. We contrast this with to the types of lexeme-sequences. The data show that only A-EBL increases the closure. But even when looking at lexemes, i.e. empirical knowledge, the A-EBL acquires richer information than D-EBL does.

Figure 4: The number of types of POS-sequences as approximation of the closure with C_{seed}, A-EBL and D-EBL. Below the number of type of LEXEME-sequences.

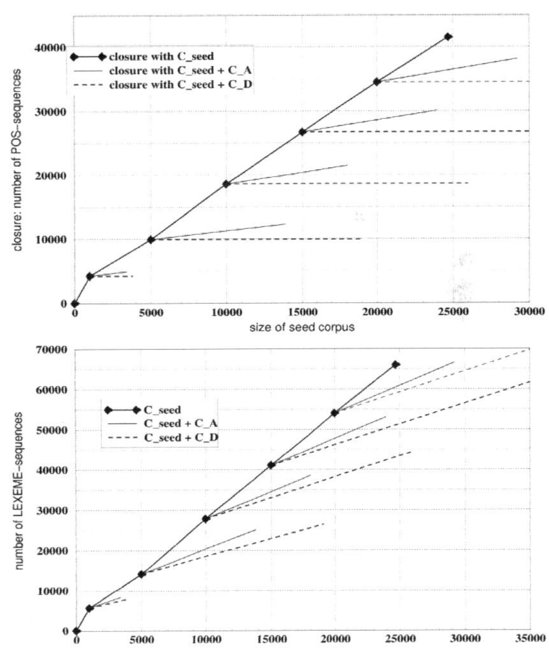

The representatives of the cached parses is gauged by the percentage of top NPs and VPs (including Ss) as top-nodes. Fig 5 shows the bias of cached parses which is more pronounced with D-EBL than with A-EBL.

Figure 5: The proportion of top-NPs and top-VP(S) in abduced and deduced corpora.

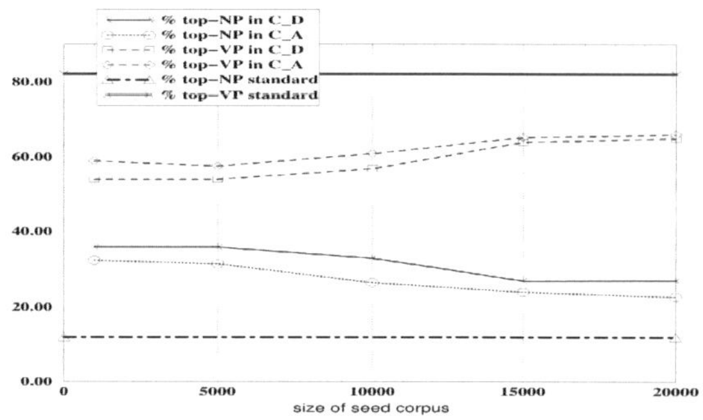

3.3 Evaluating Parsing

The experiments consist in evaluating the parsing accuracy and speed for each $\mathcal{C}_{seed} \cup \mathcal{C}_{o_{1000_{deduct}}} \ldots \mathcal{C}_{seed} \cup \mathcal{C}_{o_{20.000_{abduct}}}$.

Figure 6: The parsing accuracy with abductive EBL ($C_{seed} + C_A$) and deductive EBL ($C_{seed} + C_D$).

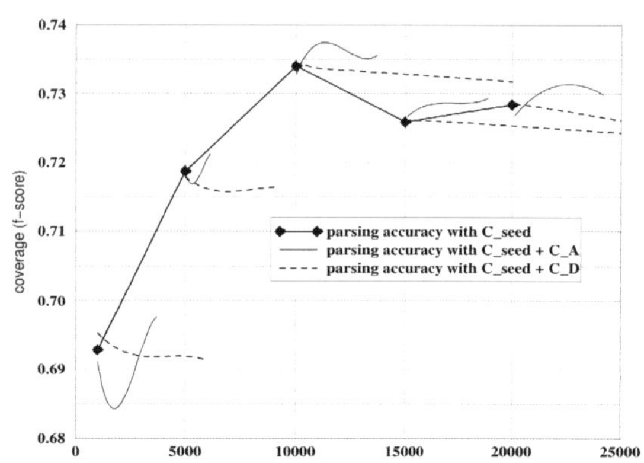

We test the parsing accuracy on 300 untrained and randomly selected sentences using the f-score on unlabeled dependency relations. Fig. 6 shows parsing accuracy depending on the size of the seed-corpus. The graphs show side branches where we introduce the EBL-derived training material. This allows comparing the effect of A-EBL, D-EBL and hand-coded trees (the baseline). Fig. 7 shows the parsing speed in words per second (Processor:1000 MHz, Memory:128 MB) for the same experiments. Rising lines indicate a speed-up in parsing. We have interpolated and smoothed the curves.

Figure 7: The parsing time with A-EBL ($C_{seed} + C_A$) and D-EBL ($C_{seed} + C_D$).

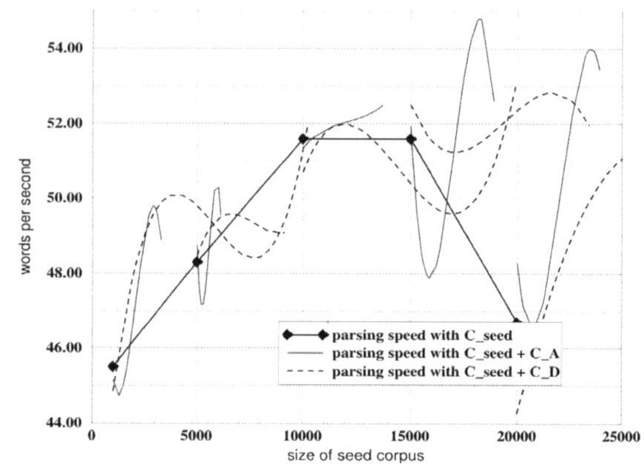

The experimental results confirm the drop in parsing accuracy with D-EBL. This fact is consistent across all experiments. With A-EBL, the parsing accuracy increases beyond the level of departure.

The data also show a speed-up in parsing. This speed-up is more pronounced and less data-hungry with A-EBL. Improving accuracy and efficiency are thus not mutually exclusive, at least for A-EBL.

4 Conclusions

Explanation-based Learning has been used to speed-up natural language parsing. We show that the loss in accuracy results from the deductive basis of parsers, not the EBL framework. D-EBL does not extend the deductive closure and acquires only empirical (disambiguation) knowledge. The accuracy declines due to cached errors, the statistical bias the filters introduce and the usage of shortcuts with limited contextual information.

Alternatively, if the parser uses abduction, the deductive closure of the parser enlarges. This makes accuracy improvements possible - not a logical consequence. In practice, the extended deductive closure compensates for negative factors such as wrong parses or unbalanced distributions in the cache.

On a more abstract level, the paper treats the problem of automatic knowledge acquisition for Chinese NLP. Theory and practice show that abduction-based NLP applications acquire new knowledge and increase accuracy and speed. Future research will maximize the gains.

References

Steven Abney. 1996. Partial Parsing via Finite-State Cascades. In *Proceedings of the ESSLLI '96 Robust Parsing Workshop*.

Rens Bod and Ronald M. Kaplan. 1998. A probabilistic corpus-driven model for lexical functional analysis. In *COLING-ACL'98*.

Michael Carl and Philippe Langlais. 2003. Tuning general translation knowledge to a sublanguage. In *Proceedings of CLAW 2003*, Dublin, Ireland, May, 15-17.

Hsing-Wu Chang. 1994. Word segmentation and sentence parsing in reading Chinese. In *Advances in the Study of Chinese Language Processing*, National Taiwan University, Taipei.

Keh-Jiann Chen. 1996. A model for robust Chinese parser. *Computational Linguistics and Chinese Language*, 1(1):183–204.

Yanis Dimopoulos and Antonis Kakas. 1996. Abduction and inductive learning. In L. De Taedt, editor, *Advances in Inductive Logic Programming*, pages 144–171. IOS Press.

Chu-Ren Huang and Keh-Jiann Chen. 1992. A Chinese corpus for linguistics research. In *COLING'92*, Nantes, France.

Chu-Ren Huang, Feng-Yi Chen, Keh-Jiann Chen, Zhaoming Gao, and Kuang-Yu Chen. 2000. Sinica treebank: Design criteria, annotation guidelines and online interface. In M. Palmer, M. Marcus, A. K. Joshi, and F. Xia, editors, *Proceedings of the Second Chinese Language Processing Workshop*, Hong Kong, October. ACL.

Aravind K. Joshi. 2003. Tree-adjoining grammars. In R. Mitkov, editor, *The Oxford Handbook of Computational Linguistics*. Oxford University Press, Oxford.

Yves Lepage. 1999. Open set experiments with direct analysis by analogy. In *Proceedings NLPRS'99 (Natural Language Processing Pacific Rim Symposium)*, pages 363–368, Beijing.

Gary F. Marcus, Steven Pinker, Michael Ullman, Michelle Hollander, John T. Rosen, and Fei Xu. 1992. *Overregularization in Language Learning*. Monographs of the Society for Research in Child Development, 57 (No. 4, Serial No. 228).

Steven Minton. 1990. Quantitative results concerning the utility problem of explanation-based learning. *Artificial Intelligence*, 42:363–393.

Tom S. Mitchel, R. Keller, and S. Kedar-Cabelli. 1986. Explanation-based generalization: A unifying view. *Machine Learning*, 1(1).

Günter Neumann. 1994. Application of explanation-based learning for efficient processing of constraint-based grammars. In *The 10th Conference on Artificial Intelligence for Applications*, San Antonio, Texas.

Manny Rayner and Christer Samuelsson. 1994. Corpus-based grammar specification for fast analysis. In *Spoken Language Translator: First Year Report*, SRI Technical Report CRC-043, pg. 41-54.

Khalil Sima'an. 1997. Explanation-based leaning of partial-parsers. In W. Daelemans, A. van den Bosch, and A. Weijters, editors, *Workshop Notes of the ECML/ML Workshop on Empirical Learning of Natural Language Processing Tasks*, pages 137–146, Prague, Czech Republic, April.

Bangalore Srinivas and Aravind K. Joshi. 1995. Some novel applications of explanation-based learning to parsing lexicalized tree-adjoining grammars. In *33th Annual Meeting of the ACL*, Cambridge, MA.

Bangalore Srinivas and Aravind K. Joshi. 1999. Supertagging: An approach to almost parsing. *Computational Linguistics*, 25(2):237–265.

Oliver Streiter, Judith Knapp, and Leonhard Voltmer. 2003. Gymn@zilla: A browser-like repository for open learning resources. In *ED-Media, World Conference on Educational Multimedia, Hypermedia & Telecommunications*, Honolulu, Hawaii, June, 23-28.

Oliver Streiter. 2002a. Abduction, induction and memorizing in corpus-based parsing. In *ESSLLI-2002 Workshop on "Machine Learning Approaches in Computational Linguistics"*, pages 73–90, Trento, Italy, August 5-9.

Oliver Streiter. 2002b. Treebank development with deductive and abductive explanation-based learning: Exploratory experiments. In *Workshop on Treebanks and Linguistic Theories 2002*, Sozopol, Bulgaria, September 20-21.

Prasad Tadepalli. 1991. A formalization of explanation-based macro-operator learning. In *IJCAI, Proceedings of the International Joint Conference of Artificial Intelligence*, pages 616–622, Sydney, Australia. Morgan Kaufmann.

Chunfa Yuang, Changming Huang, and Shimei Pan. 1992. Knowledge acquisition and Chinese parsing based on corpus. In *COLING'92*.

Jakub Zavrel and Walter Daelemans. 1997. Memory-based learning: Using similarity for smoothing. In W. Daelemans, A. van den Bosch, and A. Weijters, editors, *Workshop Notes of the ECML/ML Workshop on Empirical Learning of Natural Language Processing Tasks*, pages 71–84, Prague, Czech Republic, April.

The Semantic Knowledge-base of Contemporary Chinese and its Applications in WSD*

Hui Wang
Institute of Computational Linguistics
Peking University
Beijing 100871, China
whui@pku.edu.cn

Shiwen Yu
Institute of Computational Linguistics
Peking University
Beijing 100871, China
yusw@pku.edu.cn

Abstract

The Semantic Knowledge-base of Contemporary Chinese (SKCC) is a large scale Chinese semantic resource developed by the Institute of Computational Linguistics of Peking University. It provides a large amount of semantic information such as semantic hierarchy and collocation features for 66,539 Chinese words and their English counterparts. Its POS and semantic classification represent the latest progress in Chinese linguistics and language engineering. The descriptions of semantic attributes are fairly thorough, comprehensive and authoritative. The paper introduces the outline of SKCC, and indicates that it is effective for word sense disambiguation in MT applications and is likely to be important for general Chinese language processing.

Key words: Semantic knowledge-base, lexical semantic, computational lexicography, word sense disambiguation （WSD）, Chinese language processing

1 Introduction

Semantic resources play an important role in many areas of Natural Language Processing (NLP). The Institute of Computational Linguistics (ICL) of Peking University has been engaged in research and development of the Semantic Knowledge-base of Contemporary Chinese (SKCC) in the last eight years. This lexicon-building project was a collaboration with the Institute of Computing Technology, Chinese Academy of Sciences during 1994-1998, and resulted in a machine-readable bilingual lexicon suitable for use with Machine Translation applications, which contained a fairly complete characterization of the semantic classification, valence specifications and collocation properties for 49 thousands Chinese words and their English counterparts (Wang Hui, 1998).

Since 2001, the further development of SKCC has been co-conducted by ICL and Chinese Department of Peking University. At present, SKCC has made great progress. Not only is the scale extended to 66,539 entries, but also the quality has been immensely improved. The semantic classification in the updated edition of SKCC is the embodiment of the very latest progress in Chinese linguistics and language engineering, while the semantic descriptions are comprehensive and thorough. It can provide rich lexical semantic information for various NLP applications.

2 Outline of SKCC

2.1 Scale and Structure

SKCC consists of one general database and six sub-databases. The general database contains shared attributes of all the 66,539 entries, while the sub-databases provide detailed descriptions of the

* Supported by China National Fundamental Research Program (973) (PN: G1998030507-4).

distinctive semantic attributes associated with the parts of speech (POS). For example, the verb database has 16 attribute fields, noun database and adjective database has 15 attribute fields respectively.

Databasc Name	Entrics	Attributc fields	Attributc value
nouns	38,478	15	5
verbs	21,142	16	3
adjective	5,577	15	8
pronouns	236	15	3
adverbs	997	11	1
numerals	109	11	1
General	66,539	8	5
Total	133,07	**91**	**1**

Table 1 Scale of SKCC

All of the six sub-databases can be linked to the general database through four key fields, namely ENTRY, POS, HOMOMORPHISM and SENSE. As a result, the son knots can inherit all information from their father knots (Figure 1).

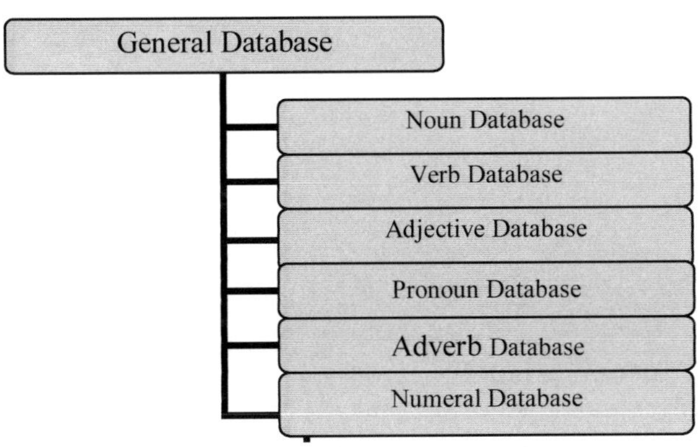

Figure 1 Main structure of SKCC

2.2 Semantic Hierarchy

One of the most outstanding characteristics of SKCC is that its semantic hierarchy is based on grammatical analysis, rather than merely on general knowledge (as illustrated in Figure 2 below). This classification system represents the latest progress in Chinese semantics. It is very useful for NLP applications(Zhan Weidong, 1997), as well as compatible with various semantic resources, such as Wordnet (Christiane Fellbaum. 1998), Chinese concept dictionary (CCD)(Yu Jiangsheng, 2002), HowNet(Dong Zhendong, 2000) etc. Currently, the classification of all of the 66,539 entries has already been completed.

(1) Verbs

- state
- emotion/cognition
- event
  - change
  - weather
  - body functions
  - perception
  - consumption
  - motion
  - creation
  - contact
  - possession
  - communication
  - competition
  - social behavior
  - other event

(2) Adjectives

- description of event
- property of object
  - measurable value
    - concentration
    - speed
    - temperature
    - speed
    - length
    - height
    - width
    - depth
    - rigidity
    - humidity
    - thickness
    - tightness
    - size
    - value
  - immeasurable value
    - vision
    - tactility
    - tone
    - taste
    - shape
    - quality
    - content
  - color
- property of human
  - age
  - character
  - relation
  - condition
- property of space
  - one dimension
  - two dimension
  - three dimension
- property of time

(3) Nouns

- entity
  - organism
    - person
      - individual
        - profession
        - identity
        - relation
        - name
      - group
        - organization
        - society
    - animal
      - beast
      - bird …
    - plant
      - tree
      - flower …
    - microbe
  - object
    - artifact
      - building
      - works
      - food
      - clothes
      - bill
      - instrument
        - tool
        - vehicle
        - sports- instrument
        - furniture
        - …
      - …
    - natural object
      - celestial body
      - weather
      - geography
        - land
        - water
      - …
    - excrement
    - shape
  - part
    - body-part
    - object-part
- abstraction
  - attribute
    - measurable
    - immeasurable
      - property of human
      - description of event
      - property of object
  - information
  - field
  - physiological state
  - motivation
  - rule
  - psycho feature
    - feelings
    - cognition
- process
  - event
  - natural phenomenon
    - visible phenomenon
    - audible phenomenon
- time
  - specific time
  - relative time
- space
  - location
  - direction

(4) adverbs

- degree
- range
- time
- location
- frequency
- manner
- negation
- modality

(5) numerals

- cardinal number
- ordinal number
- amount
- auxiliary

Figure 2 Semantic hierarchy in SKCC

2.3 Comprehensive Semantic Descriptions

There is close correlation between lexical meaning and its distribution. Oriented to MT and IR, one aim of SKCC is to provide detailed semantic description and collocation behavior that in many cases is likely to be uniquely associated with a single sense. For example, following attribute fields have been filled with values in the verb database (see table 2).

ENTRY	Commonly used Chinese word or idiom phrase
PRONUNCIATION	Chinese Pinyin with tones such as "chi3zi5" for "尺子"(ruler)
PART OF SPEECH	POS tagging of per word or idiom
SUB-CATEGORY	Sub-category tagging of per word or idiom
POSs	All POS tagging of per word
HOMOMORPHISM	Homograph number
SENSE	Sense number of per polysemous word
DEFINITION	Sense definition
SEMANTIC CATEGORY	Semantic categories of per word or idiom. A word can be tagged with two or more semantic categories. For instance, the noun "青菜" (greengrocery) belong to "plant | food" categories.
VALENCE	Valence number of each entry. For example, "咳嗽"(cough) is a one-valence verb，while "吃"(eat) is a two-valence one, "给"(give) is three-valence.
AGENT	Actor of action or motion.
OBJECT	Object of action.
DATIVE	Beneficiary or suffer of action.
TRANSLATION	English counterpart of per word or idiom.
ECAT	POS tagging of per English word or phrase.
ILLUSTRATIONS	Corpus-derived example sentences showing authentic contexts of a word or idiom.

Table 2 Semantic attributes in the verb database of SKCC

To sum up, the above attributes fall into five kinds of information below:

(1) Basic information of entry, such as vocabulary item, part of speech, sub-category, homograph and pronunciation;

(2) Descriptions of word meaning, including sense number, definition, and semantic categories;

(3) Semantic valence, thematic roles and combinatorial properties for per words; this is the most important part of SKCC and especially useful for WSD and lexical semantics research;

(4) English translation and its POS tagging. If a Chinese word has two or more English counterparts, it will be regarded as different entries respectively, and the collocation information will also be given in relevant fields. This can significantly improve the quality of Chinese-English MT system.

(5) Corpus-derived authentic examples of a word in context, showing how it is used, how phrases are formed around it, and so on.

3 Application in WSD

As a large-scale lexical knowledge base, SKCC combines the features of many of the other resources commonly exploited in NLP work: it includes definitions and English translations for individual senses of words within it, as in a bilingual dictionary; it organizes lexical concepts into a conceptual hierarchy, like a thesaurus; and it includes other links among words according to several semantic relations, including semantic role, collocation information etc. As such it currently provides the broadest set of lexical information in a single resource. The kind of information recorded and made available through SKCC is of a type usable for various NLP applications, including machine translation, automatic abstraction, information retrieval, hypertext navigation, thematic analysis, and text processing.

In this section, we shall focus on the automatic disambiguation of Chinese word senses involving SKCC since it is most troublesome, and essential for all the above NLP applications (Ide, 1998).

3.1 Determination of the polysemous words and homographs

In general terms, word sense disambiguation (WSD) task necessarily involves two steps: (1) the determination of all the polysemous words and homographs in the text or discourse; and (2) a means to assign each occurrence of a word to the appropriate sense.

Step (1) can be easily accomplished by reliance on SKCC. Firstly, each entry denotes one single sense of per word in SKCC. Thus, if a word has two or more senses, it will be regard as different entries, and the "SENSE" field will be filled with different number (as "菜" in table 3).

ENTRY	菜 1	菜 2
POS	n	n
SENSE	1	2
DEFINITION	vegetable	cooked vegetable, egg, fish, meat...etc
TRANSLATION	vegetable	dish
ILLUSTRATIONS	种～ grow vegetables 野～ potherb	荤～ meat or fish 四～一汤 four dishes and a bowl of soup

Table 3 Two senses of Chinese noun "菜"

Secondly, SKCC marked all of the homographs in "HOMOMORPHISM" field, such as two verbs "看"with different pronunciation in table 4.

ENTRY	看 1	看 2
PRONUNCIATION	Kan4	Kan1
HOMOMORPHISM	A	B
DEFINITION	see; watch; look at	look after; take care of
TRANSLATION	see	look after

Table 4 Homographs in SKCC

Therefore, if either of the "SENSE" and "HOMOMORPHISM" fields is filled with value in SKCC, the entry must be a polysemous word or homograph.

3.2 WSD based on semantic categories

The senses of most Chinese polysemous words and homographs belong to different semantic categories, and have different syntagmatic features in context (Wang Hui, 2002) . SKCC gives detailed description of such information in "AGENT" and/or "OBJECT" fields as illustrated in table 5 below.

ENTRY	清淡 1	清淡 2
POS	a	a
SENSE	1	2
DEFINITION	(of food, drink, smell) light; weak	(of business) slack
SEMANTIC CATEGORY	taste	condition
AGENT	food | drink| plant	"business"
TRANSLATION	light	slack

Table 5 Polysemous adjectives in SKCC

Based on the above description, the target word "清淡" in following POS-tagged text can be accurately disambiguated:

[1] 一/m 杯/q 清淡/a 的/u 龙井茶/n
A cup of light Longjing tea.

[2] 农忙时/t 进城/v 的/u 人/n 不/d 多/a， 生意/n 比较/d 清淡/a。
When the season is busy, few farmers go to town and the business is rather slack.

In sentence[1], the word modified by "清淡" is the noun"茶"(tea) , which is a kind of "drink"; while the word"清淡" in sentence [2] is a predicate of "business" . According to the different values in "AGENT" field, it is easy to judge that these two "清淡" belong to two semantic categories, viz. the former is "light", and the latter is "slack".

3.3 WSD based on collocation information

As for the polysemous words or homographs belonging to the same semantic category, the difference between them usually manifests at the collocation level. According to a study in cognitive science, people often disambiguate word sense using only a few other words in a given context (frequently only one additional word) (Choueka, 1983). Thus, the relationships between one word and others can be effectively used to resolve ambiguity. For example, Chinese verb "找" has two senses: one is "寻找" (look for) and the other is "退还" (give change). Only when the verb cooccurs with the noun "钱" (money), it can be interpreted as "give change"; Otherwise, it means "look for" (see table 6).

ENTRY	找 [1]	找 [2]
HOMOMORPHISM	A	B
SENSE	1	2
DEFINITION	look for; seek try to find;	give change
AGENT	person	entity
OBJECT	entity	"money"
DATIVE		person
TRANSLATION	look for	give change

Table 6 Different senses of verb "找"

According to table 6, the verb "找" in sentence [1] below must be "look for", because its object is "人" (person), a kind of "entity"; while "找"in sentence [2] has two objects, namely, indirect object "我" (me) and direct object "钱"(money). Thus, its meaning is "give change".

[1]他们/r 将/d 出去/v 找/v 人/n。
They will go out to look for sb.

[2]售货员/n 还/d 没有/d 找/v 我/r 钱/n 呢
The seller has not given change to me.

By making full use of SKCC and a large scale POS-tagged corpus of Chinese, a multi-levels WSD model is developed and has already been used in a Chinese-English MT application.

4 Conclusion

SKCC is a well-structured Chinese-English bilingual semantic resource, as described in the paper, it has more than 66,000 Chinese words and their English counterparts classified, and the accurate description of about 1.5 million attributes further enriched the abundance of lexical semantic knowledge. It not only provides a deductive system of word meaning and valuable semantic knowledge for Chinese language processing, but also has great theoretical significance in lexical semantics and computational lexicography research.

Acknowledgement

We appreciate all the members participated in SKCC project, especially Prof. Lu Jianming, Dr. Zhan Weidong, Mr. Li Kangnian and Dr. Chang Baobao. The blithesome collaboration with Dr. Ying Chenjin and Mr. Guo qingjian from Chinese Department is memorable for all of us. Lastly, thanks our colleagues and friends for their kindly discussion with the authors.

References

Choueka, Y. and S. Lusignan, 1983. "A Connectionist Scheme for Modeling Word Sense Disambiguation," *Cognition and Brain Theory*. 6 (1). pp.89-120.

Christiane Fellbaum. 1998. WordNet: an electronic lexical database. Mass: MIT Press.

Dong Zhendong, Dong Qiang. 200. "Hownet". http:// www.keenage.com.

Ide, Nancy; Jean Véronis. 1998. "Introduction to the Special Issue on Word Sense Disambiguation: The State of the Art", *Computational Linguistics*. Vol.24, No.1. pp1-40

Wang Hui, Zhan Weidong, Liu Qun. 1998. "Design of Semantic Dictionary of Modern Chinese". *Proceedings from 1998 International Conference on Chinese Information Processing*. Beijing: Tsinghua University Press. pp361-367.

Wang Hui. 2002. "Chinese Word Sense Disambiguation in Machine Translation". *Proceedings from Chinese National Symposium on Machine Translation.* Beijing: Publishing House of Electronics Industry. pp.34-43.

Yu Jiangsheng, Yu Shiwen. 2002. "Structure and Design of CCD". Chinese Information Processing. 16 (4): 12-20.

Zhan Weidong, Liu Qun. 1997. "The important role of semantic classification in Chinese-English MT". Language Engineering. Tsinghua University Press. 286-291.

Learning Verb-Noun Relations to Improve Parsing

Andi Wu
Microsoft Research
One Microsoft Way, Redmond, WA 98052
andiwu@microsoft.com

Abstract

The verb-noun sequence in Chinese often creates ambiguities in parsing. These ambiguities can usually be resolved if we know in advance whether the verb and the noun tend to be in the verb-object relation or the modifier-head relation. In this paper, we describe a learning procedure whereby such knowledge can be automatically acquired. Using an existing (imperfect) parser with a chart filter and a tree filter, a large corpus, and the log-likelihood-ratio (LLR) algorithm, we were able to acquire verb-noun pairs which typically occur either in verb-object relations or modifier-head relations. The learned pairs are then used in the parsing process for disambiguation. Evaluation shows that the accuracy of the original parser improves significantly with the use of the automatically acquired knowledge.

1 Introduction

Computer analysis of natural language sentences is a challenging task largely because of the ambiguities in natural language syntax. In Chinese, the lack of inflectional morphology often makes the resolution of those ambiguities even more difficult. One type of ambiguity is found in the verb-noun sequence which can appear in at least two different relations, the verb-object relation and the modifier-head relation, as illustrated in the following phrases.

(1) 登记 手续 的 费用
dengji shouxu de feiyong
register procedure DE expense
"the expense of the registration procedure"

(2) 办理 手续 的 费用
banli shouxu de feiyong
handle procedure DE expense
"the expense of going through the procedure"

In (1), the verb-noun sequence "登记 手续" is an example of the modifier-head relation while "办理 手续" in (2) is an example of the verb-object relation. The correct analyses of these two phrases are given in Figure 1 and Figure 2, where "RELCL" stands for "relative clause":

Figure 1. Correct analysis of (1)

Figure 2. Correct analysis of (2)

However, with the set of grammar rules that cover the above phrases and without any semantic or collocational knowledge of the words involved, there is nothing to prevent us from the wrong analyses in Figure 3 and Figure 4.

Figure 3. Wrong analysis of (1)

Figure 4. Wrong analysis of (2)

To rule out these wrong parses, we need to know that 登记 is a typical modifier of 手续 while 办理 typically takes 手续 as an object. The question is how to acquire such knowledge automatically. In the rest of this paper, we will present a learning procedure that learns those relations by processing a large corpus with a chart-filter, a tree-filter and an LLR filter. The approach is in the spirit of Smadja (1993) on retrieving collocations from text corpora, but is more integrated with parsing. We will show in the evaluation section how much the learned knowledge can help improve sentence analysis.

2 The Learning Procedure

The syntactic ambiguity associated with the verb-noun sequence can be either local or global. The kind of ambiguity we have observed in (1) and (2) is global in nature, which exists even if this noun phrase is plugged into a larger structure or complete sentence. There are also local ambiguities where the ambiguity disappears once the verb-noun sequence is put into a broader context. In the following examples, the sentences in (3) and (4) can only receive the analyses in Figure 5 and Figure 6 respectively.

(3) 这 是 新 的 登记 手续。
zhe shi xin de dengji shouxu
this be new DE register procedure
"This is a new registration procedure."

(4) 你 不 必 办理 手续。
ni bu bi banli shouxu
you not must handle procedure
"You don't have to go through the procedure."

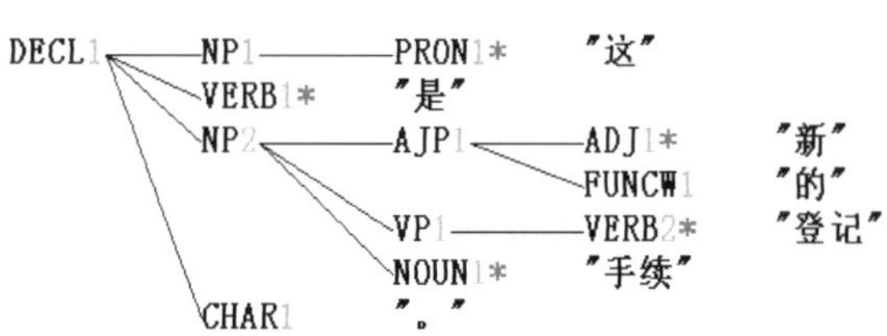

Figure 5. Parse tree of (3)

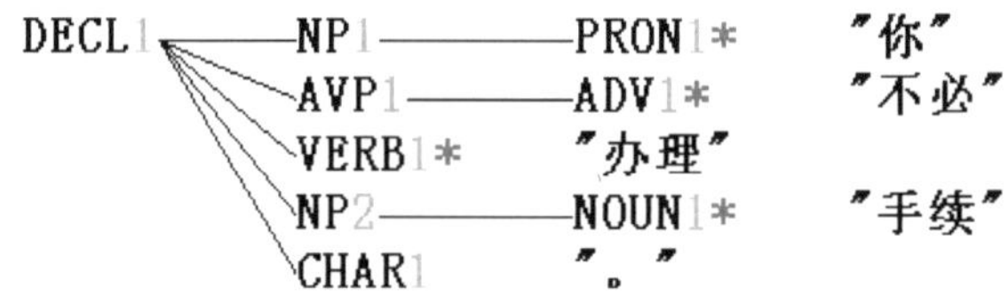

Figure 6. Parse tree of (4)

In the processing of a large corpus, sentences with global ambiguities only have a random chance of being analyzed correctly, but sentences with local ambiguities can often receive correct analyses. Although local ambiguities will create some confusion in the parsing process, increase the size of the parsing chart, and slow down processing, they can be resolved in the end unless we run out of resources (in terms of time and space) before the analysis is complete. Therefore, there should be sufficient number of cases in the corpus where the relationship between the verb and the noun is clear. An obvious strategy we can adopt here is to learn from the clear cases and use the learned knowledge to help resolve the unclear cases. If a verb-noun pair appears predominantly in the verb-object relationship or the modifier head relationship throughout the corpus, we should prefer this relationship everywhere else.

A simple way to learn such knowledge is by using a tree-filter to collect all instances of each verb-noun pair in the parse trees of a corpus, counting the number of times they appear in each relationship, and then comparing their frequencies to decide which relationship is the predominant one for a given pair. Once we have the information that "登记" is typically a modifier of "手续" and "办理" typically takes "手续" as an object, for instance, the sentence in (1) will only receive the analysis in Figure 1 and (2) only the analysis in Figure 2. However, this only works in idealized situations where the parser is doing an almost perfect job, in which case no learning would be necessary. In reality, the parse trees are not always reliable and the relations extracted from the parses can contain a fair amount of noise. It is not hard to imagine that a certain verb-noun pair may occur only a couple of times in the corpus and they are misanalyzed in every instance. If such noise is not filtered out, the knowledge we acquire will mislead us and minimize the benefit we get from this approach.

An obvious solution to this problem is to ignore all the low frequency pairs and keep the high frequency ones only, as wrong analyses tend to be random. But the cut-off point is difficult to set if we are only looking at the raw frequencies, whose range is hard to predict. The cut-off point will be too low for some pairs and too high for others. We need a normalizing factor to turn the raw frequencies into relative frequencies. Instead of asking "which relation is more frequent for a given pair?", the question should be "of all the instances of a given verb-noun pair in the corpus, which relation has a higher percentage of occurrence?". The normalizing factor should then be the total count of a verb-noun pair in the corpus regardless of the syntactic relations between them. The normalized frequency of a relation for a given pair is thus the number of times this pair is assigned this relation in the parses divided by this normalizing factor. For example, if 登记 手续 occurs 10 times in the corpus and is analyzed as verb-object 3 times and modifier-head 7 times, the normalized frequencies for these two relations will be 30% and 70% respectively. What we have now is actually the probability of a given pair occurring in a given relationship. This probability may not be very accurate, given the fact that the parse trees are not always correct, but it should a good approximation, assuming that the corpus is large enough and most of the potential ambiguities in the corpus are local rather than global in nature.

But how do we count the number of verb-noun pairs in a corpus? A simple bigram count will unjustly favor the modifier-head relation. While the verb and the noun are usually adjacent when the verb modifies the noun, they can be far apart when the noun is the object of the verb, as illustrated in (5).

(5) 他们 正在 <u>办理</u> 去 台湾 参加
tamen zhengzai banli qu taiwan canjia
they PROG handle go Taiwan participate
第十九届 国际 计算 语言学
dishijiujie guoji jisuan yuyanxue
19th international compute linguistics
会议 的 <u>手续</u>。
huiyi de shouxu
conference DE procedure
"They are going through the procedures for going to Taipei for the 19th International Conference on Computational Linguistics."

To get a true normalizing factor, we must count all the potential dependencies, both local and long-distance. This is required also because the tree-filter we use to collect pair relations consider both local and long-distance dependencies as well. Since simple string matching is not able to get the potential long-distance pairs, we resorted to the use of a chart-filter. As the parser we use is a chart parser, all the potential constituents are stored in the chart, though only a small subset of those will end up in the parse tree. Among the constituents created in the chart for the sentence in (5), for instance, we are supposed to find [办理] and [去台湾参加第十九届国际计算语言学会议的手续] which are adjacent to each other. The fact that 手续 is the head of the second phrase then makes 手续 adjacent to 办理. We will therefore be able to get one count of 办理 followed by 手续 from (5) despite the long span of intervening words between them. The use of the chart-filter thus enables us to make our normalizing factor more accurate. The probability of a given verb-noun pair occurring in a given relation is now the total count of this relation in the parse trees throughout the corpus divided by the total count of all the potential relations found in all the charts created during the processing of this corpus.

The cut-off point we finally used is 50%, i.e. a pair+relation will be kept in our knowledge base if the probability obtained this way is more than 50%. This may seem low, but it is higher than we think considering the fact that verb-object and modifier-head are not the only relations that can hold between a verb and a noun. In (6), for example, 办理 is not related to 手续 in either way in spite of their adjacency.

(6) 他们 去 上海 办理 手续 所需
tamen qu shanghai banli shouxu suoxu
they go Shanghai handle procedure need
的 公证 材料。
de gongzheng cailiao
DE notarize material

"They went to Shanghai to handle the notarized material needed for the procedure."

We will still find the 办理 手续 pair in the chart, but it is not expected to appear in either the verb-object relation or modifier-head relation in the parse tree. Therefore, the baseline probability for any pair+relation might be far below 50% and more than 50% is a good indicator that a given pair does typically occur in a given relation. We can also choose to keep all the pairs with their probabilities in the knowledge base and let the probabilities be integrated into the probability of the complete parse tree at the time of parse ranking.

The results we obtained from the above procedure are quite clean, in the sense that most of the pairs that are classified into the two types of relations with a probability greater than 50% are correct. Here are some sample pairs that we learned.

Verb-Object:

检验 真理	test - truth
配置 资源	allocate - recourses
经营 业务	manage - business
奉献 爱心	offer - love
欺骗 行人	cheat - pedestrians

Modifier-Head:

检验 标准	testing - standard
配置 方案	allocation - plan
经营 方式	management - mode
奉献 精神	offering - spirit
欺骗 行为	cheating - behavior

However, there are pairs that are correct but not "typical" enough, especially in the verb-object relations. Here are some examples:

具有 意义	have - meaning
具有 效力	have - impact
具有 色彩	have - color
具有 作用	have - function
具有 功效	have - effect

…

These are truly verb-object relations, but we may not want to keep them in our knowledge base for the following reasons. First of all, the verbs in such cases usually can take a wide range of objects and the strength of association between the verb and the object is weak. In other words, the objects are not "typical". Secondly, those verbs tend not to occur in the modifier-head relation with a following noun and we gain very little in terms of disambiguation by storing those pairs in the knowledge base. To prune away those pairs, we used the log-likelihood-ratio algorithm (Dunning, 1993) to compute the degree of association between the verb and the noun in each pair. Pairs where there is high "mutual information" between the verb and noun would receive higher scores while pairs where the verb can co-occur with many different nouns would receive lower scores. Pairs with association scores below a certain threshold were then thrown out. This not only makes the remaining pairs more "typical" but helps to clean out more garbage. The resulting knowledge base therefore has higher quality.

3 Evaluation

The knowledge acquired by the method described in the previous section is used in subsequent sentence analysis to prefer those parses where the verb-noun sequence is analyzed in the same way as specified in the knowledge base. When processing a large corpus, what we typically do is analyzing the corpus twice. The first pass is the learning phase where we acquire additional knowledge by parsing the corpus. The knowledge acquired is used in the second pass to get better parses. This is one example of the general approach of "improving parsing by parsing", as described in (Wu *et al* 2002).

To find out how much the learned knowledge contributes to the improvement of parsing, we performed a human evaluation. In the evaluation, we used our existing sentence analyzer (Heidorn 2000, Jensen *et al* 1993, Wu and Jiang 1998) to process a corpus of 271,690 sentences to learn the verb-noun relations. We then parsed the same sentences first without the additional knowledge and then with the acquired knowledge. Comparing the outputs, we found that 16,445 (6%) of the sentences had different analyses in the two passes. We then randomly selected 500 sentences from those "diff" sentences and presented them to a linguist from an independent agency who, given two different parses of the same sentence, was asked to pick the parse she judged to be more accurate. The order in which the parses were presented was randomized so that the evaluator had no idea as to which tree was from the first pass and which one from the second pass.

The linguist's judgment showed that, with the additional knowledge that we acquired, 350 (70%) of those sentences parsed better with the additional knowledge, 85 (17%) parsed worse, and 65 (13%) had parses that were equally good or bad. In other words, the accuracy of sentence analysis improved significantly with the learning procedure discussed in this paper.

Here is an example where the parse became better when the automatically acquired knowledge is used. Due to space limitation, only the parses of a fraction of the sentence is given here:

(7) 要 遵照 国家 测试 标准
yao zunzhao guojia ceshi biaozhun
want follow nation testing standard
"(You) must follow the national testing standards."

Because of the fact that 遵照 is ambiguous between a verb ("follow") and a preposition ("in accordance with"), this sentence fragment got the parse tree in Figure 7 before the learned knowledge was used, where 标准 was misanalyzed as the object of 测试:

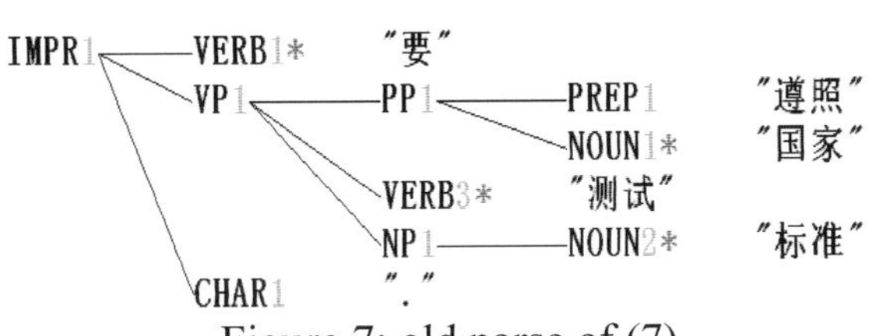

Figure 7: old parse of (7)

During the learning process, we acquired "测试-标准" as a typical pair where the two words are in the modifier-head relationship. Once this pair was added to our knowledge base, we got the correct parse, where 遵照 is analyzed as a verb and 测试 as a modifier of 标准:

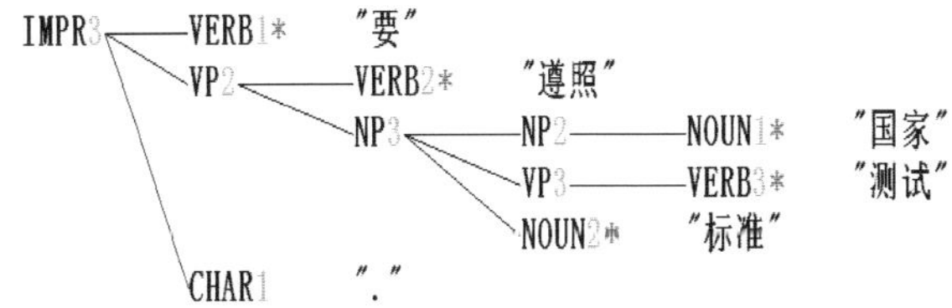

Figure 8: New tree of (7)

We later inspected the sentences where the parses became worse and found two sources for the regressions. The main source was of course errors in the learned results, since they had not been manually checked. The second source was an engineering problem: the use of the acquired knowledge required the use of additional memory and consequently exceeded some system limitations when the sentences were very long.

4 Future work

The approach described in this paper can be applied to the learning of many other typical syntactic relations between words. We have already used it to learn noun-noun pairs where the first noun is a typical modifier of the second noun. This has helped us to rule out incorrect parses where the two nouns were not put into the same constituent. Other relations we have been trying to learn include:

- Noun-noun pairs where the two nouns are in conjunction (e.g. 新郎 新娘 "bride and bridegroom");
- Verb-verb pairs where the two verbs are in conjunction (e.g. 调查 研究 "investigate and study");
- Adjective-adjective pairs where two adjectives are in conjunction (e.g. 年轻 漂亮 "young and beautiful");
- Noun-verb pairs where the noun is a typical subject of the verb.

Knowledge of this kind, once acquired, will benefit not only parsing, but other NLP applications as well, such as machine translation and information retrieval.

In terms of parsing, the benefit we get there is similar to what we get in lexicalized statistical parsing where parsing decisions can be based on specific lexical items. However, the training of a statistical parser requires a tree bank which is expensive to create while our approach does not. Our approach does require an existing parser, but this parser does not have to be perfect and can be improved as the learning goes on. Once the parser is reasonably good, what we need is just raw text, which is available in large quantities.

5 Conclusion

We have shown in this paper that parsing quality can be improved by using the parser as an automatic learner which acquires new knowledge in the first pass to help analysis in the second pass. We demonstrated this through the learning of typical verb-object and modifier-head relations. With the use of a chart-filter, a tree-filter and the LLR algorithm, we are able to acquire such knowledge with high accuracy. Evaluation shows that the quality of sentence analysis can improve significantly with the help of the automatically acquired knowledge.

References

Dunning, T. 1993. Accurate methods for the statistics of surprise and coincidence. *Computational Linguistics*, 19(1): 61-74.

Heidorn, G. E. 2000. Intelligent writing assistance, in *A Handbook of Natural Language Processing: Techniques and Applications for the Processing of Language as Text*, Dale R., Moisl H., and Somers H. eds., Marcel Dekker, New York, pp. 181-207.

Jensen, K., G. Heidorn and S. Richardson. 1993. *Natural Language Processing: the PLNLP Approach".* Kluwer Academic Publishers, Boston.

Smadja, F. 1993. Retrieving collocations from text: Xtract. *Computational Linguistics*, 19(1): 143-177.

Wu, Andi, J. Pentheroudakis and Z. Jiang, 2002. Dynamic lexical acquisition in Chinese sentence analysis. In *Proceedings of the 19th International Conference on Computational Linguistics*, pp. 1308-1312, Taipei, Taiwan.

Wu, Andi, J. and Z. Jiang, 1998. Word segmentation in sentence analysis, in *Proceedings of 1998 International Conference on Chinese Information Processing*, pp. 46-51.169-180, Beijing, China.

Single Character Chinese Named Entity Recognition

Xiaodan Zhu, Mu Li, Jianfeng Gao and Chang-Ning Huang
Microsoft Research, Asia
Beijing 100080, China
`xdzhu@msrchina.research.microsoft.com`
`{t-muli,jfgao,cnhuang}@microsoft.com`

Abstract

Single character named entity (SCNE) is a name entity (NE) composed of one Chinese character, such as "中" *(zhong1, China)* and "俄" *(e2,Russia)*. SCNE is very common in written Chinese text. However, due to the lack of in-depth research, SCNE is a major source of errors in named entity recognition (NER). This paper formulates the SCNE recognition within the source-channel model framework. Our experiments show very encouraging results: an F-score of 81.01% for single character location name recognition, and an F-score of 68.02% for single character person name recognition. An alternative view of the SCNE recognition problem is to formulate it as a classification task. We construct two classifiers based on maximum entropy model (ME) and vector space model (VSM), respectively. We compare all proposed approaches, showing that the source-channel model performs the best in most cases.

1 Introduction

The research of named entity recognition (NER) becomes very popular in recent years due to its wide applications and the Message Understanding Conference (MUC) which provides a standard test-bed for NER evaluation. Recent research on English NER includes (Collins, 2002; Isozaki, 2002; Zhou, 2002; etc.). Chinese NER research includes (Liu, 2001; Zheng, 2000; Yu, 1998; Chen, 1998; Shen, 1995; Sun, 1994; Zhang, 1992 etc.)

In Chinese NEs, there is a special kind of NE, called single character named entity (SCNE), on which there is little in-depth research. SCNE is a NE composed of only one Chinese character, such as the location name "中" *(zhong1,China)* and "俄" *(e2,Russia)* in the phrase "中俄贸易" *(zhong1-e2-mao4-yi4, trade between China and Russia)*. SCNE is very common in written Chinese text. For instance, SCNE accounts for 8.17% of all NE tokens according to our statistics on a 10MB corpus. However, due to the lack of research, SCNE is a major source of errors in NER. Among three state-of-the-art systems we have, the best F-scores of single character location (SCL) and single character person (SCP) are 43.63% and 43.48% respectively. This paper formulates the SCNE recognition within the source-channel model framework. Our results show very encouraging performance. We achieve an F-score of 81.01% for SCL recognition and an F-score of 68.02% for SCP recognition. An alternative view of the SCNE recognition problem is to formulate it as a classification task. For example, "中" is a SCNE in "中俄贸易", but not in "北京四中"*(bei3-jing1-si4-zhong1, Beijing No.4 High School)*. We then construct two classifiers respectively based on two statistical models: maximum entropy model (ME) and vector space model (VSM). We compare these two classifiers with the source-channel model, showing that the source-channel model is slightly better. We then compare the source-channel model with other three state-of-the-art NER systems.

The remainder of this paper is structured as follows: Section 2 introduces the task of SCNE recognition and related work. Section 3 and 4 propose the source-channel model and two classifiers for SCNE recognition, respectively. Section 5 presents experimental results and error analysis. Section 6 gives conclusion.

2 SCNE Recognition and Related Work

We consider three types of SCNE in this paper: single character location name (SCL), person name (SCP), and organization name (SCO). Below are examples:

1. **SCL**: "*中*"and "*俄*" in "*中俄贸易*"
2. **SCP**: "*周*" *(zhou1, Zhou)* in "*周总理*" *(zhou1-zong3-li3,Premier Zhou),*
3. **SCO**: "*国*" *(guo2, Kuomingtang Party) and* "*共*" *(gong4, Communist Party) in* "*国共合作*" *(Guo2-gong4-he2-zuo4, Cooperation between Kuomingtang Part and Communist Party)*

SCNE is very common in written Chinese text. As shown in Table 1, SCNE accounts for 8.17% of all NE tokens on the 10MB corpus. Especially, 14.65% of location names are SCLs. However, due to the lack of research, SCNE is a major source of errors in NER. In our experiments described below, we focus on SCL and SCP, while SCO is not considered because of its small number in the data.

	# SCNE	# NE	#SCNE / #NE
PN	5,892	129,317	4.56%
LN	32,483	221,713	14.65%
ON	356	122,779	0.29%
Total	38,731	473,809	8.17%

Table 1. Proportion of SCNE in NE

To our knowledge, most NER systems do not report SCNE recognition results separately. Some systems (e.g. Liu, 2001) even do not include SCNE in recognition task. SCNE recognition is achieved using the same technologies as for NER, which can be roughly classified into rule-based methods and statistical-based methods, while most of state-of-the-art systems use hybrid approaches.

Wang (1999) and Chen (1998) used linguistic rules to detect NE with the help of the statistics from dictionary. Ji(2001), Zheng (2000), Shen(1995) and Sun(1994) used statistics from dictionaries and large corpus to generate PN or LN candidates, and used linguistic rules to filter the result, and Yu (1998) used language model to filter. Liu (2001) applied statistical and linguistic knowledge alternatively in a seven-step procedure. Unfortunately, most of these results are incomparable due to the different test sets used, except the results of Chen (1998) and Yu (1998). They took part in Multilingual Entity Task (MET-2) on Chinese, held together with MUC-7. Between them, Yu (1998)'s results are slightly better. However, these two comparable systems did not report their results on SCNE separately. To evaluate our results, we compare with three state-of-the-art system we have. These systems include: MSWS, PBWS and LCWS. The former two are developed by Microsoft® and the last one comes from by Beijing Language University.

3 SCNE Recognition Using an Improved Source-Channel Model

3.1 Improved Source-Channel Model[1]

We first conduct SCNE recognition within a framework of improved source-channel models, which is applied to Chinese word segmentation. We define Chinese words as one of the following four types: (1) entries in a lexicon, (2) morphologically derived words, (3) named entity (NE), and (4) factoid. Examples are

1. lexicon word: *朋友 (peng2-you3, friend).*
2. morph-derived word: *高高兴兴 (gao1-gao1-xing4-xing4 , happily)*
3. named entity: *微软公司(wei1-ruan3-gong1-si1, Microsoft Corporation)*
4. factoid[2]: *1 月 9 日 (yi1-yue4-jiu3-ri4, Jan 9th)*

Chinese NER is achieved within the framework. To make our later discussion on SCNE clear, we introduce the model briefly.

We are given Chinese sentence S, which is a character string. For all possible word segmentations W, we will choose the one which achieves the highest conditional probability W* = argmax$_w$ $P(W|S)$. According to Bayes' law and dropping the constant denominator, we acquire the following equation:

[1] This follows the description of (Gao, 2003).

[2] We define ten types of factoid: date, time (TIME), percentage, money, number (NUM), measure, e-mail, phone number, and WWW.

$$W^* = \arg\max_W P(W)P(S \mid W) \quad (1)$$

Following our Chinese word definition, we define word class C as follows: (1) each lexicon word is defined as a class; (2) each morphologically derived word is defined as a class; (3) each type of named entities is defined as a class, e.g. all person names belong to a class PN, and (4) each type of factoids is defined as a class, e.g. all time expressions belong to a class TIME. We therefore convert the word segmentation W into a word class sequence C. Eq. 1 can then be rewritten as:

$$C^* = \arg\max_C P(C)P(S \mid C) . \quad (2)$$

Eq. 2 is the basic form of the source-channel models for Chinese word segmentation. The models assume that a Chinese sentence S is generated as follows: First, a person chooses a sequence of concepts (i.e., word classes *C*) to output, according to the probability distribution *P*(*C*); then the person attempts to express each concept by choosing a sequence of characters, according to the probability distribution $P(S|C)$.

We use different types of channel models for different types of Chinese words. This brings several advantages. First, different linguistic constraints can be easily added to corresponding channel models (see Figure 1). These constraints can be dynamic linguistic knowledge acquired through statistics or intuitive rules compiled by linguists. Second, this framework is data-driven, which makes it easy to adapt to other languages. We have three channel models for PN, LN and ON respectively. (see Figure 1)

However, although Eq. 2 suggests that channel model probability and source model probability can be combined through simple multiplication, in practice some weighting is desirable. There are two reasons. First, some channel models are poorly estimated, owing to the sub-optimal assumptions we make for simplicity and the insufficiency of the training corpus. Combining the channel model probability with poorly estimated source model probabilities according to Eq. 2 would give the context model too little weight. Second, as seen in Figure 1, the channel models of different word classes are constructed in different ways (e.g. name entity models are *n*-gram models trained on corpora, and factoid models are compiled using linguistic knowledge). Therefore, the quantities of channel model probabilities are likely to have vastly different dynamic ranges among different word classes. One way to balance these probability quantities is to add several *channel model weight CW*, each for one word class, to adjust the channel model probability $P(S|C)$ to $P(S|C)^{CW}$. In our experiments, these weights are determined empirically on a development set.

Given the source-channel models, the procedure of word segmentation involves two steps: first, given an input string *S*, all word candidates are generated (and stored in a lattice). Each candidate is tagged with its class and the probability $P(S'|C)$, where *S'* is any substring of *S*. Second, Viterbi search is used to select (from the lattice) the most probable word segmentation (i.e. word class sequence C^*) according to Eq. 2.

Word class	Channel model	Linguistic Constraints
Lexicon word (LW)	$P(S\|LW)=1$ if *S* forms a lexicon entry, 0 otherwise.	Word lexicon
Morphologically derived word (MW)	$P(S\|MW)=1$ if *S* forms a morph lexicon entry, 0 otherwise.	Morph-lexicon
Person name (PN)	Character bigram	family name list, Chinese PN patterns
Location name (LN)	Character bigram	LN keyword list, LN lexicon, LN abbr. list
Organization name (ON)	Word class bigram	ON keyword list, ON abbr. List
Factoid (FT)	$P(S\|G)=1$ if *S* can be parsed using a factoid grammar *G*, 0 otherwise	Factoid rules (presented by FSTs).

Figure 1. Channel models (Gao, 2003)

3.2 Improved Model for SCNE Recognition

Although our results show that the source-channel models achieve the state-of-the-art word segmentation performance, they cannot handle SCNE very well. Error analysis shows that 11.6% person name errors come from SCP, and 47.7% location names come from SCL. There are two reasons accounting for it: First, SCNE is generated in a different way from that of multi-character NE. Second, the context of SCNE is different from other NE. For example, SCNE usually appears one after another such as *"中俄贸易"*. But this is not the case for multi-character NE.

To solve the first problem, we add two new channel models to Figure 1, that is, define each type of SCNE (i.e. SCL and SCP) as a individual class (i.e. NE_SCL and NE_SCP) with its channel probability $P(S_j|NE\_SCL)$, and $P(S_j|NE\_SCP)$. $P(S_j|NE\_SCL)$ is calculated by Eq. 3.

$$P(S_j \mid NE\_SCL) = \frac{|SCL(S_j)|}{\sum_{i=1}^{n} |SCL(S_i)|} \quad (3)$$

Here, S_j is a character in SCL list which is extracted from training corpus. $|SCL(S_j)|$ is the number of tokens S_j , which are labeled as SCL in training corpus. n is the size of SCL list, which includes 177 SCL. Similarly, $P(S_j|NE\_SCP)$ is calculated by Eq. 4, and the SCP list includes 151 SCP.

$$P(S_j \mid NE\_SCP) = \frac{|SCP(S_j)|}{\sum_{i=1}^{n} |SCP(S_i)|} \quad (4)$$

We also use two *CW* to balance their channel probabilities with other NE's.

To solve the second problem, we trained a new source model $P(C)$ on the re-annotated training corpus, where all SCNE are tagged by SCL or SCP. For example, *"周"* in *"周总理"*is tagged as SCP instead of PN, and *"中"* in *"中俄"* is tagged as SCL in stead of LN.

4 Character-based Classifiers

In this section, SCNE recognition is formulated as a binary classification problem. Our motivations are two folds. First, most NER systems do not use source-channel model, so our method described in the previous section cannot be applied. However, if we define SCNE as a binary classification problem, it would be possible to build a separate recognizer which can be used together with any NER systems. Second, we are interested in comparing the performance of source-channel models with that of other methods.

For each Chinese character, a classifier is built to estimate how likely an occurrence of this Chinese character in a text is a SCNE. Some examples of these Chinese character as well as their probabilities of being a SCNE is shown in Table 2.

SCL	#SCL/#All Tokens	SCP	#SCP/#All Tokens
沪	0.60465	冯	0.24342
俄	0.31612	阮	0.23810
蜀	0.23810	崔	0.13913
华	0.17516	乾	0.12500
港	0.12841	裴	0.11111
…	…	…	…
深	0.00454	易	0.00033
宁	0.00436	米	0.00030
加	0.00421	施	0.00030
孟	0.00261	常	0.00020
希	0.00228	安	0.00017

Table 2. The probability of a character as SCNE

We can see that the probabilities of being a SCNE of many characters are very small. Thus, SCNE recognition is an 'unbalanced' classification problem. That is, in most cases, it is safer to assume that a character is not a SCNE.

We construct two classifiers respectively based on two statistical models: maximum entropy model (ME) and vector space model (VSM). Local context characters (i.e. left or right characters within a window) are used as features.

4.1 Maximum Entropy

ME provides a good framework to integrate various features from different knowledge sources. Each feature is typically represented as a binary constraint *f*. All features are then combined using a log-linear model shown in Eq. 5.

$$P_\lambda(y \mid x) = \frac{1}{Z_\lambda(x)} \exp\left(\sum_i \lambda_i f_i(x, y)\right) \quad (5)$$

where λ_i is a weight of the feature f_i, and $Z(x)$ is a normalization factor.

Weights (λ) are estimated using the maximum entropy principle: to satisfy constraints on observed data and assume a uniform distribution (with the maximum entropy) on unseen data. The training algorithm we used is the improved iterative scaling (IIS) described in (Berger et al, 1996)[3]. The context features include six characters: three on the left of the SCNE, and three on the right. Given the context features, the ME classifier would estimate the probability of the candidate being a SCNE. In our example, we treat candidates with the probability larger than 0.5 as SCNEs. To get the precision-recall curve, we can vary the probability threshold from 0.1 to 0.9.

4.2 Vector Space Model

VSM is another model we used to detect SCNE. Similar to ME, we use six surrounding characters as the features, as shown in Figure 2.

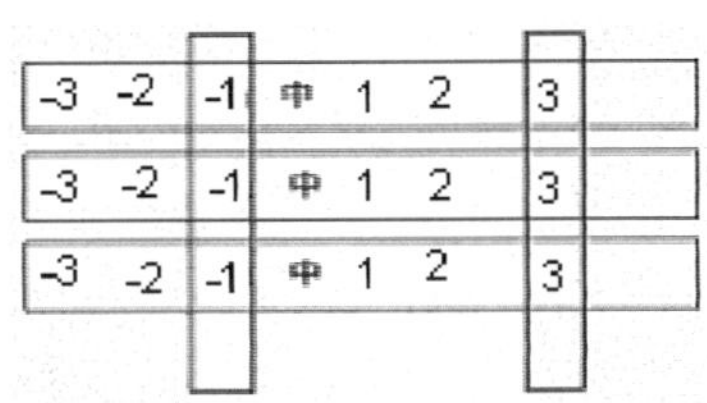

Figure 2. Context window

In this approach, we apply the standard *tf-idf* weighting technique with one minor adaptation: the same character appearing in different positions within the context window is considered as different terms. For example, character *Cj* appearing at position *i*, $i \in \{-3,-2,-1,1,2,3\}$, is regarded as term *Cji*,. Term weighting of *Cji* is acquired with Eq.6.

$$Wei(C_{ji}) = TF(C_{ji}) * IDF(C_{ji}) * PW_i \qquad (6)$$

With this adaptation, we can apply an additional weighting coefficient *PWi* to different position, so as to reflect the importance of different positions. *PWi* is determined in a heuristic way as shown in Table.3 with the underlying principle that the closer the context character is to the SCNE candidate, the larger *PWi* is.

[3] Thank Joshua Goodman for providing the ME toolkit.

Pos	-3	-2	-1	1	2	3
PWi	1	4	7	7	4	1

Table 3. Weights assigned to deferent positions

A precision/recall curve can be obtained by multiplying a factor to one of the two cosine distances we get, before comparing them.

5 Experiment results

5.1 Evaluation Methodology

To achieve a reliable evaluation, we developed an annotated test set. First, we discuss a standard of Chinese NE and SCNE. Most previous researches define their own standards; hence results of different systems are not comparable. Recently, two widely accepted standards were developed. They are (1) MET-2 (Multilingual Entity Task)[4] for Chinese and Japanese NE, and (2) IEER-99' [5] for Chinese NE. IEER-99 is a slightly modified version of MET-2. Our NE/SCNE standard is based on these two well-known standards.

Second, we manually annotated a 10MB training corpus and a 1MB test corpus. The texts are randomly selected from People's Daily, including articles from 10 subjects and 5 writing styles. This test set is much larger than MET-2 test data (which is about 106 KB), and contains more SCNE for evaluation.

The evaluation metrics we used include precision (P), recall (R), and F-score. F-score is calculated as $\frac{(\beta^2+1.0)*P*R}{(\beta^2*P)+R}$, while β=1 in our experiments.

5.2 Results of Source-Channel Models

We show the SCNE recognition results using the source-channel models described in Section 3. Two versions of NE models are used. M1 is the original model described in Section 3.1. M2 is the one adapted for SCNE, shown in Section 3.2. The results in Table 4 show that obvious improvement can be achieved on SCL and SCP after adapting source-channel models for SCNE. As shown in Table 5, the improvement of SCL and SCP has significant impact on performance of LN and PN

[4] http://www.itl.nist.gov/iaui/894.02/related_projects/muc/
[5] http://www.nist.gov/speech/tests/ie-er/er_99/er_99.htm

recognition. We can see that the increase of F-score of LN is 5.13%, and PN is 0.92% absolutely.

	SCL			SCP		
	P%	R%	F	P%	R%	F
M1	83.77	15.25	25.80	*	*	*
M2	84.38	77.90	81.01	76.14	61.47	68.02

* No SCP is detected

Table 4. Improvement of SCL and SCP recognition

	LN			PN		
	P%	R%	F	P%	R%	F
M1	88.60	71.35	79.04	83.23	76.17	79.54
M2	88.20	80.49	84.17	83.51	77.63	80.46

Table 5. Improvement of LN and PN recognition

5.3 Results of Different Methods

In Figures 3 and 4, we compare the results of the source-channel models with two classifiers described in Section 4: ME and VSM.

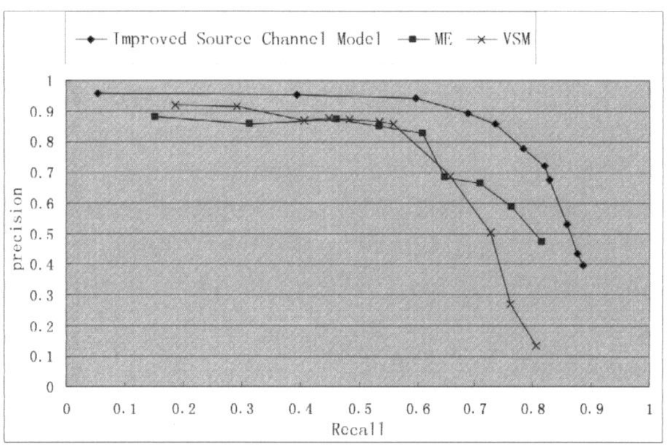

Figure 3. Result of different methods on SCL

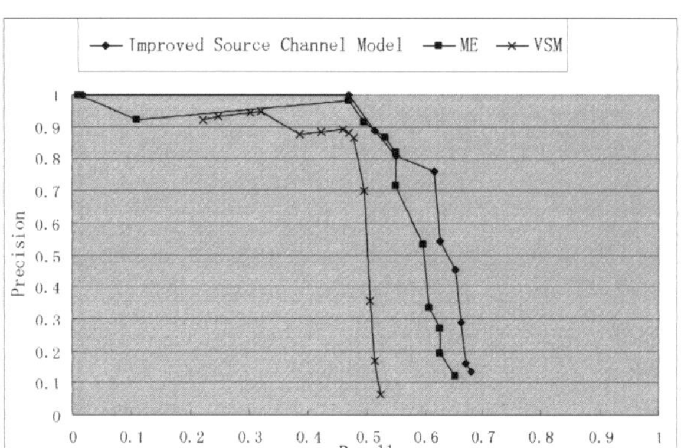

Figure 4. Result of different methods on SCP

We can see that source-channel model achieves the best result. This can be interpreted as follows. The source-channel models use more information than the other two methods. The feature set of ME or VSM classifiers includes only six surrounding characters while the source-channel models use much rich global and local information as shown in Figure 1. Based on our analysis, we believe that even enlarging the window size of the local context, the performance gain of these classifiers is very limited, because most error tags cannot be correctly classified using local context features. We can then say with confidence that the source-channel models can achieve comparable results with ME and VSM even if they used more local context.

5.4 Comparison with Other State-of-The-Art Systems

The section compares the performance of the source-channel models M2, with three state-of-the-art systems: **MSWS, LCWS** and **PBWS.**

1. The **MSWS** system is one of the best available products. It is released by Microsoft® (as a set of Windows APIs). **MSWS** first conducts the word breaking using MM (augmented by heuristic rules for disambiguation), then conducts factoid detection and NER using rules.
2. The **LCWS** system is one of the best research systems in mainland China. It is released by Beijing Language University. The system works similarly to **MSWS**, but has a larger dictionary containing more PNs and LNs.
3. The **PBWS** system is a rule-based Chinese parser, which can also output the NER results. It explores high-level linguistic knowledge such as syntactic structure for Chinese word segmentation and NER.

To compare the results across different systems, we have to consider the problem that they might have different tagging format or spec. For example, the LCWS system tags the two-character string "*中俄*" as a location name, and tags "*周总理*" other than "*周*" as a person name. We then manually convert all tagging results of these three systems according to our spec. The results are shown in Table 6.

	SCL			SCP		
	P%	R%	F	R%	P%	F
MSWS	*	*	*	71.42	31.25	43.48
LCWS	100.0	21.43	35.30	66.67	25.00	36.36
PBWS	92.31	28.57	43.63	100.0	18.75	31.58
M2	84.38	77.90	81.01	76.14	61.47	68.02

* No SCL is detected

Table 6. Comparison with other systems

We can see that our system (M2) achieves the best results in both SCL and SCP recognition. PBWS has the second best result in recognizing SCL (43.63%), and MSWS in SCP (43.48%). However, they achieved the worst result on SCP and SCL, respectively.

5.5 Error Analysis

Through human checking, we list the typical errors as follows:

1. Ambiguity between NE: *"美中贸易全国委员会"(mei3-zhong1-mao4-yi4-quan2-guo2-wei3-yuan2-hui4, National Committee on United States-China Relations)* is a ON, but *"美", "中"* are usually wrongly recognized as SCL. On the contrary, *"日中友好七团体"(ri4- zhong1-you3-hao3-qi1-tuan2-ti3, seven Janpan-China friendship organizations)* is tagged as ON falsely. So *"日"(ri4,Japan), "中"* are missed.
2. SCNE list acquire from training data cannot covers some cases in test data: *"中卡足球赛 "(zhong1-ka3-zu2-qiu2-sai4, China-Qatar soccer match), "卡"(ka3, Qatar)* here is stand for *"卡塔尔"(ka3-ta1-er3, Qatar),* which is out of SCL list.
3. Other errors: *"中巴驶出大门"(zhong1-ba1-shi3-chu1-da4-men2, the middle bus drives out from the gate), "中"(zhong1, middle), "巴" (ba1, bus)*are recognized falsely as SCL. Because*"中"* and *"巴"* can also stand for *China* and *Pakistan. "巴"* can even stand for other countries such as *"巴西"（ba1-xi1, Brazil）*.

Errors in (1) account for about 40% of all errors. SCNE is usually a part of multi-character NE, such as *"美", "中" in "美中贸易全国委员会"*.Viterbi search has to make a decision: recognizing the multi-character NE, or recognizing SCNE. Current features we used seem not powful enough to resovle this ambiguity well. Errors in (3) come from another kind of ambiguities such as ambiguity between SCNE and normal lexicon words. They are partly caused by noises in training data, because SCNE are very likely to be neglected by annotators, which makes training data more sparse. Both errors in (1) and (3) are not easy to handle.

Our immediate work is to cope with errors in (2), which account for about 8.9% of all errors. We can obtain additional SCNE entries from resources such as abbreviation dictionaries. However, the procedure to select SENE entries should be careful, because the SCNE characters we do not cover currently might be rare to act as SCNE, and difficult to recall. Besides, unsupervised methods can be applied to the task, considering insufficiency of the training data of the task.

6 Conclusion

Although SCNE is very common in written Chinese text, due to the lack of in-depth research, SCNE is a major source of errors in NER. This paper formulates the SCNE recognition within the source-channel model framework. Our experiments show very encouraging results: an F-score of 81.01% for single character location name recognition, an F-score of 68.02% for single character person name recognition. An alternative view of the SCNE recognition problem is to formulate it as a classification task. We construct two classifiers respectively based on maximum entropy model (ME) and vector space model (VSM), respectively. We compare all proposed approaches, showing that the source-channel model performs the best in most cases.

References

A. Berger, S. Della Pietra and V. Della Pietra, 1996. A maximum entropy approach to natural language processing. *Computational Linguistics* 22(1):39-71.

Andrew Borthwick, John Sterling, Eugene Agichtein, and Ralph Grishman. 1998. NYU: Description of the MENE Named Entity System as Used in MUC-7. *Proceedings of the Seventh Message Understanding Conference (MUC-7)*

Hsin-Hsi Chen, Yung-Wei Ding, Shih-Chung Tsai and Guo-Wei Bian, 1998. Description of the NTU System used for MET-2, *Proceedings of the Seventh Message Understanding Conference (MUC-7).*

Michael Collins, 2002. Ranking Algorithm for Named-Entity Extraction: Boosting and Voted Perceptron. *Proceedings of 40th Annual Meeting of Association for Computational Linguistics.*

Jianfeng Gao, Mu Li and Chang-Ning Huang, 2003. Improved Source-Channel Models for Chinese Word Segmentation. *Proceedings of 41th Annual Meeting of Association for Computational Linguistics.*

Hideki Isozaki and Hideto Kazawa, 2002. Efficient Support Vector Classifier for Named Entity Recognition, *Proceedings of 19th International Conference on Computational Linguistics.*

Heng Ji, Zhensheng Luo, 2001. Inverse Name Frequency Model and Rule Based Chinese Name Identification. (In Chinese) *Natural Language Understanding and Machine Translation.* Tsinghua University Press. pp. 123 -128.

Kaiying Liu, 2001. Research on Chinese Proper Noun and Internet Words Recognition. (In Chinese) *Proceedings of Conference of the 20th Anniversary of CIPSC.* Tsinghua University Press. pp. 7-13.

Song Rou, Benjamin K T'sou, 2001. Primary Study on Chinese Proper Noun. (In Chinese) *Proceedings of Conference of the 20th Anniversary of CIPSC.* Tsinghua University Press,14-19.

Dayang Shen, Maosong Sun, 1995. Chinese Location Name Recognition. (In Chinese) *Development and Applications of Computational Linguistics.* Tsinghua University Press.

Jian Sun, Jianfeng Gao, Lei Zhang, Ming Zhou, and Changning Huang, 2002. Chinese named entity identification using class-based language model. *COLING 2002.* Taipei, Taiwan, August 24-25, 2002.

Maosong Sun, Changning Huang, Haiyan Gao, Jie Fang, 1994. Chinese Person Name Recognition. (In Chinese) *Journal of Chinese Information Processing.*

Xing Wang, Degen Huang, Yuansheng Yang, 1999. Identifying Chinese Names Based on Combination of Statistics and Rules. (In Chinese) *proceedings of JSCL-99.* Tsinghua University Press. pp. 155 -161

Shihong Yu, Shuanhu Bai and Paul Wu. Description of the Kent Ridge Digital Labs System Used for MUC-7. *Proceedings of the Seventh Message Understanding Conference (MUC-7)*, 1998.

Junsheng Zhang, 1992. Chinese Person Name Recognition. (In Chinese) *Journal of Chinese Information Processing.* 9(2) .

Jiahen Zheng, Xin Li, Hongye Tan, 2000. The Researh of Chinese Names Recognition Based on Corpus,. (In Chinese) *Journal of Chinese Information Processing.* 14(1): 7-12

Guodong Zhou and Jian Su, 2002. Named Entity Recognition using an HMM-based Chunk Tagger. *Proceedings of 40th Annual Meeting of Association for Computational Linguistics.*

The First International Chinese Word Segmentation Bakeoff

Richard Sproat
AT&T Labs – Research
180 Park Avenue, Florham Park, NJ, 07932, USA
rws@research.att.com

Thomas Emerson
Basis Technology
150 CambridgePark Drive
Cambridge, MA 02140, USA
tree@basistech.com

Abstract

This paper presents the results from the ACL-SIGHAN-sponsored First International Chinese Word Segmentation Bakeoff held in 2003 and reported in conjunction with the Second SIGHAN Workshop on Chinese Language Processing, Sapporo, Japan. We give the motivation for having an international segmentation contest (given that there have been two within-China contests to date) and we report on the results of this first international contest, analyze these results, and make some recommendations for the future.

1 Introduction

Chinese word segmentation is a difficult problem that has received a lot of attention in the literature; reviews of some of the various approaches can be found in (Wang et al., 1990; Wu and Tseng, 1993; Sproat and Shih, 2001). The problem with this literature has always been that it is very hard to compare systems, due to the lack of any common standard test set. Thus, an approach that seems very promising based on its published report is nonetheless hard to compare fairly with other systems, since the systems are often tested on their own selected test corpora. Part of the problem is also that there is no single accepted segmentation standard: There are several, including the four standards used in this evaluation.

A number of segmentation contests have been held in recent years within Mainland China, in the context of more general evaluations for Chinese-English machine translation. See (Yao, 2001; Yao, 2002) for the first and second of these; the third evaluation will be held in August 2003. The test corpora were segmented according to the Chinese national standard GB 13715 (GB/T 13715–92, 1993), though some lenience was granted in the case of plausible alternative segmentations (Yao, 2001); so while GB 13715 specifies the segmentation 毛/泽东 for *Mao Zedong*, 毛泽东 was also allowed. Accuracies in the mid 80's to mid 90's were reported for the four systems that participated in the first evaluation, with higher scores (many in the high nineties) being reported for the second evaluation.

The motivations for holding the current contest are twofold. First of all, by making the contest international, we are encouraging participation from people and institutions who work on Chinese word segmentation anywhere in the world. The final set of participants in the bakeoff include two from Mainland China, three from Hong Kong, one from Japan, one from Singapore, one from Taiwan and four from the United States.

Secondly, as we have already noted, there are at least four distinct standards in active use in the sense that large corpora are being developed according to those standards; see Section 2.1. It has also been observed that different segmentation standards are appropriate for different purposes; that the segmentation standard that one might prefer for information retrieval applications is likely to be different from the one that one would prefer for text-to-speech synthesis; see (Wu, 2003) for useful discussion. Thus, while we do not subscribe to the view that any of the extant standards are, in fact, appropriate for any particular application, nevertheless, it seems desirable to have a contest where people are tested against more than one standard.

A third point is that we decided early on that we would not be lenient in our scoring, so that alternative segmentations as in the case of 毛泽东 *Mao Zedong*, cited above, would not be allowed. While it would be fairly straightforward (in many cases) to automatically score both alternatives, we felt we could provide a more objective measure if we went strictly by the particular segmentation standard being tested on, and simply did not get into the business of deciding upon allowable alternatives.

Comparing segmenters is difficult. This is not only because of differences in segmentation standards but also due to differences in the design of systems: Systems based exclusively (or even primarily) on lexical and grammatical analysis will often be at a disadvantage during the comparison compared to systems trained exclusively on the training data. Competitions also may fail to predict the performance of the segmenter on new texts outside the training and testing sets. The handling of out-of-vocabulary words becomes a much larger issue in these situations than is accounted for within the test environment: A system that performs admirably in the competition may perform poorly on texts from different registers.

Another issue that is not accounted for in the current collection of evaluations is the handling of short strings with minimal context, such as queries submitted to a search engine. This has been studied indirectly through the cross-language information retrieval work performed for the TREC 5 and TREC 6 competitions (Smeaton and Wilkinson, 1997; Wilkinson, 1998).

This report summarizes the results of this First International Chinese Word Segmentation Bakeoff, provides some analysis of the results, and makes specific recommendations for future bakeoffs. One thing we do not do here is get into the details of specific systems; each of the participants was required to provide a four page description of their system along with detailed discussion of their results, and these papers are published in this volume.

2 Details of the contest

2.1 Corpora

The corpora are detailed in Table 1. Links to descriptions of the corpora can be found at `http://www.sighan.org/bakeoff2003/bakeoff_instr.html`; publications on specific corpora are (Huang et al., 1997) (Academia Sinica), (Xia, 1999) (Chinese Treebank); the Beijing University standard is very similar to that outlined in (GB/T 13715–92, 1993). Table 1 lists the abbreviations for the four corpora that will be used throughout this paper. The suffixes "o" and "c" will be used to denote open and closed tracks, respectively: Thus "ASo,c" denotes the Academia Sinica corpus, both open and closed tracks; and "PKc" denotes the Beijing University corpus, closed track.

During the course of this bakeoff, a number of inconsistencies in segmentation were noted in the CTB corpus by one of the participants. This was done early enough so that it was possible for the CTB developers to correct some of the more common cases, both in the training and the test data. The revised training data was posted for participants, and the revised test data was used during the testing phase.

Inconsistencies were also noted by another participant for the AS corpus. Unfortunately this came too late in the process to correct the data. However, some informal tests on the revised testing data indicated that the differences were minor.

2.2 Rules and Procedures

The contest followed a strict set of guidelines and a rigid timetable. The detailed instructions for the bakeoff can be found at `http://www.sighan.org/bakeoff2003/bakeoff_instr.html` (with simplified and traditional Chinese versions also available). Training material was available starting March 15, testing material was available April 22, and the results had to be returned to the SIGHAN ftp site by April 25 no later than 17:00 EDT.

Upon initial registration sites were required to declare which corpora they would be training and testing on, and whether they would be participating in the open or closed tracks (or both) on each corpus,

Corpus	Abbrev.	Encoding	# Train. Words	# Test. Words
Academia Sinica	**AS**	Big Five (MS Codepage 950)	5.8M	12K
U. Penn Chinese Treebank	**CTB**	EUC-CN (GB 2312-80)	250K	40K
Hong Kong CityU	**HK**	Big Five (HKSCS)	240K	35K
Beijing University	**PK**	GBK (MS Codepage 936)	1.1M	17K

Table 1: Corpora used.

where these were defined as follows:

- For the **open** test sites were allowed to train on the training set for a particular corpus, and in addition they could use any other material including material from other training corpora, proprietary dictionaries, material from the WWW and so forth. However, if a site selected the open track the site was required to explain what percentage of the results came from which sources. For example, if the system did particularly well on out-of-vocabulary words then the participants were required to explain if, for example, those results could mostly be attributed to having a good dictionary.

- In the **closed** test, participants could only use training material from the training data for the particular corpus being testing on. No other material was allowed.

Other obvious restrictions applied: Participants were prohibited from testing on corpora from their own sites, and by signing up for a particular track, participants were declaring implicitly that they had not previously seen the test corpus for that track.

Scoring was completely automatic. Note that the scoring software does not correct for cases where a participant converted from one coding scheme into another, and any such cases were counted as errors. Results were returned to participants within a couple of days of submission of the segmented test data. The script used for scoring can be downloaded from `http://www.sighan.org/bakeoff2003/score`; it is a simple Perl script that depends upon a version of *diff* (e.g. GNU diffutils 2.7.2), that supports the *-y* flag for side-by-side output format.

2.3 Participating sites

Participating sites are shown in Table 2. These are a subset of the sites who had registered for the bake-off, as some sites withdrew due to technical difficulties.

3 Further details of the corpora

An unfortunate, and sometimes unforseen, complexity in dealing with Chinese text on the computer is the plethora of character sets and character encodings used throughout Greater China. This is demonstrated in the Encoding column of Table 1:

1. Both AS and HK utilize complex-form (or "traditional") characters, using variants of the Big Five character set. The Academia Sinica corpus is composed almost entirely of characters in pure Big Five (four characters, 0xFB5B, 0xFA76, 0xFB7A, and 0xFAAF are outside the encoding range of Big Five), while the City University corpus utilizes 38 (34 unique) characters from the Hong Kong Supplementary Character Set (HKSCS) extension to Big Five.

2. The CTB and PK corpora each use simple-form (or "simplified") characters, using the EUC-CN encoding of the GB 2312-80 character set. However, The PKU corpus includes characters that are not part of GB 2312-80, but are encoded in GBK. GBK is an extension of GB 2312-80 that incorporates some 18,000 hanzi found in Unicode 2.1 within the GB-2312 code space. Only Microsoft's CP936 implements GBK.

This variation of encoding is exacerbated by the usual lack of specific declaration in the files. Generally a file is said to be "Big Five" or "GB", when in actuality the file is encoded in a variation of these. This is problematic in systems that utilize Unicode

Site ID	Site Name	Domain	Contact	Tracks			
S01	Inst. of Comp. Tech.,CAS	CN	Huaping ZHANG	AS**o**	CTB**o**,c	HKc	PK**o**,c
S02	ICL, Beijing U	CN	Baobao CHANG		CTB**o**,c		
S03	HK Polytechnic University	HK	Qin LU	AS**o**	CTB**o**	HK**o**	PK**o**
S04	U of Hong Kong	HK	Guohong FU				PK**o**,c
S05	HK CityU	HK	Chunyu KIT	ASc	CTBc		PKc
S06	Nara IST	JP	Chooi Ling GOH	ASc	CTBc	HKc	PKc
S07	Inst. for Infocomm Research	SG	Guodong ZHOU				PKc
S08	CKIP Ac. Sinica Taiwan	TW	Wei Yun MA			HK**o**,c	PK**o**,c
S09	UC Berkeley	US	Aitao CHEN	ASc			PKc
S10	Microsoft Research	US	Andi WU		CTB**o**,c		PK**o**,c
S11	SYSTRAN Software, Inc.	US	Jin YANG	AS**o**	CTB**o**	HK**o**	PK**o**
S12	U Penn	US	Nianwen XUE	ASc		HKc	

Table 2: Participating sites and associated tracks.

internally, since transcoding back to the original encoding may lose information.

4 Results

4.1 Baseline and topline experiments

We computed a baseline for each of the corpora by compiling a dictionary of all and only the words in the training portion of the corpus. We then used this dictionary with a simple maximum matching algorithm to segment the test corpus. The results of this experiment are presented in Table 3. In this and subsequent tables, we list the *word count* for the test corpus, test *recall* (R), test *precision* (P), *F score*[1], the *out-of-vocabulary* (OOV) rate for the test corpus, the *recall on OOV* words (R_{OOV}), and the *recall on in-vocabulary* (R_{iv}) words. Per normal usage, OOV is defined as the set of words in the test corpus not occurring in the training corpus.[2] We expect systems to do *at least* as well as this baseline.

As a nominal *topline* we ran the same maximum matching experiments, but this time populating the dictionary only with words from the test corpus; this is of course a "cheating" experiment since one could not reasonably know exactly the set of words that occur in the test corpus. Since this is better than one could hope for in practice, we would expect systems to generally underperform this topline. The results of this "cheating" experiment are given in Table 4.[3]

4.2 Raw scores

4.2.1 Closed Tests

Results for the closed tests are presented in Tables 5–8. Column headings are as above, except for "c_r", and "c_p" for which see Section 4.3.

4.2.2 Open Tests

Results for the open tests are presented in Tables 9–12; again, see Section 4.3 for the explanation of "c_r", and "c_p".

4.3 Statistical significance of the results

Let us assume that the recall rates for the various system represent the probability p that a word will be successfully identified, and let us further assume that a binomial distribution is appropriate for this experiment. Given the Central Limit Theorem for Bernouilli trials — e.g. (Grinstead and Snell, 1997, page 330), then the 95% confidence interval is given

[1] We use a balanced F score, so that $F = 2PR/(P + R)$.

[2] Note that the OOV recall in Table 3 should in theory be 0.0, but is not always zero because the maximum matching algorithm might get lucky. In particular, if the dictionary contains no word starting with some character c, then the maximum matching algorithm with move on to the next character, leaving c segmented as a word on its own. If it happens that c is in fact a single-character word, then the algorithm will have fortuitously done the right thing.

[3] If one did have the exact list of words occurring in the test corpus, one could still do better than the maximum matching algorithm, since the maximum matching algorithm cannot in general correctly resolve cases where more than one segmentation is possible given the dictionary. However as we can see from the scores in Table 4, such cases constitute at most about 1.5%.

Corpus	word count	R	P	F	OOV	R_{oov}	R_{iv}
AS	11,985	0.917	0.912	0.915	0.022	0.000	0.938
CTB	39,922	0.800	0.663	0.725	0.181	0.062	0.962
HK	34,955	0.908	0.830	0.867	0.071	0.037	0.974
PK	17,194	0.909	0.829	0.867	0.069	0.050	0.972

Table 3: **Baseline** scores: Results for maximum matching using only words from training data

Corpus	word count	R	P	F	OOV	R_{oov}	R_{iv}
AS	11,985	0.990	0.993	0.992	0.022	0.988	0.990
CTB	39,922	0.982	0.988	0.985	0.181	0.990	0.980
HK	34,955	0.986	0.991	0.989	0.071	0.996	0.985
PK	17,194	0.995	0.996	0.995	0.069	1.000	0.994

Table 4: **Topline** ("cheating") scores: Results for maximum matching using only words from testing data data

as $\pm 2\sqrt{p(1-p)/n}$, where n is the number of trials (words). The values for $\pm 2\sqrt{p(1-p)/n}$ are given in Tables 5–12, under the heading "c_r". They can be interpreted as follows: To decide whether two sites are significantly different (at the 95% confidence level) in their performance on a particular task, one just has to compute whether their confidence intervals overlap. Similarly one can treat the precision rates as the probability that a character string that has been identified as a word is really a word; these precision-based confidences are given as "c_p" in the tables.

It seems reasonable to treat two systems as significantly different (at the 95% confidence level), if at least one of their recall-based or precision-based confidences are different. Using this criterion all systems are significantly different from each other except that on PK closed S10 is not significantly different from S09, and S07 is not significantly different from S04.

5 Discussion

5.1 Differences between "open" and "closed" performance

In Figure 1 we plot the F scores for all systems, all tracks. We include as "BASE", and "TOP" the baseline and topline scores discussed previously. In most cases people performed above the baseline, though well below the ideal topline; note though that the two participants in the Academia Sinica open track underperformed the baseline.

Performance on the Penn Chinese Treebank (CTB) corpus was generally lower than all the other corpora; omitting S02, which only ran on CTBo,c the scores for the other systems were uniformly higher on other corpora than they were on CTB, the single exception being S11 which did better on CTBo than on HKo. The baseline for CTB is also much lower than the baseline for other corpora, so one might be inclined to ascribe the generally lower performance to the smaller training data for this corpus. Also, the OOV rate for this corpus is much higher than all of the other corpora, and since error rates are generally higher on OOV, this is surely a contributing factor. However, this would only explain why CTB showed lower performance on the closed test; on the open test, one might expect the size of the training data to matter less, but there were still large differences between several systems' performance on CTB and their performance on other corpora. Note also that the topline for CTB is also lower than for the other corpora. What all of this suggests is that the CTB may simply be less consistent than the other corpora in its segmentation; indeed one of the participants (Andi Wu) noted a number of inconsistencies in both the training and the test data (though inconsistencies were also noted

Site	word count	R	c_r	P	c_p	**F**	OOV	R_{oov}	R_{iv}
S09	11,985	0.966	±0.0033	0.956	±0.0037	0.961	0.022	0.364	0.980
S12	11,985	0.961	±0.0035	0.958	±0.0037	0.959	0.022	0.729	0.966
S06	11,985	0.944	±0.0042	0.945	±0.0042	0.945	0.022	0.574	0.952
S05	11,985	0.952	±0.0039	0.931	±0.0046	0.942	0.022	0.043	0.972
S01	11,985	0.953	±0.0039	0.924	±0.0048	0.938	0.022	0.178	0.970

Table 5: Scores for AS closed, sorted by F.

Site	word count	R	c_r	P	c_p	**F**	OOV	R_{oov}	R_{iv}
S01	39,922	0.886	±0.0032	0.875	±0.0033	0.881	0.181	0.705	0.927
S02	39,922	0.892	±0.0031	0.856	±0.0035	0.874	0.181	0.644	0.947
S10	39,922	0.867	±0.0034	0.797	±0.0040	0.831	0.181	0.431	0.963
S06	39,922	0.852	±0.0036	0.807	±0.0040	0.829	0.181	0.412	0.949
S05	39,922	0.800	±0.0040	0.674	±0.0047	0.732	0.181	0.076	0.959

Table 6: Scores for CTB closed, sorted by F.

for the AS corpus).[4]

Systems that ran on both closed and open tracks for the same corpus generally did better on the open track, indicating (not surprisingly) that using additional data can help. However, the lower-than-baseline performance of S03 and S11 on ASo may reflect issues with tuning of these additional resources to the particular standard in question.

Finally note that the top performance of any system on any track was S09 on ASc (F=0.961). Since performances close to our ideal topline have occasionally been reported in the literature it is worth bearing the results of this bakeoff in mind when reading such reports.

5.2 Differences on OOV

Figure 2 plots the recall on out-of-vocabulary words (R_{oov}) for all systems and all tracks. For this measure, the performance of the baseline is only above 0.0 fortuitously, as we noted in Section 4.1. Similarly the topline performance is only less than 1.0 in cases where there are two or more possible decompositions of a string, and where the option with the longest prefix is not the correct one.

It is with OOV recall that we see the widest variation among systems, which in turn is consistent with the observation that dealing with unknown words is the major outstanding problem of Chinese word segmentation. While some systems performed little better than the baseline, others had a very respectable 0.80 recall on OOV. Again, there was clearly a benefit for many systems in using additional resources than what is in the training data: A number of systems that were run on both closed and open tracks showed significant improvements in the open track. For the closed-track entries that did well on OOV, one must conclude that they have effective unknown-word detection methods.

6 Summary and recommendations

We feel that this First International Chinese Word Segmentation Bakeoff has been useful in that it has provided us with a good sense of the range of performance of various systems, both from academic and industrial institutions. There is clearly no single *best* system, insofar as there is no system that con-

[4]For example, Wu notes that 二十世纪 (*20th Century*) is consistently segmented as two words in the training data, but as one word in the test data. Similarly 副总经理 (*(corporate) vice president*) is segmented as one word in training data but as two words (副/总经理) in the testing data. As a final example, superlatives such as 最佳 (*best*) should be segmented as a single word if the adjective is monosyllabic, and it is not being used predicatively; however this principle is not consistently applied.

Wu also notes that the test data is different from the training data in several respects. Most of the training data comprise texts about Mainland China, whereas most of the testing data is about Taiwan. The test data contains classes of items, such as URL's and English page designations ("p. 64"), that never appeared in the test data.

Site	word count	R	c_r	P	c_p	**F**	OOV	R_{oov}	R_{iv}
S08	34,955	0.947	±0.0024	0.934	±0.0027	0.940	0.071	0.625	0.972
S06	34,955	0.940	±0.0025	0.908	±0.0031	0.924	0.071	0.415	0.980
S12	34955	0.917	±0.0030	0.915	±0.0030	0.916	0.071	0.670	0.936
S01	34,955	0.931	±0.0027	0.873	±0.0036	0.901	0.071	0.243	0.984

Table 7: Scores for HK closed, sorted by F.

Site	word count	R	c_r	P	c_p	**F**	OOV	R_{oov}	R_{iv}
S01	17,194	0.962	±0.0029	0.940	±0.0036	0.951	0.069	0.724	0.979
S10	17,194	0.955	±0.0032	0.938	±0.0037	0.947	0.069	0.680	0.976
S09	17,194	0.955	±0.0032	0.938	±0.0037	0.946	0.069	0.647	0.977
S07	17,194	0.936	±0.0037	0.945	±0.0035	0.940	0.069	0.763	0.949
S04	17,194	0.936	±0.0037	0.942	±0.0036	0.939	0.069	0.675	0.955
S08	17,194	0.939	±0.0037	0.934	±0.0038	0.936	0.069	0.642	0.961
S06	17,194	0.933	±0.0038	0.916	±0.0042	0.924	0.069	0.357	0.975
S05	17,194	0.923	±0.0041	0.867	±0.0052	0.894	0.069	0.159	0.980

Table 8: Scores for PK closed, sorted by F.

sistently outperformed all the others on all tracks. Even if there were, the most one could say is that for the four different segmentation standards and associated corpora, this particular system outperformed the others: But there could be no implication that said system would be the most appropriate for all applications.

One thing that we have not explicitly discussed in this paper is which type of *approach* shows the most promise, given the different submissions. While we are familiar with the approaches taken in several of the tested systems, we leave it up to the individual participants to describe their approaches and hopefully elucidate which aspects of their approaches are most responsible for their successes and failures; the participants' papers all appear in this volume. We leave it up to the research community as a whole to decide whether one approach or another shows most promise.

We believe that there should be future competitions of this kind, possibly not every year, but certainly every couple of years and we have some specific recommendations on how things might be improved in such future competitions:

1. It may be a good idea to insist that all participants participate in all tracks, subject of course to the restriction that participants may not be evaluated on data from their own institution. The decision this time to let people pick and choose was motivated in part by the concern that if we insisted that people participate in all tracks, some participants might be less inclined to participate. It was also motivated in part by the different Chinese coding schemes used by the various corpora, and the possibility that someone's system might work on one coding scheme, but not the other.

   However with sufficient planning, perhaps giving people a longer period of time for training their systems than was possible with this contest, it should be possible to impose this restriction without scaring away potential participants.

2. We would like to see more testing data developed for the next bakeoff. While the test sets turned out to be large enough to measure significant differences between systems in most cases, a larger test set would allow even better statistics. In some cases, more training data will also be needed.

   Given the problems noted by some of the participants with some of the data, we would also

Site	word count	R	c_r	P	c_p	**F**	OOV	R_{oov}	R_{iv}
S11	11,985	0.915	±0.0051	0.894	±0.0056	0.904	0.022	0.426	0.926
S03	11,985	0.892	±0.0057	0.853	±0.0065	0.872	0.022	0.236	0.906

Table 9: Scores for AS open, sorted by F.

Site	word count	R	c_r	P	c_r	**F**	OOV	R_{oov}	R_{iv}
S02	39,922	0.916	±0.0028	0.907	±0.0029	0.912	0.181	0.766	0.949
S10	39,922	0.911	±0.0029	0.891	±0.0031	0.901	0.181	0.738	0.949
S11	39,922	0.891	±0.0031	0.877	±0.0033	0.884	0.181	0.733	0.925
S01	39,922	0.887	±0.0032	0.876	±0.0033	0.881	0.181	0.707	0.927
S03	39,922	0.853	±0.0035	0.806	±0.0040	0.829	0.181	0.578	0.914

Table 10: Scores for CTB open, sorted by F.

like to see more consistently annotated training and test data, and test data that is more representative of what was seen in the training data.

3. We would like to expand the testing data to include texts of various lengths, particularly short strings, in order to emulate query strings seen in commercial search engines.

4. Finally, one question that we did not ask that should have been asked was whether the tested system is used as part of a commercial product or not. It is often believed of natural language and speech applications that deployed commercial systems are about a generation behind the systems being developed in research laboratories. It would be interesting to know if this is true in the domain of Chinese word segmentation, which should be possible to find out if we get a good balance of both.

For the present, we will make the training and test data for the bakeoff available via `http://www.sighan.org/bakeoff2003` (subject to the restrictions of the content providers), so that others can better study the results of this contest.

Acknowledgements

First and foremost we wish to thank the following institutions for providing the training and testing data for this bakeoff:

- Institute of Linguistics, Academia Sinica.
- Institute of Computational Linguistics, Beijing University.
- Language Information Sciences Research Centre, City University of Hong Kong.
- The Chinese Treebank Project, University of Pennsylvania, and the Linguistic Data Consortium.

Without the generous contribution of these resources, this competition would not have been possible.

We would also like to thank Martha Palmer for making funds available to pay for translations of the detailed bakeoff instructions, and to Fu-Dong Chiou, Susan Converse and Nianwen Xue for their work on the translations. Andi Wu and Aitao Chen provided useful feedback on errors in some of the corpora. The first author wishes to thank Bill DuMouchel of AT&T Labs for advice on the statistics. We also wish to thank Professor Tianshun Yao of Northeast (Dongbei) University for sending us the reports of the Chinese national competitions. Finally we thank Fei Xia and Qing Ma for their work on the Second meeting of SIGHAN of which this bakeoff is a part.

References

GB/T 13715–92. 1993. Contemporary Chinese language word-segmentation specification for information processing. Technical report, , Beijing.

Site	word count	R	c_r	P	c_r	**F**	OOV	R_{oov}	R_{iv}
S08	34,955	0.958	±0.0021	0.954	±0.0022	0.956	0.071	0.788	0.971
S03	34,955	0.909	±0.0031	0.863	±0.0037	0.886	0.071	0.579	0.935
S11	34,955	0.898	±0.0032	0.860	±0.0037	0.879	0.071	0.616	0.920

Table 11: Scores for HK open, sorted by F.

Site	word count	R	c_r	P	c_r	**F**	OOV	R_{oov}	R_{iv}
S10	17,194	0.963	±0.0029	0.956	±0.0031	0.959	0.069	0.799	0.975
S01	17,194	0.963	±0.0029	0.943	±0.0035	0.953	0.069	0.743	0.980
S08	17,194	0.939	±0.0037	0.938	±0.0037	0.938	0.069	0.675	0.959
S04	17,194	0.933	±0.0038	0.942	±0.0036	0.937	0.069	0.712	0.949
S03	17,194	0.940	±0.0036	0.911	±0.0043	0.925	0.069	0.647	0.962
S11	17,194	0.905	±0.0045	0.869	±0.0051	0.886	0.069	0.503	0.934

Table 12: Scores for PK open, sorted by F.

Charles Grinstead and J. Laurie Snell. 1997. *Introduction to Probability*. American Mathematical Society, Providence, RI, 2nd edition.

Chu-Ren Huang, Keh-Jiann Chen, Chang Lili, and Feng-yi Chen. 1997. Segmentation standard for Chinese natural language processing. *International Journal of Computational Linguistics and Chinese Language Processing*, 2(2):47–62.

Alan Smeaton and Ross Wilkinson. 1997. Spanish and chinese document retrieval at TREC-5. In E.M. Vorhees and D.K. Harman, editors, *Proceedings of the Fifth Text REtrieval Conference*.

Richard Sproat and Chilin Shih. 2001. Corpus-based methods in Chinese morphology and phonology. Technical report, Linguistic Society of America Summer Institute, Santa Barbara, CA. `http://www.research.att.com/~rws/newindex/notes.pdf`.

Yongheng Wang, Haiju Su, and Yan Mo. 1990. Automatic processing of Chinese words. *Journal of Chinese Information Processing*, 4(4):1–11.

Ross Wilkinson. 1998. Chinese document retrieval at TREC-6. In E.M. Vorhees and D.K. Harman, editors, *Proceedings of the Sixth Text REtrieval Conference*.

Zimin Wu and Gwyneth Tseng. 1993. Chinese text segmentation for text retrieval: Achievements and problems. *Journal of the American Society for Information Science*, 44(9):532–542.

Andi Wu. 2003. Customizable segmentation of morphologically derived words in Chinese. *International Journal of Computational Linguistics and Chinese Language Processing*, 8(1): forthcoming.

Fei Xia. 1999. Segmentation guideline, Chinese Treebank Project. Technical report, University of Pennsylvania. `http://morph.ldc.upenn.edu/ctb/`.

Tianshun Yao (姚天顺). 2001. 汉英机器翻译评测系统 (第一次评测总结与汇报). Technical report, Northeast University (东北大学), China, January.

Tianshun Yao (姚天顺). 2002. 汉英机器翻译评测系统 (第二阶段评测方案). Technical report, Northeast University (东北大学), China, August.

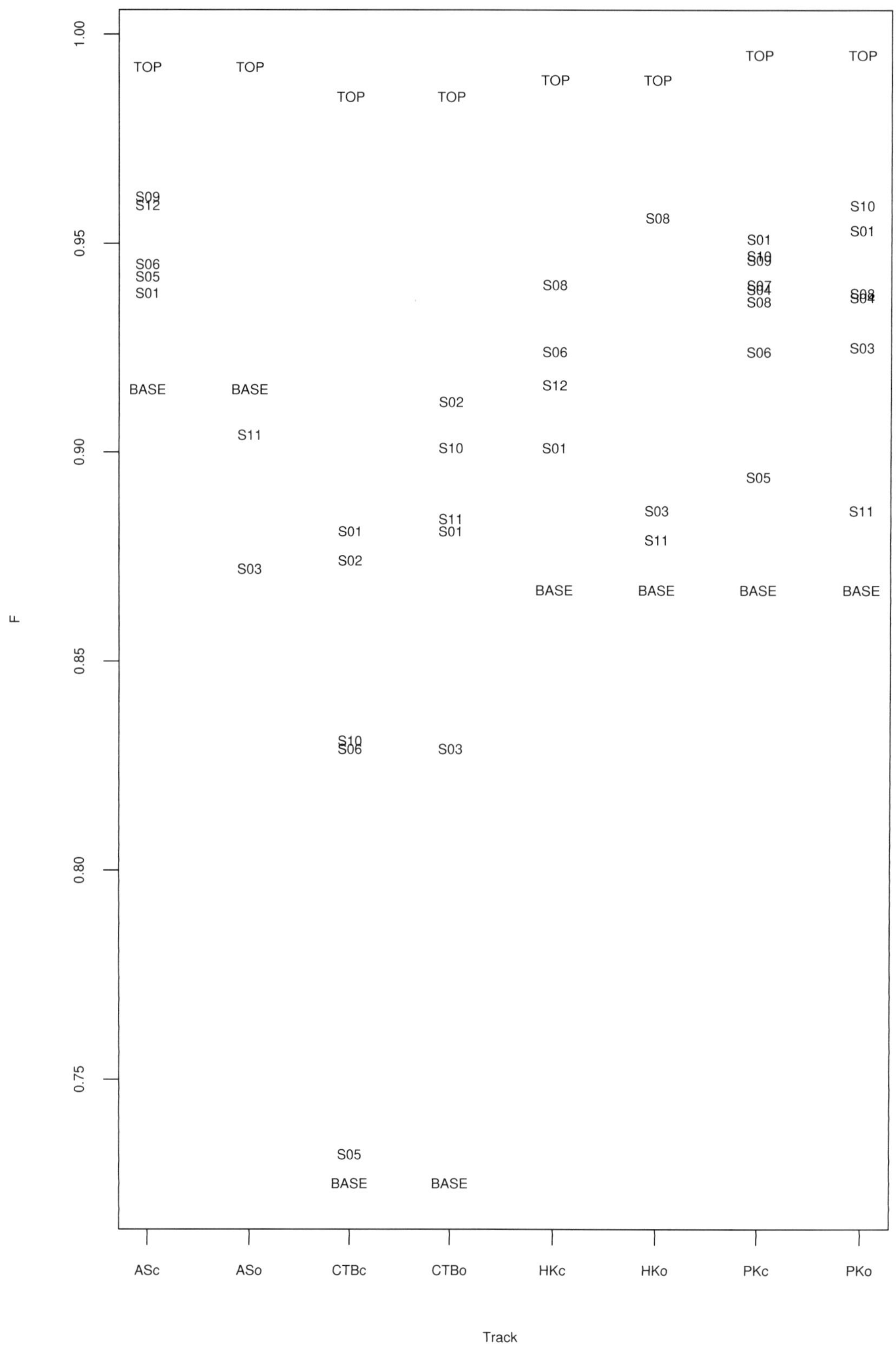

Figure 1: F scores for all systems, all tracks.

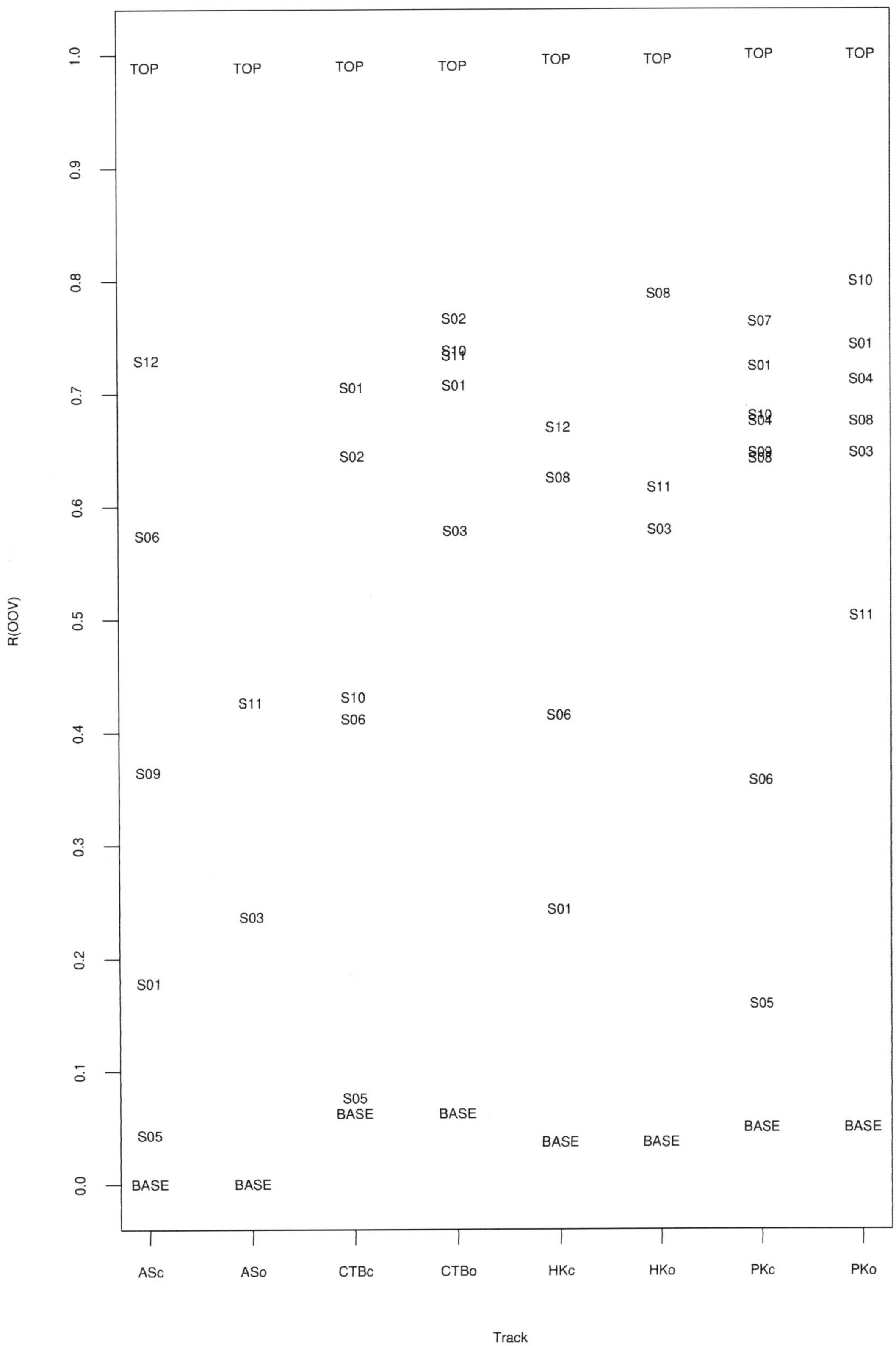

Figure 2: R_{oov} scores for all systems, all tracks.

Combining Segmenter and Chunker for Chinese Word Segmentation

Masayuki Asahara, Chooi Ling Goh, Xiaojie Wang, Yuji Matsumoto
Graduate School of Information Science
Nara Institute of Science and Technology, Japan
{masayu-a,ling-g,xiaoji-w,matsu}@is.aist-nara.ac.jp

Abstract

Our proposed method is to use a Hidden Markov Model-based word segmenter and a Support Vector Machine-based chunker for Chinese word segmentation. Firstly, input sentences are analyzed by the Hidden Markov Model-based word segmenter. The word segmenter produces n-best word candidates together with some class information and confidence measures. Secondly, the extracted words are broken into character units and each character is annotated with the possible word class and the position in the word, which are then used as the features for the chunker. Finally, the Support Vector Machine-based chunker brings character units together into words so as to determine the word boundaries.

1 Methods

We participate in the closed test for all four sets of data in Chinese Word Segmentation Bakeoff. Our method is based on the following two steps:

1. The input sentence is segmented into a word sequence by Hidden Markov Model-based word segmenter. The segmenter assigns a word class with a confidence measure for each word at the hidden states. The model is trained by Baum-Welch algorithm.

2. Each character in the sentence is annotated with the word class tag and the position in the word. The n-best word candidates derived from the word segmenter are also extracted as the features. A support vector machine-based chunker corrects the errors made by the segmenter using the extracted features.

We will describe each of these steps in more details.

1.1 Hidden Markov Model-based Word Segmenter

Our word segmenter is based on Hidden Markov Model (HMM). We first decide the number of hidden states (classes) and assume that the each word can belong to all the classes with some probability. The problem is defined as a search for the sequence of word classes $C = c_1, \ldots, c_n$ given a word sequence $W = w_1, \ldots, w_n$. The target is to find W and C for a given input S that maximizes the following probability:

$$arg \max_{W,C} P(W|C)P(C)$$

We assume that the word probability $P(W|C)$ is constrained only by its word class, and that the class probability $P(C)$ is constrained only by the class of the preceding word. These probabilities are estimated by the Baum-Welch algorithm using the training material (See (Manning and Schütze., 1999)). The learning process is based on the Baum-Welch algorithm and is the same as the well-known use of HMM for part-of-speech tagging problem, except that the number of states are arbitrarily determined and the initial probabilities are randomly assigned in our model.

1.2 Correction by Support Vector Machine-based Chunker

While the HMM-based word segmenter achieves good accuracy for known words, it cannot identify compound words and out-of-vocabulary words. Therefore, we introduce a Support Vector Machine(below SVM)-based chunker (Kudo and Matsumoto, 2001) to cover the errors made by the segmenter. The SVM-based chunker re-assigns new word boundaries to the output of the segmenter.

An SVM (Vapnik, 1998) is a binary classifier. Suppose we have a set of training data for a binary class problem: $(\mathbf{x}_1, y_1), \ldots, (\mathbf{x}_N, y_N)$, where $\mathbf{x}_i \in R^n$ is a feature vector of the i th sample in the training data and

$y_i \in \{+1, -1\}$ is the label of the sample. The goal is to find a decision function which accurately predicts y for an unseen $\mathbf{x}$. An SVM classifier gives a decision function $f(\mathbf{x})$ for an input vector $\mathbf{x}$ where

$$f(\mathbf{x}) = sign(\sum_{\mathbf{z}_i \in SV} \alpha_i y_i K(\mathbf{x}, \mathbf{z}_i) + b).$$

$f(\mathbf{x}) = +1$ means that $\mathbf{x}$ is a positive member, and $f(\mathbf{x}) = -1$ means that $\mathbf{x}$ is a negative member. The vectors $\mathbf{z}_i$ are called support vectors, which receive a non-zero weight α_i. Support vectors and the parameters are determined by solving a quadratic programming problem. $K(\mathbf{x}, \mathbf{z})$ is a kernel function which maps vectors into a higher dimensional space. We use a polynomial kernel of degree 2 given by $K(\mathbf{x}, \mathbf{z}) = (1 + \mathbf{x} \cdot \mathbf{z})^2$.

The SVM classifier determines the position tag for each character. We introduce the word class tag as the feature, which is generated by the word segmenter. Since we perform chunking by character units, the feature used by the classifier will be the information for the character unit.

The training data for our SVM-based chunker is constructed from the output of the HMM-based word segmenter defined in the previous section. In the current setting, the HMM produces all the possible tags (class labels) for each of the word within a predefined probability bound. All the words in the output are then segmented into characters, and each of the characters is tagged with pairs of a word class and a position tag. For example, in the paired tag "0-B", "0" is a class label of the word which the character belongs to and "B" indicates the character's position in the word. The number of classes is determined in advance of the HMM learning. The position tag consists of the following four tags (S/B/E/I): S means a single-character word; B is the first character in a multi-character word; E is the last character in a multi-character word; I is the intermediate character in a multi-character word longer than 2 characters. As shown in Figure 1, we set the HMM-based word segmenter to produce the classes of n-best word candidates to take into account multiple possibility of word boundaries.

The correct word boundary can be defined by assigning either of two kinds of tags to each of the characters. Look at the rightmost column of Figure 1 named as "Chunker Outputs." The label "B" in this column shows that the character is the first character of a *correct* word, and "I" shows that the character is the other part of a word. This means that the preceding positions of "B" tags are the word boundaries.

Those two tags correspond to the two classes of the SVM chunker: In the training (and test) phrase, we use window size of two characters to the left and right direction to learn (and estimate) the class for a character. For example, the shadowed parts in Figure 1 are used as the features to learn (or estimate) the word boundary tag "I" for the character "判".

Characters	Word Segmenter Outputs				Chunker Outputs
	Best	2nd Best	3rd Best	4th Best	
政	0-B	1-S	*	*	B
治	0-E	3-S	*	*	I
谈	1-B	4-S	*	*	B
判	1-E	4-S	1-S	2-S	I
是	0-S	*	*	*	B
推	0-B	4-S	*	*	B
动	0-E	3-S	*	*	I
两	2-B	4-S	*	*	B
岸	2-E	4-S	2-S	0-S	I
关	3-B	0-S	*	*	B
系	3-I	4-S	*	*	I
发	0-B	2-S	*	*	B
展	0-E	0-S	*	*	I
的	1-S	*	*	*	B
关	1-B	*	*	*	B
键	1-E	*	*	*	I
EOS					

Figure 1: The Extracted Features for the Chunker

2 Model Validation

To find out the best setting of learning, we would like to determine "the number of word classes" and "the depth of n-best word candidates" by using some sort of confidence measure. We perform validation experiments for these two types of parameters by using the training material provided.

2.1 Validation Tests for HMM-based Word Segmenter

The first validation experiment is to determine "the number of word classes" of the HMM. 80% of the material is used for the HMM training, and the other 20% is used as the validation set. We test two settings for the number of classes – 5 & 10. The results are shown in Table 1.

Table 1: Validation Results for HMM

Data	# of classes	Rec.	Prec.	F
AS	5	0.845	0.768	0.804
AS	10	0.900	0.857	0.878
CTB	5	0.909	0.844	0.875
CTB	10	0.912	0.848	0.879
HK	5	0.867	0.742	0.799
HK	10	0.867	0.741	0.799
PK	5	0.942	0.902	0.921
PK	10	0.944	0.905	0.924

In most cases, models perform slightly better with the increasing of the number of classes. When the corpus size is large like the Academia Sinica data, this tendency becomes more significant.

Whereas it is known that the Baum Welch algorithm is very sensitive to the initialization of the classes, we randomly assigned the initial classes without making much effort. There are two reasons: (1) Since the word segmenter outputs are used as the clues to the chunker in our method, we only need some consistent class annotations. (2) The initial classes did not affect on the word segmentation accuracy in our pilot experiments.

2.2 Validation Tests for SVM-based Chunker

The second validation test is for the chunking model to determine both "the number of word classes" and "the depth of the n-best candidates". 80% of the material used for the HMM training, another 10% is used for the chunking model training and the last 10% is used for the validation test. The results are shown in Table 2, 3 and 4. Since the training of this model is time- and resource-consuming, the Academia Sinica data being very large could not get enough time to finish the validation test.

Table 2: Validation Results (CTB) for Chunking

# of classes	n-best	Rec.	Prec.	F
5	1	0.957	0.930	0.943
5	**2**	**0.957**	**0.931**	**0.944**
5	3	0.957	0.930	0.943
5	4	0.957	0.930	0.943
10	1	0.956	0.929	0.943
10	2	0.957	0.928	0.942
10	3	0.956	0.929	0.942
10	4	0.955	0.928	0.941

Table 3: Validation Results (HK) for Chunking

# of classes	n-best	Rec.	Prec.	F
5	1	0.853	0.793	0.822
5	2	0.859	0.799	0.828
5	3	0.859	0.799	0.828
5	**4**	**0.859**	**0.800**	**0.828**
10	1	0.856	0.793	0.823
10	2	0.858	0.797	0.826
10	3	0.857	0.796	0.826
10	4	0.858	0.797	0.826

The results show that the chunker actually improves the word segmentation accuracy compared with the output of the HMM word segmenter for these three data sets. The segmentation errors made by the word segmenter for compound words and unknown words are corrected. The improvement in Chinese Treebank (CTB) data set is significant, because the data set contains many compound words.

Table 4: Validation Results (PK) for Chunking

# of classes	n-best	Rec.	Prec.	F
5	1	0.960	0.934	0.947
5	2	0.961	0.935	0.948
5	**3**	**0.962**	**0.936**	**0.949**
5	4	0.962	0.935	0.948
10	1	0.961	0.932	0.946
10	2	0.962	0.935	0.948
10	3	0.961	0.934	0.947
10	4	0.961	0.934	0.947

There is no significant difference in the results between the different depths of n-best answers. Still, we choose the best model for the test materials among them. If we need to have a faster analyzer, we should employ only the best answer of the word segmentation.

For the HMM, the larger number of classes tends to get better accuracy than smaller ones. However, for the chunking model, the result is the other way round. The model with the smaller number of classes gets slightly better accuracy. So, there should be trade-off between smaller and larger number of classes.

3 Final Models for Test Material

For the final models, 80% of the training material is used for HMM training and 100% of the material is used for the chunking model training. The parameters, namely "the number of word classes" and "the depth of n-best word candidates", are determined by the validation tests described in Section 2. While there is no significant difference between the depths of n-best answers, we choose the best model among them for the testing. The parameters are shown in Table 7.

We cannot create the model using all the original Academia Sinica data because of its large size. Therefore, we use 80% of the data for HMM training (5 classes) and only 10% for chunking model training (with only the best candidates).

Table 7: The Models for the Test Material
– with respect to F-Measure in Our Validation Test

Data	# of classes	n-best	F
AS	5	1	N/A
CTB	5	2	0.943
HK	5	4	0.828
PK	5	3	0.948

Table 5: Throughput Speeds (characters per second)

Data	Word Seg.	(# of words)	Fea. Ext.	(n-best)	Chunker	(# of SV)	Total Speed
AS	57000	(462750)	7640	(Only Best)	279	(96452)	241
CTB	54400	(77324)	4040	(to 2nd Best)	894	(16736)	671
HK	38900	(93231)	3870	(to 4th Best)	649	(14904)	524
PK	57400	(215865)	6209	(to 3rd Best)	254	(49736)	200

Table 6: Results for the Test Materials

Data	T. Rec.	T. Prec.	F	OOV Rec.	IV Rec.	Ranking
AS	0.944	0.945	0.945	0.574	0.952	3rd/6
CTB	0.852	0.807	0.829	0.412	0.949	8th/10
HK	0.940	0.908	0.924	0.415	0.980	5th/6
PK	0.933	0.916	0.924	0.357	0.975	2nd/4

4 Throughput Speeds

As described, our system is based on three modules: HMM-based word segmenter, Feature extractor and SVM-based chunker. The word segmenter is composed by *ChaSen* (written in C/C++) (Matsumoto et. al., 2003) which is adopted for GB/Big5 encoding. The feature extractor is written in Perl. The SVM-based chunker is composed by *YamCha* (written in C++) (Kudo and Matsumoto, 2001).

Table 5 shows the speeds [1] of the three modules individually and of the total system. "# of words" means the size of the word segmenter lexicon. Note that, if a word belongs to more than one class, we regard them as different words in our definition. "# of SV" means the number of support vectors in the chunker. The total system speed depends highly on that of the chunker. It is known that the speed of SVM classifiers depends on the number of support vectors and the number of features.

5 Conclusion

We presented our method for Chinese Word Segmentation Bakeoff in 2nd SIGHAN Workshop. The results for the test materials are shown in Table 6. The proposed method is purely corpus-based statistical/machine learning method. Although we did not incorporate any heuristic rules (e.g. part-of-speeches, functional words and concatenation for numbers) into the model, the method achieved considerable accuracy for the word segmentation task.

Acknowledgments

We thank Mr. Taku Kudo of NAIST for his development of the SVM-based chunker *YamCha*.

[1] The throughput speeds are measured on a machine: Intel(R) Xeon(TM) CPU 2.80GHz $\times$ 2, Memory 4GB, RedHat Linux 9.

References

T. Kudo and Y. Matsumoto. 2001. Chunking with Support Vector Machines. In *Proc. of NAACL 2001*, pages 192–199.

C. D. Manning and H. Schütze. 1999. *Foundation of Statistical Natural Language Processing*. Chapter 9. Markov Models, pages 317–340.

Y. Matsumoto, A. Kitauchi, T. Yamashita, Y. Hirano, K. Takaoka and M. Asahara 2003. Morphological Analyzer ChaSen-2.3.0 Users Manual Tech. Report. Nara Institute of Science and Technology, Japan.

L. A. Ramshaw and M. P. Marcus. 1995 Text chunking using transformation-bases learning In *Proc. of the 3rd Workshop on Very Large Corpora*, pages 83–94.

V. N. Vapnik. 1998. *Statistical Learning Theory.* A Wiley-Interscience Publication.

Chinese Word Segmentation Using Minimal Linguistic Knowledge

Aitao Chen
School of Information Management and Systems
University of California at Berkeley
Berkeley, CA 94720, USA
aitao@sims.berkeley.edu

Abstract

This paper presents a primarily data-driven Chinese word segmentation system and its performances on the closed track using two corpora at the first international Chinese word segmentation bakeoff. The system consists of a new words recognizer, a base segmentation algorithm, and procedures for combining single characters, suffixes, and checking segmentation consistencies.

1 Introduction

At the first Chinese word segmentation bakeoff, we participated in the closed track using the Academia Sinica corpus (AS for short) and the Beijing University corpus (PK for short). We will refer to the segmented texts in the training corpus as the *training data*, and to both the unsegmented testing texts and the segmented texts (the reference texts) as the *testing data*. For details on the word segmentation bakeoff, see (Sproat and Emerson, 2003).

2 Word segmentation

New texts are segmented in four steps which are described in this section. New words are automatically extracted from the unsegmented testing texts and added to the base dictionary consisting of words from the training data before the testing texts are segmented, line by line.

2.1 Base segmentation algorithm

Given a dictionary and a sentence, our base segmentation algorithm finds all possible segmentations of the sentence with respect to the dictionary, computes the probability of each segmentation, and chooses the segmentation with the highest probability. If a sentence of n characters, $S = c_1c_2 \ldots c_n$, has a segmentation of m words, $S = w_1w_2 \ldots w_m$, then the probability of the segmentation is estimated as $p(S,T) = p(w_1w_2 \ldots w_m) \approx \prod_{i=1}^{m} p(w_i)$, where T denotes a segmentation of a sentence. The probability of a word is estimated from the training corpus as $p(w) \approx \frac{N(w)}{N}$, where $N(w)$ is the number of times that the word w occurs in the training corpus, and N is the number of words in the training corpus. When a word is not in the dictionary, a frequency of 0.5 is assigned to the new word. The dynamic programming technique is applied to find the segmentation of the highest probability of a sentence without first enumerating all possible segmentations of the sentence with respect to the dictionary. Consider the text fragment 牡丹花木, with respect to a dictionary containing the words 牡丹, 牡丹花, 花木, 花 and 木, it has three segmentations: (1) 牡丹 / 花木; (2) 牡丹花 / 木; and (3) 牡丹 / 花 / 木. The probabilities of the three segmentations are computed as: (1) p(牡丹)*p(花木); (2) p(牡丹花)*p(木); (3) p(牡丹)*p(花)*p(木). The probability of a word is estimated by its relative frequency in the training data. Assume the first segmentation has the highest probability, then the text fragment will be segmented into 牡丹 / 花木.

2.2 Combining single characters

New words are usually two or more characters long and are often segmented into single characters. For example, the word 空阔 is segmented into 空 / 阔 when it is not in the dictionary. After a sentence is segmented using the base algorithm, the consecutive single Hanzi characters are combined into a word if the in-word probabilities of the single characters are over a threshold which is empirically determined from the training data. The *in-word* probability of a character is the probability that the character occurs in a word of two or more characters.

Some Hanzi characters, such as 的 and 了, occur as words on their own in segmented texts much more frequently than in words of two or more characters. For example, in the PK training corpus, the character 了 occurs as a word on its own 11,559 times, but in a word only 875 times. On the other hand, some Hanzi characters usually do not occur alone as words, instead they occur as part of a word. As an example, the character 国 occurs in a word 17,108 times, but as a word alone only 794 times in the PK training data. For each character in the training data, we compute its in-word probability as follow: $p(C_{inword}) = \frac{N(C_{inword})}{N(C)}$, where $N(C)$ is the number of times that character C occurs in the training data, and $N(C_{inword})$ is the number of times that character C is in a word of two or more characters.

We do not want to combine the single characters that occur as words alone more often than not. For both the PK training data and the AS training data, we divided the training data into two parts, two thirds for training, and one third for system development. We found that setting the threshold of the in-word probability to 0.85 or around works best on the development data. After the initial segmentation of a sentence, the consecutive single-characters are combined into one word if their in-word probabilities are over the threshold of 0.85. The text fragment 人人身着迷彩服 contains a new word 迷彩服 which is not in the PK training data. After the initial segmentation, the text is segmented into 人人 / 身着 / 迷 / 彩 / 服 /, which is subsequently changed into 人人 / 身着 / 迷彩服 after combining the three consecutive characters. The in-word probabilities for the three characters 迷, 彩, and 服 are 0.94, 0.98, and 0.99, respectively.

2.3 Combining suffixes

A small set of characters , such as 者, 性 and 化, frequently occur as the last character in words. We selected 145 such characters from the PK training corpus, and 113 from the AS corpus. After combining single characters, we combine a suffix character with the word preceding it if the preceding word is at least two-character long.

2.4 Consistency check

The last step is to perform consistency checks. A segmented sentence, after combining single characters and suffixes, is checked against the training data to make sure that a text fragment in a testing sentence is segmented in the same way as in the training data if it also occurs in the training data. From the PK training corpus, we created a *phrase segmentation table* consisting of word quadgrams, trigrams, bigrams, and unigrams, together with their segmentations and frequencies. Our phrase table created from the AS corpus does not include word quad-grams to reduce the size of the phrase table. For example, from the training text 明天 / 就 / 是 / 元旦, we create the following entries (only some are listed to save space):

text fragment	freq	segmentation
明天就是元旦	1	明天 / 就 / 是 / 元旦
明天就是	1	明天 / 就 / 是
就是元旦	1	就 / 是 / 元旦
就是	1	就 / 是
元旦	1	元旦

After a new sentence is processed by the first three steps, we look up every word quad-grams of the segmented sentence in the phrase segmentation table. When a word quadgram is found in the phrase segmentation table with a different segmentation, we replace the segmentation of the word quad-gram in the segmented sentence by its segmentation found in the phrase table. This process is continued to word trigrams, word bigrams, and word unigrams. The idea is that if a text fragment in a new sentence is found in the training data, then it should be segmented in the same way as in the training data. As an example, in the PK testing data, the sentence 明天就是农历羊年的大年初一。 is segmented into 明天 / 就是 / 农历 / 羊 / 年 / 的 / 大年初一 / 。 after the first three steps (the two characters 羊 and 年 are not, but should be, combined because the in-word probability of character 羊, which is 0.71, is below the pre-defined threshold of 0.85). The word bigram 明天就是 is found in the phrase segmentation table with a different segmentation, 明天 / 就 / 是. So the segmentation 明天 / 就是 is changed to the segmentation 明天 / 就 / 是 in the final segmented sentence. In essence, when a text fragment has two or more segmentations, its surrounding context, which can be the preceding word, the following word, or both, is utilized to choose the most appropriate segmentation. When a text fragment in a testing sentence never occurred in the same context in the training data, then the most frequent segmentation found in the training data is chosen. Consider the text 就是 again, in the testing data, ，就是事先 is segmented into ， / 就是 / 事先 by our base algorithm. In this case, 就是 never occurred in the context of ，就是事先, ，就是 or 就是事先. The consistency check step changes ， / 就是 / 事先 into ， / 就 / 是 / 事先 since 就是 is segmented into 就 / 是 515 times, but is treated as one word 就是 105 times in the training data.

3 New words recognition

We developed a few procedures to identify new words in the testing data. Our first procedure is designed to recognize numbers, dates, percent, time, foreign words, etc. We defined a set of characters consisting of characters such as the digits '0' to '9' (in ASCII and GB), the letters 'a' to 'z', 'A' to 'Z' (in ASCII and GB), '零一二三四五六七八九十百千万亿．点分之第年％, and the like. Any consecutive sequence of the characters that are in this predefined set of characters is extracted and post-processed. A set of rules is implemented in the post-processor. One such rule is that if an extracted text fragments ends with the character 年 and contains any character in 十百千万亿第, then remove the ending character 年 and keep the remaining fragment as a word. For example, our recognizer will extract the text fragment 四百八十年 and 第九年 since all the characters are in the pre-defined set of characters. The post-processor will strip off the trailing character 年, and return 四百八十 and 第九 as words. For personal names, we developed a program to extract the names preceding texts such as （高山族） and （女）, a program to detect and extract names in a sequence of names separated by the Chinese punctuation "、", such as 这些作品是吕厚民、侯波、吕相友、, a program to extract

	steps	dict	R	P	F	R_{oov}	R_{iv}
1	1	pkd1	0.919	0.838	0.877	0.050	0.984
2	1	pkd2	0.940	0.892	0.915	0.347	0.984
3	1	pkd3	0.949	0.920	0.934	0.507	0.982
4	1-2	pkd3	0.950	0.935	0.942	0.610	0.975
5	1-3	pkd3	0.951	0.940	0.945	0.655	0.972
6	1-4	pkd3	**0.955**	**0.938**	**0.946**	**0.647**	**0.977**

Table 1: Results for the closed track using the PK corpus.

personal names (Chinese or foreign) following title or profession names, such as 刘诗昆 in the text 著名钢琴家刘诗昆, and a program to extract Chinese personal names based on the preceding word and the following word. For example, the string 孙晓明 in 工作的孙晓明说 is most likely a personal name (in this case, it is) since 孙 is a Chinese family name, the string is three-character long (a typical Chinese personal name is either three or two-character long). Furthermore, the preceding word 的 and the following word 说 are highly unlikely to appear in a Chinese personal name. For the personal names extracted from the PK testing data, if the name is two or three-character long, and if the first character or two is a Chinese family name, then the family name is separated from the given name. The family names are not separated from the given names for the personal names extracted from the AS testing data. In some cases, we find it difficult to decide whether or not the first character should be removed from a personal name. Consider the personal name 叶利钦 which looks like a Chinese personal name since the first character is a Chinese family name, and the name is three-character long. If it is a translated foreign name (in this case, it is), then the name should not be split into family name and given name. But if it is the name of a Chinese personal name, then the family name 叶 should be separated from the given name. For place names, we developed a simple program to extract names of cities, counties, towns, villages, streets, etc, by extracting the strings of up to three characters appearing between two place name designators. For example, from the text 江西临川市洋洲镇洋洲村, our program will extract 洋洲镇 and 洋洲村.

4 Results

The last row (in boldface) in Table 1 gives our official results for the PK closed track. Other rows in the table present the results under different experimental conditions. The column labeled *steps* refers to the executed steps of our Chinese word segmentation algorithm. Step 1 segments a text using the base segmentation algorithm, step 2 combines single characters, step 3 attaches suffixes to the preceding words, and step 4 performs consistency checks. The four steps are described in details in section 2. The column labeled *dict* gives the dictionary used in each experiment. The *pkd1* consists of only the words from the PK training corpus, *pkd2* consists of the words in pkd1 and the words converted from pkd1 by changing the GB encoding to ASCII encoding for the numeric digits and the English letters, and *pkd3* consists of the words in pkd2 and the words automatically extracted from the PK testing texts using the procedures described in section 3. The columns labeled *R*, *P* and *F* give the recall, precision, and F score, respectively. The columns labeled R_{oov} and R_{iv} show the recall on out-of-vocabulary words and the recall on in-vocabulary words, respectively. All evaluation scores reported in this paper are computed using the score program written by Richard Sproat. We refer readers to (Sproat and Emerson, 2003) for details on the evaluation measures. For example, row 4 in table 1 gives the results using pkd3 dictionary when a sentence is segmented by the base algorithm, and then the single characters in the initial segmentation are combined, but suffixes are not attached and consistency check is not performed. The last row in table 2 presents our official results for the closed track using the AS corpus. The *asd1* dictionary contains only the words from the AS training corpus, while the *asd2* consists of the words in *asd1* and the new words automatically extracted from the AS testing texts using the new words recognition described in section 3. The results show that new words recognition and joining single characters contributed the most to the increase in precision, while the consistency check contributed the most to the increase in recall. Table 3 gives the results of the maximum matching using only the words in the training data. While the difference between the F-scores of the maximum matching and the base algorithm is small for the PK corpus, the F-score difference for the AS corpus is much larger. Our base algorithm performed substantially better than the maximum matching for the AS corpus. The performances of our base algorithm on the testing data using the words from the training data are presented in row 1 in table 1 for the PK corpus, and row 1 in table 2 for the AS corpus.

	steps	dict	R	P	F	R_{oov}	R_{iv}
1	1	asd1	0.950	0.936	0.943	0.000	0.970
2	1	asd2	0.950	0.943	0.947	0.132	0.968
3	1-2	asd2	0.951	0.952	0.951	0.337	0.964
4	1-3	asd2	0.949	0.952	0.951	0.372	0.961
5	1-4	asd2	**0.966**	**0.956**	**0.961**	**0.364**	**0.980**

Table 2: Results for the closed track using the AS corpus.

corpus	dict	R	P	F	R_{oov}	R_{iv}
AS	asd1	0.917	0.912	0.915	0.000	0.938
PK	pkd1	0.909	0.829	0.867	0.050	0.972

Table 3: Performances of the maximum matching (forward) using words from the training data.

5 Discussions

In this section we will examine in some details the problem of segmentation inconsistencies within the training data, within the testing data, and between training data and testing data. Due to space limit, we will only report our findings in the PK corpus though the same kinds of inconsistencies also occur in the AS corpus. We understand that it is difficult, or even impossible, to completely eliminate segmentation inconsistencies. However, perhaps we could learn more about the impact of segmentation inconsistencies on a system's performance by taking a close look at the problem.

We wrote a program that takes as input a segmented corpus and prints out the shortest text fragments in the corpus that have two or more segmentations. For each text fragment, the program also prints out how the text fragment is segmented, and how many times it is segmented in a particular way. While some of the text fragments, such as 等同 and 才能, truly have two different segmentations, depending on the contexts in which they occur or the meanings of the text fragments, others are segmented inconsistently. We ran this program on the PK testing data and found 21 unique shortest text fragments, which occur 87 times in total, that have two different segmentations. Some of the text fragments, such as 黄金周, are inconsistently segmented. The fragment 黄金周 occurs twice in the testing data and is segmented into 黄金 / 周 in one case, but treated as one word in the other case. We found 1,500 unique shortest text fragments in the PK training data that have two or more segmentations, and 97 unique shortest text fragments that are segmented differently in the training data and in the testing data. For example, the text 冰清玉洁 is treated as one word in the training data, but is segmented into 冰 / 清 / 玉 / 洁 in the testing data. We found 11,136 unique shortest text fragments that have two or more segmentations in the AS training data, 21 unique shortest text fragments that have two or more segmentations in the AS testing data, and 38 unique shortest text fragments that have different segmentations in the AS training data and in the AS testing data.

Segmentation inconsistencies not only exists within training and testing data, but also between training and testing data. For example, the text fragment 极大地 occurs 35 times in the PK training data and is consistently segmented into " 极大 / 地, but the same text fragment, occurring twice in the testing data, is segmented into 极 / 大 / 地 in both cases. The text 最新 occurs 67 times in the training data and is treated as one word 最新 in all 67 cases, but the same text, occurring 4 times in the testing data, is segmented into 最 / 新 in all 4 cases. The text 除夕夜 occurs 16 times in the training data, and is treated as one word in all cases, but in the testing data, it is treated as one word in three cases and segmented into 除夕 / 夜 in one case. The text 抱有 is segmented into 抱 / 有 in 8 cases, but treated as one word in one case in the training data. A couple of text fragments seem to be incorrectly segmented. The text 塞尔维亚族人 in the testing data is segmented into 塞尔维亚 / 族人, and the text 共庆春节 segmented into 共 / 庆春节.

Our segmented texts of the *PK* testing data differ from the reference segmented texts for 580 text fragments (427 unique). Out of these 580 text fragments, 126 text fragments are among the shortest text fragments that have one segmentation in the training data, but another in the testing data. This implies that up to 21.7% of the mistakes committed by our system may have been impacted by the segmentation inconsistencies between the PK training data and the PK testing data. Since there are only 38 unique shortest text fragments found in the AS corpus that are segmented differently in the training data and the testing data , the inconsistency problem probably had less impact on our AS results. Out of the same 580 text fragments, 359 text fragments (62%) are new words in the PK testing data. For example, the proper name 巴拉迪, which is a new word, is incorrectly segmented into 巴 / 拉迪 by our system. Another example is the new word 时好时坏 which is treated as one word in the testing data, but is segmented into 时 / 好 / 时 / 坏 by our system. Some of the longer text fragments that are incorrectly segmented may also involve new words, so at least 62%, but under 80%, of the incorrectly segmented text fragments are either new words or involve new words.

6 Conclusion

We have presented our word segmentation system and the results for the closed track using the *AS* corpus and the *PK* corpus. The new words recognition, combining single characters, and checking consistencies contributed the most to the increase in precision and recall over the performance of the base segmentation algorithm, which works better than maximum matching. For the closed track experiment using the *PK* corpus, we found that 62% of the text fragments that are incorrectly segmented by our system are actually new words, which clearly shows that to further improve the performance of our system, a better new words recognition algorithm is necessary. Our failure analysis also indicates that up to 21.7% of the mistakes made by our system for the PK closed track may have been impacted by the segmentation inconsistencies between the training and testing data.

References

Richard Sproat and Tom Emerson. 2003. *The First International Chinese Word Segmentation Bakeoff*. In proceedings of the Second SIGHAN Workshop on Chinese Language Processing, July 11-12, 2003, Sapporo, Japan.

Chinese Word Segmentation at Peking University

Duan Huiming Bai Xiaojing Chang Baobao Yu Shiwen
Institute of Computational Linguistics, Peking University
{duenhm, baixj, chbb, yusw}@pku.edu.cn

Abstract

Word segmentation is the first step in Chinese information processing, and the performance of the segmenter, therefore, has a direct and great influence on the processing steps that follow. Different segmenters will give different results when handling issues like word boundary. And we will present in this paper that there is no need for an absolute definition of word boundary for all segmenters, and that different results of segmentation shall be acceptable if they can help to reach a correct syntactic analysis in the end.

Keyword: automatic Chinese word segmentation, word segmentation evaluation, corpus, natural language processing

1. Introduction

On behalf of the Institute of Computational Linguistics, Peking University, we would like to thank ACL-SIGHAN for sponsoring the First International Chinese Word Segmentation Bakeoff, which provides us an opportunity to present our achievement of the past decade.

We know for sure that it is very difficult to settle on a scientific and appropriate method of evaluation, and it might be even more difficult than word segmentation itself. We are also clear that each step in Chinese information processing requires great efforts, and a satisfactory result in word segmentation, though critical, does not necessarily guarantee good results in the following steps.

From the test results of this evaluation, we are very gratified to see that we have done a good job both as a test corpus provider and as a participant. According to the rule, we did not test on the corpus we provided, but it is quite encouraging that our supply tops the test corpus list to be elected by other participants.

Section 2 and Section 3 describes our work in the Bakeoff as the test corpus provider and the participant respectively.

2. The test corpus provider

2.1 Corpus

The corpus we provided to the sponsor includes:

- A training set from People's Daily (January, 1998)
- A test set from People's Daily (Page 4 of January 1, 1998)

Data from People's Daily features standard Chinese, little language error, a wide coverage of linguistic phenomenon and topics, which are required for statistic training. Meanwhile, the corpus we provided is a latest version manually validated, hence a high level of correctness and consistency.

2.2 Specification

When processing a corpus, we need a detailed and carefully designed specification for guidance. And when using the corpus for NLP evaluation, we also need such a specification to ensure a fair contest for different systems within a common framework.

We provided the latest version of our specification, which has been published in the *Journal of Chinese Information Processing*. Based on our experience of large-scale corpus processing in recent years, the current version gave us different perspectives in a consistent way, and we hope it will also help others in this field know better of our segmented and POS-tagged corpus.

3. The participant

3.1 Training and testing

Our research on word segmentation has been focusing on People's Daily. As we are one of the two providers of Chinese corpora in GB code in this Bakeoff, we had to test on the Penn Chinese treebank.

Not all the training and test corpus we got came from the Mainland China. Some were GB data converted from BIG5 texts of Taiwan. It is commonly known that in the Mainland, Hong Kong and Taiwai, the Chinese langauge is used diversely not only in the sense of different coding systems, but in respect of different wordings as well.

While training our segmenter, we studied the guidelines and training corpus of Penn Chinese treebank, tracing the differences and working on them. The main difference between the work of U. Penn and that of ours is notion of "word". For instance:

Differences of "Word"	U. Penn	PKU
Chinese name	刘卫东，彭少阳	刘　卫东，彭　少阳
Number + "多|余……"	11.6 万余，八千七百多万	11.6 万　余，八千七百　多　万
Monosyllabic verb + complement	砌出，填上，读完	砌　出，填　上，读　完
Time word	十时三十分，９０年代	十时　三十分，９０　年代
Noun + suffix "们"	大学生们，企业家们	大学生　们，企业家　们
Disyllabic verb + "于"	领先于，受命于	领先　于，受命　于
… …		

These are different combinations in regard of words which follow certain patterns, and can therefore be handled easily by applying rules to the grogram. The real difficulty for us, however, is the following items:

U. Penn	PKU
有线　电视	有线电视
中央　军委	中央军委
中华　民族	中华民族
人民　日报	人民日报
知识　产权	知识产权
一　条　龙	一条龙
… …	… …

The Open Track allows us to use our own recourses, so we had to find the lexical correspondence to reduce the negtive effect caused by the difference between Penn Chinese treebank and our own corpus. However, as the training corpus is small, we could not remove all the negative effect, and the untackled problems remained to affect our test result.

Further, as we have been working on language data from the Mainland China, the lexicon of our segmenter does not contain words used in Taiwan. Such being the case, we added into our lexicon the entries that were not known (i.e., not found in the training set) and could not be handled by the rule-based makeshift either. But because we are not very familiar with the Chinese language used in Taiwan, we could not make a complete patch due to the limit of time.

3.2 Result analysis

From the test result that the sponsor provided, we can see our segmenter failed to score when the notion of "word" and the recognition of unknown words are involved.

Example 1:
[U. Penn] 实施 初期 将 以 **除罪化** 与 小额 贸易 合法化 为主 ， 在 观察 小三通 对 **金 马** 地区 治安 与 产业 影响 后 ， 才 会 考虑 在 第二 阶段 开放 商业性 行为 ， 至于 大 三通 的 实施 ， 尚 没有 明确 的 时间表 。
[PKU] 实施 初期 将 以 **除 罪 化** 与 小额 贸易 合法化 为主 ， 在 观察 小三通 对 **金马** 地区 治安 与 产业 影响 后 ， 才 会 考虑 在 第二 阶段 开放 商业性 行为 ， 至于 大 三通 的 实施 ， 尚 没有 明确 的 时间表 。

Example 2:
[U. Penn] 一 家 **宽频** 公司 负责 管理 两 个 大型 鱼缸 的 赖 小姐 更 表示 ， 公司 受 景气 影响 ， 不免 人人 节衣缩食 ， 但 每 个 月 五 、 六千 元 的 鱼缸 清理费 可 不 曾 少 过 ， 更 别 提 不时 得 补充 鱼 、 饲料 等 费用 。
[PKU] 一 家 **宽 频** 公司 负责 管理 两 个 大型 鱼缸 的 赖 小姐 更 表示 ， 公司 受 景气 影响 ， 不免 人人 节衣缩食 ， 但 每 个 月 五 、 六千 元 的 鱼缸 清理费 可不 曾 少 过 ， 更 别提 不时 得 补充 鱼 、 饲料 等 费用 。

In addition, there are also cognitive differences concerning the objective world, which did come up to influence our fine score.

Example 3:
[U. Penn] 吴思华 则 以 英特尔 为 例 ， 说明 知识 「 点 矽 成 金 」 的 威力 ： 一 张 名片 大小 的 CPU ， 说穿 了 就 是 一 块 烧 有 复杂 电路图 的 **矽 晶 板** 。
[PKU] 吴思华 则 以 英特尔 为 例 ， 说明 知识 「 点 矽 成金 」 的 威力 ： 一 张 名片 大小 的 CPU ， 说穿 了 就 是 一 块 烧 有 复杂 电路图 的 **矽晶板** 。

Example 4:
[U. Penn] 啊 ， 外太空人 入侵 ？ 别 紧张 ， 这 是 新 车 大展 中 ， 观众 戴 着 特制 的 「 **虚拟 实 境** 」 头盔 ， 体会 一下 自己 驾驶 新型 车 的 超炫 快感 。
[PKU] 啊 ， 外 太空人 入侵 ？ 别 紧张 ， 这 是 新车 大展 中 ， 观众 戴 着 特制 的 「 **虚拟 实境** 」 头盔 ， 体会 一下 自己 驾驶 新型 车 的 超 炫 快感 。

The recognition of unknown words has long been a bottleneck for word segmentation technique. So far we have not found a good solution, but we are confident about a progress in this respect in the near future.

4. Conclusion

Word segmentation is the first step yet a key step in Chinese information processing, but we have not found a perfect solution up till now. From an engineering perspective, we think there is no need for a unique result of segmentation. All roads lead to Rome. The approach you take, technical or non-technical, will be a good one if the expected result is achieved. And it would be more desirable if the processing program in each step can tolerate or even correct the errors made in the previous step.

We learn from our experience that the computer processing of natural language is a complex issue, which requires a solid fundamental research (on the language itself) to ensure a higher accuracy of automation. It is definitely hard to achieve an increase of one percent or even less in the accuracy of word segmentation, but we are still confident and will keep working in this respect.

Finally, we would like to thank Dr. Li Baoli and Dr. Bing SWEN for their great efforts on the maintenance of our segmentation program.

Reference

Yu, Shiwen, DUAN, Hui-ming, ZHU, Xue-feng, Bing SWEN. 2002. *The Specification of Basic Processing of Contemporary Chinese Corpus*. Journal of Chinese Information Processing, Issue 5 & Issue 6, 2002.

Yu, Shiwen, et al. 2002. The Grammatical Knowledge-base of Contemporary Chinese – A Complete *Specification (Second Version)*. Beijing: Tsinghua University Press.

Liu, Yuan, et al. 1994. *Specification and Automation of Word Segmentation of Contemporary Chinese for Information Processing*. Beijing: Tsinghua University Press.

Fie Xia. 2000. *The segmentation guidelines for the Penn Chinese tree bank (3.0)*. see http://www.cis.upenn.edu/~chinese/segguide.3rd.ch.pdf

A two-stage statistical word segmentation system for Chinese

Guohong Fu
Dept of Linguistics
The University of Hong Kong
Pokfulam Road, Hong Kong
ghfu@hkucc.hku.hk

K.K. Luke
Dept of Linguistics
The University of Hong Kong
Pokfulam Road, Hong Kong
kkluke@hkusua.hku.hk

Abstract

In this paper we present a two-stage statistical word segmentation system for Chinese based on word bigram and word-formation models. This system was evaluated on Peking University corpora at the First International Chinese Word Segmentation Bakeoff. We also give results and discussions on this evaluation.

1 Introduction

Word segmentation is very important for Chinese language processing, which aims to recognize the implicit word boundaries in Chinese text. During the past decades, great success has been achieved in Chinese word segmentation (Nie, et al, 1995; Yao, 1997; Fu and Wang, 1999; Wang et al, 2000; Zhang, et al, 2002). However, there still remain two difficult problems, i.e. ambiguity resolution and unknown word (so-called OOV word) identification, while developing a practical segmentation system for large open applications.

In this paper, we present a two-stage statistical word segmentation system for Chinese. In the first stage, we employ word bigram model to segment known words (viz. the words included in the system dictionary) in input. In the second stage, we develop a hybrid algorithm to perform unknown word identification incorporating word contextual information, word-formation patterns and word juncture model.

The rest of this paper is organized as follows: Section 2 presents a word bigram solution for known word segmentation. Section 3 describes a hybrid approach for unknown word identification. In section 4, we report the results of our system at the SIGHAN evaluation program, and in the final section we give our conclusions on this work.

2 The first stage: Segmentation of known words

In a sense, known word segmentation is a process of disambiguation. In our system, we use word bigram language models and Viterbi algorithm (1967) to resolve word boundary ambiguities in known word segmentation.

For a particular input Chinese character string $C = c_1 c_2 \cdots c_n$, there is usually more than one possible segmentation $W = w_1 w_2 \cdots w_m$ according to given system dictionary. Word bigram segmentation aims to find the most appropriate segmentation $\hat{W} = w_1 w_2 \cdots w_m$ that maximizes the probability $\prod_{i=1}^{m} P_r(w_i \mid w_{i-1})$, i.e.

$$\hat{W} = \arg\max_{W} P_r(W \mid C) \approx \arg\max_{W} \prod_{i=1}^{m} P_r(w_i \mid w_{i-1}) \qquad (1)$$

where $P_r(w_i \mid w_{i-1})$ is the probability that word w_i will occur given previous word w_{i-1}, which can be easily estimated from segmented corpus using maximum likelihood estimation (MLE), i.e.

$$P_r(w_i \mid w_{i-1}) \approx \frac{Count(w_{i-1} w_i)}{Count(w_{i-1})} \qquad (2)$$

To avoid the problem of data sparseness in MLE, here we apply the linear interpolation technique (Jelinek and Mercer, 1980) to smooth the estimated word bigram probabilities.

3 The second stage: Unknown word identification

The second stage mainly concerns unknown words segmentation that remains unresolved in first stage. This section describes a hybrid algorithm for unknown word identification, which can incorporate word juncture model, word-formation patterns and contextual information. To avoid the complicated normalization of the probabilities of different dimensions, the simple superposition principle is also used in merging these models.

3.1 Word juncture model

Word juncture model score an unknown word by assigning word juncture type. Obviously, most unknown words appear as a string of known words after segmentation in first stage. Therefore, unknown word identification can be viewed as a process of re-assigning correct word juncture type to each known word pair in input. Given a known word string $W = w_1 w_2 \cdots w_n$, between each word pair $w_i w_{i+1} (1 \le i \le n-1)$ is a *word juncture*. In general, there are two types of junctures in unknown word identification, namely *word boundary* (denoted by t_B) and *non-word boundary* (denoted by t_N).

Let $t(w_i w_{i+1})$ denote the type of a word juncture $w_i w_{i+1}$, and $P_r(t(w_i w_{i+1}))$ denote the relevant conditional probability, then

$$P_r(t(w_i w_{i+1})) \stackrel{def}{=} \frac{Count(t(w_i w_{i+1}))}{Count(w_i w_{i+1})} \quad (3)$$

Thus, the word juncture probability $P_{CJM}(w_U)$ of a particular unknown word $w_U = w_i w_{i+1} \cdots w_j$ $(1 \le i \le j \le n)$ can be calculated by

$$P_{CJM}(w_U) = P_r(t_B(w_{i-1} w_i)) \times P_r(t_B(w_j w_{j+1})) \times \prod_{l=i}^{j-1} P_r(t_N(c_l c_{l+1})) \quad (4)$$

In a sense, *word juncture model* mirrors the affinity of known word pairs in forming an unknown word. For a word juncture (w_i, w_{i+1}), the larger the probability $P_r(t_N(w_i w_{i+1}))$, the more likely the two words are merged together into one new word.

3.2 Word-formation patterns

Word-formation pattern model scores an unknown word according to the probability of how each internal known word contributes to its formation. In general, a known word w may take one of the following four patterns while forming a word: (1) w itself is a word. (2) w is the beginning of an unknown word. (3) w is at the middle of an unknown word. (4) w appears at the end of an unknown word. For convenience, we use S, B, M and E to denote the four patterns respectively. Let $pttn(w)$ denote a particular pattern of w in an unknown word and $P_r(pttn(w))$ denote the relevant probability, then

$$P_r(pttn(w)) \stackrel{def}{=} \frac{Count(pttn(w))}{Count(w)} \quad (5)$$

Obviously, $\sum_{pttn} P_r(pttn(w)) = 1$. And $1 - P_r(S(w))$ is the word-formation power of the known word w.

Let $P_{pttn}(w_U)$ be the overall word-formation pattern probability of a certain unknown word $w_U = w_1 w_2 \cdots w_l$, then

$$P_{pttn}(w_U) = \prod_{w_i \in w_U} P_r(pttn(w_i)) \quad (6)$$

Theoretically speaking, a known word can take any pattern while forming an unknown word. But it is not even in probability for different known words and different patterns. For example, the word 性 (xing4, nature) is more likely to act as the suffix of words. According to our investigation on the training corpus, the character 性 appears at the end of a multiword in more than 93% of cases.

3.3 Hybrid algorithm for unknown word identification

Current algorithm for unknown word identification consists of three major components: (1) an unknown word extractor firstly extracts a fragment of known words $w_1 w_2 \cdots w_n$ that that may have unknown words based on the related word-formation power and word juncture probability and its left and right contextual word w_L, w_R from the output of the first stage. (2) A candidate word constructor then generates a lattice of all possible new segmentations $\{W_U \mid W_U = x_1 x_2 \cdots x_m\}$ that may involve unknown words from the extracted fragment. (3) A decoder finally incorporates word juncture model $P_{WJM}(W_U)$, word-formation patterns $P_{pttn}(W_U)$ and word bigram probability

$P_{bigram}(W_U)$ to score these candidates, and then applies the Viterbi algorithm again to find the best new segmentation $\hat{W}_U = x_1 x_2 \cdots x_m$ that has the maximum score:

$$\begin{aligned}\hat{W}_U &= \arg\max_{W_U}\{P_{pttn}(W_U) + P_{CJM}(W_U) + P_{bigram}(W_U)\} \\ &= \arg\max_{W_U}\{\sum_{i=1,\cdots,n}(P_{pttn}(x_i) + P_{CJM}(x_i) + P_r(x_i \mid x_{i-1}))\}\end{aligned} \quad (7)$$

where $x_0 = w_L$ and $x_{n+1} = w_R$. Let w_U denote any unknown word in the training corpus. If x_i is an unknown word, then $P_r(x_i \mid x_{i-1}) = \frac{\sum_{w_U} Count(x_{i-1} w_U)}{Count(x_{i-1})}$.

4 Experiments

Our system participated in both closed and open tests on Peking University corpora at the First International Chinese Word Segmentation Bakeoff. This section reports the results and discussions on its evaluation.

4.1 Measures

In the evaluation program of the First International Chinese Word Segmentation Bakeoff, six measures are employed to score the performance of a word segmentation system, namely test recall (*R*), test precision (denoted by *P*), the balanced F-measure (*F*), the out-of-vocabulary (OOV) rate for the test corpus, the recall on OOV words (R_{OOV}), and the recall on in-vocabulary (R_{iv}) words. OOV is defined as the set of words in the test corpus not occurring in the training corpus in the closed test, and the set of words in the test corpus not occurring in the lexicon used in the open test.

4.2 Experimental lexicons and corpora

As shown in Table 1, we only used the training data from Peking University corpus to train our system in both the open and closed tests. As for the dictionary, we compiled a dictionary for the closed test from the training corpus, which contained 55, 226 words, and used a dictionary in the open test that contained about 65, 269 words.

Items	# words in lexicon	# train. words	# test. words
Closed	55,226	1,121,017	17,194
Open	65,269	1,121,017	17,194

Table 1: Experimental lexicons and corpora

4.3 Experimental results and discussion

Items	F	R	P	OOV	ROOV	Riv
Closed	0.939	0.936	0.942	0.069	0.675	95.5
Open	0.937	0.933	0.941	0.094	0.762	95.0

Table 2: Test results on PK corpus

Segmentation speed: There are in all about 28,458 characters in the test corpus. It takes about 3.21 and 3.07 seconds in all for our system to perform full segmentation (including known word segmentation and unknown word identification) on the closed and open test corpus respectively, running on an ACER notebook (TM632XC-P4M). This indicates that our system is able to process about 531,925~556,182 characters per minute.

Results and discussions: The results for the closed and open test are presented in Table 2. We can draw some conclusions from these results.

Firstly, the overall performance of our system is very stable in both the closed and open tests. As shown in Table 2, the out-of-vocabulary (OOV) rate is 6.9% in the closed test and 9.4% in the open test. However, the overall test F-measure drops by only 0.2 percent in the open test, compared with the closed test.

Secondly, our approach can handle most unknown words in the input. As can be seen from Table 2, the recall on OOV words are 67.5% the closed-test and 76.2% in the open-test. Wang et al (2000) and Yao (1997) have proposed a character juncture model and word-formation patterns for Chinese unknown word identification. However, their approaches can only work for the unknown words that are made up of pure monosyllable character in that they are character-based methods. To address this problem, we introduce both word juncture model and word-based word-formation patterns into our system. As a result, our system can deal with different unknown words that consist of different known words, including monosyllable characters and multiword.

Although our system is effective for most ambiguities and unknown words in the input, it has its inherent deficiencies. Firstly, to avoid data sparseness, we do not differentiate known words and unknown words while estimating word juncture models and word-formation patterns from the training corpus. This simplification may introduce some noises into these models for identifying unknown words. Our further investigations show that the precision on OOV words is still very low, i.e. 67.1% for closed test and 72.5% for open test. As a result, our system may yield a number of mistaken unknown words in the processing. Secondly, we regard known word segmentation and unknown word identification as two independent stages in our system. This strategy is obviously simple and more easily applicable. However, it does not work while the input contains a mixture of ambiguities and unknown words. For example, there was a sentence 中行长葛支行注重健身 in the test corpus, where, the string 中行长葛 is a fragment mixed with ambiguity and unknown words. The correct segmentation should be 中行/长葛/, where 中行(Zhonghang, the Bank of China) is a abbreviation of organization name, and 长葛 (Changge) is a place name. Actually, this fragment is segmented as 中/行长/葛/ in the first stage of our system. However, the unknown word identification stage does not have a mechanism to split the word 行长(Hangzhang, president) and finally resulted in wrong segmentation.

5 Conclusions

This paper presents a two-stage statistical word segmentation system for Chinese. In the first stage, word bigram model and Viterbi algorithm are applied to perform known word segmentation on input plain text, and then a hybrid approach is employed in the second stage to incorporate word bigram probabilities, word juncture model and word-based word-formation patterns to detect OOV words. The experiments on Peking University corpora have shown that the present system based on fairly simple word bigram and word-formation models can achieve a F-score of 93.7% or above. In future work, we hope to improve our strategies on estimating word juncture model and word-formation patterns and develop an integrated segmentation technique that can perform known word segmentation and unknown word identification at one time.

Acknowledgments

We would like to thank all colleagues of the First International Chinese Word Segmentation Bakeoff for their evaluations of the results and the Institute of Computational Linguistics, Peking University for providing the experimental corpora.

References

Fu, Guohong and Xiaolong Wang. 1999. Unsupervised Chinese word segmentation and unknown word identification. In: *Proceedings of NLPRS'99*, Beijing, China, 32-37.

Jelinek, Frederick, and Robert L. Mercer. 1980. Interpolated estimation of Markov source parameters from sparse data. In: *Proceedings of Workshop on Pattern Recognition in Practice*, Amsterdam, 381-397.

Nie, Jian-Yuan, M.-L. Hannan and W.-Y. Jin. 1995. Unknown word detection and segmentation of Chinese using statistical and heuristic knowledge. Communication of COLIPS, 5(1&2): 47-57.

Viterbi, A.J. 1967. Error bounds for convolutional codes and an asymmetrically optimum decoding algorithm. IEEE Transactions on Information Theory, IT-13(2): 260-269.

Wang, Xiaolong, Fu Guohong, Danial S.Yeung, James N.K.Liu, and Robert Luk. 2000. Models and algorithms of Chinese word segmentation. In: *Proceedings of the International Conference on Artificial Intelligence (IC-AI'2000)*, Las Vegas, Nevada, USA, 1279-1284.

Yao, Yuan. 1997. Statistics Based approaches towards Chinese language processing. Ph.D. thesis. National University of Singapore.

Zhang, Hua-Ping, Qun Liu, Hao Zhang, and Xue-Qi Cheng. 2002. Automatic recognition of Chinese unknown words based on roles tagging. In: *Proceedings of The First SIGHAN Workshop on Chinese Language Processing*, Taiwan, 71-77.

Integrating Ngram Model and Case-based Learning For Chinese Word Segmentation

Chunyu Kit Zhiming Xu Jonathan J. Webster
Department of Chinese, Translation and Linguistics
City University of Hong Kong
Tat Chee Ave., Kowloon, Hong Kong
{ctckit, ctxuzm, ctjjw}@cityu.edu.hk

Abstract

This paper presents our recent work for participation in the First International Chinese Word Segmentation Bakeoff (ICWSB-1). It is based on a general-purpose ngram model for word segmentation and a case-based learning approach to disambiguation. This system excels in identifying in-vocabulary (IV) words, achieving a recall of around 96-98%. Here we present our strategies for language model training and disambiguation rule learning, analyze the system's performance, and discuss areas for further improvement, e.g., out-of-vocabulary (OOV) word discovery.

1 Introduction

After about two decades of studies of Chinese word segmentation, ICWSB-1 (henceforth, the bakeoff) is the first effort to put different approaches and systems to the test and comparison on common datasets. We participated in the bakeoff with a segmentation system that is designed to integrate a general-purpose *ngram model* for probabilistic segmentation and a *case-* or *example-based learning* approach (Kit et al., 2002) for disambiguation.

The ngram model, with words extracted from training corpora, is trained with the EM algorithm (Dempster et al., 1977) using unsegmented training corpora. Originally it was developed to enhance word segmentation accuracy so as to facilitate Chinese-English word alignment for our ongoing EBMT project, where only unsegmented texts are available for training. It is expected to be robust enough to handle novel texts, independent of any segmented texts for training. To simplify the EM training, we used the uni-gram model for the bakeoff and relied on the Viterbi algorithm (Viterbi, 1967) for the most probable segmentation, instead of attempting to exhaust all possible segmentations of each sentence for a complicated full version of EM training.

The case-based learning works in a straightforward way. It first extracts case-based knowledge, as a set of context-dependent transformation rules, from the segmented training corpus, and then applies them to ambiguous strings in a test corpus in terms of the similarity of their contexts. The similarity is empirically computed in terms of the length of relevant common affixes of context strings.

The effectiveness of this integrated approach is verified by its outstanding performance on IV word identification. Its IV recall rate, ranging from 96% to 98%, stands at the top or the next to the top in all closed tests in which we have participated. Unfortunately, its overall performance is not sustainable at the same level, due to the lack of a module for OOV word detection.

This paper is intended to present the implementation of the system and analyze its performance and problems, aiming at exploration of directions for further improvement. The remaining sections are organized as follows. Section 2 presents the ngram model and its training with the EM algorithm, and Section 3 presents the case-based learning for disambiguation. The overall architecture of our system is given in Section 4, and its performance and problems are analyzed in Section 5. Section 6 concludes the paper and previews future work.

2 Ngram model and training

An ngram model can be utilized to find the most probable segmentation of a sentence. Given a Chinese sentence $s = c_1 c_2 \cdots c_m$ (also denoted as c_1^n), its probabilistic segmentation into a word sequence $w_1 w_2 \cdots w_k$ (also denoted as w_1^k) with the aid of an ngram model can be formulated as

$$\mathrm{seg}(s) = \underset{s = w_1 \circ w_2 \circ \cdots \circ w_k}{\arg\max} \prod_i^k p(w_i | w_{i-n+1}^{i-1}) \quad (1)$$

where $\circ$ denotes string concatenation, w_{i-n+1}^{i-1} the *context* (or *history*) of w_i, and n is the order of the ngram model in use. We have opted for uni-gram for the sake of simplicity. Accordingly, $p(w_i|w_{i-n+1}^{i-1})$ in (1) becomes $p(w_i)$, which is commonly estimated as follows, given a corpus $\mathcal{C}$ for training.

$$p(w_i) \doteq f(w_i) / \sum_{w \in \mathcal{C}} f(w) \quad (2)$$

In order to estimate a reliable $p(w_i)$, the ngram model needs to be trained with the EM algorithm using the available training corpus. Each EM iteration aims at approaching to a more reliable $f(w)$ for estimating $p(w)$, as follows:

$$f^{\mathrm{k}+1}(w) = \sum_{s \in \mathcal{C}} \sum_{s' \in \mathcal{S}(s)} p^{\mathrm{k}}(s')\, f^{\mathrm{k}}(w \in s') \quad (3)$$

where k denotes the current iteration, $\mathcal{S}(s)$ the set of all possible segmentations for s, and $f^{\mathrm{k}}(w \in s')$ the occurrences of w in a particular segmentation s'.

However, assuming that every sentence always has a segmentation, the following equation holds:

$$\sum_{s' \in \mathcal{S}(s)} p^{\mathrm{k}}(s') = 1 \quad (4)$$

Accordingly, we can adjust (3) as (5) with a normalization factor $\alpha = \sum_{s' \in \mathcal{S}(s)} p^{\mathrm{k}}(s')$, to avoid favoring words in shorter sentences too much. In general, shorter sentences have higher probabilities.

$$f^{\mathrm{k}+1}(w) = \sum_{s \in \mathcal{C}} \sum_{s' \in \mathcal{S}(s)} \frac{p^{\mathrm{k}}(s')}{\alpha}\, f^{\mathrm{k}}(w \in s') \quad (5)$$

Following the conventional idea to speed up the EM training, we turned to the Viterbi algorithm. The underlying philosophy is to distribute more probability to more probable events. The Viterbi segmentation, by utilizing dynamic programming techniques to go through the word trellis of a sentence efficiently, finds the most probable segmentation under the current parameter estimation of the language model, fulfilling (1)). Accordingly, (6) becomes

$$f^{\mathrm{k}+1}(w) = \sum_{s \in \mathcal{C}} p^{\mathrm{k}}(\mathrm{seg}(s))\, f^{\mathrm{k}}(w \in \mathrm{seg}(s)) \quad (6)$$

and (5) becomes

$$f^{\mathrm{k}+1}(w) = \sum_{s \in \mathcal{C}} f^{\mathrm{k}}(w \in \mathrm{seg}(s)) \quad (7)$$

where the normalization factor is skipped, for only the Viterbi segmentation is used for EM re-estimation. Equation (7) makes the EM training with the Viterbi algorithm very simple for the uni-gram model: iterate word segmentation, as (1), and word count updating, via (7), sentence by sentence through the training corpus until there is a convergence.

Since the EM algorithm converges to a local maxima only, it is critical to start the training with an initial $f^0(w)$ for each word not too far away from its "true" value. Our strategy for initializing $f^0(w)$ is to assume all possible words in the training corpus as equiprobable and count each of them as 1; and then $p^0(w)$ is derived using (2). This strategy is supposed to have a weaker bias to favor longer words than maximal matching segmentation.

For the bakeoff, the ngram model is trained with the *unsegmented* training corpora together with the test sets. It is a kind of *unsupervised* training. Adding the test set to the training data is reasonable, to allow the model to have necessary adaptation towards the test sets. Experiments show that the training converges very fast, and the segmentation performance improves significantly from iteration to iteration. For the bakeoff experiments, we carried out the training in 6 iterations, because more iterations than this have not been observed to bring any significant improvement on segmentation accuracy to the training sets.

3 Case-based learning for disambiguation

No matter how well the language model is trained, probabilistic segmentation cannot avoid mistakes on ambiguous strings, although it resolves most ambiguities by virtue of probability. For the remaining unresolved ambiguities, however, we have to resort to other strategies and/or resources. Our recent study (Kit et al., 2002) shows that *case-based learning* is an effective approach to disambiguation.

The basic idea behind the case-based learning is to utilize existing resolutions for known ambiguous strings to do disambiguation if similar ambiguities occur again. This learning strategy can be implemented in two straightforward steps:

1. Collection of correct answers from the training corpus for ambiguous strings together with their contexts, resulting in a set of context-dependent transformation rules;

2. Application of appropriate rules to ambiguous strings.

A transformation rule of this type is actually an *example* of segmentation, indicating how an ambiguous string is segmented within a particular context. It has the following general form:

$$C^l \alpha \, C^r : \alpha \rightarrow w_1 w_2 \cdots w_k$$

where α is the ambiguous string, C^l and C^r its *left* and *right* contexts, respectively, and $w_1 w_2 \cdots w_k$ the correct segmentation of α given the contexts. In our implementation, we set the context length on each side to two words.

For a particular ambiguity, the example with the most similar context in the *example* (or, *rule*) *base* is applied. The similarity is measured by the sum of the length of the common suffix and prefix of, respectively, the left and right contexts. The details of computing this similarity can be found in (Kit et al., 2002) . If no rule is applicable, its probabilistic segmentation is retained.

For the bakeoff, we have based our approach to ambiguity detection and disambiguation rule extraction on the assumption that only ambiguous strings cause mistakes: we detect the discrepancies of our probabilistic segmentation and the standard segmentation of the training corpus, and turn them into transformation rules. An advantage of this approach is that the rules so derived carry out not only disambiguation but also error correction. This links our disambiguation strategy to the application of Brill's (1993) transformation-based error-driven learning to Chinese word segmentation (Palmer, 1997; Hockenmaier and Brew, 1998).

4 System architecture

The overall architecture of our word segmentation system is presented in Figure 1.

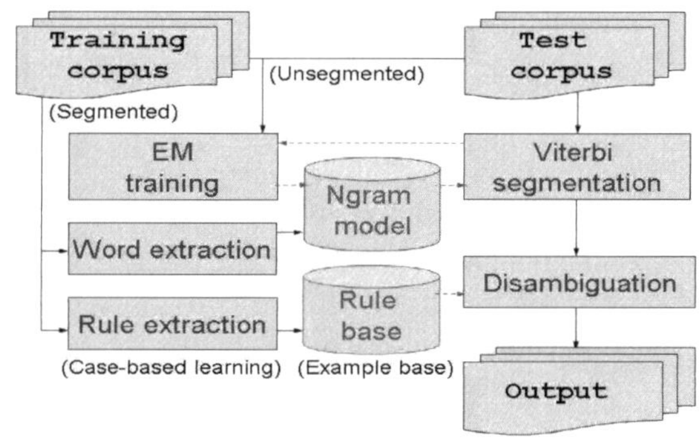

Figure 1: Overall architecture of the system

5 Performance and analysis

The performance of our system in the bakeoff is presented in Table 1 in terms of precision (P), recall (R) and F score in percentages, where "c" denotes closed tests. Its IV word identification performance is remarkable.

However, its overall performance is not in balance with this, due to the lack of a module for OOV word discovery. It only gets a small number of OOV words correct by chance. The higher OOV proportion in the test set, the worse is its F score. The relatively high R_{oov} for PK_c track is, mostly, the result of number recognition with regular expressions.

Test	P	R	F	OOV	R_{oov}	R_{iv}
SA_c	95.2	93.1	94.2	02.2	04.3	97.2
CTB_c	80.0	67.4	73.2	18.1	07.6	95.9
PK_c	92.3	86.7	89.4	06.9	15.9	98.0

Table 1: System performance, in percentages (%)

5.1 Error analysis

Most errors on IV words are due to the side-effect of the context-dependent transformation rules. The rules resolve most remaining ambiguities and correct many errors, but at the same time they also corrupt some proper segmentations. This side-effect is most likely to occur when there is inadequate context information to decide which rules to apply.

There are two strategies to remedy, or at least alleviate, this side-effect: (1) retrain probabilistic segmentation – a conservative strategy; or, (2) incorporate Brill's error-driven learning with several rounds of transformation rule extraction and application, allowing mistakes caused by some rules in previous rounds to be corrected by other rules in later rounds.

However, even worse than the above side-effect is a bug in our disambiguation module: it always applies the first available rule, leading to many unexpected errors, each of which may result in more than one erroneous word. For instance, among 430 errors made by the system in the SA closed test, some 70 are due to this bug. A number of representative examples of these errors are presented in Table 2, together with some false errors resulting from the inconsistency in the standard segmentation.

Errors	Standard	False errors	Standard
中的 (8)	中 的	第二次大戰	第二 次 大戰
只 是 (7)	只是	公元兩千年	公元 兩千年
不 能 (7)	不能	天然資源	天然 資源
個 人 (5)	個人	套裝軟體	套裝 軟體
只 有 (4)	只有	美其名爲	美其名 爲
才能 (4)	才 能	不虛此生	不 虛 此 生

Table 2: Errors and false errors

6 Conclusion and future work

We have presented our recent work for participation in ICWSB-1 based on a general-purpose ngram model for probabilistic word segmentation and a case-based learning strategy for disambiguation. The ngram model is trained using available unsegmented texts with the EM algorithm with the aid of Viterbi segmentation. The learning strategy acquires a set of context-dependent transformation rules to correct mistakes in the probabilistic segmentation of ambiguous substrings. This integrated approach demonstrates an impressive effectiveness by its outstanding performance on IV word identification. With elimination of the bug and false errors, its performance could be significantly better.

6.1 Future work

The above problem analysis points to two main directions for improvement in our future work: (1) OOV word detection; (2) a better strategy for learning and applying transformation rules to reduce the side-effect. In addition, we are also interested in studying the effectiveness of higher-order ngram models and variants of EM training for Chinese word segmentation.

Acknowledgements

The work is part of the CERG project "EBMT for HK Legal Texts" funded by HK UGC under the grant #9040482, with Jonathan J. Webster as the principal investigator and Chunyu Kit, Caesar S. Lun, Haihua Pan, King Kuai Sin and Vincent Wong as investigators. The authors wish to thank all team members for their contribution to this paper.

References

E. Brill. 1993. *A Corpus-Based Approach to Language Learning*. Ph.D. thesis, University of Pennsylvania, Philadelphia, PA.

A. P. Dempster, N. M. Laird, and D. B.Rubin. 1977. Maximum likelihood from incomplete data via the em algorithm. *Journal of the Royal Statistical Society, Series B*, 34:1–38.

J. Hockenmaier and C. Brew. 1998. Error-driven learning of Chinese word segmentation. In *PACLIC-12*, pages 218–229, Singapore. Chinese and Oriental Languages Processing Society.

C. Kit, H. Pan, and H. Chen. 2002. Learning case-based knowledge for disambiguating Chinese word segmentation: A preliminary study. In *COLING2002* workshop: *SIGHAN-1*, pages 33–39, Taipei.

D. Palmer. 1997. A trainable rule-based algorithm for word segmentation. In *ACL-97*, pages 321–328, Madrid.

A. J. Viterbi. 1967. Error bounds for convolutional codes and an asymptotically optimum decoding algorithm. *IEEE Transactions on Information Theory*, IT-13:260–267.

A Unicode based Adaptive Segmentor

Q. Lu, S. T. Chan, R. F. Xu, T. S. Chiu
Dept. Of Computing,
The Hong Kong Polytechnic University,
Hung Hom, Hong Kong
{csluqin,csrfxu}@comp.polyu.edu.hk

B. L. Li, S. W. Yu
The Institute of Computational Linguistics,
Peking University,
Beijing, China
{libi,yusw}@pku.edu.cn

Abstract

This paper presents a Unicode based Chinese word segmentor. It can handle Chinese text in Simplified, Traditional, or mixed mode. The system uses the strategy of divide-and-conquer to handle the recognition of personal names, numbers, time and numerical values, etc in the pre-processing stage. The segmentor further uses tagging information to work on disambiguation. Adopting a modular design approach, different functional parts are separately implemented using different modules and each module tackles one problem at a time providing more flexibility and extensibility. Results show that with added pre-processing modules and accessorial modules, the accuracy of the segmentor is increased and the system is easily adaptive to different applications.

1 Introduction

The most difficult problem in Chinese word segmentation is due to overlapping ambiguities [1-2]. The recognition of names, foreign names, and organizations are quite unique for Chinese. Some systems can already achieve very high accuracy [3], but they heavily rely on manual work in getting the system to be trained to work certain language environment. However, for many applications, we need to look at the cost to achieve high accuracy. In a competitive environment, we also need to have systems that are quickly adaptive to new requirements with limited resources available.

In this paper, we report a Unicode based Chinese word segmentor. The segmentor can handle Chinese text in Simplified, Traditional, or mixed mode where internally only one dictionary is needed. The system uses the strategy of divide-and-conquer to handle the recognition of personal names, numbers, time and numerical values. The system has a built-in new word extractor that can extract new words from running text, thus save time on training and getting the system quickly adaptive to new language environment. The Bakeoff results in the open text for our system in all categories have shown that it works reasonably good for all different corpora.

The rest of the paper is organized as follows. Section 2 presents our system design objectives and components. Section 3 discusses more implementation details. Section 4 gives some performance evaluations. Section 5 is the conclusion.

2 Design Objectives and Components

With the wide use of Unicode based operating systems such as Window 2000 and Window XP, we now see more and more text data written in both the Simplified form and the Traditional form to co-exist on the same system. It is also likely that text written in mixed mode. Because of this reality, the first design objective of this system is its ability to handle the segmentation of Chinese text written in either Simplified Chinese, Traditional Chinese, or mixed mode. As an example, we should be able to segment the same sentence in different forms such as the example given below:

```
Simplified:[我][后日][要][上学]
Traditional:[我][後日][要][上學]
Mixed:[我][后日][要][上學]
```

The second design objective is to adopt the modular design approach where different functional parts are separately implemented using independent modules and each module tackles one problem at a time. Using this modular approach, we can isolate problems and fine tune each module with minimal effect on other modules in the system.

Special features like adding new rules or new dictionary can be easily done without affecting other modules. Consequently, the system is more flexible and can be easily extended.

The third design objective of the system is to make the segmentor adaptive to different application domains. We consider it having more practical value if the segmentor can be easily trained using some semi-automatic process to work in different domains and work well for text with different regional variations. We consider it essential that the segmentor has tools to help it to obtain regional related information quickly even if annotated corpora are not available. For instance, when it runs text from Hong Kong, it must be able to recognize the personal names such as 陳方安生 if such a name(quadra-gram) appears in the text often.

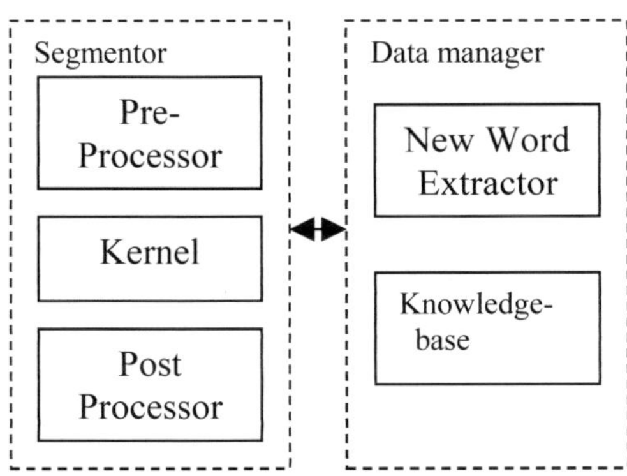

Figure 1. System components

Figure 1 shows the two major components, the segmentor and data manager. The *segmentor* is the core component of the system. It has a pre-processor, the kernel, and a post-processor. As the system has to maintain a number of tables such as the dictionaries, family name list, etc., a separate component called data manager is responsible in handling the maintenance of these data. The *pre-processor* has separate modules to handle paragraphs, ASCII code, numbers, time, and proper names including personal names, place and organizational names, and foreign names. The *kernel* supports different segmentation algorithms. It is the application or user's choice to invoke the preferred segmentation algorithms that at current time include the basic maximum matching and minimum matching in both forward and backward mode. These can also be used to build more complicated algorithms later on. In addition, the system provides segmentation using part-of-speech tagging information to help resolve ambiguity. The *post processor* applies morphological rules which cannot be easily applied using a dictionary.

The data manager helps to maintain the knowledge base in the system. It also has an accessory software called the *new word extractor* which can collect statistical information based on character bi-grams, tri-grams and quadra-grams to semi-automatically extract words and names so that they can be used by the segmentor to improve performance especially when switching to a new domain. Another characteristic of this segmentor is that it provides tagging information for segmented text. The tagging information can be optionally omitted if not needed by an application.

3 Implementation Details

The basic dictionary of this system was provided by Peking University [4] and we also used the tagging data from [4]. The data structure for our dictionaries are very similar to that discussed in [5]. As our program needs to handle both Simplified and Traditional Chinese characters, Unicode is the only solution for dealing with more than one script at the same time.

Even though it is our design objective to support both Simplified and Traditional Chinese, we do not want to keep two different sets of dictionaries for Simplified and Traditional Chinese. Even if two versions are kept, it would not serve well for text in mixed mode. For example, Traditional Chinese word of "the day after tomorrow" should be 後日, and for Simplified Chinese, it should be 后日. However sometimes we can see the word 后日 appears in a Traditional Chinese text. We cannot say that it is wrong because the sentence is still semantically correct especially in Unicode environment. Therefore the segmentor should be able to segment those words correctly such as in the examples: "[我][後日][上班]", and in "[他][后日][放假]". We must also deal with dictionary maintenance related to Chinese variants. For example, characters 強 and 强 are variants, so are 雞 and 鷄.

In order to keep the dictionary maintenance simple, our system uses a single dictionary which only keeps the so called canonical form of a word. In our system, the *canonical form* of a word is its "simplified form". We quoted the word "simplified" because only certain characters have simplified forms such as 後日 to 后日, but for 清晨, there is no simplified form. In the case of variants, we simply choose one of them as the canonical character. The canonical characters are maintained in the traditional-simplified character conversion table as well as in a variant table. Whenever a new word, *item*, is added into the dictionary, it must be added using a function *CanonicalConversion()*, which takes *item* as an input. During segmentation, the corresponding dictionary look up function will first convert the token to its canonical form before looking up in the dictionary.

The personal name recognizers (separate for Chinese names and foreign names) use the maximum-likelihood algorithm with consideration of commonly used Chinese family names, given names, and foreign name characters. It works for Chinese names of length up to 5 characters. In the following examples you can see that our system successfully recognized the name 陳方安生. This is done using our algorithm, not by putting her name in our dictionary:

[陳方安生/nr][昨晚/t][出席/v][公開/a][場合/n][發表/v][演詞/n]

Organization names and place names are recognized mainly using special purpose dictionaries. The segmentor uses tagging information to help resolve ambiguity. The disambiguation is mostly based on rules such as

p + (n + f) -> p + n + f

which would word to correct

[從/p][(馬/n 上/f)/d] -> [從/p][馬/n][上/f]

For efficiency reasons, our system uses only about 20 rules. The system is flexible enough for new rules to be added to improve performance.

The new word extractor is an accessory program to extract new words from running text based on statistical data which can either be grabbed from the internet or collected from other sources. The basic statistical data include bi-gram frequency, tri-gram frequency, and quadra-gram frequencies. In order to further example whether a bi-gram, say 差餉, is indeed a word, we further collect forward conditional frequency of 差, $freq_{forward}$(餉|差), and the back-ward conditional frequency of 餉, $freq_{backward}$(差|餉). For an i-gram token, we also use the (i+1)-gram statistics to eliminate those i-grams that are only a part of (i+1) – gram word. For instance, if the frequency of bi-gram 普洱 is very close to the frequency of tri-gram 普洱茶, it is less likely that 普洱 is a word. Of course, whether 普洱茶 is a word depends on quadra-gram results. Using the statistical result, a set of rules was applied to these i-grams to eliminate entries that are not considered new words. Minimal manual work is required to identify whether the remaining candidates are new words. Before words are added into the dictionary, part-of-speech information are added manually (although not necessary) before using the canonical function. The following table shows examples of bi-grams which are found by the new word extractor using one year Hong Kong Commercial Daily News data.

Bigram	count	forwardfreq	backwardfreq
差餉	818	0.061425	0.943483
入伙	734	0.007373	0.583002
叱吒	120	0.902256	0.794702
蜆殼	106	0.751773	0.120045
叮噹	44	0.330827	0.473118
普洱	44	0.003137	0.483516
[illegible]	15	1.000000	0.001847
[illegible]	15	1.000000	1.000000

4 Performance Evaluation

The valuation metrics used in [6] were adopted here.

$$recall = \frac{N_3}{N_1} \tag{1}$$

$$presicion = \frac{N_3}{N_2} \tag{2}$$

$$F_1(precision, recall) = \frac{2 \times recall \times precision}{recall + precision} \quad (3)$$

where N_1 denotes the number of words in the annotated corpus, N_2 denotes the number of words identified by the segmentation algorithm , and N_3 is the number of words correctly identified.

We participated in the open tests for all four corpora. The results are shown in the following table.

Data	R	P	F	R_{oov}	R_{iv}
AS	0.892	0.853	0.872	0.236	0.906
CTB	0.853	0.806	0.829	0.578	0.914
HK	0.909	0.863	0.886	0.579	0.935
PK	0.94	0.911	0.925	0.647	0.962

The worst performance in the 4 tests were for the CTB(UPenn) data. From the observation from the testing data, we found that the main problem with have with CTB data is the difference in word granularity. To confirm our observation, we have done an analysis of combining errors and overlapping errors. The results show that the ratios of combining errors in all the error types are 0.8425(AS), 0.87684(CTB), 0.82085(HK), and 0.77102(PK). The biggest problem we have with AS data, on the other hand is due to out of vocabulary mistakes. Even though our new word extractor can help us to reduce this problem, but we have not trained our system using data from Taiwan. Our best performance was on PK data because we used a very similar dictionary. The additional training of data for HK was done using one year Commercial Daily(香港商報).

The following table summarizes the execution speed of our program for the 4 different sources:

Data	No. of chars	Processing Time (sec.)	Processing Rate (char/sec)	Segmentation Rate (char/sec)
AS	18,743	4.703	3,985	7,641
CTB	62,332	10.110	6,165	7,930
HK	57,432	10.329	5,560	7,109
PK	28,458	4.829	5,893	10,970

The program initialization needs around 2.25 seconds mainly to load the dictionaries and other data into the memory before the segmentation can start. If we only count the segmentation time, the rate of segmentation on the average is around 7,500 characters for the first three corpora. It seems that the processing speed for Peking U. data is faster. This may be because the dictionaries we used are closer to the PK system, thus it would take less time to work on disambiguation.

5 Conclusion

In this paper, design and algorithms of a general-purposed Unicode based segmentor is proposed. It is able to process Simplified and Traditional Chinese appear in the same text. Sophisticated pre-processing and other auxiliary modules help segmenting text more accurately. User interactions and modules can be easily added with the help of its modular design. A built-in new word extractor is also implemented for extracting new words from running text. It saves much time on training and thus it can be quickly adapted to new environments.

Acknowledgement

We thank the PI of ***ITF Grant by ITC of HKSARG*** (ITS/024/01) entitled: *Towards Cost-Effective E-business in the News Media & Publishing Industry* for the use of HK Commercial Daily.

References

[1] Automatic Segmentation and Tagging for Chinese Text (《中文文本自動分詞和標注》) , K.Y. Liu, Commercial Press, 2000

[2] Segmentation Issues in Chinese Information Processing, 《語言文字應用》(C.N. Huang Issue No. 1, 1997)

[3] The design and Implementation of a Modern General Purpose Segmentation System (B. Lou, R. Song, W.L. Li, and Z.Y. Luo, Journal of Chinese Information Processing, Issue No. 5, 2001)

[4] 北大語言資源：語法資訊辭典 (Institute of Computational Linguistics, Peking Univ., 2002)

[5] 漢語自動分詞詞典機制的實驗研究 (孫茂松，左正平，黃昌寧，Journal of Chinese information processing vol. 14, no. 1, 2001)

[6] Chinese Word Segmentation and Information Retrieval, Palmer D., and Burger J., In AAAI Symposium Cross-Language Text and Speech Retrieval 1997

Introduction to CKIP Chinese Word Segmentation System for the First International Chinese Word Segmentation Bakeoff

Wei-Yun Ma
Institute of Information science,
Academia Sinica
ma@iis.sinica.edu.tw

Keh-Jiann Chen
Institute of Information science,
Academia Sinica
kchen@iis.sinica.edu.tw

Abstract

In this paper, we roughly described the procedures of our segmentation system, including the methods for resolving segmentation ambiguities and identifying unknown words. The CKIP group of Academia Sinica participated in testing on open and closed tracks of Beijing University (PK) and Hong Kong Cityu (HK). The evaluation results show our system performs very well in either HK open track or HK closed track and just acceptable in PK tracks. Some explanations and analysis are presented in this paper.

1 Introduction

At the first international Chinese Word Segmentation Bakeoff, Academia Sinica participated in testing on open and closed tracks of Beijing University (PK) and Hong Kong Cityu (HK). The same segmentation algorithm was applied to process these two corpora, except that character code conversion from GB to BIG5 for PK corpus and few modifications due to different segmentation standards had been made. The difference between open and closed tracks is that while processing the open track, besides of the lexicon trained from the specific corpus, we also consulted the Academia Sinica lexicon to enhance the word collection.

It is well known that there are two major difficulties in Chinese word segmentation. One is resolving the ambiguous segmentation, and the other is identifying unknown words.

Our earlier work mainly focused on the resolving of segmentation ambiguities and using regular expressions to handle the determinant-measure and reduplication compounds (Chen & Liu 1992, Chen 1999). We adopt a variation of the longest matching algorithm with several heuristic rules to resolve the ambiguities and achieve 99.77% of the success rate without counting the mistakes occurred due to the existence of unknown words. After that, we were paying more attention on the problems of extracting and identifying unknown words (Chen et.al 1997, Chen & Bai 1998, Chen & Ma 2002, Tseng & Chen 2002, Ma & Chen 2003). The process of unknown word extraction could be roughly divided into two steps, i.e. detection process and extraction process. The detection process detects possible occurrences of unknown words (Chen & Bai 1998), so that deeper morphological analysis is carried out only at the places where unknown word morphemes were detected (Chen & Ma 2002). A bottom-up merging algorithm was proposed in (Ma & Chen 2003), which utilizes hybrid statistical and linguistic information to extract unknown words effectively.

In addition to the bakeoff results evaluated by SIGHAN, we also present some other relevant experiment results and provide analysis on the system performance in the following sections.

2 System Overview

Figure 1 illustrates the block diagram of our segmentation system used in this contest. The first two steps of word segmentation algorithm are word matching and resolution for ambiguous matches. These two processes were performed in parallel. The algorithm reads the input sentences from left to right and matches the input character string with lexemes. In (Chen & Liu 1992), if an ambiguous segmentation docs occur, the matching algorithm looks ahead two more words, and the disambiguation rules for those three word chunks is applied afterward. For instance, in (1), the first matched word could be '完' or '完成'. Then the algorithm will look ahead to take all of the possible combinations of three word chunks, as shown in (2), into consideration.

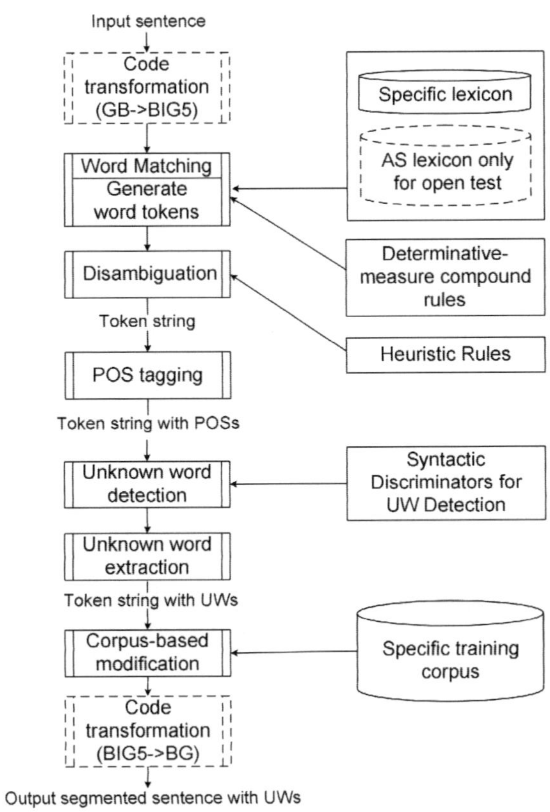

Figure 1. Flowchart of the system

(1) 完成 鑑定 報告
complete authenticate report
"complete the report about authenticating"

(2) 完 成 鑑定
完成 鑑定 報
完成 鑑定 報告

The disambiguation algorithm will select the first word of the most plausible chunks as the solution according to heuristic rules. The first heuristic rule is:

Longest Matching Rule: The most plausible segmentation is the three word sequence with the longest length.

In the above example, the longest matched three-word chunk is (1). Therefore the first segmented word is '完成'. This heuristic rules achieves as high as 99.69% accuracy and a high applicability of 93.21%, i.e. the 93.21% of the ambiguities were resolved by this rule. However there are still about 6.79% of ambiguities, i.e. the three word chunks with the same length but with different segmentations, which cannot be resolved by the maximal matching rule. The following heuristic rules were used for further resolution.

Word Length Rule: Pick the three-word chunk that has the smallest standard deviation in length of the three words.

Morphemic Rules:

(a). Pick the chunk with fewer bound morphemes.
(b). Pick the chunk with fewer characters in compound words.

Probability Rule:

(a). Pick the chunk with the high frequency monosyllabic words.
(b). Pick the chunk with the highest probability value.

After disambiguation process, an input sentence is segmented into a word sequence. Then for the needs of the following unknown word extraction, a Pos bi-gram tagging model is applied to tag Pos of words.

It is clear that unknown words in the input text will be segmented into several adjacent tokens (known words or monosyllabic morphemes). Then at unknown word detection stage, every monosyllable is decided whether it is a word or an unknown word morpheme by a set of syntactic discriminators, which are trained from a word segmented corpus.

(3) 若 能 提升 毛利率
if can increase gross profit rate
"if gross profit rate can be increased…"

(4) after first step word segmentation:
若 能 提升 毛 利 率
after unknown word detection:
若 能 提升 毛(?) 利(?) 率(?)
after unknown word extraction:
若 能 提升 毛利率

For example, the correct segmentation of (3) is shown, but the unknown word "毛利率" is segmented into three monosyllabic words after the first step of word segmentation process. In (4), The unknown word detection process will mark the sentence as "若() 能() 提升() 毛(?) 利(?) 率(?)", where (?) denotes the detected monosyllabic unknown word morpheme and () denotes common words. During extracting process, the rule matching process focuses on the morphemes marked with (?) only and tries to combine them with left/right neighbors according to the rules for unknown words. After that the unknown word "毛利率" is extracted.

We adopt a bottom-up merging algorithm (Ma & Chen 2003), which utilizes hybrid statistical and linguistic information, to extract unknown words.

3 Adaptation for Different Tracks

It is known that different segmentation standards could affect the performance of segmentation significantly. In this contest, due to limited preparing time, we mainly focused on adjusting the regular expressions for determinant-measure compounds according to the HK and PK segmentation standards.

While processing the PK track, a shortcut method of converting GB codes to BIG5 codes was adopted to cope with the problem of character coding difference. Instead of re-design or re-implement the GB segmentation system, we convert the codes of training and testing PK corpora into BIG5 versions and perform the segmentation under the BIG5 environment. The segmented results are then translated back to GB code as the final outputs. In contrast, processing of HK corpus is easier for us, because our system was designed for the BIG5 environment.

As for the lexicons, for closed test, both PK and HK lexicons are derived from the word sets of each respective training corpus. For the open test, each lexicon was enhanced by adding the lexical entries in the CKIP lexicon. The sizes of lexicons are shown in table1.

	HK	PK
# of lexical entries (HK/PK)for closed test	22K	50K
# of lexical entries (HK/PK join CKIP) for open test	140K	156 K

Note: # lexicon of (CKIP) is 133K

Table 1. The sizes of lexicons

Syntactic categories of a words were utilized in unknown word detection and extraction processes. We don't have syntactic categories for words which are not in the CKIP lexicon. Therefore, we (Chen et.al 1997, Tseng & Chen 2002) use association strength between morphemes and syntactic categories to predict the category of a new word. The accuracy rate is about 80%.

4 Evaluation Results

There are several evaluation indexes provided by SIGHAN, i.e. test recall (R), test precision (P), F score[2], the out-of-vocabulary (OOV) rate for the test corpus, the recall on OOV words (R_{oov}), and the recall on in-vocabulary (R_{iv}) words.

Tables 2 shows the evaluation results of our system in HK closed and open tracks. For both tracks, our system achieved the top ranks on F scores.

	R	P	F	OOV	R_{oov}	R_{iv}
Closed	0.947	0.934	0.940	0.071	0.625	0.972
Open	0.958	0.954	0.956	0.071	0.788	0.971

Note: The word count of testing corpus is 34955

Table 2. Scores for HK

The evaluations of our system in PK closed and open tracks are shown in table 3. For PK closed track, our system ranks 6th among 10 systems. And for PK open track, our system ranks 3rd among 8 systems.

	R	P	F	OOV	R_{oov}	R_{iv}
Closed	0.939	0.934	0.936	0.069	0.642	0.961
Open	0.939	0.938	0.938	0.069	0.675	0.959

Note: The word count of testing corpus is 34955

Table 3. Scores for PK

Because Academia Sinica corpora (AS) are provided by us, we are not allowed to participate any AS track at this contest. Therefore, in this report, we still show the performance of our system evaluating AS closed track in table 4. Our system would have the top rank if the result was compared with the other 6 participants of AS closed track.

R	P	F	OOV	R_{oov}	R_{iv}
0.968	0.966	0.967	0.022	0.657	0.975

Note: The word count of testing corpus is 11985

Table 4. Scores for AS closed

5 Discussions and Conclusions

The evaluation results show that our system performs very well in either HK closed track or HK open track. We think the key to the success is our unknown word extraction performs better than other participants. This could be observed by the results of HK closed track, the 2th and 3th system, which have better performance in R_{iv} but worse R_{oov} than our system, performs worse than our system in f score. Furthermore to have better performance, high precision for unknown word extraction is necessary, since one identification error may cause at least two segmentation errors.

The performance in PK tracks are not as well as HK. An important reason is that coding conversion may cause errors. For instance, in the conversion of the GB code of "里約" (the capital of Brazil) to its BIG5 codes, Since GB code to BIG5 conversion is a one-to-many mapping, the above example is wrongly converted to "裡約". This kind of errors do affect accuracy of the segmentation significantly, especially for the unkown word processes. To solve this problem, we think the best and direct solution is to re-implement the GB segmentation version without any code conversion.

Variation on the word segmentation standards is another reason of causing segmentation errors. Some of the standards were even not available to the public. It is better to propose a uniform word segmentation standard in the future.

Regarding evaluation index, we suggest that an error type of crossing error should be take into consideration, since noncrossing errors are more or less related to segmentation standards and crossing errors are more severe.

6 References

[1] Chen, K.J. & S.H. Liu, 1992,"Word Identification for Mandarin Chinese Sentences," *Proceedings of 14th Coling*, pp. 101-107

[2] Chen, C. J., M.H. Bai, & K.J. Chen, 1997," Category Guessing for Chinese Unknown Words," Proceedings of the Natural Language Processing Pacific Rim Symposium, 35-40, Thailand.

[3] Chen, K.J. & Ming-Hong Bai, 1998, "Unknown Word Detection for Chinese by a Corpus-based Learning Method," international Journal of Computational linguistics and Chinese Language Processing, Vol.3, #1, pp.27-44

[4] Chen, Keh-jiann,1999,"Lexical Analysis for Chinese- Difficulties and Possible Solutions", Journal of Chinese Institute of Engineers, Vol. 22. #5, pp. 561-571.

[5] Chen, K.J. & Wei-Yun Ma, 2002. Unknown Word Extraction for Chinese Documents. In Proceedings of COLING 2002, pages 169-175

[6] Tseng, H.H. & K.J. Chen, 2002. Design of Chinese Morphological Analyzer. In Proceedings of SIGHAN, pages 49-55

[7] Ma Wei-Yun & K.J. Chen, 2003. A bottom-up Merging Algorithm for Chinese Unknown Word Extraction. In Proceedings of SIGHAN

Chinese Word Segmentation in MSR-NLP

Andi Wu
Microsoft Research
One Microsoft Way, Redmond, WA 98052
andiwu@microsoft.com

Abstract

Word segmentation in MSR-NLP is an integral part of a sentence analyzer which includes basic segmentation, derivational morphology, named entity recognition, new word identification, word lattice pruning and parsing. The final segmentation is produced from the leaves of parse trees. The output can be customized to meet different segmentation standards through the value combinations of a set of parameters. The system participated in four tracks of the segmentation bakeoff -- PK-open, PK-close, CTB-open and CTB-closed – and ranked #1, #2, #2 and #3 respectively in those tracks. Analysis of the results shows that each component of the system contributed to the scores.

1 System Description

The MSR-NLP Chinese system that participated in the current segmentation bakeoff is not a stand-alone word segmenter. It is a Chinese sentence analyzer where the leaves of parse trees are displayed as the output of word segmentation. The components of this system are described below.

1.1 Basic segmentation

Each input sentence is first segmented into individual characters.[1] These characters and their combinations are then looked up in a dictionary[2] and a word lattice containing lexicalized words only is formed. Each node in the lattice is a feature matrix that contains the part of speech and other grammatical attributes. Multiple-character words may also have information for resolving segmentation ambiguities. In general, multiple-character words are assigned higher scores than the words they subsume, but words like "才能" are exceptions and such exceptional cases are usually marked in the dictionary. For some of the words that tend to overlap with other words, there is also information as to what the preferred segmentation is. For instance, the preferred segmentation for "会议员" is "会+议员" rather than "会议+员". Such information was collected from segmented corpora and stored in the dictionary. The scores are later used in word lattice pruning and parse ranking (Wu and Jiang 1998).

1.2 Derivational morphology and named entity recognition

After basic segmentation, a set of augmented phrase structure rules are applied to the word lattice to form larger word units which include:

- Words derived from morphological processes such as reduplication, affixation, compounding, merging, splitting, etc.
- Named entities such as person names, place names, company names, product names, numbers, dates, monetary units, etc.

Each of these units is a tree that reflects the history of rule application. They are added to the existing word lattice as single nodes and treated as single words by the parser. The internal structures are useful for various purposes, one of which is the customization of word segmentation: words with such structures can all be displayed as single words or multiple words depending on where the "cuts" are made in the word tree (Wu 2003).

1.3 New word identification

The expanded word lattice built in 1.2 is inspected to detect spots of possible OOV new words. Typical spots of this kind are sequences of single char-

[1] If an input line contains more than one sentence, a sentence separator is applied to break the line into individual sentences, which are then processed one by one and the results are concatenated to form a single output.

[2] The lookup is optimized so that not all possible combinations are tried.

acters that are not subsumed by longer words. We then use the following information to propose new words (Wu and Jiang, 2000).

- The probability of the character string being a sequence of independent words;
- The morphological and syntactic properties of the characters;
- Word formation rules;
- Behavior of each character in existing words (e.g. how likely is this character to be used as the second character of a two-character verb).
- The context in which the characters appear.

The proposed new words are added to the word lattice and they will get used if no successful parse can be obtained without them. When a new word proposed this way has been verified by the parser (i.e. used in a successful parse) more than *n* times, it will automatically become an entry in the dictionary. From then on, this word can be looked up directly from the dictionary instead of being proposed online. This kind of dynamic lexical acquisition has been presented in Wu *et al* (2002).

1.4 Word lattice pruning

Now that all the possible words are in the word lattice, both statistical and linguistic methods are applied to eliminate certain paths. For instance, those paths that contain one or more bound morphemes are pruned away. Single characters that are subsumed by longer words are also thrown out if their independent word probabilities are very low. The result is a much smaller lattice that resembles the n-best paths produced by a statistical word segmenter. Because the final resolution of ambiguities is expected to be done during parsing, the lattice pruning is non-greedy so that no plausible path will be excluded prematurely. Many of the ambiguities that are eliminated here can also be resolved by the parser, but the pruning greatly reduces the complexity of the parsing process, making the parser much faster and more accurate.

1.5 Parsing

The cleaned-up word lattice is then submitted to the parser as the initial entries in the parsing chart. With the assumption that a successful parse of the sentence requires a correct segmentation of the sentence, many segmentation ambiguities are expected to be resolved here. This assumption does not always hold, of course. A sentence can often be parsed in multiple ways and the top-ranking parse is not always the correct one. There are also sentences that are not covered by the grammar and therefore cannot be parsed at all. In this latter case, we back off to partial parsing and use dynamic programming to assemble a tree that consists of the largest sub-trees in the chart.

In most cases, the use of the parser results in better segmentation, but the parser can also mislead us. One of the problems is that the parser treats every input as a sentence and tries to construct an *S* out of it. As a result, even a name like "王爱民" can be analyzed as a sentence with 王 as the subject, 爱 as the verb and 民 as the object, if it appears in the wrong context (or no context).

1.6 Segmentation parameters

Due to the differences in segmentation standards, the leaves of a parse tree do not always correspond to the words in a particular standard. For instance, a Chinese full name is a single leaf in our trees, but it is supposed to be two words (family name + given name) according to the PK standard. Fortunately, most of the words whose segmentation is controversial are built dynamically in our system with their internal structures preserved. A Chinese full name, for example, is a word tree where the top node dominates two nodes: the family name and the given name. Each non-terminal node in a word tree as described in 1.2 is associated with a parameter whose value determines whether the daughters of this node are to be displayed as a singe word or multiple words. Since all the dynamic words are built by phrase structure rules and their word trees reflect the derivational history of rule application, there is a one-to-one correspondence between the types of words and the word-internal structures of those words. A segmentation parameter is associated with each type of words[3] and the value of this parameter determines how the given type of words should be segmented. This makes it possible for the system to quickly adapt to different standards (Wu 2003).

[3] There are about 50 parameters in our system.

1.7 Speed

Our system is not optimized for word segmentation in terms of speed. As we have seen, the system is a sentence analyzer and word segmentation is just the by-product of a parser. Thc speed we report here is in fact the speed of parsing.

On a single 997 MHz Pentium III machine, the system is able to process 28,740 characters per minute. The speed may vary according to sentence lengths: given texts of the same size, those containing longer sentences will take more time. The number reported here is an average of the time taken to process the test sets of the four tracks we participated in.

We have the option of turning off the parser during word segmentation. When the parser is turned off, segmentation is produced directly from the word lattice with dynamic programming which selects the shortest path. The speed in this case is about 60,000 characters per minute.

2 Evaluation

We participated in the four GB tracks in the first international Chinese word segmentation bakeoff - PK-open, PK-closed, CTB-open and CTB-closed – and ranked #1, #2, #2, and #3 respectively in those tracks. In what follows, we discuss how we got the results: what dictionaries we used, how we used the training data, how much each component contributed to the scores, and the problems that affected our performance.

2.1 Dictionaries

In the open tracks, we used our proprietary dictionary of 89,845 entries, which includes the entries of 7,017 single characters. In the closed tracks, we removed from the dictionary all the words that did not appear in the training data, but kept all the single characters. This resulted in a dictionary of 34,681 entries in the PK track and 18,207 entries in the CTB track. It should be noted that not all the words in the training data are in our dictionary. This explains why the total numbers of entries in those reduced dictionaries are smaller than the vocabulary sizes of the respective training sets even with all the single-character entries included in them.

The dictionary we use in each case is not a simple word list. Every word has one or more parts-of-speech and a number of other grammatical features. No word can be used by the parser unless it has those features. This made it very difficult for us to add all the words in the training data to the dictionary. We did use a semi-automatic process to add as many words as possible, but both the accuracy and coverage of the added grammatical features are questionable due to the lack of manual verification.

2.2 Use of the training data

We used the training data mainly to tune the segmentation parameters of our system. As has been mentioned in 1.6, there are about 50 types of morphologically derived words that are built online in our system and each type has a parameter to determine whether a given unit should be displayed as a single word or separate words. Since our default segmentation is very different from PK or CTB, and PK and CTB also follow different guidelines, we had to try different value combinations of the parameters in each case until we got the optimal settings.

The main problem in the tuning is that many morphologically derived words have been lexicalized in our dictionary and therefore do not have the word-internal structures that they would have if they had been constructed dynamically. As a result, their segmentation is beyond the control of those parameters. To solve this problem, we used the training data to automatically identify all such cases, create a word-internal structure for each of them, and store the word tree in their lexical entries.[4] This made it possible for the parameter values to apply to both the lexicalized and non-lexicalized words. This process can be fairly automatic if the annotation of the training data is completely consistent. However, as we have discovered, the training data is not as consistent as expected, which made total automation impossible.

2.3 Contribution of each component

After we received our individual scores and the reference testing data, we did some ablation ex-

[4] The work is incomplete, since the trees were created only for those words that are in the training data provided.

periments to find out the contribution of each system component in this competition. We turned off the components one at a time (except basic segmentation) and recorded the scores of each ablated system. The results are summarized in the following table, where "DM-NER" stands for "derivational morphology and named entity recognition", "NW-ID" for "new word identification and lexicalization", "pruning" for "lattice pruning" and "tuning" for "tuning of parameter values". Each cell in the table has two percentages. The top one is the F-measure and the bottom one is the OOV word recall rate.

	PK Open	PK closed	CTB open	CTB closed
Complete System	**95.9 %** **79.9 %**	**94.7 %** **68.0 %**	**90.1 %** **73.8 %**	**83.1 %** **43.1 %**
Without DM-NER	90.2 % 44.4 %	88.9 % 33.9 %	86.6 % 66.6 %	79.2 % 33.5 %
Without NW-ID	95.8 % 77.3 %	94.0 % 61.2 %	88.7 % 69.0 %	79.2 % 28.2 %
Without Pruning	92.0 % 77.5 %	90.9 % 65.9 %	85.5 % 69.0 %	78.8 % 39.5 %
Without Parsing	95.5 % 79.9 %	94.4 % 68.5 %	89.8 % 75.0 %	84.0 % 48.1 %
Without Tuning	84.8 % 43.4 %	83.9 % 33.3 %	84.8 % 72.3 %	78.4 % 43.3 %

Several interesting facts are revealed in this break-down:

- The tuning of parameter values has the biggest impact on the scores across the board.
- Derivational morphology and NE recognition is also a main contributor, especially in the PK sets, which presumably contains more named entities.
- The impact of new word identification is minimal when the OOV word rate is low, such as in the PK-open case, but becomes more and more significant as the OOV rate increases.
- Lattice pruning makes a big difference as well. Apparently it cannot be replaced by the parser in terms of the disambiguating function it performs. Another fact, which is not represented in the table, is that parsing is three times slower when lattice pruning is turned off.
- The parser has very limited impact on the scores. Looking at the data, we find that parsing did help to resolve some of the most difficult cases of ambiguities and we would not be able to get the last few points without it. But it seems that most of the common problems can be solved without the parser. In one case (CTB closed), the score is higher when the parser is turned off. This is because the parser may prefer a structure where those dynamically recognized OOV words are broken up into smaller units. For practical purposes, therefore, we may choose to leave out the parser.

2.4 Problems that affected our performance

The main problem is the definition of new words. While our system is fairly aggressive in recognizing new words, both PK and CTB are quite conservative in this respect. Expressions such as "援藏", "反腐", "耳鼻喉", "屡禁不绝" are considered single words in our system but not so in PK or CTB. This made our new word recognition do more harm than good in many cases, though the overall impact is positive. Consistency in the annotated corpora is another problem, but this affects every participant. We also had a technical problem where some sentences remained unsegmented simply because some characters are not in our dictionary.

References

Wu, Andi. 2003. Customizable segmentation of morphologically derived Words in Chinese, to appear in *Computational Linguistics and Chinese Language Processing.*, 8(2).

Wu, Andi, J. Pentheroudakis and Z. Jiang, 2002. Dynamic lexical acquisition in Chinese sentence analysis. In *Proceedings of the 19th International Conference on Computational Linguistics*, pp. 1308-1312, Taipei, Taiwan.

Wu, Andi, J. and Z. Jiang, 2000. Statistically-enhanced new word identification in a rule-based Chinese system, in *Proceedings of the 2nd Chinese Language Processing Workshop*, pp. 46-51, HKUST, Hong Kong.

Wu, Andi, J. and Z. Jiang, 1998. Word segmentation in sentence analysis, in *Proceedings of 1998 International Conference on Chinese Information Processing*, pp. 46-51.169-180, Beijing, China.

Chinese Word Segmentation as LMR Tagging

Nianwen Xue
Inst. for Research in Cognitive Science
University of Pennsylvania
Philadelphia, PA 19104, USA
xueniwen@linc.cis.upenn.edu

Libin Shen
Dept. of Computer and Info. Science
University of Pennsylvania
Philadelphia, PA 19104, USA
libin@linc.cis.upenn.edu

Abstract

In this paper we present Chinese word segmentation algorithms based on the so-called LMR tagging. Our LMR taggers are implemented with the Maximum Entropy Markov Model and we then use Transformation-Based Learning to combine the results of the two LMR taggers that scan the input in opposite directions. Our system achieves F-scores of 95.9% and 91.6% on the Academia Sinica corpus and the Hong Kong City University corpus respectively.

1 Segmentation as Tagging

Unlike English text in which sentences are sequences of words delimited by white spaces, in Chinese text, sentences are represented as strings of Chinese characters or *hanzi* without similar natural delimiters. Therefore, the first step in a Chinese language processing task is to identify the sequence of words in a sentence and mark boundaries in appropriate places. This may sound simple enough but in reality identifying words in Chinese is a non-trivial problem that has drawn a large body of research in the Chinese language processing community (Fan and Tsai, 1988; Gan et al., 1996; Sproat et al., 1996; Wu, 2003; Xue, 2003).

The key to accurate automatic word identification in Chinese lies in the successful resolution of ambiguities and a proper way to handle out-of-vocabulary words. The ambiguities in Chinese word segmentation is due to the fact that a *hanzi* can occur in different word-internal positions (Xue, 2003). Given the proper context, generally provided by the sentence in which it occurs, the position of a *hanzi* can be determined. In this paper, we model the Chinese word segmentation as a *hanzi* tagging problem and use a machine-learning algorithm to determine the appropriate position for a *hanzi*. There are several reasons why we may expect this approach to work. First, Chinese words generally have fewer than four characters. As a result, the number of positions is small. Second, although each *hanzi* can in principle occur in all possible positions, not all *hanzi* behave this way. A substantial number of *hanzi* are distributed in a constrained manner. For example, 们, the plural marker, almost always occurs in the word-final position. Finally, although Chinese words cannot be exhaustively listed and new words are bound to occur in naturally occurring text, the same is not true for *hanzi*. The number of *hanzi* stays fairly constant and we do not generally expect to see new *hanzi*.

We represent the positions of a *hanzi* with four different tags (Table 1): LM for a *hanzi* that occurs on the left periphery of a word, followed by other *hanzi*, MM for a *hanzi* that occurs in the middle of a word, MR for a *hanzi* that occurs on the right periphery of word, preceded by other *hanzi*, and LR for *hanzi* that is a word by itself. We call this LMR tagging. With this approach, word segmentation is a process where each *hanzi* is assigned an LMR tag and sequences of *hanzi* are then converted into sequences of words based on the LMR tags. The use of four tags is linguistically intuitive in that LM tags morphemes that are prefixes or stems in the absence of prefixes, MR tags morphemes that are suffixes or stems in the absence of suffixes, MM tags stems with affixes and LR tags stems without affixes. Representing the distributions of *hanzi* with LMR tags also makes it easy to use machine learning algorithms which has been successfully applied to other tagging problems, such as POS-tagging and IOB tagging used in text chunking.

	Right Boundary (R)	Not Right Boundary (M)
Left Boundary (L)	LR	LM
Not Left Boundary (M)	MR	MM

Table 1: LMR Tagging

2 Tagging Algorithms

Our algorithm consists of two parts. We first implement two Maximum Entropy taggers, one of which scans the input from left to right and the other scans the input from right to left. Then we implement a Transformation Based Algorithm to combine the results of the two taggers.

2.1 The Maximum Entropy Tagger

The Maximum Entropy Markov Model (MEMM) has been successfully used in some tagging problems. MEMM models are capable of utilizing a large set of features that generative models cannot use. On the other hand, MEMM approaches scan the input incrementally as generative models do.

The Maximum Entropy Markov Model used in POS-tagging is described in detail in (Ratnaparkhi, 1996) and the LMR tagger here uses the same probability model. The probability model is defined over $H \times T$, where H is the set of possible contexts or "histories" and T is the set of possible tags. The model's joint probability of a history h and a tag t is defined as

$$p(h,t) = \pi\mu \prod_{j=1}^{k} \alpha_j^{f_j^{(h,t)}} \tag{1}$$

where π is a normalization constant, $\{\mu, \alpha_1, ..., \alpha_k\}$ are the model parameters and $\{f_1, ..., f_k\}$ are known as features, where $f_j(h,t) \in \{0,1\}$. Each feature f_j has a corresponding parameter α_j, that effectively serves as a "weight" of this feature. In the training process, given a sequence of characters $\{c_1, \cdots, c_n\}$ and their LMR tags $\{t_1, ..., t_n\}$ as training data, the purpose is to determine the parameters $\{\mu, \alpha_1, ..., \alpha_k\}$ that maximize the likelihood of the training data using p:

$$L(P) = \prod_{i=1}^{n} P(h_i, t_i) = \prod_{i=1}^{n} \pi\mu \prod_{j=1}^{k} \alpha_j^{f_j^{(h_i,t_i)}} \tag{2}$$

The success of the model in tagging depends to a large extent on the selection of suitable features. Given (h,t), a feature must encode information that helps to predict t. The features we used in our experiments are instantiations of the feature templates in (1). Feature templates (b) to (e) represent character features while (f) represents tag features. In the following list, $C_{-3}...C_3$ are characters and $T_{-3}...T_3$ are LMR tags.

(1) Feature templates
(a) Default feature
(b) The current character (C_0)
(c) The previous (next) two characters (C_{-2}, C_{-1}, C_1, C_2)
(d) The previous (next) character and the current character ($C_{-1}C_0$, C_0C_1), the previous two characters ($C_{-2}C_{-1}$), and the next two characters (C_1C_2)
(e) The previous and the next character ($C_{-1}C_1$)
(f) The tag of the previous character (T_{-1}), and the tag of the character two before the current character (T_{-2})

2.2 Transformation-Based Learning

One potential problem with the MEMM is that it can only scan the input in one direction, from left to right or from right to left. It is noted in (Lafferty et al., 2001) that non-generative finite-state models, MEMM models included, share a weakness which they call the Label Bias Problem (LBP): a transition leaving a given state compete only against all other transitions in the model. They proposed Conditional Random Fields (CRFs) as a solution to address this problem.

A partial solution to the LBP is to compute the probability of transitions in both directions. This way we can use two MEMM taggers, one of which scans the input from left to right and the other scans the input from right to left. This strategy has been successfully used in (Shen and Joshi, 2003). In that paper, pairwise voting (van Halteren et al., 1998) has been used to combine the results of two supertaggers that scan the input in the opposite directions.

The pairwise voting is not suitable in this application because we must make sure that the LMR tags assigned to consecutive words are compatible. For example, an LM tag cannot immediately follow an MM. Pairwise voting does not use any contextual information, so it cannot prevent incompatible tags from occurring. Therefore, in our experiments described here, we use the Transformation-Based Learning (Brill, 1995) to combine the results of two MEMM taggers. The feature set used in the TBL algorithm is similar to those used in the NP Chunking task in (Ngai and Florian, 2001).

3 Experiments

We conducted closed track experiments on three data sources: the Academia Sinica (AS) corpus, the Beijing University (PKU) corpus and the Hong Kong City University (CityU) corpus. We first split the training data from each of the three sources into two portions. $9/10$ of the official training data is used to train the MEMM taggers, and the other $1/10$ is held out as the development test data (the *development set*). The *development set* is used to estimate the optimal number of iterations in the MEMM training. Figure (1), (2) and (3) show the curves of F-scores on the *development set* with respect to the number of iterations in MEMM training.

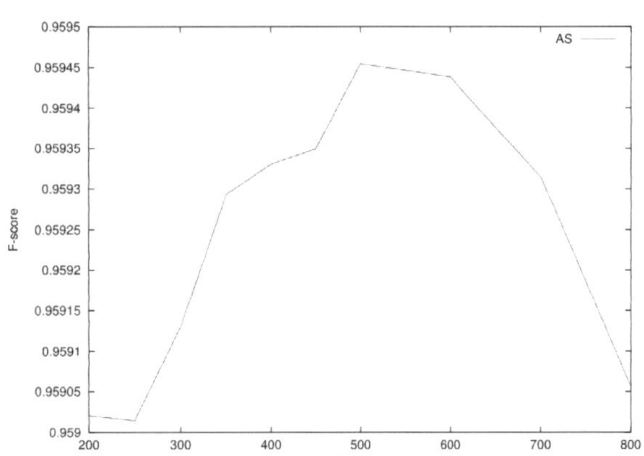

Figure 1: Learning curves on the development dataset of the Academia Sinica corpus. X-axis stands for the number of iteration in training. Y-axis stands for the F-score.

Experiments show that the MEMM models achieve the best results after 500 and 400 rounds (iterations) of training on the AS data and the PKU data respectively. However, the results on the CityU data is not very clear. From Round 100 through 200, the F-score on the *development set* almost stays unchanged. We think this is because the CityU data is from three different sources, which differ in the optimal number of iterations. We decided to train the MEMM taggers for 160 iterations the HK City University data.

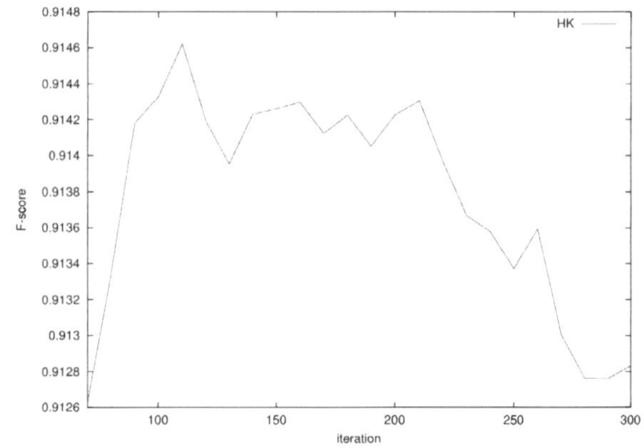

Figure 2: Learning curves on the development dataset of the HK City Univ. corpus.

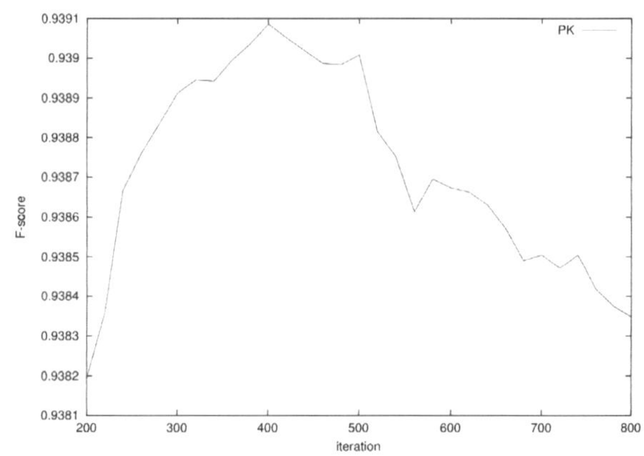

Figure 3: Learning curves on the development dataset of the Beijing Univ. corpus.

We implemented two MEMM taggers, one scans the input from left to right and one from right to left. We then used these two MEMM taggers to tag both the training and the development data. We use the LMR tagging output to train a Transformation-Based learner, using *fast TBL* (Ngai and Florian, 2001). The middle in Table 2 shows the F-score on the *development set* achieved by the MEMM tagger that scans the input from left to right and the last column is the results after the Transformation-Based Learner is applied. The results show that using Transformation-Based learning only give rise to slight improvements. It seems that the bidirectional approach does not help much for the LMR tagging. Therefore, we only submitted the results of our left-to-right MEMM tagger, retrained on the entire training sets, as our official results.

F-score	MEMM	MEMM+TBL
AS	0.9595	0.9603
HK	0.9143	N/A
PK	0.9391	0.9398

Table 2: F-score on development data

The results on the official test data is similar to what we have got on our *development set*, except that the F-score on the Beijing Univ. corpus is over 2% lower in absolute accuracy than what we expected. The reason is that in the training data of Beijing University corpus, all the numbers are encoded in GBK, while in the test data many numbers are encoded in ASCII, which are unknown to our tagger. With this problem fixed, the results of the official test data are compatible with the results on our *development set*. However, we have withdrawn our segmentation results on the Beijing University corpus.

corpus	R	P	F	R_{OOV}	R_{IV}
AS	0.961	0.958	0.959	0.729	0.966
HK	0.917	0.915	0.916	0.670	0.936

Table 3: Official Bakeoff Outcome

4 Conclusions and Future Work

Our closed track experiments on the first Sighan Bakeoff data show that the LMR algorithm produces promising results. Our system ranks the second when tested on the Academia Sinica corpus and third on the Hong Kong City University corpus. In the future, we will try to incorporate a large word list into our tagger to test its performance on open track experiments. Its high accuracy on R_{OOV} makes it a good candidate as a general purpose segmenter.

References

E. Brill. 1995. Transformation-based error-driven learning and natural language processing: A case study in part-of-speech tagging. *Computational Linguistics*, 21(4):543–565.

C. K. Fan and W. H. Tsai. 1988. Automatic word identification in chinese sentences by the relaxation technique. *Computer Processing of Chinese and Oriental Languages*, 4(1):33–56.

Kok-Wee Gan, Martha Palmer, and Kim-Teng Lua. 1996. A statistically emergent approach for language processing: Application to modeling context effects in ambiguous chinese word boundary perception. *Computational Linguistics*, 22(4):531–53.

J. Lafferty, A. McCallum, and F. Pereira. 2001. Conditional random fields: Probabilistic models for stgmentation and labeling sequence data. In *Proceedings of ICML 2001*.

G. Ngai and R. Florian. 2001. Transformation-based learning in the fast lane. In *Proceedings of NAACL-2001*, pages 40–47.

Adwait Ratnaparkhi. 1996. A maximum entropy part-of-speech tagger. In *Proceedings of the Empirical Methods in Natural Language Processing Conference*, University of Pennsylvania.

L. Shen and A. K. Joshi. 2003. A SNoW based supertagger with application to NP chunking. In *Proceedings of ACL 2003*.

R. Sproat, Chilin Shih, William Gale, and Nancy Chang. 1996. A stochastic finite-state word-segmentation algorithm for chinese. *Computational Linguistics*, 22(3):377–404.

H. van Halteren, J. Zavrel, and W. Daelmans. 1998. Improving data driven wordclass tagging by system combination. In *Proceedings of COLING-ACL 98*.

Andi Wu. 2003. Customizable segmentation of morphologically derived words in chinese. *Computational Linguistics and Chinese Language Processing*.

Nianwen Xue. 2003. Chinese word segmentation as character tagging. *Computational Linguistics and Chinese Language Processing*.

SYSTRAN's Chinese Word Segmentation

Jin Yang
SYSTRAN Software, Inc.
9333 Genesee Ave.
San Diego, CA 92121, USA
jyang@systransoft.com

Jean Senellart
SYSTRAN S.A.
1, rue du Cimetière
95230 Soisy-sous-Montmorency, France
senellart@systran.fr

Remi Zajac
SYSTRAN Software, Inc.
9333 Genesee Ave.
San Diego, CA 92121, USA
zajac@systransoft.com

Abstract

SYSTRAN's Chinese word segmentation is one important component of its Chinese-English machine translation system. The Chinese word segmentation module uses a rule-based approach, based on a large dictionary and fine-grained linguistic rules. It works on general-purpose texts from different Chinese-speaking regions, with comparable performance. SYSTRAN participated in the four open tracks in the First International Chinese Word Segmentation Bakeoff. This paper gives a general description of the segmentation module, as well as the results and analysis of its performance in the Bakeoff.

1 Introduction

Chinese word segmentation is one of the pre-processing steps of the SYSTRAN Chinese-English Machine Translation (MT) system. The development of the Chinese-English MT system began in August 1994, and this is where the Chinese word segmentation issue was first addressed. The algorithm of the early version of the segmentation module was borrowed from SYSTRAN's Japanese segmentation module. The program ran on a large word list, which contained 600,000 entries at the time[1]. The basic strategy was to list all possible matches for an entire linguistic unit, then solve the overlapping matches via linguistic rules. The development was focused on technical domains, and high accuracy was achieved after only three months of development. Since then, development has shifted to other areas of Chinese-English MT, including the enrichment of the bi-lingual word lists with part-of-speech, syntactic and semantic features. In 2001, the development of a prototype Chinese-Japanese MT system began. Although the project only lasted for three months, some important changes were made in the segmentation convention, regarding the distinction between words and phrases[2]. Along with new developments of the SYSTRAN MT engine, the segmentation engine has recently been re-implemented. The dictionary and the general approach remain unchanged, but dictionary lookup and rule matching were re-implemented using finite-state technology, and linguistic rules for the segmentation module are now expressed using a context-free-based formalism, improving maintainability. The re-implementation generates multiple segmentation results with associated probabilities. This will allow for disambiguation at a later stage of the MT process, and will widen the possibility of word segmentation for other applications.

2 System Description

2.1 Segmentation Standard

Our definition of words and our segmentation conventions are based on available standards, modified for MT purposes. The PRC standard (Liu et al., 1993) was initially used. Sample differences are listed as follows:

Type	PRC	SYSTRAN
NP	中华民族 中华人民共和国	中华 民族 中华 人民 共和国
CD	31 日	31 日
CD + M	一个 一排排	一 个 一 排 排
DI4 + CD	第一	第 一
Name	李 白 李 清照	李白 李清照

Table 1. Segmentation Divergences with the PRC Guidelines

2.2 Methodology

The SYSTRAN Chinese word segmentation module uses a rule-based approach and a large dictionary. The dictionary is derived from the

Chinese-English MT dictionary. It currently includes about 400,000 words. The basic segmentation strategy is to list all possible matches for a translation unit (typically, a sentence), then to solve overlapping matches via linguistic rules. The same segmentation module and the same dictionary are used to segment different types of text with comparable performance.

All dictionary lookup and rule matching are performed using a low level Finite State Automaton library. The segmentation speed is 3,500 characters per second using a Pentium 4 2.4GHZ processor.

Dictionary

The Chinese-English MT dictionary currently contains 400,000 words (e.g., 中华), and 200,000 multi-word expressions (e.g., 中华 人民 共和国). Only words are used for the segmentation. Specialized linguistic rules are associated with the dictionary. The dictionary is general purpose, with good coverage on several domains. Domain-specific dictionaries are also available, but were not used in the Bakeoff.

The dictionary contains words from different Chinese-speaking regions, but the representation is mostly in simplified Chinese. The traditional characters are considered as "variants", and they are not physically stored in the dictionary. For example, 意大利 and 义大利 are stored in the dictionary, and 義大利 can also be found via the character matching 義→ 义.

The dictionary is encoded in Unicode (UTF8), and all internal operations manipulate UTF8 strings. Major encoding conversions are supported, including GB2312-80, GB13000, BIG-5, BIG5-HKSCS, etc.

Training

The segmentation module has been tested and fine-tuned on general texts, and on texts in the technical and military domains (because of specific customer requirements for the MT system). Due to the wide availability of news texts, the news domain has also recently been used for training and testing.

The training process is merely reduced to the customization of a SYSTRAN MT system. In the current version of the MT system, customization is achieved by building a User Dictionary (UD). A UD supplements the main dictionary: any word that is not found in the main MT system dictionary is added in a User Dictionary.

Name-Entity Recognition and Unknown Words

Name entity recognition is still under development. Recognition of Chinese persons' names is done via linguistic rules. Foreign name recognition is not yet implemented due to the difficulty of obtaining translations.

Due to the unavailability of translations, even when an unknown word has been successfully recognized, we consider the unknown word recognition as part of the terminology extraction process. This feature was not integrated for the Bakeoff.

2.3 Evaluation

Our internal evaluation has been focused on the accuracy of segmentation using our own segmentation standard. Our evaluation process includes large-scale bilingual regression testing for the Chinese-English system, as well as regression testing of the segmenter itself using a test database of over 5MB of test items. Two criteria are used:

1. Overlapping Ambiguity Strings (OAS): the reference segmentation and the segmenter segmentation overlap for some string, e.g., AB-C and A-BC. As shown below, this typically indicates an error from our segmenter.

2. Covering Ambiguity Strings (CAS): the test strings that cover the reference strings (CAS-T: ABC and AB-C), and the reference strings that cover the test strings (CAS-R: AB-C and ABC). These cases arise mostly from a difference between equally valid segmentation standards.

No evaluation with other standards had been done before the Bakeoff.

Test	Reference	Type
崇文区　政府	崇文　区政府	OAS
冰清玉洁	冰 清 玉 洁	CAS-T
除夕之夜	除夕 之 夜	CAS-T
擦泪	擦 泪	CAS-T
精神 文明	精神文明	CAS-R
1994　年	1994 年	CAS-R
不 怕	不怕	CAS-R

Table 2. Types of Segmentation Differences

3 Discussion of the Bakeoff

3.1 Results

SYSTRAN participated in the four open tracks in the First International Chinese Word Segmentation Bakeoff http://www.sighan.org/bakeoff2003/. Each track corresponds to one corpus with its own word segementation standard. Each corpus had its own segmentation standard that was significantly different from the others. The training process included building a User Dictionary that contains words found in the training corpora, but not in the SYSTRAN dictionary. Although each of these corpora was segmented according to its own standard, we made a single UD containing all the words gathered in all corpora.

Although the ranking of the SYSTRAN segmenter is different in the four open tracks, SYSTRAN's segmentation performance is quite comparable across the four corpora. This is to be compared to the scores obtained by other participants, where good performance was typically obtained on one corpus only. SYSTRAN scores for the 4 tracks are shown in Table 3 (Sproat and Emerson, 2003).

Track	R	P	F	R_{oov}	R_{iv}
AS_o	0.915	0.894	0.904	0.426	0.926
CTB_o	0.891	0.877	0.884	0.733	0.925
HK_o	0.898	0.860	0.879	0.616	0.920
PK_o	0.905	0.869	0.886	0.503	0.934

Table 3. SYSTRAN's Scores in the Bakeoff

3.2 Discussions

The segmentation differences between the reference corpora and SYSTRAN's results are further analyzed. Table 4 shows the partition of divergences between OAS, CAS-T, and CAS-R strings:[3]

	Total	Same	OAS	CAS-T	CAS-R
AS_o	11,985	10,970	76	448	491
CTB_o	39,922	35,561	231	2,419	1,711
HK_o	34,959	31,397	217	1,436	1,909
PK_o	17,194	15,554	82	615	943

Table 4. Count of OAS and CAS Divergence

The majority of OAS divergences show incorrect segmentation from SYSTRAN. However, differences in CAS do not necessarily indicate incorrect segmentation results. The reasons can be categorized as follows: a) different segmentation standards, b) unknown word problem, c) name entity recognition problem, and d) miscellaneous[4]. The distributions of the differences are further analyzed in Table 5 and 6 for the AS_o and PK_o corpora, respectively.

CAS-R: Unique Strings=334 (total=491)			
Type	Count	Percent	Examples
Different Standards	184	55%	感觉到 不能 第十三区 廿十五日
Unknown Words	116	35%	秋颱 中菜 哭骂 院庆
Name Entity	30	9%	川崎 津巴貝 台塑
Misc.	4	1%	一百余萬
CAS-T: Unique Strings=137 (total=448)			
Type	Count	Percent	Examples
Different Standard	134	98%	喝酒 出了名 喝不喝酒
True Covering	3	2%	都會 有為

Table 5. Distribution of Divergences in the AS_o Track

CAS-R: Unique Strings=508 (total=943)			
Type	Count	Percent	Examples
Different Standards	294	58%	中共中央 这次 本届 不要 第一 2001 年
Unknown Words	90	18%	攀岩 雪浴 拥堵
Name Entity	61	12%	奥佩蒂 福彩村
Misc.	63	12%	20% 3.9 亿
CAS-T: Unique Strings=197 (total=615)			
Type	Count	Percent	Examples
Different Standards	194	98%	中国人 大吼 不夜天 赤着膊
True Covering	3	2%	高过 雪洗

Table 6. Distribution of Divergences in the PK_o Track

This analysis shows that the segmentation results are greatly impacted by the difference in the segmentation standards. Other problems include for example the encoding of numbers using single bytes instead of the standard double-byte encoding in the PKo corpus, which account for about 12% of differences in the PKo track scores.

4 Conclusion

For an open track segmentation competition like the Bakeoff, we need to achieve a balance between the following aspects:

- Segmentation standards: differences between one's own standard and the reference standard.
- Adaptation to the other standards: whether one should adapt to other standards.
- Dictionary coverage: the coverage of one's own dictionary and the dictionary obtained by training.
- Algorithm: combination of segmentation, unknown word identification, and name entity recognition.
- Speed: the time needed to segment the corpora.
- Training: time and manpower used for training each corpus and track

Few systems participated in all open tracks: only SYSTRAN and one university participated in all four. We devoted about 2 person/week for this evaluation. We rank in the top three of three open tracks, and only the PK_0 track scores are lower, probably because of encoding problems for numbers for this corpus (we did not adjust our segmenter to cope with this corpus-specific problem). Our results are very consistent for all open tracks, indicating a very robust approach to Chinese segmentation.

Analysis of results shows that SYSTRAN's Chinese word segmentation excels in the area of dictionary coverage, robustness, and speed. The vast majority of divergences with the test corpora originate from differences in segmentation standards (over 55% for CAS-R and about 98% for CAS-T). True errors range between 0% and 2% only, the rest being assigned to either the lack of unknown word processing or the lack of a name entity recognizer. Although not integrated, the unknown word identification and name entity recognition are under development as part of a terminology extraction tool.

For future Chinese word segmentation evaluations, some of the issues that arose in this Bakeoff would need to be addressed to obtain even more significant results, including word segmentation standards and encoding problems for example. We would also welcome the introduction of a surprise track, similar to the surprise track of the DARPA MT evaluations that would require participants to submit results within 24 hours on an unknown corpus.

References

Liu, Y, Tan Q. & Shen, X. 1993. Segmentation Standard for Modern Chinese Information Processing and Automatic Segmentation Methodology.

Sproat, R., & Emerson T. 2003. The First International Chinese Word Segmentation Bakeoff. In the Proceedings of the Second SIGHAN Workshop on Chinese Language Processing. ACL03.

---

[1] The word list only contained Chinese-English bilingual dictionary without any syntactic or semantic features. It also contained many compound nouns, e.g. 北京大学.

[2] Compound nouns are no longer considered as words. They were moved to the expression dictionary. For example, 北京大学 has become 北京 大学.

[3] The number of words in the reference strings is used when counting OAS and CAS divergences. For example, 除夕之夜's CAS count is three because the number of words in the reference string 除夕 之 夜 is three.

[4] Word segmentation in SYSTRAN MT systems occurs after sentence identification and normalization. During word segmentation, Chinese numbers are converted into Arabic numbers.

HHMM-based Chinese Lexical Analyzer ICTCLAS*

Hua-Ping ZHANG[1] **Hong-Kui Yu**[1] **De-Yi Xiong**[1] **Qun LIU**[1,2]
[1]Inst. of Computing Tech., The Chinese Academy of Science, Beijing, 100080 CHINA
[2]Inst. of Computational Linguistics, Peking University, Beijing, 100871 CHINA
Email: zhanghp@software.ict.ac.cn

Abstract

This document presents the results from Inst. of Computing Tech., CAS in the ACL-SIGHAN-sponsored First International Chinese Word Segmentation Bakeoff. The authors introduce the unified HHMM-based frame of our Chinese lexical analyzer ICTCLAS and explain the operation of the six tracks. Then provide the evaluation results and give more analysis. Evaluation on ICTCLAS shows that its performance is competitive. Compared with other system, ICTCLAS has ranked top both in CTB and PK closed track. In PK open track, it ranks second position. ICTCLAS BIG5 version was transformed from GB version only in two days; however, it achieved well in two BIG5 closed tracks. Through the first bakeoff, we could learn more about the development in Chinese word segmentation and become more confident on our HHMM-based approach. At the same time, we really find our problems during the evaluation. The bakeoff is interesting and helpful.

1 Introduction

ICT (Institute of Computing Technology, Chinese Academy of Sciences) participated the First International Chinese Word Segmentation Bakeoff. We have taken six tracks: Academia Sinica closed (ASc), U. Penn Chinese Tree Bank open and closed(CTBo,c), Hong Kong CityU closed (HKc), Peking University open and closed(PKo,c).

The structure of this document is as follows. The next section presents the HHMM-based framework of ICTCLAS. Next we detail the operation of six tracks. The following section provides evaluation result and gives further analysis.

2 HHMM-based Chinese lexical analysis

2.1 ICTCLAS Framework

As illustrated in Figure 1, HHMM-based Chinese lexical analysis comprises five levels: atom segmentation, simple and recursive unknown words recognition, class-based segmentation and POS tagging. In the whole frame, class-based segmentation graph, which is a directed graph designed for word segmentation, is an essential intermediate data structure that links disambiguation, unknown words recognition with word segmentation and POS tagging.

Atom segmentation, the bottom level of HHMM, is an initial step. Here, atom is defined to be the minimal segmentation unit that cannot be split in any stage. The atom consists of Chinese character, punctuation, symbol string, numeric expression and other non-Chinese char string. Any word is made up of an atom or more. Atom segmentation is to segment original text into atom sequence and it provides pure and simple source for its parent HMM. For instance, a sentence like "2002.9，ICTCLAS 的自由源码开始发布" (The free source codes of ICTCLAS was distributed in September, 2002) would be segmented as atom sequence "2002.9/，/ICTCLAS/的/自/由/源/码/开/始/发/布/". In this HMM, the original symbol is observation while the atom is state. We skip the detail of operation in that it's a simple application on the basis of HMM. POS tagging and role tagging using Viterbi are also skipped because they are classic application of HMM. Because of paper length limit, unknown words recognition is omitted. Our previous papers (Zhang et al. 2003) gave more

* ICTCLAS is the abbreviation for "Inst. of Computing Tech., Chinese Lexical Analysis System.". We published ICTCLAS as free software. The full source code and document of ICTCLAS is available at no cost for non-commercial use. Welcome researchers and technical users download ICTCLAS from Open Platform of Chinese NLP (www.nlp.org.cn).

explanation.

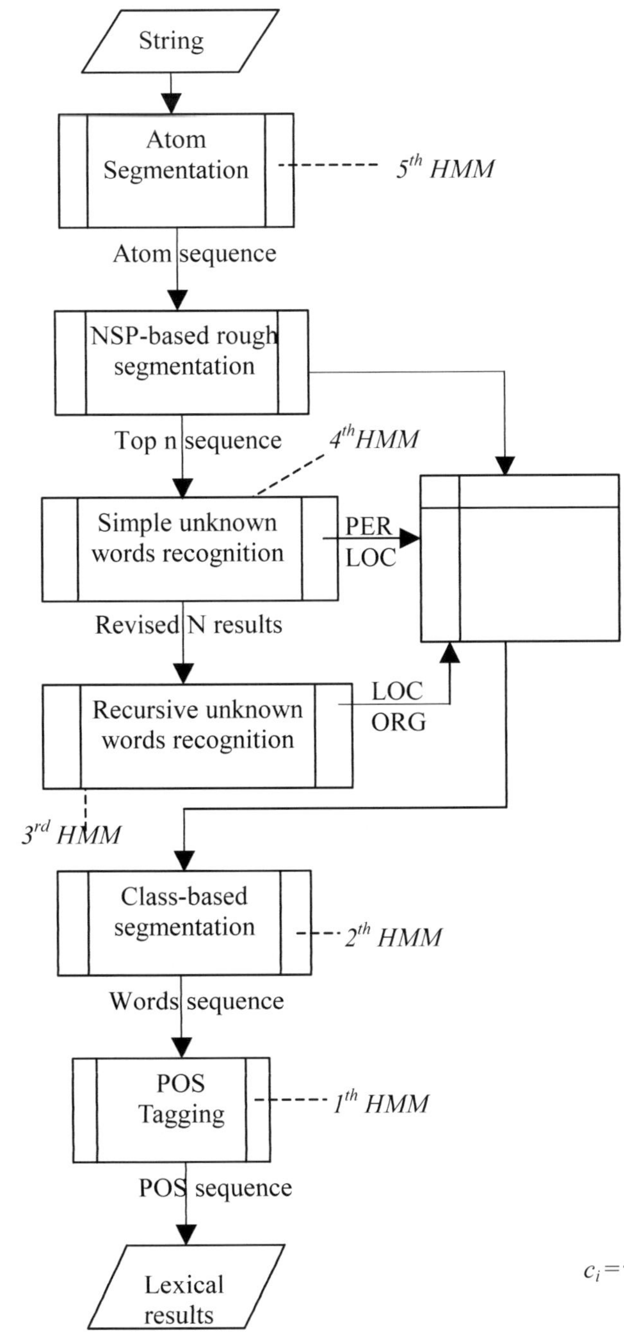

Figure 1. HHMM-based Chinese lexical analysis

2.2 Class-based HMM for word segmentation

We apply to word segmentation class-based HMM, which is a generalized approach covering both common words and unknown words.

Given a word w_i, class c_i is defined in Figure 2. Suppose |LEX| to be the lexicon size, then the total number of word classes is |LEX|+9.

Given the atom sequence A=(a_1,...a_n), let W=(w_1,...w_m) be the words sequence, C= (c_1,...c_m) be a corresponding class sequence of W, and $W^\#$ be the choice of word segmentation with the maximized probability, respectively. Then, we could get:

$$W^\# = \arg\max_W P(W|A) = \arg\max_W P(W,A)/P(A)$$

For a specific atom sequence A, P(A) is a constant and P(W,A)= P(W). So,

$$W^\# = \arg\max_W P(W)$$

On the basis of Baye's Theorem, it can be induced that:

$$W^\# = \arg\max_W P(W|C)P(C)$$

$W^\#$ can be found with another level of HMM if class c_i is viewed as state while word w_i is output. Therefore:

$$W^\# \approx \arg\max_{w_1 w_2 \ldots w_m} \prod_{i=1}^{m} p(w_i \mid c_i) p(c_i \mid c_{i-1}),$$

where c_0 is begin of sentence.

For convenience, we often use the negative log probability instead of the proper form. That is:

$$W^\# = \arg\min_W \sum_{i=1}^{m} [-\ln p(w_i \mid c_i) - \ln p(c_i \mid c_{i-1})]$$

$$c_i = \begin{cases} w_i & \text{iff } w_i \text{ is listed in the segmentation lexicon;} \\ \text{PER} & \text{iff } w_i \text{ is unlisted}^* \text{ personal name;} \\ \text{LOC} & \text{iff } w_i \text{ is unlisted location name;} \\ \text{ORG} & \text{iff } w_i \text{ is unlisted organization name;} \\ \text{TIME} & \text{iff } w_i \text{ is unlisted time expression;} \\ \text{NUM} & \text{iff } w_i \text{ is unlisted numeric expression;} \\ \text{STR} & \text{iff } w_i \text{ is unlisted symbol string;} \\ \text{BEG} & \text{iff beginning of a sentence} \\ \text{END} & \text{iff ending of a sentence} \\ \text{OTHER} & \text{otherwise.} \end{cases}$$

* "unlisted" is referred as being outside the lexicon

Figure 2: Class Definition of word w_i

According to the word class definition, if w_i is listed in lexicon, then c_i is w_i, and $p(w_i|c_i)$ is equal to 1.0. Otherwise, $p(w_i|c_i)$ is probability that class

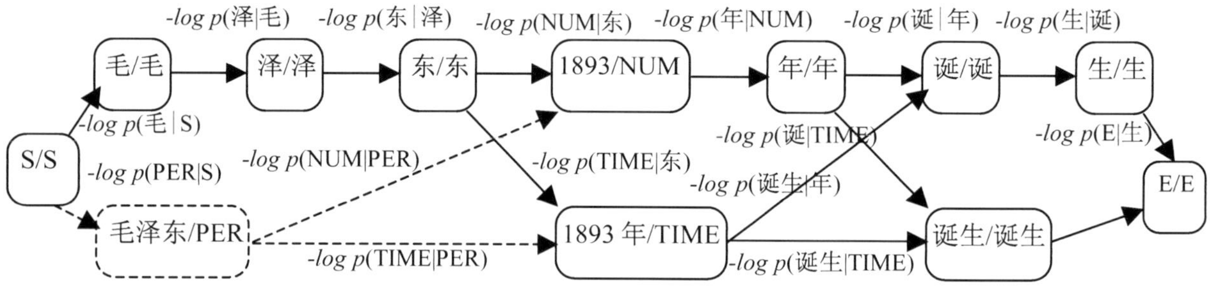

Figure3. Class-based word segmentation

Note:

1. The original sentence is "毛泽东 1893 年诞生" (Mao Ze-Dong was born in the year of 1893). Its atom sequence is "毛/泽/东/1893/年/诞/生/" after atom segmentation;
2. The node format is "word/class" (w_i / c_i) and the weight on the node is $-log\ p\ (w_i \mid c_i)$;
3. Weight on the directed edge is $-\log p\ (c_i \mid c_{i-1})$;
4. "毛泽东" (Mao Ze-Dong) is personal name outside the lexicon.The node " 毛泽东/PER" and the related edges with dash line is inserted after unknown words recognition.

c_i initially activates w_i, and it could be estimated in its child HMM for unknown words recognition.

As demonstrated in Figure 3, we provide the process of class-based word segmentation on "毛泽东 1893 年诞生" (Mao Ze-Dong was born in the year of 1893). The significance of our method is: it covers the possible ambiguity. Moreover, unknown words, which are recognized in the following steps, can be added into the segmentation graph and proceeded as any other common words.

After transformation through class-based HMM, word segmentation becomes single-source shortest paths problem. Hence the best choice $W^{\#}$ of word segmentation is easy to find using Djikstra's algorithm.

3 Tracks

Here, we would introduce the operation of some different track.

3.1 Closed Tracks

We participate all the closed tracks. As for each closed track, we first extracted all the common words and tokens that appear in the training corpus. Then build the segmentation core lexicons with the words. Those named entity words are classified into different named entities: numeric and time expression, personal names, location names, and transliterated names. According to named entities in the given corpus, we could train both class-based segmentation HMM and role-based HMM model for unknown word recognition. Therefore, the whole lexical system including unknown word detection is accomplished as shown in Figure 1.

3.2 Open Tracks

We only participate GB code open tracks. Actually, open track is similar to closed one. The only difference is the size of training data set. In Peking University open track, ICTCLAS is trained on six-month news corpus that is 5 months more than closed track. The entire corpus is also from Peking University. Except for the additional corpus, we have not employed any other special libraries or other resources.

As for CTB open track, we find that it cannot benefit from that 5 month PKU corpus. Actually, PKU standard is very different from CTB one though they seemed similar. Core lexicon extracted from Peking corpus degraded the performance on CTB testing data. Except for some named entity corpus, we could not get any more sources related to CTB standard. Therefore, CTB open track is operated in the similar way as closed track.

3.3 BIG5-coded Tracks

Before the bakeoff, BIG5-coded word segmentation has never been researched in our institute. Besides the character code, common words and sentence styles are greatly different in China mainland and Taiwan or Hong Kong. Because of time limitation, we have only spent two days on transforming our GB-coded ICTCLAS to BIG5-coded lexical analyzer. For each BIG5 closed, we extracted a BIG5-coded core lexicon. Then, the

BIG5 version ICTCLAS could work properly. The core source code is same as GB version.

4 Evaluation result

Track	ASc	CTBc	CTBo	HKc	PKc	PKo
Participant Number	6	6	7	4	10	8
Corpus Size (bytes)	38,882	125,248	125,248	114,384	56,254	56,254
True Word count	11,985	39,922	39,922	34,955	17,194	17,194
Test Word count	12,360	40,460	40,426	37,274	17,582	17,563
Insertions	434	1,789	1,755	2,439	485	458
Deletions	59	1,251	1,251	120	97	89
Substitutions	506	3,281	3,262	2,291	562	539
Nchange	999	6,321	6,268	4,850	1,144	1,086
Recall (Rank)	0.953 (3)	0.886 (2)	0.887 (4)	0.931 (3)	0.962 (1)	0.963 (1)
Precision (Rank)	0.924 (5)	0.875 (1)	0.876 (4)	0.873 (3)	0.940 (3)	0.943 (2)
F measure (Rank)	0.938 (5)	0.881 (1)	0.881 (4)	0.901 (3)	0.951 (1)	0.953 (2)
OOV rate	0.022	0.181	0.181	0.071	0.069	0.069
OOV Recall (Rank)	0.178 (5)	0.705 (1)	0.707 (5)	0.243 (4)	0.724 (2)	0.743 (2)
IV Recall(Rank)	0.970 (3)	0.927 (5)	0.927 (5)	0.984 (1)	0.979 (2)	0.980 (1)
***Time Cost (s)**	3.92	10.57	10.62	7.11	5.18	5.53
****Speed (bytes/s)**	9,919	11,849	11,794	16,088	10,860	10,173

Table 1. Evaluation result of ICTCLAS in the First International Chinese Word Segmentation Bakeoff

*Time Cost: CPU: Pentium 4, 1.6GHz; Main Memory: 192M

**Speed=Corpus Size / Time cost * 1000

Compared with other systems, ICTCLAS especially GB-coded version is competitive. In both GB-coded closed tracks, ICTCLAS ranked top. ICTCLAS also rank second position in Peking open track. Because of the lack of resources, CTB open track is almost as same as CTB closed track. The final performance in BIG5 track is not very good. As a preliminary BIG-coded system, however, we are satisfied with the result.

As is shown in Table 1, It could also be concluded that class-based segmentation HMM is effective. Excepted for CTB, IV Recall is over 97%.

5 Conclusion

Through the first bakeoff, we have learn more about the development in Chinese word segmentation and become more confident on our HHMM-based approach. At the same time, we really find our problems during the evaluation. The bakeoff is interesting and helpful. We look forward to participate forthcoming bakeoff.

6 Acknowledgements

The authors would like to thank Prof. Shiwen Yu of Peking University for the Peking corpus. And we acknowledge our debt to Gang Zou, Dr. Bin Wang, Dr. Jian Sun, Ji-Feng Li, Hao Zhang and other colleagues. Huaping Zhang would especially express gratitude to his graceful girl friend Feifei and her family for their encouragement. We also thank Richard Sproat, Qing Ma, Fei Xia and other SIGHAN colleagues for their elaborate organization and enthusiastic help in the First International Chinese Word Segmentation Bakeoff.

References

Lawrence. R.Rabiner.1989. *A Tutorial on Hidden Markov Models and Selected Applications in Speech Recognition*. Proceedings of IEEE 77(2): pp.257-286.

Shai Fine, Yoram Singer, and Naftali Tishby.1998. *The hierarchical Hidden Markov Model: Analysis and applications*. Machine Learning, 32:41

Zhang Hua-Ping, Liu Qun. *Model of Chinese Words Rough Segmentation Based on N-Shortest-Paths Method*. Journal of Chinese information processing, 2002,16(5):1-7 (in Chinese)

ZHANG Hua-Ping, LIU Qun, Zhang Hao and Cheng Xue-Qi. 2002. *Automatic Recognition of Chinese Unknown Words Recognition*. Proc. of First SigHan attached on COLING 2002

ZHANG Hua-Ping, LIU Qun, YU Hong-Kui, CHENG Xue-Qi, BAI Shuo. *Chinese Named Entity Recognition Using Role Model*. International Journal of Computational Linguistics and Chinese language processing, 2003,Vol. 8 (2)

Chunking-based Chinese Word Tokenization

GuoDong ZHOU
Institute for Infocomm Research
21 Heng Mui Keng Terrace
Singapore, 119613
zhougd@i2r.a-star.edu.sg

Abstract

This paper introduces a Chinese word tokenization system through HMM-based chunking. Experiments show that such a system can well deal with the unknown word problem in Chinese word tokenization.

1 Introduction

Word Tokenization is regarded as one of major bottlenecks in Chinese Language Processing. Normally, word tokenization is implemented through word segmentation in Chinese Language Processing literature. This is also affected in the title of this competition.

There exists two major problems in Chinese word segmentation: ambiguity and unknown word detection. While ngarm modeling and/or word co-ocurrence has been successfully applied to deal with ambiguity problem, unknown word detection has become major bottleneck in word tokenization.

This paper proposes a HMM-based chunking scheme to cope with unkown words in Chinese word tokenization. The unknown word detection is re-casted as chunking several words (single-character word or multi-character word) together to form a new word.

2 HMM-based Chunking

2.1 HMM

Given an input sequence $G_1^n = g_1 g_2 \cdots g_n$, the goal of Chunking is to find a stochastic optimal tag sequence $T_1^n = t_1 t_2 \cdots t_n$ that maximizes (Zhou and Su 2000) (2-1)

$$\log P(T_1^n \mid G_1^n) = \log P(T_1^n) + \log \frac{P(T_1^n, G_1^n)}{P(T_1^n) \cdot P(G_1^n)}$$

The second term in (2-1) is the mutual information between T_1^n and G_1^n. In order to simplify the computation of this term, we assume mutual information independence (2-2):

$$MI(T_1^n, G_1^n) = \sum_{i=1}^{n} MI(t_i, G_1^n) \text{ or}$$

$$\log \frac{P(T_1^n, G_1^n)}{P(T_1^n) \cdot P(G_1^n)} = \sum_{i=1}^{n} \log \frac{P(t_i, G_1^n)}{P(t_i) \cdot P(G_1^n)}$$

That is, an individual tag is only dependent on the token sequence G_1^n and independent on other tags in the tag sequence T_1^n. This assumption is reasonable because the dependence among the tags in the tag sequence T_1^n has already been captured by the first term in equation (2-1). Applying it to equation (2-1), we have (2-3):

$$\log P(T_1^n \mid G_1^n) = \log P(T_1^n) - \sum_{i=1}^{n} \log P(t_i) + \sum_{i=1}^{n} \log P(t_i \mid G_1^n)$$

From equation (2-3), we can see that:

- The first term can be computed by applying chain rules. In ngram modeling, each tag is assumed to be probabilistically dependent on the N-1 previous tags.
- The second term is the summation of log probabilities of all the individual tags.
- The third term corresponds to the "lexical" component (dictionary) of the tagger.

We will not discuss either the first or the second term further in this paper because ngram modeling has been well studied in the literature. We will focus on the third term $\sum_{i=1}^{n} \log P(t_i \mid G_1^n)$.

2.2 Chinese Word Tokenization

Given the previous HMM, for Chinese word tokenization, we have (Zhou and Su 2002):

- $g_i = < p_i, w_i >$; $W_1^n = w_1 w_2 \cdots w_n$ is the word sequence; $P_1^n = p_1 p_2 \cdots p_n$ is the word formation pattern sequence and p_i is the word formation pattern of w_i. Here p_i consists of:
  - The percentage of w_i occurring as a whole word (round to 10%)
  - The percentage of w_i occurring at the beginning of other words (round to 10%)
  - The percentage of w_i occurring at the end of other words (round to 10%)
  - The length of w_i
  - The occurring frequence feature, which is set to max(log(Frequence), 9).
- tag t_i : Here, a word is regarded as a chunk (called "Word-Chunk") and the tags are used to bracket and differentiate various types of Word-chunks. Chinese word tokenization can be regarded as a bracketing process while differentiation of different word types can help the bracketing process. For convenience, here the tag used in Chinese word tokenization is called "Word-chunk tag". The Word-chunk tag t_i is structural and consists of three parts:
  - **Boundary category (B)**: it is a set of four values: 0,1,2,3, where 0 means that current word is a whole entity and 1/2/3 means that current word is at the beginning/in the middle/at the end of a word.
  - **Word category (W)**: used to denote the class of the word. In our system, word is classified into two types: pure Chinese word type and mixed word type (for example, including English characters/Chinese digits/Chinesenumbers).
  - **Word Formation Pattern(P)**: Because of the limited number of boundary and word categories, the word formation pattern is added into the structural chunk tag to represent more accurate models.

3 Context-dependent Lexicons

The major problem with Chunking-based Chinese word tokenization is how to effectively approximate $P(t_i / G_1^n)$. This can be done by adding lexical entries with more contextual information into the lexicon Φ. In the following, we will discuss five context-dependent lexicons which consider different contextual information.

3.1 Context of current word formation pattern and current word

Here, we assume:

$$P(t_i / G_1^n) = \begin{cases} P(t_i / p_i w_i) & p_i w_i \in \Phi \\ P(t_i / p_i) & p_i w_i \notin \Phi \end{cases}$$

where

$\Phi = \{p_i w_i, p_i w_i \exists C\} + \{p_i, p_i \exists C\}$ and $p_i w_i$ is a word formation pattern and word pair existing in the training data C.

3.2 Context of previous word formation pattern and current word formation pattern

Here, we assume :

$$P(t_i / G_1^n) = \begin{cases} P(t_i / p_{i-1} p_i) & p_{i-1} p_i \in \Phi \\ P(t_i / p_i) & p_{i-1} p_i \notin \Phi \end{cases}$$

where

$\Phi = \{p_{i-1} p_i, p_{i-1} p_i \exists C\} + \{p_i, p_i \exists C\}$ and $p_{i-1} p_i$ is a pair of previous word formation pattern and current word formation pattern existing in the training data C.

3.3 Context of previous word formation pattern, previous word and current word formation pattern

Here, we assume :

$$P(t_i / G_1^n) = \begin{cases} P(t_i / p_{i-1}w_{i-1}p_i) & p_{i-1}w_{i-1}p_i \in \Phi \\ P(t_i / p_i) & p_{i-1}w_{i-1}p_i \notin \Phi \end{cases}$$

where

$\Phi = \{p_{i-1}w_{i-1}p_i, p_{i-1}w_{i-1}p_i \exists C\} + \{p_i, p_i \exists C\}$, where $p_{i-1}w_{i-1}p_i$ is a triple pattern existing in the training corpus.

3.4 Context of previous word formation pattern, current word formation pattern and current word

Here, we assume :

$$P(t_i / G_1^n) = \begin{cases} P(t_i / p_{i-1}p_i w_i) & p_{i-1}p_i w_i \in \Phi \\ P(t_i / p_i) & p_{i-1}p_i w_i \notin \Phi \end{cases}$$

where

$\Phi = \{p_{i-1}p_i w_i, p_{i-1}p_i w_i \exists C\} + \{p_i, p_i \exists C\}$, where $p_{i-1}p_i w_i$ is a triple pattern.

3.5 Context of previous word formation pattern, previous word, current word formation pattern and current word

Here, the context of previous word formation pattern, previous word, current word formation pattern and current word is used as a lexical entry to determine the current structural chunk tag and $\Phi = \{p_{i-1}w_{i-1}p_i w_i, p_{i-1}w_{i-1}p_i w_i \exists C\} + \{p_i, p_i \exists C\}$, where $p_{i-1}w_{i-1}p_i w_i$ is a pattern existing in the training corpus. Due to memory limitation, only lexical entries which occurs at least 3 times are kept.

4 Error-Driven Learning

In order to reduce the size of lexicon effectively, an error-driven learning approach is adopted to examine the effectiveness of lexical entries and make it possible to further improve the chunking accuracy by merging all the above context-dependent lexicons in a single lexicon.

For a new lexical entry e_i, the effectiveness $F_\Phi(e_i)$ is measured by the reduction in error which results from adding the lexical entry to the lexicon : $F_\Phi(e_i) = F_\Phi^{Error}(e_i) - F_{\Phi+\Delta\Phi}^{Error}(e_i)$. Here, $F_\Phi^{Error}(e_i)$ is the chunking error number of the lexical entry e_i for the old lexicon Φ and $F_{\Phi+\Delta\Phi}^{Error}(e_i)$ is the chunking error number of the lexical entry e_i for the new lexicon $\Phi + \Delta\Phi$ where $e_i \in \Delta\Phi$ ($\Delta\Phi$ is the list of new lexical entries added to the old lexicon Φ). If $F_\Phi(e_i) > 0$, we define the lexical entry e_i as positive for lexicon Φ . Otherwise, the lexical entry e_i is negative for lexicon Φ .

5 Implementation

In training process, only the words occurs at least 5 times are kept in the training corpus and in the word table while those less-freqently occurred words are separated into short words (most of such short words are single-character words) to simulate the chunking. That is, those less-frequently words are regarded as chunked from several short words.

In word tokenization process, the Chunking-based Chinese word tokenization can be implemented as follows:

1) Given an input sentence, a lattice of word and word formation pattern pair is generated by skimming the sentence from left-to-right, looking up the word table to determine all the possible words, and determining the word formation pattern for each possible word.
2) Viterbi algorithm is applied to decode the lattice to find the most possible tag sequence.
3) In this way, the given sentence is chunked into words with word category information discarded.

6 Experimental Results

Table 1 shows the performance of our chunking-based Chinese word tokenization in the competition.

	PK (closed, official)	CTB (closed, unofficial)
Precision	94.5	90.7
Recall	93.6	89.6
F	94.0	90.1
OOV	6.9	18.1
Recall on OOV	76.3	75.2
Recall on In-Voc	94.9	92.7
Speed on P1.8G	420 KB/min	390 KB/min

The most important advantage of chunking-based Chinese word segmentation is the ability to cope with the unknown words. Table 1 shows that about 75% of the unknown words can be detected correctly using the chunking approach on the PK and CTB corpus.

7 Conclusion

This paper proposes a HMM-based chunking scheme to cope with the unkown words in Chinese word tokenization. In the meantime, error-driven learning is applied to effectively incorporate various context-dependent information. Experiments show that such a system can well deal with the unknown word problem in Chinese word tokenization.

References

Rabiner L. 1989. A Tutorial on Hidden Markov Models and Selected Applications in Speech Recognition. *IEEE 77(*2), pages257-285.

Viterbi A.J. 1967. Error Bounds for Convolutional Codes and an Asymptotically Optimum Decoding Algorithm. *IEEE Transactions on Information Theory,* IT 13(2), 260-269.

Zhou GuoDong and Su Jian. 2000. Error-driven HMM-based Chunk Tagger with Context-dependent Lexicon. *Proceedings of the Joint Conference on Empirical Methods on Natural Language Processing and Very Large Corpus (EMNLP/ VLC'2000).* Hong Kong, 7-8 Oct.

AUTHOR INDEX

Association for Computational Linguistics
209 N. Eighth Street
Stroudsburg, Pennsylvania 18360